THE BOW AND THE CLUB

JULIUS EVOLA

THE BOW AND THE CLUB

TRANSLATED BY SERGIO KNIPE

ARKTOS
LONDON 2018

Published in 2018 by Arktos Media Ltd.

www.arktos.com

Printed in the United Kingdom.

Originally published as *L'arco e la clava*. Italy, 1968.

TRANSLATION	Sergio Knipe
EDITOR	John Bruce Leonard
COVER	Andreas Nilsson
LAYOUT	Daniel Friberg
	Tor Westman
ISBN	978-1-912079-09-4 (Softcover)
	978-1-912079-08-7 (Hardback)
	978-1-912079-07-0 (Ebook)

CONTENTS

Introduction vii

1. The Civilisation of Space and the Civilisation of Time 1

2. The Breed of the Evasive Man 10

3. The Third Sex 16

4. Negrified America 26

5. The Decay of Words 39

6. The Psychoanalysis of Skiing 61

7. The Myth and Fallacy of Irrationalism 66

8. The Olympian Ideal and Natural Law 83

9. The Taste for Vulgarity 97

10. The Laughter of the Gods 109

11. The Concept of Initiation 121

12. Freedom of Sex and Freedom from Sex 152

13. Romanness, Germanicness,
and the 'Light of the North' 190

14. Subliminal Influences and 'Intelligent Stupidity' 215

15. The Myth of East and West
and the 'Meeting of Religions' 230

16. The Youth, the Beats, and Right-Wing Anarchists 275

17. Initiatic Centres and History 299

18. The Metaphysics of Sex and the 'One' 308

19. What 'Tradition' Is 323

Index 331

INTRODUCTION

1

The title of the present volume leaves no doubt about the intent of its author: *The Bow and the Club* is a call to battle.

This impression is strengthened by what Evola himself tells us about its title. In the year 1930, Evola founded and directed a journal called *La Torre* (*The Tower*) which, as he himself affirms it, 'sought to gather the few people capable of a revolt against contemporary civilisation' (*The Path of Cinnabar*, 'My Experience with *La Torre* and Its Implications'). It included a section called *L'arco e la clava*, *The Bow and the Club*, which offered a trenchant attack on the press of the time. Evola would resurrect this most evocative phrase some decades hence to head the present collection of essays. He explained the intent of this title most succinctly: 'the bow, to strike at what is far; the club, to beat down what is near.'

The martial element of this book, surely, could not be clearer; it is indeed one of the ubiquitous veins of the present compendium. Virgil's *arma virumque cano* might have been scribed beneath its title; Evola is here at his finest as a cultural warrior in the greatest sense of the term, and a significant portion of his work is dedicated to instilling that same lofty spirit in his readers, particularly in the youngest and most promising of them. The reader will find that in the brief course of these brief essays Evola has laid his hand upon the sickened nerves of modernity, and has closed his fist hard. This book offers a thoroughgoing critique of the atmosphere contemporary with Evola's writing—and given that nothing has improved since his time, and everything worsened, his words are even more vital now than when he indited them, half a century ago. Even when he speaks of authors whose names have been all been forgotten in the mere decades standing between this book's publication in 1968 and our own day, the ideas and problems they represent remain wholly relevant, and need for the attitude he embodies is tenfold as urgent.

The Bow and the Club enjoyed a success in Italy which was wholly unusual for an Evolian title. The reason is not hard to divine. As Sergio Knipe's excellent translation renders in faithful and elegant English, this book is one of the most beautiful of the Evolian oeuvre, and also one of the most accessible. Together with the last book Evola was ever to publish, *Recognitions*, this book forms a gate of entry into the world that is Evola's philosophy; these two works are uniquely suited as introductions to what one might call, in good Evolian language, the *Evolian orientation*. The other works of Evola which might lend themselves to such a task are riddled with special problems: *Revolt Against the Modern World* is in many ways too daunting and, indeed, *dis*orienting for anyone unaccustomed to Evola's approach to 'history' and to the world in general; *The Path of Cinnabar*, while being in certain respects excellently suited to the task of introduction, is in many places very personal, and one who comes to Evola without knowing anything about him might occasionally wonder why he should be bothered to care. Moreover, many of the books written by Evola are problematic from the start, insofar as they dedicate themselves to material which lies in 'ancient history', or even *pre*history. Modernity is intoxicated with itself, and often does not know how to take even two steps backward in time; it fumbles so soon as it touches the best things of even two or three centuries ago, not to speak of two or three millennia—and certainly not to speak of anything remoter than that.

But both *The Bow and the Club* and *Recognitions* stand firm and determined in the contemporary fray itself, taking up arms against the figures and ideals of the present moment. In the right spirit of 'conservative revolution', they challenge the present with unwavering reference to the past. They confront modernity head on and unapologetically, and for the clarity of their protest and the unflinching and unequivocal quality of their revolt they are as refreshing as a sup of water in a year of drought. Evola even resuscitates at a blow the propriety of 'reaction': 'As if, when certain parties "act", others should refrain from reacting and instead turn the other cheek like good Christians and say "Well done, keep it up!"' There is something bracing in all of this, something which stirs the slumbering martial spirit in us. More, there is something *didactic* in it, something which *teaches* the warrior's spirit.

In a certain sense, indeed, this book can be taken as the gift of a worthy and wise elder to the best and most promising youth: Evola would show how 'the bow and the club' are to be wielded. It is no accident that the concern for youth runs as a constant preoccupation throughout both this book (see, for instance, Chapters 6, 11, and 16) and through the chapters of *Recognitions*. In both these books, Evola the educator steps forth. A generation of Italians responded willingly to his offer; we may pray that this is an augur of things to come. It is most welcome, then, that so fine a translation should at last reach an English public, upon the brink of our hour of need.

2

A word on the order and problems of the present book. *The Bow and the Club* together with *Recognitions* are two of the last books that Evola published in his lifetime: between their publication stand but a collection of poetry and a work on Taoism. *The Bow and the Club* and *Recognitions* are also unique in the properly Evolian oeuvre for their character as anthologies of essays on a variety of topics; while most of the works penned by Evola rigorously pursue singular and well-defined themes, and do so with a simultaneous breadth, intricacy, and depth of vision, these two works appear at first glance dispersive and arbitrarily arranged. It is easy to suppose that they represent the decline of Evola's last years, a failing of his once intense and concentrated intellectual vision — the product of an aging man who could no longer gather the enormous energy necessary for such powerful, sweeping studies as *Revolt Against the Modern World* and *Men Among the Ruins. The Bow and the Club* and *Recognitions* have been all too often neglected for this, as though their lack of singular theme were to be considered a defect — as though the same trait could not as easily be considered, in a certain light, their *strength*.

In the first place, as can be seen from even a superficial reading of, for instance, Chapters 1, 2, and 19, the essays in the present volume are truly remarkable for their diamond-dense reproduction of a lifetime of study and contemplation. Precisely the *contrary* of dispersion and waning energy, each essay represents a culmination of centralising powers, an inner light focused upon a point so keenly as to *burn*. One struggles to think of any other instances in all our literature of statements at once so clear, so brief, so articulate, and so complete, of such fundamental and fundamentally complex questions as the relation between modernity and tradition (Chapters 1 and 19), the rich tensions between North Europe and South Europe (Chapter 13), the essential difference between the Occident and the Orient (Chapter 15), or the problems of initiation (Chapters 11 and 17). The stylistic control and stern, mastered power of vision required to produce such hard and luminous jewels demonstrates beyond any doubt that these works are to be seen, not as the *afterword* to Evola's productive life, but in a certain sense as its most lapidary and condensed synthesis.

Which leads us to another essential question: the question of the order in *The Bow and the Club*. As we have noted, it is tempting to assume that Evola, having arrived at his waning years of life, and desirous of making some final contribution, had but gathered up a variety of his essays, tossed them into a pair of volumes, and distributed them just so. A mere glance at the titles of the chapters in this book might encourage such a view: Evola seems to jump from Tradition to sex, from East to West, from Black America to Hyperborean Rome, from 'the evasive man' to skiing, with no rhyme nor reason. But this analysis disregards certain basic inevitable questions, as: why *these* essays, and not others? Why *this* order, and not another?

It is needless to say that a man like Evola did nothing in his life haphazardly, and certainly nothing that he wrote was penned without discretion and awareness. We know, moreover, that this work was arranged and edited with deliberation over a lengthy period of time, and that some of the essays within it had never been published before, but were written expressly for the present work. We are then constrained to depart from the presupposition, unquestionably warranted by analysis of the evident care displayed by Evola's entire existence, that these books were assembled with conscious design; they were, to take the word in its older and nobler sense, the consequence of an *architecture.*

The order of the essays in *The Bow and the Club* is dependent on the problems that they address. Because of the literary excellence of Evola's prose, to expound on these problems would require a book considerably longer than the one the reader holds in his hands. We can do no more than indicate some of the most intriguing problems which the master's words have suggested to our eyes.

We begin from what is most obvious, from the title itself. The majority of Evolian titles define (with Evola's usual rigor) the precise theme of the book they head. There are but few exceptions to this — most notably the *Path of Cinnabar,* which title limns its theme but obscurely. The title *The Bow and the Club,* on the other hand, seems to give no substantial idea of what the work might be about.

We begin then with the weapons themselves. One wonders that, of all the weapons at his disposal, Evola might have symbolised this work with the club—that brute instrument of beating—rather than, say, a rapier, or even more generically a sword. *L'arco e la spada* hardly rings less pleasantly to the ear than *L'arco e la clava*. Indeed, no one contemplating a comparison with Evola's style would spontaneously choose a cudgel as its symbol. Evola cuts straight to the nerve; his writing, as his thinking, is swift and deft, far from the awkward and unwieldy swing of the blunt bludgeon. The bow, moreover, is an instrument of a decidedly different nature; it is precision itself, making for a curious contrast which begs interpretation.

The first account that might be given for the title is that Evola speaks here of two different kinds of arms for confronting two different kinds of problems or enemies. There are those which circumstand us, which appear before and around us—perhaps even within us—and there those which stand distant to us. Hence 'the bow, to strike at what is far; the club, to beat down what is near'. In the penultimate chapter of this book, for instance, 'The Metaphysics of Sex and the "One"', Evola might well be battling a 'distant' foe—that is, one who shares so few of Evola's presuppositions that he is compelled to affirm that the author in question belongs 'to an intellectual world which is foreign to him'.

But what are we to do about the enemies that are 'near'? Certainly, Evola takes the so-called 'Guénonians' of Turin hard to task, as well as the theosophists and anthroposophists, as well as the increasingly effeminate men and manly women of his day, as well as the 'baleful popes' of a recent Catholicism. But once again, it is more fitting to call his remarks in all these cases 'cutting' than brutal or savage.

Moreover, there is also a third category of critique to be found in this book, which forms indeed one of the most important of its portions; and this category cannot be said to have anything to do with enemies near *or* far. I am referring for instance to Evola's disputes with the true Traditionalists or with his fellow esotericists, which are essentially friendly disputes. Indeed, even as regards his 'enemies', Evola's statement on his approach in the penultimate chapter of this book is anything but warlike: it epitomises, to the contrary, a civil and peaceable attitude: 'If a writer is capable of recognising the ultimate assumptions of his own thought...and grasps the fundamental difference between them and those of another writer, the only sensible thing for him to do is to follow his own path without seeking to interfere with an intellectual world that is foreign to him'. What could the club or the bow, what could the martial pose itself, have to do with a statement such as that?

Then we are compelled to seek another account. Let us suppose for a moment that with the 'bow' and the 'club' Evola is not referring at all to two kinds of weapons or enemies or even problems, but to two categories of intellectual or spiritual action (spiritual, it goes without saying, understood in a high and Evolian sense). The first, that represented by the club, is the action demanded by our present age: namely, an action of destruction and demolishment, an action requiring a brutal weapon capable of smashing this rotten day inward and bursting apart its very underpinnings, of sweeping everything away. This action must take place on the practical and intellectual planes, but every bit as much within one's own inward and privatest soul as well — in that realm wherein it is all too simple to 'live and let live', and wherein, out of carelessness or laziness, one adopts the principles of corrosion and degeneration almost without being aware of it. The club thus indicates a strengthening of the sinews and brawn in body and spirit, a more manly approach to life and to the deep and destructive problems particular to our modernity.

The bow, on the other hand, refers to our *aims*, to our *goals*; as when Nietzsche speaks of the tense bow of modern Europe. ('With so tense a bow we can now shoot for the most distant goals', Nietzsche tells us.) Precision is wanted here, for we must have clarity about where it is we are going and what we are trying to achieve. And indeed it is

most noteworthy that many of the essays in this book are attacks, *not*
on modernity itself, not on the subversive forces at work in modernity,
*but on those very individuals who have 'attacked' modernity, but in the
wrong way.* From the scandalous 'libertine' writings of a Miller or a
Lawrence to the 'rebellious' lifestyles of the Beats; from the dark temp-
tations of the Promethean attitude to the vague vagaries of the mystics;
from those who critique the West on the grounds of a superficial and
inadequate comprehension of the East, to extremely high-level disputes with René Guénon and the Traditionalists themselves — Evola is
engaging here in a kind of rectifying action, on the level of thought and
on the level of doctrine (and consequently also *action*), and once more
especially with eye to the promising youth who might read his words.
The bow represents our ability to shoot for distant targets; but we must
have the sight necessary for that work, else its precision is vain and it
transforms itself into a worthless arc of wood. The 'bow' is thus symbol
for the future and what we would make of it, in an arc drawn from the
deepest yesterday to the highest tomorrow — shot, as it were, from the
earth toward the sun. The bow is meant to show those have eyes to see,
the *true* purpose, the *true* aim.

Taken together, then, these symbolic weapons indicate the scope
and the force of Evola's critique. From these considerations, we are able
to return to our original position with due clarity: *The Bow and the
Club* is indeed a warrior's critique, penned for warriors or for those
who might become warriors. It thus takes 'action' as its aim; it is an
embodiment of that 'ray which issues forth and proceeds' from the
originating center, which Evola, in the profound fifteenth chapter of
this book, indicates as the principle defining feature of the best part
of the West as compared to the East. This kind of action cannot but
dream idly on the Tradition, nor seek simply to return to the divine
center, but it must also confront itself with the reality surrounding it
to see how this reality can and should be altered. At the same time, it
cannot concentrate its thought or its action exclusively on that reality,

on the 'phenomenal world', but it must have a rigorous and continually conscious connection with a metaphysical position, which leads back to the divine center itself. For to accept modernity in *principle* and to battle it in *consequence*, is to engage in that half-hearted labor, that effort doomed to failure and paralysis and self-compromising self-sacrifice, which we have seen finally overwhelm the better part of the contemporary conservative 'right' in late years.

There is one final observation which bears mention here. The bow and the club, taken together, conjure a specific figure from Classical Antiquity — a figure of the Western tradition, whose name comes down to us associated with these arms precisely: none other than Heracles. Heracles, before setting forth upon his famous Twelve Labors, was gifted a bow by Apollo and a club by Haephestus, which two weapons were to become heraldic of his name, so that it is difficult to find any artistic portrayal of that hero which does not feature the one or the other. Heracles was said moreover to excel in the art of both; and especially with regard to what has been written above, it is worth mentioning that when he became wrathful, as often happened, he would threaten to shoot the sun. This same Heracles is mentioned but once in the present book, yet in a context which could not be more suggestive: it is Heracles who frees the chained Prometheus after killing the eagle with his bow, thus reconciling the rebellious Titan to the Olympian Zeus; it is Heracles who 'in Antiquity embodied man, the hero, who has made the *other* choice, that of allying himself with the Olympian powers'.

Is it merely accident which has placed *this* chapter at the precise numerical center of this book? Is it but chance that the reference to Heracles, echoed in the work's very title, is located at the heart of a book which opens with the classification of Modernity as 'civilisation of time' and closes with the definition of Tradition as 'a force...which transcends historical contingencies'? One is permitted to doubt that a man such as Evola would have let such a reference, such a 'coincidence', pass unwittingly.

The superficial teaching of this is evident enough. We are invited, throughout this book, to put ourselves on the side of the Olympians, and to partake, insofar as it is given us to do so, of the 'Laughter of the Gods', *against* Prometheus and his 'titanic cunning'. Evola spurs us, in this latter day and these last times, to embody in our own beings and our own acts the spirit of the 'embodied man', the hero Heracles. Or if we cannot in this straying and swiftly declining 'Iron Age' become anything like the golden heroes of an Olympian light, at least we may strive in that direction. As Evola tells us, 'The "Olympian" orientation is just as possible as the Promethean one'. And it might be that herein, too, is contained hint of a possible answer to one of the highest and most intriguing riddles of this book — the riddle to which Evola directs us in such striking terms in the third to last of these essays.

As for what might lie beneath all this, beyond it, or *within* it — we are compelled to leave that where it rightfully belongs, in the sphere of the reader's own will and desire, and in the arc of his most personal effort. Evola has not failed to provide indications of where we might look, if we would enter these mysteries. And this entire book, taken in a certain light — taken, we are tempted to say, in the 'Olympian' light — might itself be considered precisely such an indication.

John Bruce Leonard

Cagliari, January 31, 2018

1. THE CIVILISATION OF SPACE AND THE CIVILISATION OF TIME

The traces left by certain great primordial civilisations — traces left often only in stone — possess a significance which is rarely perceived. Looking upon the remains of the archaic Graeco-Roman world and beyond — of Egypt, of Persia, of China, down to the last emerging and immobile vestiges of worlds submerged and swept away, those mysterious megalithic monuments scattered across deserts, wild areas and forests — or, to consider the opposite limit on the chronological spectrum of history, down to certain expressions of the European Middle Ages — looking upon all of this, one wonders whether the miraculous survival of such testimonies may not stand as a symbol, rather than simply as the consequence of a lucky combination of external circumstances.

This impression is further strengthened when we consider the general character of the life of those civilisations to which most of these traces belong, which is to say the general character of what may be described as 'traditional' life. This life has endured throughout the centuries and generations, essentially remaining faithful to the same principles, the same kind of institutions, and the same world-view. Though it is open to adaptation and exterior changes in the face of calamitous events, it is nonetheless unalterable in its core, its animating principle, its spirit, and its overall nature.

It is chiefly the East which this traditional world brings to mind. Consider what China and India were like until relatively recent times, or indeed Japan until an even more recent past. Generally speaking, the further back we go in time, the more vital, universal and powerful we find this kind of civilisation to be; so much so that the East alone must be regarded as that part of the world in which, thanks to lucky circumstances, traditional civilisation survived longer and developed better than anywhere else. It is as though the rule of time were partly suspended in civilisations of this sort. They seem to have been born not so much in time, as in *space*. They possess an 'atemporal' character.

According to the formula most current nowadays, the civilisations just described are 'stationary' civilisations — 'static' or 'immobilist' civilisations. In fact, they are civilisations whose very material vestiges are apparently destined to outlast all the modern world's monuments or idealistic creations. For the latter hardly have the power to endure more than half a century: the words 'progress' and 'dynamism' mean nothing in relation to them but a mere subjection to contingency, to the movement of incessant change, of a rapid rise and a sharp and equally rapid decline. These processes do not obey any truly organic inner law; they are not enclosed within any limits, but they acquire a momentum of their own, so that they ultimately carry away the very people who have triggered them: such is the distinguishing feature of this different world, in all of its sectors. Yet despite all this, these processes have been turned into a kind of criterion for measuring everything which ought to be described as a 'civilisation' in an eminent sense, within the framework of a historiography marked by arrogant and disparaging value judgements of the kind already indicated.

It is quite typical, in this connection, to mistake for immobility what in civilisations with a traditional orientation possessed a very different meaning: immutability. Those civilisations were civilisations of *being*. They showed their strength precisely in their identity, in their triumph over becoming, over 'history', change, and the amorphous flow of things. These civilisations plunged deep, beyond the shifting and treacherous waters, and in the deep they firmly rooted themselves.

The opposition between modern civilisations and traditional ones may be summarised as follows: *modern civilisations devour space, whereas traditional civilisations devoured time.*

The former — modern civilisations — are dizzying in their fever for movement and for the conquest of space. This has led to the creation of an endless arsenal of mechanical means to reduce all distances, shorten all intervals, and contract into a sense of ubiquity whatever is scattered across a multitude of places. This is a frenzied need for possession; a dark angst towards all that is detached, isolated, deep or remote; an impulse to expand, circulate, associate with others and find oneself in any which place — anywhere except within oneself. Science and technology, which have been promoted by this irrational existential impulse, in turn strengthen it, nourish it, and exacerbate it: exchanges, forms of communication, ultrasonic speeds, radio and television, standardisation, cosmopolitanism, internationalism, unlimited production, the American spirit, the 'modern' spirit.

The net is swiftly being extended, strengthened and perfected. Terrestrial space practically no longer conceals any mysteries. All paths by land, water and aether have been disclosed. The human gaze has probed the remotest heavens, the infinitely great and the infinitely small. One no longer speaks of other lands, but rather of other planets. On our own planet, action is carried everywhere in a flash. A din of a thousand voices that gradually merge into a uniform, monotonous and impersonal rhythm. These are the latest effects of what has been termed Western 'Faustianism', which is not unrelated to the myth of revolution in all its various aspects, the technocratic included — all formulated within the framework of a degenerated messianism.

By contrast, traditional civilisations were dizzying in their stability, in their identity, in their subsisting in an unwavering and changeless fashion in the midst of the current of time and history: so much so that they even succeeded in lending sensible, tangible expression to eternity. They stood as islands or bastions in time; operating within them were forces that consumed time and history. For this reason, it is incorrect to say that they 'were': it would be more correct to say that they quite simply *are*. If they seem to withdraw and almost vanish into a remote past, which at times even acquires mythical contours, this is only the mirage reaching whomever is carried away by an unstoppable current which leads him further and further from the domains of spiritual stability. This idea moreover corresponds perfectly to the image of the 'double perspective' provided by an ancient traditional teaching: the 'immobile land' moves and withdraws from whomever goes with the waters, while the waters move and withdraw from whomever firmly resides in the 'immobile land'.

If one understands this image by viewing it in relation not to the physical plane but to the spiritual plane, one thereby perceives the correct hierarchy of values; thus we cast our gaze beyond the horizon which confines our contemporaries. What seemed to be past becomes present, by virtue of an essential relating of historical (and hence con-tingent) forms to meta-historical contents. What has been referred to as 'static' proves to be overflowing with a dizzying life. *The others* — they are the fallen, those who have lost their centre. Changeism, historicism, evolutionism, and so on, all seem like the thrills of the shipwrecked, truths applying to whatever flees (*où fuyez-vous en avant, imbéciles?* Bernanos),[1] to whatever lacks inner consistency and ignores what

---

1   The citation is French: 'Whither are you fleeing, fools?' It is taken from an es-say by French novelist Georges Bernanos (1888–1948) entitled *La France contre les robots* (*France Against the Robots*). The original French differs slightly from Evola's reproduction: '*Que fuyez-vous donc, imbéciles?*' meaning 'From what are you feeling, fools?' The response which Bernanos furnishes very much accords however with Evola's argument in the present chapter: 'Alas! You are fleeing from yourselves... One understands nothing of modern civilisation if one does not first admit that it is a universal conspiracy against every kind of interior life'. Bernanos is perhaps best remembered for his novel *Diary of a Country Priest*, which treats of a young but ailing pastor who, assigned to a troubled country parish, struggles against spiritual temptation and faithlessness. Bernanos was a Roman Catholic, a monarchist and an anti-democrat, who nonetheless manifested great intolerance

this means or even what the origin of all elevations and achievements is. By such achievements, I mean here not merely an intangible and often invisible spiritual culmination, but achievements which rather expressed themselves through events, epic deeds and the cycles of civilisations which even in their silent and scattered stone vestiges seem to adumbrate something supra-temporal and eternal. To this we should further add certain traditional artistic creations, monolithic, rough and mighty creations utterly foreign to all subjectivity — often anonymous creations that constitute almost an extension of elemental forces.

Finally, it is worth recalling the conception of time which traditional civilisations had: not an irreversible linear conception but a cyclical, periodical one. A range of customs, rites and institutions distinguish both higher civilisations as well as the echoes which survive of them in certain 'primitive' peoples (one may wish to refer here to the material collected in the history of religion — Hubert, Mauss, Eliade, and others).[2] These reveal a constant intention to bring time back to its origins (hence the cycle), which means destroying everything that represents mere becoming, curbing it, or making it express or reflect supra-historical, sacred or metaphysical structures, often connected to myth. It was in such terms — as a 'mobile image of eternity' — that time acquired value and meaning, not as 'history'. Returning to the

---

for the politics of his epoch: though he fought in the First World War, he spent the entirety of the Second in self-imposed exile in South America.

2   Henri Hubert (1872–1927) was a French archaeologist and sociologist of comparative religion. Most of his research centered on pre-Christian faiths, and particularly the religion of the Celts. He was a friend and collaborator of Marcel Mauss (1872–1950), best remembered for his comparative analyses of gift exchanges in various cultures, though his work with Hubert focused rather on magic and sacrifice. The brilliant Romanian religious historian and novelist Mircea Eliade was a somewhat later thinker (1907–1986) whose broad work in comparative religion included a study precisely of the traditional belief in the cyclical nature of time. Eliade was decidedly a thinker of the Right, and drew a degree of his inspiration from Evola himself, with whom he kept a long correspondence.

origins meant renewing oneself, drawing upon the spring of eternal youth, and confirming one's spiritual stability, against temporality. The great cycles of nature encouraged such an attitude. The 'historical awareness' that is inseparable from the situation of 'modern' civilisations only seals this fracture, this fall of man into temporality. Yet it is presented as one of the conquests of the last mankind,[3] which is to say of crepuscular mankind.

Concerning certain discoveries, even such as allegedly fall within the range of scientific objectivity, it is not at all uncommon that they, as the origins of those general conceptions destined to revolutionise an age, constitute a symptom; so much so that their occurrence in one particular period rather than another cannot be regarded a matter of chance. With reference to the natural sciences, for example, it is widely known that according to the most recent theory en vogue — that of Einstein and his followers — it makes little difference whether we say that the Earth moves around the Sun or vice-versa: it is only a matter of preferring a greater or lesser complexity in the astrophysical calculations used to establish relational systems.[4] Now, with the 'Copernican

---

3   Italian: dell'uomo ultimo. The Italian is ambiguous; it can mean both 'the most recent man' and also 'the final man'. Given Evola's general philosophy this ambiguity is almost certainly intended, and is probably meant as a reminder of the fact that we are living in the last times, the decades at the 'close of a cycle', as he says elsewhere. In reference to man, it might also be the Italian for the translation of the German der letzte Mensch, Nietzsche's Last Man (see Thus Spoke Zarathustra, First Part, 'Zarathustra's Prologue'). This little word thus takes on a peculiar importance. In the present translation, ultimo has been uniformly translated as 'last' to preserve the original ambiguity.

4   Hence the name given to the Theory of Relativity of Albert Einstein (1879–1955). Indeed, even more radically yet, according to Einsteinian physics it is possible to take any arbitrary point or perspective as the center of the entire universe, such as the Earth, the Sun, the Moon, or a stone rolling down a hill; all that changes is the efficiency and clarity of the mathematical calculations which follow. This, as Evola indicates, stands in marked contrast to all past astronomical or physical theories, including those of Nicolaus Copernicus (1473–1543), which proposed

discovery', it ceased to be 'true' that the Earth is the firm and immobile centre of the heavenly bodies, and it became 'true' that the Earth moves and, following its own law, travels through cosmic space, an irrelevant part of a dispersed or indefinitely expanding universe. It seems highly significant that this discovery occurred more or less in the age of the Renaissance and of Humanism, which is to say in the age of the most crucial upheavals in the emergence of a new civilisation, whose individuals were progressively to lose all connections with what 'is' and to fall away from all forms of spiritual centredness in their adoption of the perspective of becoming, of history, of transformation, of the uncontrollable and unpredictable current of 'life'. (The most peculiar thing is that the beginning of this upheaval was marked by the claim — the illusion — that it had finally discovered, affirmed and glorified 'man' — hence the term 'Humanism'; in fact, everything was reduced to the 'merely human', thereby impoverishing the possibilities of any opening to and integration within the 'more than human'.)

This is not the only symbolic upheaval that could be mentioned in this connection. With regard to the example just adduced — the 'Copernican revolution' — one point is worth noting: in the traditional world no so-called 'objective' truth was granted importance; truths of this sort might be taken into account, but only secondarily, according to their actual relativity on the one hand, and to their human value on the other, ever bearing in mind criteria of what would be opportune for the general way of perceiving things. A traditional theory about nature may have been 'wrong' from the point of view of modern science (at a given stage of its development); yet its value — the reason why it was chosen — lay in its suitability as a means of expressing something true on a different and more interesting level. For example, the geocentric theory grasped an aspect of sensible reality that might serve as a sup-

---

always a *true* center, a *true* perspective. It might be said that the Copernican Revolution shifted the center of the universe from the Earth to the Sun, while the Einsteinian Revolution abolished the center altogether.

port for a truth of a different sort, an unassailable truth, namely the truth regarding 'being', spiritual centredness, as the principle governing the true essence of man.

Let this suffice for a morphological clarification of the antithesis between the civilisation of space and the civilisation of time. From this antithesis it would also be easy to infer the corresponding typological and existential antithesis between the man of the former civilisation and the man of the latter. And should we wish to move on to the problem of the crisis of the present age based on what has been argued so far, it should be quite clear just how useless any criticism, reaction or aspiration toward rectifying action will be, unless an inner change of polarity has first taken place in man himself, or at any rate in a certain number of men capable of exercising a significant influence. This change may be described as a *metanoia*,[5] to use the ancient term, meaning a shift towards the dimension of 'being', of 'what is' — a dimension which has been lost and dissolved in modern man, to the point that he hardly knows what inner stability or centredness is, and hence also calmness and a higher sense of security. Instead, a hidden sense of angst is becoming increasingly common, of disquietude and of emptiness, despite the widespread use, in all domains, of recently invented spiritual anaesthetics. A sense of 'being', of stability, is bound to produce also a sense of limits through a principle effective even in a more external domain, as a means of asserting oneself over forces and processes that have become more powerful than those individuals that have rashly set them in motion within the temporal realm.

---

5   From the Ancient Greek μετάνοια, 'changing one's mind' (lit. 'beyond the mind'). This is a prominent Biblical theme, and is generally translated in the Bible by the word 'repentance'. Its original meaning, probably also among the Christians, was a change of heart or a profound spiritual conversion; and this is clearly the meaning it takes on in Evola's use, as demonstrated by Evola's indications here.

Taking our civilisation as a whole, it is indeed difficult to say where any firm points of reference could be found in a civilisation which, like the modern one, is entirely — and to an unprecedented degree — a civilisation of time. It is moreover quite obvious that not so much a rectification, as the end of one form and the emergence of a new one is now possible. Thus we can at most reasonably consider only a change in orientation in some specific domain; in particular, we can consider the goal that a few differentiated men, as though through an awakening, might still set themselves, and invisibly accomplish.[6]

---

6   [Evola's note. —*Ed.*] The differentiated type, distinguished by the possession of the dimension of 'being', is the point of reference for existential orientations suitable for an age of dissolution such as the present one — orientations which I formulated in my book *Ride the Tiger* (1961).

2. THE BREED OF
THE EVASIVE MAN

An analogy has been drawn since ancient times between the human being and the larger organism of the State. The traditional conception of the State — a conception both organic and complex — has always reflected the natural hierarchy of faculties which distinguishes the complete human being. Here the purely physical and corporeal element is supported by life forces which are governed by the life of the spirit and character, while above the whole being stands the spiritual and intellectual principle, which the Stoics referred to as the inner sovereign, the *hegemonikon*.[1]

Bearing these points in mind, every democracy necessarily appears as a regressive phenomenon, a system in which every normal relationship is inverted. The *hegemonikon* is non-existent. Determination occurs from from below. A real centre is missing. This revocable pseudo-authority at the service of what lies below — i.e. of the purely material, 'social', economic and quantitative aspect of a people — corresponds, according to this analogy, to the situation in an individual being of a mind and a spiritual principle which exist solely on account of and for the sake of bodily needs.

The advent of democracy therefore signals something far more serious than it might seem to today from a purely political perspec-

---

1   Ancient Greek, ἡγεμονικόν: 'the authoritative or ruling part of the soul or universe'.

10

tive — that is, the mistake and foolish infatuation of a society digging its own grave. Indeed, it might be argued that the 'democratic' climate is, in the long run, bound to exert a regressive influence on the very personality of man, even in 'existential' terms — precisely by virtue of the aforementioned correspondences between the individual as a small organism and the State as a large organism.

Confirmation of this idea may be found by examining various aspects of contemporary society. Plato has stated that those who have no master within themselves at least ought to have a master outside them. But what has been extolled as the 'liberation' of this or that people and its 'democratic progress', which is brought — often even through the use of violence (as occurred after the World War) — by doing away with all principles of sovereignty, all genuine authority and all order from above, is matched today in a significant number of individuals by a 'liberation' amounting to the elimination of any inner 'form', any sort of character, any kind of rectitude. What we find, in other words, is the decline or absence in the individual of that central power which I have already referred to with the evocative Classical denomination of *hegemonikon*. This does not apply to the ethical sphere alone, but also to the field of common behaviour, of individual psychology, and of one's existential structure. The result is the spread of an unstable and formless type — what may well be described as *the breed of the evasive man*. This is a breed that deserves to be described in more detail than I can possibly do here; a full description would even draw upon scientific and experimental methods.

The type of man belonging to this breed not only cannot stand any inner discipline and hates the prospect of facing himself, but he is also incapable of taking any serious commitment, of following a well-defined line of conduct, of showing any character. Partly, he does not wish to do so; partly, he cannot. Indeed, it is interesting to note that this feebleness is not always of the unscrupulous self-serving sort, typical of the kind of man who says: 'In this age one cannot afford to show any character.' In many cases, the behaviour of the people in question is even detrimental to them. It is significant, moreover, that the shattered type of individual I am talking about is increasingly taking root both in places that were the least suited to it in terms of race and tradition (I am chiefly referring to central Europe and to the Nordic countries, and to some extent to Britain too) and among classes, such as the aristocracy and the artisan class, whose members until just recently still preserved a certain inner form.

The decline of all 'professional honour' also reflects the same pattern of disintegration — the sort of honour which in the practical field represented a valuable expression of one's moral conscience as well as a degree of nobility. The pleasure of producing things according to one's art, by doing one's best, in an earnest and honourable fashion, is replaced by the basest kind of interest, which does not shy from adulteration and fraud. Most typical of all are food frauds, which nowadays have become blatant and widespread as never before. An often criminal irresponsibility comes into play here; yet it is also a matter of obliqueness, of a drop of one's inner level, of the vanishing of that sense of honour which in former times distinguished even the humblest guilds. (In a certain sector, parallel with industrialisation, this sense of honour is replaced by a proletarian character and by social blackmailing from the so-called 'working class', those mere 'sellers of labour'.)

As already noted, the phenomenon does not concern the moral sphere alone. Feebleness, evasiveness, light-hearted irresponsibility and casual unfairness are also displayed in relation to trivial, everyday matters of life. One promises something — to write, phone, take care of this or that — and then fails to act on it. One is not punctual. In more serious cases, memory itself is affected: forgetfulness, absent-mindedness, a difficulty to concentrate. Specialists have noted that the young generations have a poorer memory, and various bizarre or adjunct reasons have been invoked to explain this fact. But the real cause actually lies in the aforementioned alteration of the overall climate, which would appear to be leading to a genuine alteration of people's psychological make-up. We can grasp the deeper implications of this phenomenon if we bear in mind Weininger's insightful observations on the relation between ethics, logic and memory[2] — on the meaning of memory on a higher rather than merely psychological level (memory being closely associated with the unity of the human person, with its resistance to dispersion over time, to the flow of time; as such, it also possesses an ethical and ontological value — which is why a particular strengthening of memory comes into play in ascetic disciplines of a higher order, as in Buddhism for instance).

The evasive breed of man displays a natural tendency towards lying, often gratuitously so, for no real reason; this is one of its specifically 'feminine' traits. And if someone reproaches a man of this breed on account of such behaviour, he will either react with surprise, since it comes so naturally to him, or feel irked and react with a sort of huff. Such a man does not wish to be 'bothered'. With a little attention, one will easily find confirmation of this sort of neurosis within the circle of one's own social relations. And one will also note that many people who only yesterday seemed to be friends or men with a certain inner composure, have now become — in the aftermath of the War — quite unrecognisable.

It is not even worth discussing the world of petty politicians, with its wheeling and dealing and the corruption that has always been the hallmark of parliamentary democracies, but which has emerged in a

---

2   Otto Weininger was a Jewish Austrian philosopher. He was born in 1880, but in 1903 committed suicide at the green age of 23. His motive remains mysterious; evidently he had had the thought of killing himself for years prior, and one of the more plausible motivations which are adduced to explain his act was a certain self-loathing on account of his Jewish heritage. He wrote several books in his short life, but he is most famous for his brilliant *Sex and Character*, which remains notorious to this day for its intrepid but harsh judgement of Jews and women. The Italian editor for the present work provides the following reference here: Otto Weininger, *Sex and Character*, Part II, Chapter 6.

particularly prominent and blatant form today. For it is all too evident just what role is played here by the breed of the evasive man, which is always the same despite its wide range of labels and parties. Indeed, it is worth noting that those professing ideas of the 'Right' often constitute no exception, since these ideas frequently make up a separate compartment in such people, with no direct contact to — and no practical consequences for — their actual life. Rather, it is worth mentioning here the petty corruption that one finds, especially in the sexual field, among the new and 'emancipated' generations. This goes more or less in the direction of the ideal of '*dolce vita*'.[3] The phenomenon may be traced back to the same cause: feebleness and inconstancy. It does not correspond to something genuinely non-conformist, to the affirmation of a higher sort of freedom, of a more pronounced personality. Ultimately, it is the effect of letting oneself go in a form of passiveness, a banal drop in level. I will return to this point when studying the background of certain sexological ideological currents en vogue nowadays. The space that ought to be filled by one's 'inner sovereign' — possibly in contrast to all exterior laws, hypocrisy or lies, through the law of one's own being (Stirner, Nietzsche, Ibsen)[4] — is empty. One lives from day

---

3   The Italian term is often translated as 'the sweet life', but is better rendered as 'sweet living'. Outside of Italy, the term is associated most commonly with the eponymous film by Federico Fellini, which itself took the name — as well as inspiration for its theme and many of its events — from the historical period in Italy around the close of the 50s. This brief but memorable period was characterised by a kind of carefree thoughtlessness and rampant hedonism.

4   The three men named here all in their own way promoted a kind of self-reliant championing of one's innermost and truest self, against all the deceits and conceits of the world surrounding. Max Stirner (born Johann Caspar Schmidt, 1806–1856) was a German philosopher, known almost exclusively for his 1845 work *The Ego and its Own*, which has been variously interpreted as a work of amoral nihilism, a proto-anarchical tract, and an early form of existentialism. It can certainly be taken above all as a work of individualism (as its very title does not blush to announce). The philosophy of Friedrich Nietzsche (1844–1900) is

to day, foolishly. Hence the disgust and boredom that one feels in rare moments of awareness.

The lack of an external authority and of true leaders within the organism of the State, and the lack of an inner form in the individual — the two things go hand in hand, the one strengthening the other, so much so that they may well be two different aspects of a single phenomenon marking the progressive and democratic times in which we live.

---

often, and not altogether erroneously, encapsulated in a phrase taken from *Thus Spake Zarathustra*, 'Become what you are' (Fourth and Last Part, 'The Honey Sacrifice'; the phrase itself is in fact an importation from Pindar, Second Pythian Ode, line 72). The implication of this phrase is clearly that most of us are *not* what we are — that is, our lives are determined, not in strict adherence to what is deepest and most personal to us, but rather by the often frivolous, hypocritical, and mendacious social customs surrounding us. Henrik Ibsen (1828–1906) was a Norwegian playwright, whose enormous influence extended well beyond the borders of his homeland. One of his major themes was the individual standing against the masses and mores of the day, as exemplified perhaps most strikingly in his play *An Enemy of the People.*

3. THE THIRD SEX

1

There is no doubt that the increase in homosexuality as well as the inroads made by what has been called the 'third sex' constitutes a phenomenon typical of the last period,[1] and not only in Italy.

As regards homosexuality,[2] one peculiar trait is worth noting: it is no longer limited, as was largely the case in the past, to the upper classes — artists, aesthetes, decadent pursuers of perversions and deviant experiences — but has come to affect also the so-called 'simple folk' and the lower classes. Only the middle class has been spared, at least to some extent.

It is not worth investigating here the problem of homosexuality itself. In one of my works,[3] I have conducted a systematic study of every

---

1   Italian: *tempi ultimi.*

2   Here — and throughout the present chapter — Evola very explicitly avails himself of the Italian words *pederastia* and *pederasta*, which, despite their evident similarity to the English 'pederasty' and 'pederast', are generally used to indicate homosexuality as such, rather than the relations between men and boys in particular, as they almost exclusively do in English. However, these Italian words have a decidedly negative connotation which it is impossible to render elegantly in English. In the present translation, the common neutral English terms have been preferred, and 'pederasty' is reserved exclusively for the practices of the Ancient Greeks. But the reader is invited, as he proceeds, to keep in mind Evola's derogatory tone.

3   [Evola's note. —Ed.] *Eros and the Mysteries of Love: The Metaphysics of Sex,* Inner Traditions International, New York, 1991.

possible form of eroticism, not confining myself to 'normal' forms but also drawing attention to all those which distinguished other ages and civilisations. However, this book hardly makes any mention of homosexuality at all. The reason for this is that starting from the very concept of sexuality, even in its broader sense, and leaving aside all social prejudices, it is not easy to elucidate the phenomenon of homosexuality. It essentially falls within the category of 'pathology' understood in a broad and objective sense, and not merely for its opposition to what current ideas of bourgeois morality take to be 'healthy'. I will briefly frame the question by distinguishing two of its aspects. The second of these will lead us to the sociological level and, in a way, to the kind of considerations made in the previous chapter.

In the work just mentioned, I set out from the idea that all 'normal' sexuality derives from the psycho-physical states engendered by the opposition of two principles operating like magnetic poles, the masculine and the feminine. I am speaking here of 'masculine' and 'feminine' *in an absolute sense*, meaning two principles governing what is ultimately a metaphysical — and not just a physical — order. These principles may be present to widely varying degrees in men and women. Indeed, in real life 'absolute' men and women are found just about as often as the abstract triangle of pure geometry. We rather find beings in whom either the masculine quality is predominant ('men') or the feminine one is ('women'), but in whom the opposite quality is never completely absent. The basic law of sexual attraction, already presented by Plato and Schopenhauer, and later clearly formulated by Weininger,[4] is that sexual attraction in its most typical forms stems from the encounter between a man and a woman such that the sum of the masculine and feminine parts contained in each makes up an absolute man and an absolute woman. To illustrate this with an example, a man who is

---

4   [Evola's note. —*Ed.*] See Plato, *The Symposium*; Arthur Schopenhauer, *The Metaphysics of Sexual Love*; Otto Weininger, *Sex and Character*.

three quarters man and one quarter woman will find himself irresist-
ibly, magnetically attracted to a woman who is three quarters woman
and one quarter man: for the sum in this case would be precisely one
absolute man and one absolute woman, combined into one. This law
applies to every intense, deep and 'elementary' eroticism between the
two sexes; it does not concern degraded, watered-down, bourgeois or
merely 'ideal' and sentimental forms of love and sexuality.

Now, the law in question also allows us to identify those cases in
which homosexuality is understandable and 'natural': these are the cases
in which the sex of two individuals is not very differentiated. Let us
take, for example, a man who is only 55% 'man' and for the remainder
'woman'. His natural counterpart will be a being who is 55% 'woman'
and for the remainder 'man'; but a being of this sort will hardly differ
from a man, and since one must consider not just the external, physical
sex but also (or even especially) the interior one, this being may well be
physiologically male — and the same applies to a woman in a similar
case. Such poorly differentiated 'sexuations' may be associated with the
concept of a 'third sex', although these are clearly only extreme cases.
This would explain the origin and foundation of the relations between
homosexual men or between lesbians as 'natural' phenomena, deriving
from a peculiar, congenital conformation and from the very same law
that, when applied to a different conformation, leads to normal sexual
relations. In these cases alone, there is little point in stigmatising homosexuality as a 'corruption' (since for beings such as those mentioned
here so-called 'natural' relations would not be natural at all, but contrary
to *their* nature). Likewise, it would be pointless to trust the efficacy of
prophylactic measures or therapies, if one — quite reasonably — does
not believe that such measures are capable of altering what in biology is
referred to as the constitutional type, the individual's congenital psycho-
physical constitution. If one were to formulate a moral judgement with
regard to the corresponding state of affairs in these extreme cases, one
ought to censure chiefly male homosexuality, since it entails the degra-

dation of one of the two men as a 'person' and his sexual use as a woman. This is not the case with lesbians: if it is true that, as the ancients used to say, *tota mulier sexus*[5] — if, that is, sexuality is the essential undercurrent of feminine nature — then a relation between two women is not quite as degrading, provided it is a relationship between two equally feminine women and not the grotesque caricature of a normal heterosexual relationship, with one woman playing the part of the man.

If this general picture does not explain *all* cases of homosexuality, this is due to the fact that a fair share of them fall within a different category, that of abnormal forms in the precise sense: they are determined by extrinsic factors, which require a different evaluation. If we were to take a broader look at the phenomenon, as it presents itself from a historical perspective and among other peoples, in many cases we would have to take into account a different range of factors. I mean to say that such phenomena can no longer be explained by invoking the sexual attraction engendered by any sort of polarity between the masculine principle and the feminine one (considered in themselves that is, independently of the different degrees to which they may be present in individual men and women). For instance, male homosexuality in the Classical world constitutes an altogether different phenomenon. As is widely known, Plato sought to define it as an aesthetic factor. In this case, it is clear that, strictly speaking, we are not dealing with erotic attraction at all. For in such cases the kind of rapture and elation usually triggered by a creature of the opposite gender, according to the law of polarity of the

---

5   Latin: 'woman is wholly sex', the meaning of which Evola aptly summarises here. Though the phrase made a notable appearance in the Christian scholastic tradition, and formed the basis of much of the Christian animus against women (woman as temptress, woman as sexually insatiable), the saying also reveals the less moralistic view of women common to the Ancients. According to this last view, sexuality was fundamental to the feminine nature for the essential connection of the same to pregnancy and childbirth. This is certainly related to the traditional role that women were delegated in the societies of Classical Antiquity, as well as to the high social premium placed on the chastity of women in Roman times especially.

sexes, is instead activated by other objects, which serve as a mere support or trigger for the phenomenon in question. Thus Plato speaks of *eros* as a form of 'divine madness', or μανία, which is akin to other forms of madness unrelated to sex, and which becomes increasingly detached from the corporeal, or indeed carnal, level. Plato establishes a progression in which the rapture and love stirred by an ephebe only represent the lowest degree (since in the other degrees these feelings are elicited by spiritual beauty) in the ascent to the idea of pure, abstract and heavenly beauty.[6]

---

6   Eros (Ancient Greek: ἔρως) is best translated as 'love', but indicates rather something like what we would call, drawing from the same root, 'erotic love'. In truth, the Greek word means 'desire', and thus implicates sexual or romantic love in particular; but let it be noted that this is a very superficial understanding of a concept which figures centrally in Ancient Greek culture. The Greek idea of μανία is something like inspired or (as Evola has it here) divine madness; it appears in an extremely suggestive moment in Plato's *Phaedrus* (see 243d-257b), toward the beginning of one of the rare Socratic speeches. An ephebe (Ancient Greek: ἔφηβος) was an adolescent boy — or better say a boy on the cusp between adolescence and adulthood, which transitional period was to be superseded through an initiation into maturity and full citizenship. Though this period would generally correspond to the age of about seventeen to eighteen, physiological cues were taken to be more important than age itself: an ephebe would not be considered a man until he could grow a beard, which naturally would come sooner with some and later with others. A key part of the ephebe's initiation in certain epochs and regions of Ancient Greece was his relationship with an older man, who would act as his mentor and role model. Apropos Evola's present theme, it is worth noting that though we tend to identify this relationship with our modern forms of homosexuality, this is extremely misleading for a great many reasons. Here we can note only one of the most important of these: the Greeks, who agreed essentially with a part of Evola's critique of male homosexuality above, generally despised sodomy, since it compromised the honour of the ephebe, and preferred intercrural pederasty. Their stance on this matter is tangible in Plato's dialogue *Gorgias*, in which Socrates scandalously uses the case of the catamite, the passive male recipient of sodomy, to indicate the most shameful role imaginable (see *Gorgias*, 494e). Plato treats the theme of eros in various parts of his oeuvre, but most famously and most exhaustively in *The Symposium*, to which Evola makes

Just to what extent this homosexual 'Platonic love' (which at its lowest degree would be 'purer', since it does not have a woman as its object and hence cannot serve any reproductive purposes) may be invoked to justify the practice of ancient pederasty is an altogether different question. Certainly, it can hardly be invoked at all in relation to the decadent period of Roman history.

Plato's theory finds an echo in certain Muslim milieus. However, it would be difficult to associate it with the kind of homosexuality that is so widespread among the Turks. In the Ottoman army for instance (at any rate in the past, as the case reported by Colonel Lawrence suggests)[7] it seems as though any attempt on a soldier's part not to yield to his officer's desire was practically regarded as an act of insubordination. Furthermore, in this case it seems as though another factor has sometimes been at work, a factor which has nothing to do with sexuality in itself: according to a certain person's confession which was recently reported to me (once again, from the Turkish area), what is effective here is the thrill caused in the active homosexual by a 'feeling of power'. But this background is far from clear in itself, given all the number of ways in which the *libido dominandi*,[8] or desire to domi-

---

special reference here. See in particular Socrates' speech on Diotima's ladder: 202e — 212c.

7   That is, the famed T. E. Lawrence (1888–1935), commonly known as Lawrence of Arabia for his important role in the Arab Revolt during World War I, excellently portrayed in David Lean's film *Lawrence of Arabia*. Lawrence, a soldier, a scholar, a sometime translator of Homer, wrote an uncommonly beautiful memoir on his wartime experiences entitled *The Seven Pillars*, which includes the passages to which Evola here alludes: see Introduction, Chapter VI. It is also possible that Evola is referring to Lawrence's rape at the hands of a Turkish officer: see Book VI, Chapter LXXX.

8   Latin: 'the lust or will to rule'. Though Evola uses the term to refer to sexual matters, it actually comes from Augustine's *City of God*, Book 1, Pr., in which he says of the earthly city that it is *ipsa ei dominandi libido dominatur*, 'itself ruled by its lust to rule'. (Translation mine. Augustine also states most inter-

nate, can be exercised and satisfied even in normal relationships with women. Homosexuality in Japan presents a similar problem.

Generally speaking, none of these phenomena can be explained as extreme examples of the above-mentioned law of sexual complementarity, for the condition of a weakly differentiated sex in both partners does not occur in them. In homosexual couples, we might find one partner who is markedly virile for example (i.e. who might show the 'masculine' quality to a high degree), rather than a relationship between two representatives of the intermediate hybrid form of the 'third sex'.

The phenomenon of the deflection of erotic love, which makes its emergence possible outside the normal conditions of sexual attraction (the polarity and hence magnetism between the two sexes) — and therefore in a way also the phenomenon of its displacement, or transfer, onto a different object (a phenomenon clearly established by psychoanalysis) — can therefore provide an 'additive' explanation of homosexuality. But a few considerations of a different sort are also necessary here.

2

We previously considered the constitution of individuals with regard to sex (their 'sexuation', the degree to which they are men or women) as something preformed and fixed. Now we must broaden the picture to include those cases in which certain changes become possible as a consequence of regressive processes, possibly favoured by certain general conditions in the environment, society, and civilisation.

To begin with, we must form a more precise idea about sex, which may be defined as follows. The fact that we find 100% male or 100% fe-

---

estingly — Paragraph XXX — that the Roman people possessed this will to a greater extent than any other people.)

male individuals only in exceptional cases, and that in each individual we find residues of the other sex, is related to the fact — well-known in biology — that the embryo is initially not sexually differentiated at all, but presents traits belonging to both sexes. 'Sexuation' is produced only in a subsequent process (which seems to begin in the fifth or sixth month of gestation): then the traits of one gender prevail and increasingly develop, while those of the opposite gender atrophy or remain latent (as is widely known, in the purely somatic sphere residues of the other sex are to be found, as for instance in the half-developed breasts of males and in the female clitoris). Thus, once the development is complete, the sex of the male or female individual must be regarded as the effect of a predominant force which leaves its mark on this process, neutralising and excluding the originally coexistent possibilities of the other sex, particularly in the bodily, physiological sphere (in the psychological sphere, the margin of fluctuation can be far broader).

Now, the dominant power responsible for sexuation may weaken due to a process of regression. Then, just as happens in the political sphere at the weakening of a central authority in a society, all the lower forces which had hitherto been held in check may free themselves and resurface; in the individual, latent traits of the other sex may emerge and, with them, a bisexual inclination. Thus we will once again find the condition of the 'third sex', obviously a particularly fertile soil for the phenomenon of homosexuality. Its precondition, then, is an inner yielding, a collapse of one's 'inner form' or, rather, of that forming power which manifests itself not only in sexuation but also in one's character and personality — in one's having, in general, 'a particular persona'.

We can understand, then, why the development of homosexuality even among popular strata, potentially in endemic forms, is a sign of the times, one that logically falls among those phenomena which make the modern world regressive. This leads us back to the considerations made in the previous chapter.

In an egalitarian and democraticised society (in the broader sense of the term); in a society in which there are no longer any casts, functional organic classes or Orders; in a society in which 'culture' is standardised, extrinsic, utilitarian, and tradition is no longer a living, forming force; in a society in which Pindar's 'be thyself' has become but a meaningless phrase;[9] in a society in which character amounts to a luxury that only fools can afford, whereas inner weakness is the norm; in a society, finally, in which whatever lies above racial, ethnic and national difference has been replaced by what effectively lies below all this and which, therefore, has a shapeless and hybrid character — in such a society, forces are at work that in the long run are bound to influence the very constitution of individuals, thus affecting everything typical and differentiated, even in the psycho-physical field.

'Democracy' is not a mere political and social fact; it is a general climate which, in the long term, is destined to have regressive consequences on the existential level itself. In the particular domain of the sexes, this can promote the kind of inner decay, the kind of weakening of the inner power of sexuation that, as already noted, represents the premise for the emergence and spread of the 'third sex' and, with it, of many truly striking forms of homosexuality in contemporary society.[10] On the other hand, another consequence of all this is the visible trivialisation and 'primitivisation' of normal sexual relations between young members of the latest generations (on account of reduced tension due to the lower degree of polarity). Even certain strange phenomena which were apparently very rare in the past, such

---

9   Taken from Pindar's Second Pythian Ode, line 72: γένοι᾽ οἷος ἐσσὶ μαθών ('Become what you are, having learned what that is', translation mine).

10   [Evola's note. For the Aristotle reference here, see *On the Generation of Animals*, Book 1, Chapter 20 —*Ed.*] In accordance with all this, it seems as though the increase in the number of lesbians today is almost negligible compared to that of gays: for it is man who embodies the principle on which 'form' rests, as already acknowledged by Aristotle.

as sex changes — men taking on female bodies and vice-versa — may be understood in the same terms and traced back to the same causes: it is as though in today's general climate the potentialities of the opposite gender contained within each of us had acquired an exceptional possibility of resurfacing and activating itself on account of the weakening of that central force which, even biologically, defines one's 'type', to the point of replacing and changing the sex one was born with.

If the argument made so far is a convincing one, in this case too we are only to take this as a sign of the times and to acknowledge the utter inanity of all moralising and socially repressive conformist measures. It is impossible to hold together the sand running through our fingers, no matter how hard we try. Rather, we ought to reach the level of first causes — of which everything else in all the various domains, including that of the phenomena just considered, is only a consequence — and act at that level, so as to produce an essential change. But this is tantamount to saying that the principle of everything ought to be the overcoming of the present civilisation and society, and the restoration of a differentiated, organic and well-structured type of social organisation through the intervention of a forming, living, central force. Now, this prospect increasingly seems like sheer utopia, since 'progress' in all fields today tends increasingly in the opposite direction. Those who inwardly do not belong — and do not wish to belong — to this world have no choice but to note those general relations of cause and effect that escape our contemporaries in their blindness, and to calmly take stock of all that is sprouting forth, according to a clear logic, from the soil of a decaying world.

4. NEGRIFIED AMERICA

Not long ago, the newspapers announced that according to some calculations, half of the population of Manhattan will be black by 1970, and that in the five boroughs that make up the entire city of New York, 28% of the inhabitants will be of coloured race.[1] Developments in the same direction have been registered in other cities and areas of

---

1   Needless to say, these predictions have not come to pass in so extreme a manner as this. According to the 2010 census, about a fourth of the present population of New York City (taking all five boroughs) is black; the 2000 census reports the lowest percentage in Staten Island (about a tenth of the population as black) and the highest in Brooklyn (just over a third of the population as black). Some 18% of Manhattan in 2000 was black. It is interesting to speculate as to what might have curbed the stark demographic trends widely recognised at the time of Evola's writing. One of the factors involved is certainly the displacement of blacks from increasingly affluent neighborhoods, particularly in Manhattan and Brooklyn. Another factor which has undoubtedly had a huge impact is the legalisation of abortion in New York in the 70s, and the widening influence of Planned Parenthood beginning so early as the late 50s. In a particularly striking case, more black babies were aborted in New York City in 2012 than were born. Despite the retardation of these trends, however, the black population in New York City is greater than in any other metropolitan area in the United States, and though its percentage has declined in absolute terms in the most recent decades (due primarily to the growing immigration of Hispanic and Asian ethnicities), it has grown with respect to the fast declining white population, which according to the 2010 census now makes up a mere third of the total population of the city. And it is equally needless to say that the overall demographic movement in the whole of the United States continues in the direction that Evola here laments.

the United States. We are witnessing a negrification, a mongrelisation, and a decline of the white race in the face of faster-breeding inferior races.

Of course, from the democratic point of view, there is nothing wrong with that: on the contrary. We are all acquainted with the zeal and intransigence of American proponents of so-called 'racial integration', which can only further speed the process. Not only do they advocate complete interracial social fraternisation, not only do they want the Negro to have free access to any public and political office (so that we may even expect, in the future, a black president of the United States), but they also have no objection to Negroes mixing their blood with that of white Americans. A characteristic example of propaganda for this agenda is the play entitled *Deep Are the Roots* (in other words: of racial 'prejudice'), which Italian radio has felt the need to subject us to on more than one occasion.[2]

The 'integrationists' who draw these conclusions — as logical as they are aberrant — from the dogma of egalitarian democracy, and who, while talking at full blast about freedom, in fact advocate a truly coer-

---

2   The play in question was written in 1945 by the communists Arnaud d'Usseau and James Gow, and treats of a theme which has (in any number of different forms) subsequently become a commonplace in Hollywood: the morally impeccable black man fighting against the utterly irrational prejudice of bigoted whites. In *Deep Are the Roots*, Brett, a black soldier, returns to his home in the South after serving (with distinction, naturally) in World War II. The dashing young veteran wins the love not just of one, but of *both* the daughters of the obligatory conservative white Senator of his hometown. The eldest of these daughters most progressively would have Brett go to college to get himself an education, but the intrepid young war hero chooses to remain to fight for right in his hometown instead. He selects the younger of the two daughters, causing the elder to ally herself most wickedly with her scheming father in a malevolent plot to destroy the blameless Brett. The plot proceeds apace, to a climax which is, surely, either happy or unhappy.

cive system,[3] are still opposed, especially in the South, by certain groups that have no intention of giving a green light to the advance of the black race and the 'negrification' of their country. However, these latter groups fail to realise the extent of the phenomenon, for they notice it only in its most material and tangible form. They fail to see the extent to which America is 'negrified' not only racially and demographically, but above all in its civilisation, in the behaviour and tastes of the Americans, even when there has been no actual mixing with Negro blood.

---

3   [Evola's note. —*Ed.*] Forced 'integration' is a blatant violation of the principle of freedom, and that violation is only secondarily a matter of 'race'. No family has ever been denied the right not to welcome strangers it dislikes into its home or to stay apart from them (whatever the reason may be for such dislike); but fraternisation with Negroes in public life is now being imposed — ironically in the name of liberty, of a one-sided freedom. So-called segregation — apartheid — is deplored, even though it is the only reasonable system, and one that harms nobody: let each remain in his own realm, among his own. It is unbelievable what 'progress' has brought about in the degenerate white race: the British, who until recently were extreme practical racists, to the point of believing that beyond the English Channel there dwelt almost a different humanity, so that in their colonies they haughtily held themselves apart even from 'coloured' representatives of ancient civilisations superior to their own (India, China, etc.)– these same British have at the time of this writing, as a result of the 'anti-colonialist' infatuation, forced their compatriots in Rhodesia to secede from the Commonwealth, applying sanctions against them because the Rhodesians refuse to yield to the imposition of granting an equal and indiscriminate democratic vote to the mass of the black population, which would have forced them out of the land that had they alone had civilised.

As for the US, if it is indeed the case, as some claim, that the anti-segregationists are motivated by a guilt complex for the wrongs done to blacks in the former regime of slavery — as if all the blood shed by whites in the fratricidal Civil War (officially fought for the freedom of the blacks) were not enough — why do they not request that one of the fifty states of the Union be emptied and ceded, so that all American blacks could be moved there, allowing them to rule themselves and do whatever they want without bothering or contaminating anyone? That would be the best solution.

The US has been compared, not without justification, to a melting-pot. It actually presents us with a case in which a human type of largely uniform and constant characteristics was formed from out of a highly heterogeneous raw material. Emigrating to America, men of the most diverse peoples receive the same imprint; after two generations, except in rare cases, they lose almost all of their original characteristics, reproducing a type which is fairly homogeneous in terms of mentality, sensibility, and behaviour: the American type.

In this regard, theories such as those formulated by Frobenius and Spengler, who have asserted a close relationship between the forms of a given culture and a kind of 'soul' bound to the natural environment, to the 'landscape' and the original population, do not seem applicable.[4] Otherwise, an essential part ought to have been played in American culture by the indigenous element, which consists of Amerindians, the redskins. The red Indians were proud races with their own style, their own dignity, sensibility and forms of religiosity; not without justification, a traditionalist writer, F. Schuon, spoke of the presence in their

---

4   Leo Frobenius (1873–1938) was a German ethnologist and archaeologist, and one of the major theoreticians of the idea of *Kulturkreise*, 'Culture Circles'. This idea was meant to explain the diffusion of cultures throughout the world with reference to their geographical locations. Though in his earlier work, the geographical element was less pronounced (Frobenius believed that cultures could as it were migrate and transmit their cultures to others) the geographical element gradually attained centrality in his views. Oswald Spengler (1880–1936) was the author of the celebrated *Decline of the West*, a seminal study in the growth and decline of cultures in world history. Spengler took a degree of inspiration from Frobenius' work; he similarly believed that a culture, even in its racial traits, receives the morphological stamp of the landscape in which it arises and the soil upon which it is reared, though he understood 'landscape' and 'soil' in a mystico-spiritual more than in a materialistic sense. The specific relation of race and geography in Spengler's thought is a matter of some interest, and a deal of contention surrounds it.

being, of something 'aquiline and solar'.[5] And we will not hesitate to assert that had it been their spirit — in its best aspects and on an appropriate plane — to appreciably imbue the human material thrown into the 'American melting pot', the level of American civilisation would probably be higher.[6]

Instead, besides its Puritan-Protestant component (which, in turn, as a result of its fetishistic emphasis on the Old Testament, possesses many Judaised, degenerate traits), it seems that precisely the Negro element, in its primitivism, has set the tone in important aspects of the American psyche. It is already significant that when speaking of American folklore, it is to the Negroes one refers, as if they were the original inhabitants of the country. Thus, the famous *Porgy and Bess* by the Jew Gershwin, which deals exclusively with blacks, is considered in the US to be a classic work inspired by 'American folklore'. The

---

5   Frithjof Schuon (1907–1998) was a Swiss metaphysician who first embarked on his spiritual quest with the study of the Hindu scriptures. At an early age he met Guénon, who convinced him to move to Paris and to begin to study Arabic. The translator provides the following reference: Frithjof Schuon, *The Feathered Sun: Plains Indians in Art and Philosophy* (Bloomington, IN: World Wisdom Books, 1990), pp. 39–40.

6   [Evola's note. —Ed.] A certain man of letters with intellectual pretensions, one Salvatore Quasimodo, has deplored the 'racist' ideas expounded here, and has accused me, among other things, of self-contradiction, because while I stand against Negroes, I nonetheless respect Amerindians. He has no suspicion of the fact that a 'healthy racism' has nothing to do with the prejudice of 'white skin'; it is essentially a matter of a hierarchy of values, according to which we say 'no' to Negroes, to all that pertains to them and to all Negro contamination (the Negro races, in this hierarchy, are just above Australian primitives, and according to a well-known morphology correspond mainly to the type of 'nocturnal' and 'telluric' races, as opposed to the 'diurnal' type), while on the other hand, given what the white race has been reduced to in the age of colonial mercantilist expansion, we would certainly be willing to concede superiority over 'whites' to the higher Hindu, Chinese, and Japanese types, and to some Arabs strains, despite the fact that they do not have white skin.

composer has declared that he lived for some time among American blacks in preparation for this work.[7]

But the phenomenon of popular and dance music is even more conspicuous and generalised. Fitzgerald was not wrong when he said that in one of its main aspects, American civilisation can be called a civilisation of jazz, i.e., of negrified music and dance.[8] In this domain, very singular 'elective affinities' have led America, by way of a process of regression and primitivisation, to imitate the Negroes. Assuming there is a need for frenzied rhythms and forms as a legitimate compensation for the mechanical and materialistic soullessness of modern civilisation, one would have done much better to look to the many sources available in Europe: we have elsewhere mentioned, for example, the dance rhythms of South Eastern Europe, which often have something truly Dionysian about them. But America has chosen to imitate the blacks and the Afro-Cubans, and from America this contagion has gradually spread to all other countries.

---

7   The no doubt appealingly named *Porgy and Bess* is one of two 'operas' produced by George Gershwin (1898–1937) in the course of his short career. It follows the vicissitudes of a number of penurious blacks in the city slums, and therefore features a winning cast of beggars, drug addicts, drug dealers, and violent drunkards. Gershwin himself called it a 'folk opera', whatever that is supposed to mean, and with it he somehow hoped to fuse the jazz and classical traditions into one. He envisioned an exclusively black cast, as he felt that only a black would be able to understand his musical vision; his wishes were somewhat complicated by the fact that a great many blacks somehow did not like being condescended to in such a fashion by an artsy Jew. In perhaps the single element of the work which kept to good operatic tradition, *Porgy and Bess* ran some four hours in its original form. Oddly, this proved a strain on the better part of its intended public, and the work was later considerably abridged. The shortened form enjoyed much greater success than its more endless original.

8   Reference to the American F. Scott Fitzgerald (1896–1940), one of the best remembered authors of the so-called Jazz Age (name which he himself coined), who, despite concluding only four novels in his relatively short life, has suffered nothing in terms of celebrity since his untimely death.

The Negro component of the American psyche was already noticed, in his time, by the psychoanalyst C. G. Jung. A few of his observations are worth quoting:[9]

> Another thing that struck me [in the American] was the great influence of the Negro, a psychological influence naturally, not due to the mixing of blood. The emotional way an American expresses himself, especially the way he laughs, can best be studied in the illustrated supplements of the American papers; the inimitable Teddy Roosevelt laugh is found in its primordial form in the American Negro. The peculiar walk with loose joints, or the swinging of the hips so frequently observed in Americans, also comes from the Negro.[10] American music draws its main inspiration from the Negro, and so does the dance. The expression of religious feeling, the revival meetings, the Holy Rollers and other abnormalities are strongly influenced by the Negro. The vivacity of the average American, which shows itself not only at baseball games but quite particularly in his extraordinary love of talking — the ceaseless gabble of American papers is an eloquent example of this — is scarcely to be derived from his Germanic forefathers, but is far more like the chattering of a Negro village. The almost total lack of privacy and the

---

9   Taken from the essay 'Mind and Earth' by the Swiss psychiatrist C. G. Jung (1875–1961), whose influence in his field is probably matched only by Freud. It might be mentioned apropos the present theme that Jung in another essay ('The Complications of American Psychology', originally 'Your Negroid and Indian Behavior') relates how, on walking through the streets of the American city of Buffalo, he was struck with the resemblance of the Americans with the Indians. (At first, he even took this as a sign of long intermixing between the two groups, but was disabused of this impression by his American companion.) In the passage in question, he seems to subscribe to the views which Evola above assigns to Spengler and Frobenius. But in fundamental agreement with Evola, he asks in 'Mind and Earth': 'Does the body react to America, and the psyche to Africa?' Jung's take on the American situation was somewhat more ambiguous, however, than Evola's.

10 [Evola's note. —*Ed.*] One may add the absolutely Negro character of the movements of American comedians and *variété* dancers.

all-devouring mass sociability remind one of primitive life in open huts, where there is complete identity with all members of the tribe.

The passage continues along the same lines, and Jung ends up wondering if the inhabitants of the new continent could still be considered to be Europeans. But his observations can be developed even further.

That brutality which is unquestionably characteristic of Americans can well be said to have a Negro character. In the happy days of what Eisenhower was not ashamed to call the 'Crusade in Europe',[11] as well as in the early days of the occupation, we had the occasion to observe the typical forms of that brutality; but we also saw that at times, American 'whites' went even farther in this respect than their Negro comrades, whose infantalism, however, they often shared.

Generally speaking, the taste for brutality now seems to be ingrained in the American mindset. It is true that the most brutal of all sports, boxing, originated in England, but it is in the United States that its most aberrant forms have developed, and it is there that it has become the object of a collective obsession, which was quickly transmitted to other nations. Concerning this taste for getting into fights and coming to blows in the most savage manner, it suffices however to consider the greater part of American films and popular detective stories: vulgar fist-fighting is a constant theme, evidently because it corresponds to the tastes of American audiences and readers, for whom it seems to be the symbol of true masculinity. On the other hand, America, the world leader, has more than any other nation relegated the traditional duel to the status of ridiculous European antiquated rubbish. The duel is a method of settling disputes following strict rules, without resorting to the primitive brute force of the mere arm and fist. There is no need to point out the striking contrast between this American brutality and

---

11   That is, the days of American intervention in World War II. The wartime memoirs of President Dwight D. Eisenhower (1890–1969) were indeed entitled *Crusade in Europe*.

the ideal behaviour of the English gentleman, despite the fact that the English made up a component of the original people of the United States.

Modern Western man, to a large extent a regressive type, is comparable in various respects to a crustacean; he is as 'hard' on the outside — as a man of action, as an unscrupulous entrepreneur, as an organiser, and so forth — as he is 'soft' and formless in his internal substance. Now, this is true to the highest degree of Americans, who represent the degenerate Western type carried to its extreme. But here we find another of their affinities with the Negro. Inconsistent sentimentality, banal pathos, especially in love affairs, put Americans much closer to Negroes than to truly civilised Europeans. Of this, observers can easily find clear evidence in a number of typical American novels and again, songs, as well as in cinema and everyday life.

The fact that American eroticism is as pandemic as it is primitive (technically speaking), has also been deplored by American girls and women. Which brings us to yet another convergence with characteristic features of the Negro races, in which the occasionally obsessive part which eroticism and sexuality have played from the earliest times is associated with primitivism; thus, these races — unlike Orientals, the ancient Western world and certain other peoples — have never known an *ars amatoria* worthy of the name.[12] The much-vaunted high sexual performance of Negroes is really only of a crudely quantitative priapic character.

Another obvious aspect of American primitivism concerns the concept of 'bigness'. Werner Sombart has successfully put his finger

---

12   Latin: 'art of love'. This was originally the title of Ovid's instructional poetry on the right relation between the sexes, but the 'art of love' makes its appearance throughout European history in a most characteristic fashion. In one of its most illustrious forms, it appears centrally in the chivalry of the Late Middle Ages.

on it in saying that 'they mistake bigness for greatness'.[13] Now, this trait is not found in all non-European peoples or peoples of colour. For example, an authentic Arab of the old race, a redskin, or an East Asian (leaving aside those individuals among them who have already been Europeanised) are not overly impressed by merely material, quantitative, ostentatious size, including that related to machinery, technology and the economy. This is a trait found only in truly primitive and childish races like that of the Negro. It is no exaggeration to assert that the foolish pride of Americans in spectacular 'bigness', in the 'achievements' of their civilisation, reek of the Negro psyche.

Here, we ought to mention the oft-repeated nonsense about Americans being a 'young race', with the tacit corollary that they are the race of the future. It is true that a myopic gaze easily mistakes regressive childishness for true youth. Strictly speaking, according to the traditional conception, this perspective must be inverted. Despite appearances, recent peoples, since they came last, are the most removed from their origins, and as such must be considered to be the most senile and decadent peoples. This view, moreover, corresponds to the organic world.[14] It explains the paradoxical similarities of supposedly 'young' peoples, understood as late-comers, with those genuinely primitive races which have remained outside of world history, and it explains as well the taste for primitivism and the return to primitivism. We have

---

13 Werner Sombart (1863–1941), who was well regarded by Evola, was the author of various works on economics and sociology. The quotation here reported appears in Sombart's *Der Bourgeois*, but is actually taken from another author: the Englishman Viscount James Bryce, who made this statement in his important work on American institutions, *The American Commonwealth*. Evola treats the question of American (and hence modern) infantalism more extensively in Chapter 25 of his final book, *Recognitions* (also available from Arktos Media Ltd).

14 [Evola's note. —*Ed.*] Returning to what was argued in the first chapter, one might mention the opposite conception, according to which it is the periodical return to one's origins that gives the quality of 'youthfulness'.

already remarked upon the American predilection, through elective affinity, for Negro and sub-tropical music; but the same phenomenon is apparent in other domains of more recent culture and art. We could consider, for example, the glorification of *négritude* by existentialists, intellectuals, and 'progressive' artists in France.[15]

It follows that Europeans, including the imitators of higher non-European civilisations, demonstrate in turn the same primitive and provincial mentality when they profess admiration for America, when they let themselves be impressed by America, when they stupidly allow themselves to be Americanised and enthusiastically believe that this means catching up with the march of progress, as a sign of their liberation and open-mindedness.

This 'catching up' includes the social and cultural 'integration' of the Negro, which is spreading in Europe itself and even in Italy, promoted through the subliminal effects of imported films (where blacks and whites are shown mixing in social functions, as judges, police officers, lawyers, etc.) and television, in spectacles showing black dancers and singers mixed up with white ones, so that the general public is gradually accustomed to interracial fraternisation and loses every remaining natural sense of race and every feeling of distance. The hysteria caused by the shapeless, screaming mass of flesh that is the Negress Ella Fitzgerald during her performances in Italy is a phenomenon is as sad as it is indicative. As is the fact that the most blatant glorification of Negro 'culture', of *négritude*, comes from a German, Janheinz Jahn, in a book entitled *Muntu*, issued by a venerable old publishing house in Germany (the homeland of

---

15 *Négritude* was a movement formed by a number of black intellectuals in France in the first half of the twentieth century, which gradually spread to the wider artistic culture of France and thence Europe. It focused on literary criticism of Marxist orientation and sought to instill a Pan-African sense of identity in blacks across the world — effort which, to judge from the present atmosphere, does not seem to have been altogether wasted.

Aryan racism!).[16] A well-known left-wing Italian publisher, Einaudi, was quick to spread it in our country as well, in a translation in two editions. This ranting book goes to the point of claiming that Negro 'culture' would be a excellent means of reviving and restoring the 'materialistic civilisation' of the West...

Regarding the elective affinities of Americans, we would like to mention one more point. If in the United States of America there was one thing that seemed to be positive and to present some sort of hope, it was the phenomenon of a new generation that championed a kind of rebellious, anarchistic, nihilistic, and anti-conformist existentialism: the so-called Beat generation, the Beats, the hipsters and the like, which we will discuss more elsewhere. But this movement is characterised by its fraternising with blacks, in a veritable religion of Negro jazz and deliberate race-mixing, including white women having sexual relations with Negroes. In a well-known essay, Norman Mailer, who was one of its main exponents, actually established a kind of equivalence between the Negro and the human type of the generation in question, even defining the latter as a 'white negro'. Fausto Gianfranceschi has very rightly written in this regard:[17] 'There is a parallel between the fascination exerted by Negro "culture", in the terms described by

---

16 Ella Fitzgerald (1917–1996) was a famous American jazz singer. Janheinz Jahn was a German scholar who occupied himself extensively with Sub-Saharan Africa. The German publishing house mentioned here was Eugen Diederichs Verlag. *Muntu* was translated in English under the title *Muntu: African Culture and the Western World*. It might be described as a long and somewhat triumphalistic study of generalised African 'culture' and its interaction with the culture of the West.

17 Normal Mailer (1923–2007), who is discussed further in Chapter 16 below, was an American novelist and journalist who won the Pulitzer Prize for his 1979 work *The Executioner's Song*. Mailer indeed wrote an essay entitled 'The White Negro', which was meant to be at once an analysis of and a call to arms for the 'hipster' (defined at one point as a 'philosophical psychopath'). Fausto Gianfranceschi (1928–2012) was an Italian writer who associated with neofascism in his youth, and remained throughout his life a man of the Right. Partially

Mailer, and the effect of Friedrich Nietzsche's message at the turn of the century. The starting point is the same concern with shattering fossilised conformity through the immediate awareness of vital and existential facts; but what confusion, what degradation, if the Negro, as seen today with jazz and the sexual orgasm, is placed on the pedestal of the "Superman"!'[18]

Pour la bonne bouche,[19] we will conclude with a significant statement by a far from superficial American author, James Burnham (in *The Struggle for the World*):[20] 'There is in American life a strain of callow brutality. This betrays itself no less in the lynching and gangsterism at home than in the arrogance and hooliganism of soldiers or tourists abroad. The provincialism of the American mind expresses itself in a lack of sensitivity toward other peoples and other cultures. There is in many Americans an ignorant contempt for ideas and tradition and history, a complacency with the trifles of merely material triumph. Who, listening a few hours to the American radio, could repress a shudder if he thought that the price of survival [of a non-communist society] would be the Americanisation of the world?' And unfortunately, to a certain extent, this is already happening.

---

for that reason, no doubt, his works have never been translated into English. The present quotation is taken from his *L'uomo in allarme*.

18 [Evola's note. —Ed.] Of course, only one aspect of Nietzscheanism is here taken into consideration. The degree of confusion that reigned in American existentialism can be seen in the fact that some, while on the one hand making common cause with the Negro, on the other hand were attracted by the transcendence of the Far Eastern esoteric school of Zen.

19 French: 'saving the best til last', or 'in closing'. Lit., 'for a good mouthful'.

20 James Burnham (1905–1987) was an American political theorist best known for his work *The Managerial Revolution*. The work referenced here was rather an alarums at the rise of communism, which attempted to incite the United States and Great Britain to join in a unified struggle against the red menace.

5. THE DECAY OF WORDS

One of the indications that the course of history has not at all amounted to a form of progress on any level apart from the purely material, is the poverty of modern languages compared to many ancient ones. In terms of structural organicity, articulation and flexibility, not one of the so-called 'living' Western languages can compare, for example, to ancient Latin or Sanskrit. Among the European languages only German, perhaps, has preserved some features of its archaic structure (which is why the German language is said to be 'so difficult'), whereas English and the Scandinavian languages have undergone a process of erosion and levelling. Generally speaking, it may be argued that the ancient languages just mentioned were three-dimensional, whereas modern ones are two-dimensional. Here too time has exerted a corrosive influence; it has made languages 'practical' and 'fluid', to the detriment of their structural coherence. This is but a reflection of what has occurred in many other areas of culture and life.

Words too have a history, and often the change they undergo in terms of content provides an interesting measure of corresponding changes in their speakers' general sensibility and world-view. In particular, it might be interesting to compare the meaning possessed by certain words in the ancient Latin language with that of many corresponding terms which have outwardly remained almost the same in

Italian and often other Romance languages.[1] Generally speaking, one observes a drop in level here. The more ancient meaning has either been lost or only survives in a residual form in particular uses of the word or expression, which no longer correspond to what has become its general and dominant meaning; or else they have been utterly distorted and frequently trivialised. I shall provide a few examples.

1 — *Virtus*. The most typical and best known case is perhaps the word *virtus*. 'Virtue' in a modern sense has almost nothing to do with ancient *virtus*. *Virtus* meant strength of mind, courage, prowess, virile steadfastness. It was connected to *vir*, a term describing man in the strict sense — not in the generic and naturalistic one.[2] In modern languages, the same word has instead acquired an essentially moralistic meaning, one very frequently associated with sexual prejudices, to the point that Vilfredo Pareto coined the term 'virtuism' with reference to it, to describe bourgeois puritan and sexophobic morality.[3] What is

---

1   As the reader will see, many if not all of the examples Evola provides have made a similar pattern in English as they have in Italian. English, however, has been somewhat more fortunate in certain of the cases that follow. We owe this happy turn in part to the lexical richness of our multi-rooted language, and in part to the fact that words of Latin origin in English are already imbued with a sense of formality and distance which to some extent protects them from common pawing. Despite this, English, too, has declined steeply and dramatically in the recent centuries. A few reflections on English in particular will be offered in the footnotes that follow for the benefit of this translation's readers.

2   That is to say, the Latin word *vir* indicates man in the specific and gendered sense of masculinity, rather than 'human being' generally, which was represented by the Latin word *homo*. (All subsequent translations in the footnotes for the present chapter are of Latin terms, unless otherwise specified.)

3   Pareto (1848–1923) was an Italian political scientist and sociologist. He wrote in both Italian and French, and in 1911 published a work in French named *Le virtuisme*, which later issued in Italian under the title *Il mito virtuista e la letteratura immorale* (*The Virtuistic Myth and Immoral Literature*). This book has yet to be translated into English.

generally meant today by a 'virtuous person' is something very different from expressions like *vir virtute praeditus*, with their very effective reiteration.[4] And this difference frequently turns into a kind of antithesis. Indeed, a steadfast, proud, fearless and heroic spirit is the opposite of a 'virtuous' person in the modern, moralistic and conformist sense.

The meaning of *virtus* as an efficacious force has only been preserved in certain specific modern expressions: the 'virtues' of a plant or a drug, 'by virtue' of this or that.

2 — *Honestus*. Connected to the idea of *honos*,[5] in Antiquity this term mainly meant 'honourable', 'noble', 'of noble rank'. What is preserved of this in the corresponding modern term? An 'honest' person now means a 'decent' member of bourgeois society, someone who does not do anything really bad. The phrase *'nato da onesti genitori'* today takes on an almost ironic nuance,[6] whereas in ancient Rome it was used specifically to designate nobility of birth, which often also corresponded to biological nobility. *Vir honesta facie* meant a man of fine appearance, just as the Sanskrit term *arya* referred both to a person worthy of honour and to a nobility that was as much of the mind as it was of the body.[7]

3 — *Gentilis*, *gentilitas*. Today, these terms bring the gentleman to mind, an affable and well-mannered person. The ancient terms, however, referred to the concept of *gens*, stock, race, caste or lineage. For the Romans, someone was *gentilis* when he possessed qualities deriving from a differentiated lineage and blood. These might — yet only as a reflection — determine a demeanour of detached courtesy,

---

4   'A man gifted with virtue'.

5   'Honor, reputation, dignity'.

6   The phrase is Italian, meaning 'born of honest parents'.

7   The word *arya*, from which the term 'Aryan' derives, literally means 'noble'.

something very different from 'good manners', which even a parvenu can acquire by studying etiquette — and different too from the vague modern notion of 'kindness'.[8] Few people today are able to grasp the fuller and deeper meaning of expressions such as 'a gentle spirit' and the like, which survive as isolated extensions of the original meaning in the language of writers of the past.

4 — *Genialitas.* Who is a 'genius' today? A predominantly individualistic man who is imaginative and full of original ideas. At the extreme, there is the artistic 'genius' that in humanistic and bourgeois civilisation represents an object of fetishistic worship, to the point that the 'genius' — more so than the hero, the ascetic or aristocrat — has often been regarded, within this civilisation, as the highest type of man. The Latin term *genialis*, instead, alludes to something that is not at all individualistic and 'humanistic'. It comes from the word *genius*, which originally designated the formative and generative, inner, spiritual and mystical force of a given *gens* or blood lineage. One could argue, therefore, that the qualities of *genialitas* in the ancient sense had a certain relationship with qualities that are 'racial' in the higher sense of the word. By contrast to the modern sense of the word, the element of 'genius' distinguishes itself from the individualistic and the arbitrary; it is bound to a deep root, it obeys an inner necessity through faithfulness to the already supra-personal forces of blood and race — forces that, as is well-known, were connected in any patrician lineage to a sacred tradition.

5 — *Pietas.* There is no real need to state what we mean by a 'pious person' today. One thinks of a more or less humanitarian, sentimental

---

8   The reference is lost in translation: the Italian word is *gentilezza*. One might consider the English word 'gentility', which in English, however, retains decided connotations of high birth — connections to the *gentry*, to use another etymologically related word that has not been utterly shorn of its original acceptation.

attitude — 'pious' is almost synonymous with compassionate.[9] In the ancient Latin tongue, *pietas* instead pertained to the realm of the sacred. It designated the special relationship that the Roman had first of all with the the gods, and secondly with other elements of the world of Tradition, including the State itself. Before the gods, it meant an attitude of calm, dignified veneration: a sense of belonging and, at the same time, of respect, of mindful concern, even of duty and loyalty: an intensified form of the feeling elicited by the stern figure of the *pater familias* (hence *pietas filialis*).[10] As already mentioned, *pietas* could also manifest itself in the political domain: *pietas in patriam* meant loyalty and duty towards the State and the fatherland. In some cases, the term also takes on the meaning of *iustitia*.[11] He who is foreign to *pietas* is unjust, almost impious, and does not know his place — the place he must hold within a higher order which is both divine and human.

6 — *Innocentia*. This word, too, evoked ideas of clarity and strength; according to its prevalent meaning in antiquity, it expressed purity of soul, integrity, disinterestedness, and righteousness. It did not merely

---

9   Though the present considerations are certainly valid for English as well, it should also be noted that the words 'pious' and 'piety' in English have preserved their original sense somewhat better than the Italian equivalents, which are used with greater frequency and looseness. There is a certain seriousness in these words in English, while other related words which ought to be equally weighty have not been so fortunate in their 'evolution' (one thinks, for instance, of the abuse made of 'spirituality' and 'faith' in our day).

10   The 'father of the family' and 'filial piety', respectively. The *pater familias* was of course much more than the mere masculine parent of the family; he was rather the oldest living male of a given family, and therefore was considered the head of the household, over which he enjoyed in many ways an almost absolute authority. *Pietas filialis* was the compliment of this idea — the obedience and loyalty which the children of owed to their parents, and particularly to their father, to the *pater familias*.

11   Also written *justitia*, the word means 'justice'.

have the negative sense of 'not guilty'. It was free of the shade of banality found in the phrase 'innocent soul' today, which is almost synonymous with 'simpleton'. In other Romance languages, such as French for example, the same term, *innocent*, even designates idiots, poor souls that are congenitally feeble-minded and dazed.[12]

7 — Patientia. The modern meaning of the term, compared to the ancient one, once again shows signs of dulling and weakening. A 'patient' person today is someone who does not get angry, who is not irritated, who shows tolerance. In Latin, *patientia* designated one of the primary 'virtues' of the Roman: it encompassed the idea of an inner strength, an unshakable firmness; it alluded to the capacity to stand one's ground, to maintain an unwavering spirit in the face any setback or adversity. This is why the race of Rome was said to possess the power to accomplish great things as well as to endure[13] equally great adversities (cf. Livy's famous saying: *et facere et pati fortia romanum est*).[14] The modern meaning, compared to the older, proves completely watered down. Today, even a donkey is taken as an example of a typically 'patient' nature.

8 — Humilitas. With the religion that has come to dominate the West, 'humility' has become a 'virtue' — certainly not in a Roman sense. It is glorified by its very contrast to the kind of dignity, strength and calm awareness described above. In ancient Rome, *humilitas* stood for the very opposite of all *virtus*. It meant baseness, wretchedness, lowliness, abjection, cowardice, and dishonour — so that death or exile were

---

12   Our English 'innocence' is frequently associated rather with childishness, infancy, and ignorance; Evola's point is thus very applicable to our own use.

13   Italian: *patire*.

14   'It is Roman to act and to endure valiantly', taken from the *History of Rome* by the great Roman historian Livy (BC 64 or 69-AD 12 or 17). See Book 2, Chapter 12.

considered preferable to 'humility': *humilitati vel exilium vel mortem anteponenda esse.* Associations of ideas such as *mens humilis et prava*, 'a low and evil mind', were common. The expression *humilitas causam dicentium* refers to the inferior and guilty condition of those being brought before a court. Here, too, the idea of race or caste comes into play: *humilis natus parentis* meant born of the people, in the pejorative, plebeian sense, by contrast to noble birth, and hence in a sense that diverges significantly from the modern one of the expression 'of humble origins', especially considering that practically the sole criterion for social positions today is the economic one. In any case, a Roman of the good old days would never have dreamed of making a virtue of *humilitas*, let alone of boasting of it or of preaching it to others. As for a certain 'morality of humility', one might recall the remark of a Roman emperor, that nothing is more despicable than the pride of those who say they are humble — which does not mean that arrogance and presumptuousness are to be encouraged.[15]

9 — *Ingenium.* The modern word has only preserved part of the ancient sense of the term and, once again, its least interesting aspect. In Latin, *ingenium* also signified perspicacity, sharpness of mind, sagacity, and foresight — but at the same time, it referred to one's character, to that which in each person is organic, innate, and really one's own.[16] *Vana ingenia* could therefore refer to persons without character; *redire ad*

---

15   The emperor in question is Marcus Aurelius (AD 121–180), whose famed *Meditations* contains the phrase here alluded to. See Book 12, Section 27: 'For that arrogance which grows in arrogance for its own lack of arrogance is most irksome of all' (translation mine). The book was written in Ancient Greek, and so the word *humilitas* does not appear in the original. However, to Evola's point, Aurelius was a good Stoic, and believed that modesty was to be counted among the virtues. This Stoic modesty (αἰδημοσύνη), however, has little or nothing to do with Christian humility.

16   The first meaning, though certainly not the second, is contained in our English word 'ingenious'.

ingenium could mean to return to one's own nature, to a lifestyle consistent with what one really is. This more important sense has been lost in the modern word, which has acquired almost the opposite meaning. Indeed, if we understand 'ingeniousness' in an intellectualistic and dialectic sense, it clearly stands in contrast to the second meaning of the ancient term, which refers to one's character, to a style that conforms with one's own nature. The modern term indicates superficiality by contrast to what is organic; a restless, brilliant and inventive mobility of the mind, in contrast to a rigorous way of thinking perfectly suited to one's own character.

10 — *Labor.* So far as the changes in the value attached to words goes, changes that clearly indicate a radical change in world-view, the most typical case is perhaps the term *labor*. In Latin, this word had a mainly negative meaning. Although in some cases it could refer to activity in general — as in the expression *labor rei militaris*, activity in the army — its predominant meaning expressed the idea of toil, exhaustion, unpleasant effort, and sometimes even misfortune, torment, a burden, a punishment. The Greek term *ponos* had an analogous meaning.[17] Thus, *laborare* could also mean to suffer, to be anguished or tormented. *Quid ego laboravi?* means: 'Why did I torment myself?' *Laborare ex renis, ex capite* means: to suffer from backache or headache. *Labor itineris* means: the fatigue and inconvenience of travel — and so on.

The Roman, then, would never have thought of making *labor* a sort of virtue and social ideal. Yet Roman civilisation can hardly be described as a civilisation of slackers, loafers, and 'idlers'. The truth is that at that time there was a sense of distance. 'Work' stood in

---

17   Our English word 'pain' ultimately derives from this etymology. The negative connotation of the Latin *labor* gives rise to our English word 'laborious', as well as our use of the word 'labor' for childbirth (this use existed also in Latin, but has, interestingly, been lost in Italian).

contrast to *agere*, action in the higher sense. 'Work' corresponded to the dark, material, servile and insignificant forms of human activity, and referred to those for whom activity was determined exclusively by need, necessity or an unfortunate fate (the ancient world also had a metaphysics of slavery). Opposed to such people were those who act in the proper sense of the term, those who devote themselves to free, non-physical, conscious, deliberate and to some extent disinterested forms of action. Indeed, the term 'work' was not applied in the case of a person who exercised material activities, but rather it was applied with a certain qualitative character, and on the basis of an authentic and free vocation; such a person was an *artifex* (there was also the term *opifex*), and this view was also retained in later times, in the climate and style of the traditional craft guilds.

The change in the meaning and value of the word in question is therefore a very clear sign of the plebeian character that has increasingly come to dominate the Western world, a civilisation increasingly shaped by what are in any complete social hierarchy the lowest strata. The modern 'cult of work' is all the more aberrant because today, more than ever, in our regime of industrialisation, mechanisation and anonymous mass production, work has necessarily lost any higher value it might have had. Despite this, we have come to speak of a 'religion of work', of a 'humanism of work' and even of a 'labour state', making work a kind of insolent ethical and social imperative for everyone, to which one almost wants to answer defiantly with the Spanish saying *El hombre que trabaja pierde un tiempo precioso* ('The man who works loses precious time').

More generally, I have already noted on another occasion that the traditional world stands in contrast to the modern by virtue of the fact that whereas in the former 'work' could take the form of an 'action' or art, in the modern world even action and art sometimes take on the character of 'work' — that is, of a coerced, opaque and interested activity performed, not according to a vocation, but according to need and, above all, for profit, for *lucre*.

11 — *Otium*. This term has undergone a change exactly inverse to that of the preceding one: almost without exception, it has acquired a pejorative meaning. According to modern usage, someone is idle[18] when he is useless to himself and to others. To be idle is more or less the same as to be indolent, distracted, inactive, listless, and prone to the '*dolce far niente*' of today's mandolin-playing Italy for tourists.[19] However, the Latin *otium* once meant a period of free time essentially corresponding to a meditative state of concentration, calm, and transparent contemplation. Idleness[20] in the negative sense — which was also known in antiquity — indicated only what this can lead to when misused: only in such cases could the Romans say, for example, *hebescere otio* or *otio diffluere*, that is to become stupid or dissipated through idleness. But this is not the predominant sense. Cicero, Seneca, and other Classical authors chiefly understood *otium* as the healthy and normal counterpart to all forms of action, and even as a necessary condition for action to truly be action, and not agitation, business (*negotium*) or 'work'.

We could also refer to the Greeks, as Cicero wrote: *Graeci non solum ingenio atque doctrina, sed etiam otio studioque abundantes* — 'The Greeks are rich not only in innate gifts and learning but also in *otium* and diligence'. Of Scipio the Elder it was said: *Nunquam se minus*

---

18   The Italian is *ozioso*, a word echoed in our far less common English term 'otiose'. English is, however, somewhat more fortunate in this respect: our word 'leisure', which has certainly suffered a shameful degradation of its own, nonetheless preserves the positive sense contained in the Latin *otium*, though it in fact derives from another root: the Latin word *licere*, meaning 'to allow'. We thus have two words in English to indicate the negative and the positive side of one and the same concept: idleness and leisure, respectively.

19   The phrase is Italian for 'sweet idleness' (literally, 'sweet doing nothing').

20   Italian: *ozio*.

otiosum esse quam cum otiosus esset, aut minus solum esse quam cum solus esset — 'He was never less idle than when he was idle, and never less alone than when he enjoyed solitude', which stresses an active (in a higher sense) type of 'idleness' and solitude. And Sallust wrote: *Maius commodum ex otio meo quam ex aliorum negotiis reipublicae venturum* — 'My leisure will be more useful to the State than the busyness of others.' To Seneca we owe a treatise entitled *De otio*, in which 'idleness' gradually takes on the character of pure contemplation.

It is worth mentioning some of the characteristic ideas expounded in this treatise. According to Seneca, there are two States: a greater State, without exterior and contingent limits, which encompasses both men and gods; and the particular, earthly State, to which one belongs by birth.

Now, Seneca says, there are men who serve the two States at once, others who serve only the greater State, and others that serve only the earthly State. The greater State can also be served through 'idleness', if not better through idleness — by investigating what constitutes *virtus*, strength and virile dignity: *huius maiori rei publicae et in otio deservire possumus, imno vero nescio an in otium melius, ut quaeremus quid sit virtus*. *Otium* is closely linked to the tranquillity of mind of the sage, to the inner calm that allows one to attain the summits of contemplation. If understood in its correct, traditional sense, contemplation is not an escape from the world or a distraction, but an immersion within oneself and elevation to the perception of the metaphysical order that every true man must never cease to keep in sight when living and struggling in an earthly State.

Moreover, even in Catholicism (before the Church came up with Christ the Worker — to be honoured on May 1 — and before it 'opened itself to the left') one found the phrase *sacrum otium*, 'sacred idleness', which referred precisely to a contemplative activity. But in a civilisation in which all action has taken on the dull, physical, mechanical and mercenary traits of work, even when that work is done in one's mind ('intellectual workers', who naturally also have their 'unions' and fight for the 'demands of their professional sector'), the positive and traditional meaning of contemplation was bound to be lost. This is why in relation to modern civilisation we should speak not of an 'active civilisation' but of a restless and neurotic one. As compensation for 'work' and a reaction against the strain of a life that has been reduced to a vain acting and producing, Classical *otium* — contemplation, silence, the state of calm and pause allowing one to return to oneself and find oneself again — is foreign to modern man. No: all he knows is 'distraction' (the literal meaning of which is 'dispersion');[21] he looks for sensations, for new tensions, and new stimuli — almost as psychic narcotics. Anything, as long as he can escape himself, as long as he can avoid finding himself alone with himself, isolated from the noise of the outside world and interaction with his 'neighbour'. Hence the radio, television, cinema, cruises, the frenzy of sports or political rallies in a regime of the masses, the need to hear things, to chase after the latest or most sensational news, 'supporters' of all kinds, and so on. Every expedient seems to have been diabolically brought into play in order to destroy any kind of genuine inner life, to prevent any internal defence of one's personality, so that, almost like an artificially galvanised being, the individual will let himself be swept away by the collective current, which — naturally, according to the famous 'meaning of history' — moves forward according to an unlimited progress.[22]

12 — *Theoria*. Through an association of ideas, this brings to mind the collapse which the meaning of the Greek term *theoria* has undergone. To speak of 'theories' today is more or less to refer to 'abstractions', things far removed from of reality, 'intellectual' matters; a great poet even wrote: 'All theory is grey, my friend. But forever green is the tree

---

21   The etymology of the word 'distraction' is indeed 'a pulling apart'.

22   I cannot resist noting that all of this was written *before* the advent of the internet and the 'smartphone'.

of life.'[23] Again, we find an alteration and a weakening of meaning. According to its ancient meaning, θεωρία does not signify abstract intellectuality but a fulfilling vision, something particularly active, the act of the highest principle in man, the νοῦς, or Olympian intellect (which will be discussed in another chapter).[24]

13 — Servitium. The verb *servio, servire* in Latin also has the positive sense of 'to be faithful'. However, the predominant meaning is the negative one, 'to be a servant'; it is this latter sense, in any case, that lies at the basis of the other word, *servitium*, which specifically meant slavery, serfdom, as it derived from *servus* = slave. In modern times, the word 'to serve' has become increasingly widespread, while losing this negative and demeaning connotation, to the point that, especially among the Anglo-Saxon peoples, service as 'social service' has almost become a kind of ethic, the only truly modern ethic. And just as people have not sensed the absurdity of speaking of 'intellectual workers', they have come to see the sovereign as 'the first servant of the nation'.

In this respect too it is worth noting that, just as the Romans clearly were not a race of 'idlers', they also present us with the highest examples of political loyalty, of loyalty to the State and to its leaders. However, the tone is very different. The change in the soul of words is not a matter of chance. The fact that words like *labor*, *servitium*, and *otium* have become common in their modern sense is a subtle yet eloquent

---

23 See Goethe's *Faust*, Part I, lines 2038–2039. It should certainly be noted, however, that Goethe puts these words into the mouth of Mephistopheles, who in the scene in question is evidently attempting to corrupt a young student. It is therefore not immediately evident that Goethe himself subscribes to this sentiment; and indeed, if one takes the Devil as the force which draws *down*, which is at least suggested many parts of Goethe's great poem, then it may well be that Goethe indicates here, albeit poetically, a basic *agreement* with Evola.

24 See Chapter 7 below.

sign of a shift of perspective, which has certainly not occurred in the direction of virile, aristocratic, and qualitative vocations.

14 — *Stipendium*. We hardly need to mention what the word 'stipend' means today. One immediately thinks of an employee, of bureaucracy, of pay-day for civil servants. In ancient Rome, the same term referred almost exclusively to the army. *Stipendium merere* meant to be in the military, under the orders of a particular leader or commander. *Emeritis stipendis* meant after having completed military service; *homo nullius stipendii* meant one who had not known the discipline of arms. *Stipendis multa habere* meant to boast many campaigns, many military enterprises.[25] Here too, the difference is a significant one.

The complete meaning of other Latin words, such as *studium* and *studiosus*, currently only survives in certain special turns of phrase, such as the Italian expression '*fare con studio*', meaning to do something on purpose or with a certain diligence. The Latin term conveyed the idea of intensity, warmth, and keenly felt interest, which has been obscured in the modern word, which brings to mind more or less arid intellectual or scholastic disciplines. The Latin *studium* could even mean love, desire, a vivid inclination. *In re studium ponere* meant taking something to heart, taking a deep and keen interest in it. *Studium bellandi* meant the pleasure, the love of combat. *Homo agendi studiosus* was one who loves action — recalling what was said earlier about *labor*, he was the opposite of the man for whom action can only mean 'work' — What should we make, today, of an expression like *studiosi Caesaris*? It did not mean those who study Caesar, but those who fol-

---

25 The literal translations of these Latin phrases are as follows: 'to earn one's stipend' (*stipendium merere*); 'meriting of stipends' (*emeritis stipendis*); 'a man without stipends' (*homo nullius stipendii*); and 'to have many stipends' (*stipendis multa habere*).

low him, who admire him, which take his side, and who are devoted and loyal to him.[26]

Other words whose ancient meaning has been forgotten are, for example, *docilitas*, which did not mean docility, but good disposition or ability to learn, to assimilate a teaching or principle; also *ingenuus*, which did not at all the mean ingenuous, but referred to the free-born man, to a non-servile condition. It is more or less widely known that the Latin word *humanitas* did not mean 'humanity' in the democratic and decayed sense of today, but cultivation of the self, fullness of life and of experience — and this, originally, not even in the 'humanist' sense à la Humboldt.[27] Another rather telling example: *certus*. In the ancient Latin tongue, the notion of certainty, of something certain, was often connected to the idea of a conscious decision. *Certum est mihi* means: it is my firm resolve. *Certus gladio* is he who can rely on his sword, who knows how to use it. A well-known phrase is *diebus certis*, which does not mean 'on certain days' but on the fixed, established days. This could lead us to considerations about a particular conception of certainty: an active conception, certainty as dependent on what lies within our power to decide. Much in the same spirit, Giambattista Vico enunciated the formula *verum et factum convertuntur* — but everything was to end later in the digressions of neo-Hegelian 'absolute idealism'.[28] I will bring these observations to a close by examining

---

26 Another most characteristic expression in this sense is Tacitus' famous phrase *sine ira e studio*, meaning 'without ire and without zeal' — in short, with inner self-mastery.

27 Wilhelm von Humboldt (1767–1835) was a Prussian diplomat and an intellectual, and one of the figures of the so-called 'New Humanism' in Germany. A characteristic phrase, taken from his unfinished treatise on education: 'The ultimate task of our existence is to give the fullest possible content to the concept of humanity in our own person'.

28 *Verum et factum convertuntur* is *Latin, meaning* 'the true and the made are convertible' ('convertible' is a Scholastic term meaning 'interchangeable'). Giambattista Vico (1668–1744) was an Italian philosopher and historian, best

the original content of three ancient Roman notions, those of *fatum*, *felicitas*, and *fortuna*.

15. Fatum. According to the most common modern usage of the term, 'fate' is a blind power looming over men which imposes itself on them by making what they least of all desire come true, possibly pushing them towards tragedy and misfortune. Hence the term 'fatalism', the opposite of any attitude of free, effective initiative. According to the fatalistic world-view, the individual is nothing; his actions, despite his apparent free will, are either predestined or vain, and events unfold according to a law or power that transcends him and that does not take him into any account whatsoever. The adjective 'fatal' has a prevalently negative meaning: 'fatal' outcome, 'fatal' accident, the 'fatal hour of death', and so on.[29]

---

known for his 1725 work *The New Science*, one of the first attempts at a philosophy of history. The present reference is to his 1710 work *De antiquissima Italorum sapientia, ex linguae latinae originibus eruenda* (On the Most Ancient Wisdom of the Italians, Unearthed from the Origins of the Latin Language); see Chapter 1, Part 1. Some care is however warranted here: Vico's concept stands dangerously close to the modern notion according to which we only understand what we make; whereas the ancient conception which Evola references is even the *contrary* of this, namely, that we only make what we understand, that we can only build upon the real elements of the cosmos which we have rightly comprehended. A review of the progress of Vico's *De antiquissima Italorum sapientia* indicates that Vico in truth argued the modern conception *under the guise* of the ancient, so that it would really be no surprise that his theories were later swallowed by the historicism of the German philosopher Georg Wilhelm Friedrich Hegel (1770–1831). The 'absolute idealism' of the neo-Hegelians (Italian exemplars include Benedetto Croce and Giovanni Gentile) culminated in a kind of complicated quasi-solipsism, as exemplified in the Gentilian proposition that the world is posited by the *I*, the absolute *I*, the 'I-pure-act'.

29 Most interestingly, a very similar alteration of our English word 'doom' can be observed. Doom in its original form meant law, decree, but also a judgement, a willed decision — perhaps on the part of the gods or superhuman powers,

According to its ancient meaning, *fatum* instead essentially corresponded to the law of the continuous development of the world; this law was not deemed blind, irrational, and automatic — 'fatal' in the modern sense of the word — but full of meaning, and proceeding from an intelligent will, above all the will of the Olympian powers. Like the Indo-European *rta*,[30] Roman *fatum* referred to the notion of the world as a cosmos and order, and in particular to the concept of history as a development of causes and events reflecting a higher meaning. Even the Fates of the Greek tradition, while presenting some evil and 'infernal' aspects (due to the influence of pre-Hellenic and pre-Indo-European cults), often appear as personifications of the intelligent and just law that governs the universe in certain of its manifestations.

However, the idea of *fatum* acquired particular importance above all in Rome. The reason for this is that Roman civilisation was, of all traditional and sacred civilisations, the one that focused especially on the plane of action and historical reality. Rome was less concerned with knowing the cosmic order as a supra-temporal and metaphysical law than it was with knowing it as a force operating within reality, as a divine will ordering events. This was linked to *fatum* in the Roman sense. This expression comes from the verb *fari*, which also gives the word *fas*, right as divine law. Thus, *fatum* alludes to the 'word' — meaning the revealed word, first and foremost that of the Olympian deities, which allows men to know the right norm (*fas*) and also announces what is going to occur. Regarding this second aspect, oracles — through which a special traditional art sought to discern, in embryonic form, whatever corresponded to situations in the process of

---

but perhaps also on the part of a wise man or a powerful man (hence wis*dom*, king*dom*). It now almost without exception indicates a terrible end, brought by an almost blind fate.

30 The Sanskrit word *Ṛta* indicates the perfect or excellent order of the universe, by which everything that exists is organised. Most suggestively, the word also means 'truth'.

being realised — were also called *fata*; these were almost the revealed word of the gods.

Given all this, we must remember, with regard to the matters we are examining, that man's relationship to the general order of the world in ancient Rome and in traditional civilisations in general was very different from the one that later came to predominate. Although the idea of a universal law and a divine will did not erase the notion of human freedom, ancient man was constantly concerned about shaping his life and actions in such a way that they might continue the cosmic order — that they might represent, so to speak, an extension or further development of that order. Starting from *pietas*, which is to say, in Roman terms, the acknowledgement and veneration of divine forces, man set himself the task of foreseeing the direction of these forces in history, in such a way as to bring his actions into accordance with them, making them as effective and meaningful as possible. Hence the important role played in the Roman world, even in the field of public affairs and the military art, by oracles and omens. The Roman was firmly convinced that the worst mishaps, including military defeats, depended not so much on human blunders, weaknesses, or errors, as they did on neglect of the omens — meaning, essentially, the fact of having acted in a disorderly and arbitrary fashion, following merely human criteria, severing one's connections with the higher world (in Roman terms, acting without *religio*, i.e. without a connection),[31] without regard for the 'expedient directions' and 'right moment' ensuring a '*felicitous*' action. Note that *fortuna* and *felicitas* are often, in ancient Rome, only the other side of *fatum*, its specifi-

---

31   One possible etymology of the word 'religion' offered by certain early Christian writers is from the Latin verb *religare*, meaning 'to bind fast', which is the etymology supposed by Evola here. Cicero suggested a derivation from the Latin *relegere*, meaning 'to read again, to undertake again', emphasising the importance of rite and ritual in religious belief, the constant renewal and return to the origins.

cally positive side. The men, the leaders or the people who use their freedom to act in accordance with the divine forces hidden in things are successful, they succeed, they triumph — and in antiquity this is what being 'fortunate' and 'felicity' meant. A modern historian, Franz Altheim, believed he could discern in this attitude the effective cause of Rome's greatness.[32]

In order to further clarify the link between 'fate' and human action, we can refer to modern technology. There are certain laws governing things and phenomena which can be known or ignored, which can be taken into account or neglected. In the face of these laws, man remains fundamentally free. He can even act in a manner contrary to what these laws advise, thus meeting failure in his action or else achieving his goal only after an enormous waste of energy and every kind of difficulty. Modern technology corresponds to the opposite option: one seeks to know the laws of things so as to be able to make use of them, letting them show the path of least resistance and maximum efficiency in the achievement of a given objective.

Things are no different when spiritual and 'divine' forces rather than the laws of matter are in question. Ancient man believed that it was essential to know or at least to sense these forces, in order to get an idea of the conditions propitious for a given action, and possibly an idea of what he should or should not do. For him, challenging fate, rising up against destiny, was not something 'Promethean' in the Romantic sense glorified by the moderns: it was simply foolish. For ancient man, impiety (meaning the opposite of *pietas*, i.e. the lack of *religio*, of a 'connection' with, and respectful understanding of, the cosmic order) was more or less equivalent to stupidity, childishness, and fatuousness. The comparison with modern technology is flawed in one respect: the laws of historical reality did not present themselves

---

32   The German historian Franz Altheim (1898–1976) was also a student of philology who spent some time in Italy in pursuit of his historical research.

as inanimately 'objective' and completely detached from man and his goals. One might say: the objective, divine order connected to 'fate' extends up to a certain limit, beyond which it ceases to be decisive and only amounts to a tendency (hence the well-known astrological formula: *astra inclinant non determinant, i.e. the stars influence but do not determine*). This is the point at which the human and historical world, properly speaking, begins. Normally, this world should be continuous with the previous one: in other words, human will should carry the 'divine' will further. Whether this occurs or not essentially depends on freedom: one must will it. If it does occur, that which was only potentiality is realised through human action. The human world will then manifest itself as a continuation of the divine order, and history itself will take the form of a revelation and a 'sacred history'. Man, in this case, will no longer have any value in himself, will no longer act for his own sake, but will be invested with divine dignity, and the whole human world will somehow acquire a higher dimension.

It is evident, therefore, that we are dealing with something quite different from 'fatalism'. Just as any action that goes against 'fate' is foolish and irrational, any action in harmony with 'fate' is not only effective, but also transfiguring. Whoever fails to take *fatum* into account is almost invariably destined to be passively carried along by events; he who knows *fatum*, makes it his own and grafts himself onto it, is instead led to accomplish a higher purpose, by possessing more than a merely individual significance. This is the meaning of the ancient maxim that *fata 'nolentem trahunt, volentem ducunt'.*[33]

In the ancient Roman world and in ancient Roman history, there are numerous episodes, situations and institutions that convey the sense of a 'fateful' encounter between the human world and the divine one, of forces from above that flow through history and manifest themselves in human actions. To limit ourselves to one example, we

---

33   'Fate "drags the unwilling, leads the willing"'.

might recall that 'the culmination of the Roman cult of Jupiter was an action in which the god manifested his victorious essence in a man, the *vir triumphalis*. Jupiter is not just the cause of victory, but is himself the victor; the triumph is not celebrated in his honour, but he himself is the triumphant one. It is for this reason that the *imperator* wears the god's insignia' (K. Kerényi, F. Altheim).[34] To realise the divine in one's actions and life — sometimes prudently, sometimes boldly — was a guiding principle that ancient Rome applied also to the political order. Likewise, some authors have rightly noted the degree to which Rome lacked myths in the abstract and supra-historical sense prevalent in some other civilisations; in Rome myth becomes history, just as history, in turn, takes on a 'fateful' aspect and becomes myth.

An important consequence follows from this. What is realised in such cases is ultimately an identity. It is no longer a matter of a divine word that can either be heeded or not. Rather, this is a kind of unfolding whereby human will appears to coincide with that of higher forces. Here we are in the presence of a very particular, objective, almost transcendental concept of freedom. By opposing *fatum*, I can of course lay claim to a free will, but this is a sterile freedom, a mere 'gesture', since it cannot have any deep effect on the fabric of reality. By contrast, when I act in such a way that my will continues a higher order, that is, when it becomes the instrument by which that order is realised in history, in such a state of coincidence or attunement, what I will may possibly become a command directed at objective forces that otherwise would

---

34 I have been unable to source the reference here. Both the Hungarian Károly Kerényi (1897–1973) and the German Franz Altheim mentioned in the footnote 32 above authored numerous works in German on classical religions and mythology, but I find no book co-authored by the two, though they were evidently schoolmates in the University of Frankfurt. Altheim wrote a number of works dealing particularly with Roman religion, including one *History of the Roman Religion* (1938).

not easily be dominated, or would have no regard for what human beings desire or hope for.

Now, we may wonder: how did we come to this modern notion of fate as an obscure and blind force? Like many other such changes, this shift is far from random. It reflects a change in people's inner level and can essentially be explained by the rise of individualism and 'humanism' understood in a general sense, which is to say by reference to a civilisation and world-view based exclusively on what is human and earthly. It is evident that once this break occurred one could then perceive, no longer an intelligible order of the world, but only the power of something obscure and alien. 'Fate' thus became the general symbol of all the deeper forces at work, over which man — for all his mastery of the physical world — has little power, since he no longer understands them and has cut himself off from them; but it also symbolises those forces that man, through his own attitude, has released and made sovereign in certain domains of existence.

With this study of the ancient and modern notions of *fatum*, I will end my series of examples. They should suffice to give the reader an idea of how important and interesting an enlightened philology would be, since — as already noted — words have a soul and life, and a return to their origins can often open up surprising perspectives. This work, however, would be even more fruitful if, instead of merely going back from modern 'Romance' languages to the ancient Latin tongue, it connected Latin itself to the much broader, common family of Indo-European languages, of which Latin, in its fundamental elements, represents but one distinct branch.

6. THE PSYCHOANALYSIS OF SKIING

The importance that sport has generally acquired in modern life is a significant phenomenon, and is one of the markers of the shift of the Western soul towards very different interests from those that were predominant in the 19th century. Modern sport would therefore deserve a dedicated study. Moreover, it would be interesting to compare modern sport and its general significance with its counterpart in the ancient Western, Greek and Roman world, as well as in non-European civilisations. As regards this second point, I have provided some essential points of reference in another work of mine.[1] As for modern sport, I only wish to draw attention here to one particular variety of it, namely skiing.

This sport is a rather recent trend. In Nordic countries skiing had enjoyed a certain popularity, yet not as a real sport (it apparently only made its début as a sport at Oslo in 1870, when people from Telemark used this means of transport to outstrip their opponents in a race, causing a general stir);[2] rather, skiing was used as a practical device, not unlike sledges and poles, which came in handy in areas that were covered in snow for much of the year. By contrast, the enjoyment of skiing in itself, as a thrilling activity, only spread among the younger

---

1   See *Revolt Against the Modern World*, Part 1, Chapter 18, 'Games and Victory'.

2   Telemark is a region in Sweden, and has given its name to the Telemark style of skiing.

generations in major non-Nordic Western countries, including Britain, in recent times — roughly, in the inter-war period. The sudden success and great popularity of this sport, and the spontaneous interest and enthusiasm which men and women alike display toward it, are distinctive elements that beg the question of whether this phenomenon may be due not only to extrinsic factors but also to the general orientation of modern life.

Let us explore this possibility by asking ourselves: what is the essential psychological trait associated with skiing as a sport? What is the 'moment' in this sport to which everything else, in most cases, is subordinated? The answer is quite obvious: the *descent*. This emerges quite clearly when we compare this to the salient point and meaning of another sport that is practised in largely the same environment as skiing, namely mountaineering.

In mountaineering the essential element, the focus of interest of the sport, is constituted by the act of *ascending*; in skiing this instead corresponds to *descending*. The dominant motif in mountaineering is conquest; the attainment of the peak, the point beyond which one cannot go any higher, marks the end of the truly interesting stage for the rock or ice-wall climber (let us leave aside here the technical-acrobatic deviations displayed by a certain kind of recent mountaineering). The opposite takes place in the case of skiing: if one ascends, this is mostly in order to descend. The hours of toil required to reach a certain altitude are only faced in order to then take the 'downhill run', the *Abfahrt*, the swift skiing descent.[3] Thus in the more modern and fashionable winter sport stations the problem has been solved by building cableways, chair lifts and sledge lifts that meet the real interest of skiers by effortlessly taking them up, allowing them then to ski down in a few minutes and to take the same cableway — or a different one — once again in order

---

3   The term is German, and outside of the context of skiing essentially means 'departure' (*ab* = off, away; *Fahrt* = journey).

to face another descent, until they have had enough. Consequently, whereas mountaineering is characterised by the *thrill of the ascent*, as a struggle and conquest, the sport of skiing is characterised by the thrill of descent with its speed and, if one may put it so, its fall time.

This last point is worth emphasising. A person's way of relating to his or her own body varies significantly from mountaineering to skiing. Mountaineering entails a far more direct perception of one's own body, with acts of balancing, efforts, thrusts and moves that require complete control over the body, and careful and well-planned manoeuvres to be performed in relation to the various challenges posed by climbing and ascending, by choosing and clinging to a handhold, and by the resistance of a step cut into the ice. In skiing we find something quite different: a person's way of relating to his or her own body is certainly subject to the force of gravity and may be compared to the relation between a car driven at a certain speed and its driver; once he has 'set off', the skier must do one thing alone: guide himself through appropriate movements in order to regulate his speed and direction. This will lead him to master his reflexes (making them instinctive, reliable and quick after much taxing training), thereby allowing him to control his descent, more or less like a driver who enjoys speeding down a street filled with pedestrians and other vehicles without slowing down, using his quick reflexes to avoid this or that obstacle and brush past it, almost playfully, before moving on to continue his race. The impression produced by a skilled skier is precisely of this sort.

As regards the more inward aspect of the phenomenon, i.e. what it ultimately gives the human spirit, it is worth recalling the impression felt by someone who puts on a pair of skies for the first time. This is the impression of having the ground slip away from under one's feet, of *falling*. The same feeling resurfaces when one strives to master the most difficult forms of this sport: swift downhill runs or jumps. Hence, I believe it is possible to argue that the deepest meaning of skiing lies in the following fact: the instinctual feeling of physical fear, with the reflex it triggers of withdrawing or hanging onto something, is overcome and transformed into a feeling of elation and pleasure, and developed into the impulse of going ever faster and playing in various different ways with the speed and acceleration that the force of gravity exerts on bodies. In this respect, skiing may be defined as *the technique, game, and thrill of falling*. By practising this sport, one develops a certain physical daring or fearlessness, but of a particular sort, quite distinct from the daring of the mountaineer, or even opposite to it in terms of its meaning: we may well say that it is an essentially 'modern' kind of daring.

The above term encapsulates not only the symbolic meaning of the sport of skiing, but probably the deep, underlying reason for its sudden popularity as well. Of all the many types of sport, skiing ranks among those most devoid of any relation to the symbols of the previous world-view. So to draw upon the comparison we made previously, whereas the ancient traditions of all peoples are replete with symbols related to the mountain as the goal of an ascent and site of transfiguration — despite the fact that mountaineering was not really practised in ancient times at all — they contain nothing that may be associated with the sport of skiing.[4] It is essentially the 'modern' soul that feels at ease with this sport: the soul drunk with speed, 'becoming', and accelerating or indeed frantic motion — what until recently was praised as the motion of 'progress' and 'intense living', and which has in fact been nothing but a kind of collapse and downfall. The thrill of this motion, combined with a cerebral and abstract feeling that one is in control of forces which have been unleashed and which one really no longer possesses, is typical of the modern way in which the Ego grasps the sharpest perception of itself. I believe that this existential orientation,

---

4   For those interested, Evola offered a specific metaphysical study of mountainclimbing in a number of essays which were compiled posthumously as *Meditazioni delle vette*, translated in 1998 into English as *Meditations on the Peaks*.

be it only as a reflection, contributes to the enthusiasm for skiing as a sport and that it distinguishes it in particular from mountaineering — conceived as a physical and sporting expression of the opposite symbol, the symbol of ascending, elevating oneself, and conquering the forces of gravity, which is to say the forces at work in a fall.

The acknowledgement of all this does not necessarily lead to a particular value judgement. Indeed, from a more external perspective, one may assign skiing the same recognition that one assigns certain aspects of that 'naturism' which has become popular in recent times: as a winter sport, when practised seriously (without the snobbishness and foolishness associated with the fashionable centres of such sport, with their carnivalesque clothes, and all the rest), skiing can certainly help compensate, in a way, for the damage inflicted on many men's organism nowadays by life in big cities, as well as contribute to a certain psycho-physical activation in the young. But even if one were to directly perceive the inner side of the enthusiasm for skiing in the problematic terms I have just outlined, this — at least in the case of a certain differentiated human type — is not bound to be an entirely negative thing. The maxim which applies to such a type of person, especially in the present day, may also apply within the profane domain of skiing: no experience is to be avoided, but everything must be experienced, yet in a detached way. One is *to keep abreast of the wave*, confirming one's freedom.

7. THE MYTH AND FALLACY
OF IRRATIONALISM

Whereas the worship of reason was the hallmark of the previous age, the present times are certainly marked by a multifaceted irrationalism. The emphasis has shifted onto what seems to be irreducible to *ratio* and the intellect.[1] A mystique of 'Life' has been proclaimed, of the vital impulse and of pure immanence. Direct experience, sheer existence, and action in all their forms have come to be promoted. In opposition to the alleged sovereignty of clear thought, primacy has been affirmed for everything within the very depths of the human being which cannot be traced back to thought. Typical positions include those of Ludwig Klages and Oswald Spengler; these men would appear to be incapable of conceiving the spirit, *Geist*, as anything other than the abstract intellect — something which, in their view, stands in contrast to 'life' and the soul, to what is connected to the blood, to the soil, and to the primary background of existence, the superior right of which, they hold, now ought to be acknowledged.[2]

---

1   *Ratio*, from which we derive our word 'rationality', is Latin for 'reason', though it has connotations also of method and rule (a *ratio* can be taken as the rational principle of a thing, which thus determined that thing's quality and character).

2   Klages (1872–1956) was a German psychologist and nominee for the Nobel Prize in Literature. In his thought he advocated an extreme version of Nietzschean 'life philosophy' — and it is also well worth mentioning that much if not all the impetus for the transformations which Evola indicts throughout this chapter can be traced back to Nietzsche in one way or another — which is not to say

Existentialism tows the same line when it proclaims the primacy of existence over essence,[3] which — once again — is misleadingly identified with conceptuality, with what relates to the categories of the intellect. It is moreover obvious that psychoanalysis essentially adopts the same general orientation: its hallmark is the emphasising and promoting of what it regards as being primary, primary by virtue of its belonging to the obscure realm of the unconscious and preconscious, in which the real driving force of one's being is believed to reside.

As a consequence of all this, recent years have witnessed a renewed interest in the world of myths and symbols, which is seen as the expression of a primary psycho-vital substrate, irreducible to *ratio*. A particular place should be assigned, within this framework, to C. G. Jung's theory of the so-called 'archetypes', which are based on an irrationalist contamination of this concept of ancient metaphysics.[4]

---

that Nietzsche himself would have approved of all its manifestations. Klages held that *Geist* (a German word which is impossible to translate into English, but which means something like spirit and mind together) was life-destroying, while the *Seele*, the vital spirit, was life-affirming. For Spengler, see note 4 to Chapter 4 of the present work. The radical and very influential Spenglerian distinction between *Kultur* and *Zivilisation*, the first being the youthful and irrational expression of still potent life forces, the second the ossified, decayed, rationalistic decline of the same, certainly reflects elements of that thought which Evola here critiques.

3   Evola refers here to the position of certain Existentialists (see e.g. Sartre, *Existentialism is a Humanism*) who hold that 'existence precedes essence', meaning that a man *is* before he *is something in particular*. This view indicates a radical existential freedom at the very heart of human existence — a freedom so radical indeed that it cannot help but be, at least sometimes and possibly in its most complete expression, utterly irrational. Camus' *The Stranger*, in which a man, evidently for no reason whatsoever, murders another, is sometimes taken as an artistic portrayal of this idea.

4   For Jung, see note 9 to Chapter 4 above. Jung's idea of archetypes is complex, but might be summed up as follows: archetypes, for Jung, are certain symbols

In several respects, the polemical character of modern irrationalism, which verges on aggressiveness, is quite clear. It expresses a
revolt against the kind of rationality that in the bourgeois age had
been conceived as an ordering principle, as a symbol of progress with
respect to the previous periods, and even as a guarantee of safety for
collective living, since rationality was expected to eliminate all that is
arbitrary, accidental, and impulsive. In particular, irrationalism rejects
the mechanised and soulless view of the world which has acted as as
a fatal counterpart to all the material achievements of modern man.
The polemical character of irrationalism in itself suggests we should be
distrustful of any phenomenon that constitutes a mere reaction — for
reactions to one unbalance almost inevitably end up replacing it with
another, without ever attaining anything truly positive. It would be
appropriate, therefore, to consider the relations between the rational
and the irrational.

First of all, it should be noted that irrationalism falls prey to the
same fallacy as rationalism insofar as it maintains that the sphere of
abstract thought and rationalism has an independent existence. Thus
the irrational is set in contrast to the rational, and 'life', or existence,
or instinct, or the unconscious, to the intellect; and it seems as though
people are incapable of envisaging anything above and beyond these
limiting oppositions. All this attests to a clear drop in level, and it
engenders a vicious circle.

It is necessary on the contrary to hold that both 'reason' (together
with all the various forms of modern intellectualistic consciousness) and
its irrationalist counterpart do not constitute anything primary, but are
rather the products of a dissociation — interconnected products that lack
an independent existence. Their opposition is only true from a certain
point of view, and only if we accept the assumption that they are dis-

---

which recur universally in human history (as in the art, mythology, and dreams
of peoples and individuals) and can thus be understood as deriving from the
'collective unconscious' of humanity.

sociated from a reality higher than and anterior to either of them. This unity is the true centre of the human being in his *normal* state — normal, that is, in a higher sense. It does not at all fall within some twilight zone which can be reached by approaching point zero in one's personal consciousness, as Jung suggests when he speaks of the so-called 'individuation process,' or the only sphere where the dubious union between one's consciousness and the collective unconscious can occur. It must rather be defined as the spiritual realm in the proper and legitimate sense.

There is a certain philosophy of civilisation according to which the domain of clear thought was pervaded in primordial times by an imaginative activity, an activity which created myths and emotionally charged images. Only in a subsequent period (subsequent in a historical and chronological sense for some people, but in an 'ideal' sense for others) did intellectual consciousness differentiate itself by emerging out of the haze of the mythical experience and grasping the clear and stark forms of concepts essentially as philosophy knows them. In primordial times, therefore, there was a unity or indistinctness between what was to subsequently differentiate itself into the immediacy of the creative artistic act on the one hand and the mediation of rational reflective thought on the other. Spengler holds a similar view, which provides the general backdrop to his entire morphology of civilisations: the primordial condition is pure experience governed by *time*, while the subsequent stage is the world of *space* and nature which takes shape through the categories of 'awakeness.'[5] These theories too are based on a fundamental misunderstanding of reality; they are digressions of an arbitrary speculative thought that ignores the central experience of 'traditional' man, who ought to be regarded as the true, normal human being.

In primordial times, there existed an essentially spiritual and supra-rational ideal of knowledge, which we might call the ideal of meta-

---

5   See for instance Spengler's *Decline of the West*, Chapter IV.

physical clarity. This played a central role — particularly in the cycle of all higher Indo-European societies. In the ancient world, it is reflected by everything which was identified with or adumbrated by the symbolism of light, of celestial brightness, of the regions and entities of a higher realm. This had as little to do with 'reason' as with the irrational, mere imagination, or the projections of the 'collective unconscious'. One might speak here of an *Olympian* nucleus corresponding to what is actually the primordial element of all higher ancient civilisations, of their mythologies, and — to some extent — even of their institutions. Looking back at the Greek civilisation of the historical age, terms such as λόγος and νοῦς can only inadequately be translated as 'reason' and 'intellect' in the modern sense.[6] Essentially, these terms point to the metaphysical level, whereas their intellectualistic meaning belongs to a relatively recent period and must be regarded as a sort of reflection or transposition. This emerges in a particularly clear way in the Greek conception of κόσμος νοητός (intelligible world, associated with 'archetypes' — in the genuine and not Jungian sense), where the intel-

---

6   Λόγος (logos) meant a great many things in Ancient Greek, including reason, speech, discourse, argument, language, and word (consider the first line of the Book of John in the New Testament: Ἐν ἀρχῇ ἦν ὁ λόγος, 'In the beginning was the Word'). Plato's Socrates makes innumerable references to the λόγος, and often incites his interlocutors to follow or to obey it. The term makes its debut in philosophy with Heraclitus, and features in several of his more enigmatic statements (see fragments 1 and 50). Νοῦς (nous), on the other hand, is that part of the human soul which was capable of comprehending the real, the true. It is translated as 'mind', 'intellect', even 'spirit'. Nietzsche, for instance, in the Preface to *Beyond Good and Evil*, is referring to the νοῦς when he states that Plato's greatest error was the 'invention of the pure spirit': *Plato's Erfindung vom reinen Geiste* (see note 2 above). Plato's Socrates seems at many points to ascribe to νοῦς the divine ability to directly perceive the truth; Aristotle, in his *On the Soul*, provides a philosophical account for this idea.

ligible aspect is connected to the ontological and metaphysical one within a fundamental unitary experience.[7]

There is a consensus regarding the essentially 'intelligible content' of myths and symbols, yet not regarding philosophical speculation and the kind of later rational or erudite clarification of the irrational and imaginary. What we have, instead, are meanings of a higher and objective sort, extensions of a genuine super-conciousness soaring within a space beyond history, in the world of principles, or ἀρχαί.[8] On this level, the action of the intellect coincided and was consubstantial with the action of being — in a real sense, and not as in certain modern theories of knowledge, which lack any confirmation in actual experience. (The fact that I have referred to Greek terms here should not be taken to suggest that these are exclusively Greek views: I have used such terms simply because the Greek tradition has more clearly expressed what is also to be found in other civilisations.)

In the light of all this, it may also be argued that myths and symbols exercised a special power, that they also manifested themselves as forces that carried the soul and 'integrated' all the various functions

---

7   Κόσμος (cosmos) means the ordered whole of existence, and was taken by the Greeks in contrast to the χάος, chaos. Νοητός derives from νοῦς (see previous footnote), so that the entire phrase means something like the ubiquitous and articulated order which can be directly apprehended by the mind of man. The reference to 'archetypes' here might well be to the enigmatic Platonic theory of forms or ideas, according to which everything that is real is but the pale reflection or perceptible image of divine archetypes.

8   Ἀρχή (plural ἀρχαί) is another Ancient Greek word which is difficult if not impossible to translate. It means the beginning or the origin of a thing; hence also the principle of a thing. And since this principle, this origin, this beginning, might be taken as determining the course and character of the thing in question, it came also to mean rule, governance, even empire or realm. (As in footnote 6 above, here again consider the first line of the Johannine Gospel: Ἐν ἀρχῇ ἦν ὁ λόγος; consider also the English words architect and archetype.) Most intriguingly, we thus find in ἀρχή a concept in which intellect and power intersect in a most vivid way.

of the human being — as Vico more or less realised in relation to the
'heroic ages', an expression which for him is synonymous with 'mythical ages'.[9] What this means is that myths and symbols also contained
that power, that potential, which is attributed to the 'irrational'. It was
therefore a kind of experience that grasped whatever manifested itself
to the senses according to a higher meaning and in an intelligible
light. This experience was not a hazy 'mystical' one, but rather an
action in the higher sense, which essentially entailed the destruction,
the burning out, of all that is infrasensible[10] and unconscious. I have
thus spoken of 'extensions of a super-consciousness' — which reveals
the utterly deviant character of the aforementioned interpretations of
myths and symbols in terms of vital irrationality and the unconscious.
One should not conclude from the acknowledgement of this dynamic
counterpart to the myths of the traditional world that they possessed
a purely irrational and emotional content. Both this counterpart and
their other aspect, as images and forms of the imagination, must be
regarded as secondary. The essential nucleus is rather to be found on a
different level, suffused by the light of the metaphysical and primordial.

I realise that many readers will find it difficult to grasp all this,
since we are dealing with perspectives that have long been lost and
which are foreign to today's 'culture'. Yet these references are essential
for finding one's bearings, as well as for grasping the true meaning of
contemporary irrationalism.

In the field of the history of civilisations, therefore, the theory of
a 'mythical era', irrationally conceived as lying in a primordial time,
is absolutely wrong (such a theory serves as a worthy counterpart to
Darwinism, and Benedetto Croce too has drawn upon it in order to

---

9   For Vico, see note 28 to Chapter 5 above. On Vico's understanding of the 'heroic
     age', see for instance *The New Science*, Chapter VI, beginning.

10   [Translator's note. —*Ed.*] That is, all that falls below the level of the senses.

'interpret' Giambattista Vico).[11] However, one must acknowledge that in certain stages or periods of an ancient civilisation, what is ideally secondary in practice occasionally acquired a primary role, in such a way that myths were mostly experienced in terms of their imaginative, emotional and sub-rational aspect. In such cases, we find a degeneration of the original form of an experience and of a kind of knowledge that preserved their genuine and normal character only among certain closed elites.

The same applies to the world of primitive peoples, who for the most part are but the degenerated and twilight remnants of very ancient, extinct cultures. Just as the higher type of the sage and initiate has been replaced among them by the witch-doctor, medicine man and shaman, so in their world a sort of demonising of symbols and myths has occurred, creating a kind of nocturnal consciousness. All that survives are the psychic and magical corpses of the symbols and myths of these peoples, their ghosts, so to speak, in the form of dynamic complexes which, having lost their luminous and intelligible spiritual nucleus, produce dark ecstasies. This has been completely ignored both by ethnologists and by many historians of religion, who have put everything in the same basket, nor realising that to place material collected from savage tribes alongside evidence from higher civilisations is to contaminate the latter. Certain purely formal correspondences, akin to those between an object and its shadow, have led them to commit the most deplorable mistakes. Let us add that what lies in the subconscious of civilised man and tends to burst forth in his crises and nervous collapses may be seen to possess the same character as the residues just mentioned — hence the possibility of drawing a parallel between the world of primitive peoples and that of psychopathology.

---

11   Benedetto Croce (1866–1952) was a celebrated Italian statesman, art critic, and philosopher, developer of an idealistic historicism. Croce was much influenced by Vico, and even purchased the deceased philosopher's house. The present reference is to Croce's 1913 work on Vico, *The Philosophy of Giambattista Vico*.

Such correspondences only apply within this framework, which is to say this shared level of residual regressive and degenerate forms. They have no correlation with the level pertaining to symbols and myths in higher civilisations with a metaphysical orientation; rather, the argument I outlined above holds for such higher civilisations.

To further clarify this picture, it is possible to succinctly outline the stages of the process of descent which progressively occurred in historical times. At the origin there lies what I have described as the Olympian ideal of supra-sensible light, the realm of higher, suprarational knowledge. As is well known, comparative philology has identified this in the very names, sprung from the same root and connected to the idea of luminosity, that the various higher civilisations of Indo-European origin used to describe the deity: Dyaus, Deus, Zeus, Thiuz, etc.[12] However, parallels are also to be found in other cultural areas; one might mention, for example, the conception of the Tiān and great luminous Yang in the Far-Eastern tradition. We may trace back to this stage the highest object of knowledge, the metaphysical content of myths and symbols. The next stage is distinguished by the fact that the mythical form of this content becomes more prominent and, partly, independent. This is the point at which the various mythological personifications emerge, whose inner meaning, or intelligible content, grows dimmer and dimmer, transforming into a merely religious, mythologising or even aestheticising experience, as we can see in the phases of decline in Greece and Rome. One of the effects of this initial dissociation is the activity of the imagination, which — so to speak — acts fruitlessly, which is to say without any objective (supra-

---

12   *Dyauṣ* is the sky god of the Vedic pantheon, Deus is the Latin word for 'god' (cf. Greek θεός), and Zeus is the Greek father of the gods. By Thiuz it is possible that Evola is referencing the proto-Germanic name Tiwaz, which gives us Tyr in Old Norse. In the following sentence, Tiān is a Chinese term indicating 'heaven', while Yang represents one half of the famous Yin and Yang — the half corresponding in particular to light, clarity, openness, and masculinity.

sensible) content, veering towards the subjectivism of mere art. Let us note in passing that it is in relation to these sub-products that the conception of symbols and myths emerged as arbitrary and unreal imaginative forms — a conception which long remained dominant in contemporary culture.

As regards the primary direction of these changes — a direction neither irrational nor aestheticising — the turning point for the West is represented by those aspects of Greek thought in which given conceptions — starting from that of 'intelligible world', κόσμος νοητός, and of principles conceived as metaphysical realities, ἀρχαὶ — lost their meaning as symbols pertaining to sacred knowledge, and became speculative, conceptual constructs. This ambiguity is already to be found in Plato, and was only partly overcome by the Neoplatonists. The same process later occurred with medieval Scholasticism, whose rationalism used a system of more or less sterile concepts to express the content of a supra-rational experience that lay behind the various representations and hypostases of theology. By continuing in this direction, we approach actual rationalism; the traditional ideal of supra-sensible clarity gives way to that of 'natural light' and of rational evidence (Descartes).[13] A tendency takes root to conceive reason as an

---

13   Neoplatonism refers to the school of thought which emerged after Plato's death and which, taking its orientation from his philosophy, developed a distinct spiritualistic vision of the world. Its origins can be traced back to the Third Century and the writings in particular of Plotinus, who is considered the first of the Neoplatonists; its end is dated at AD 529, when the Christian Emperor Justinian I closed the Platonic Acadamy. (This date, and indeed the event itself, are not so unambiguous, however, as many modern historians seem to believe.) After the decline of the Neoplatonists, classical thought began to wane in the West. Scholasticism, which was from the first connected to an attempt to perpetuate classical learning, arose around the ninth century (one of its founders was the Irishman Johannes Scotus Eriugena), and by 1200 had become the common basis for Medieval schooling throughout Europe. While the Neoplatonists had emerged from a dialectic principally with Plato, it was from Aristotle that

independent faculty capable of drawing from within itself the principles required to ensure certainty in the sphere of knowledge, a code of
conduct in the practical domain, and order in the social and political
field.

With regard to subsequent developments, three general directions
may be distinguished. The first is that of speculative and dialectic
abstractions which are more and more removed both from the spirit
and from concrete reality; this direction corresponds to the domain of
modern philosophy. The second direction is marked by the degrading
of the intellect through its increasingly practical and pragmatist use,
reducing it to a means of acquiring positive scientific knowledge and
to its various applications (through the mathematisation and coordi-
nation of data from sensible experience, as well as through technical
and technological organisation). Finally, the third direction is that of
the Enlightenment and its offshoots, such as modern 'critical thought'.
This is the aggressive direction whereby intellectualistic thought, in
cahoots with individualism and all the various revolutionary and anti-
traditional movements, often including scientism itself, has come to
serve as an instrument for the destruction or desacrilisation of existence, presented as the liberation of man and of the human spirit from
'obscurantism'.

Scholasticism took its main impetus, and in particular from the effort to har-
monise Aristotelian thought with Christian theology — an attempt which was
to culmine in the grand Christian apologia of St. Thomas Aquinas. The influence of Scholasticism was broken by the advent of modernity; René Descartes
(1596–1650) was surely one of the most important and influential figures in
the transition from Scholasticism to rationalism. The idea of the 'natural light'
was evidently of central importance to Descartes (see his Third Meditation in
Meditations on First Philosophy), and there can be no doubt, given the work
of preparatory universal demolition employed by that philosopher in the em-
ployment of his method, that the 'light' in question must be taken as purely
rationalistic, as Evola here suggests.

With respect to this third direction, I have noted on another occasion the significance of the change of meaning which the term 'enlightenment' has undergone.[14] I noted how it was originally related to a range of ideas analogous to those just outlined; it was neither a 'philosophy' nor a social ideology. The 'enlightened ones' were those who had received spiritual enlightenment, enabling them to participate of a kind of knowledge that transcended ordinary human faculties. One may refer here to what Scholasticism describes as *intuitio intellectualis*, Hinduism as *vidya*, Buddhism as *prajñā* or *bodhi*, and so on.[15] By its very nature, this form of experience can only be the prerogative of a few elect. It is evident, therefore, that the doctrine of 'enlightenment' found its rightful place exclusively within a hierarchical and aristocratic, and hence traditional, framework.

The inversion that the term 'enlightenment' has undergone is tangibly expressed by the relation between dogma and illumination. In positive religions, and particularly in Catholicism, dogma is akin to myth. Its intelligible content is not given directly: it is presented as the object not of knowledge but of faith (often in relation to a 'revelation'), based on an authority which places it beyond all criticism or discussion. This form is not essential, but is due to special circumstances and practical

---

14   See *The Mystery of the Grail*, (1938), § 29.

15   *Intuitio intellectualis* is a Latin term meaning 'intellectual intuition' — though here again translation into modern English is utterly inadequate. *Intuitio* was, rather than being a kind of hunch or instinctive understanding, something much more akin to the Greek νοῦς (see note 6 above), and indicated the capacity of the mind to immediately apprehend knowledge. The expression was introduced by the German mystic Nicholas of Cusa (1401–1464). In good Aristotelian tradition, it was interpreted by the Scholastics as indicating the mind's ability to understand first principles. According to the Christian Scholastics, this capacity exists in pure form in the angels and of course in God himself. The Hindu term *vidya* means 'clear or correct knowledge'. *Prajñā* means 'wisdom' or 'understanding', and *bodhi*, which derives from the same root as the name of Buddha himself, means 'awakening'.

considerations, since the same kind of knowledge is imparted in other ways in civilisations of a different sort. The peculiar situation that led to dogmatic forms at the end of Antiquity in the West is to be found in a certain spiritual degradation of the most recent European man, his marked propensity towards individualism and intellectual anarchy. From a given historical period onwards, certain forms of knowledge came to exceed the intellectual limits of the average person. So the only way to safeguard them against profane attacks was to present them in the form of dogmas. René Guénon rightly observes: 'There are people who in order not to "divagate", in the etymological sense of the word,[16] need to be kept under strict supervision, while there are others who have no such need; dogma is necessary for the first and not for the second, just as, to take another example of a slightly different kind, the forbidding of images is necessary only for people who naturally tend towards a kind of anthropomorphism [in conceiving the sacred].'[17]

Now, illumination must be understood as that which, in principle, can allow an especially qualified being to do without dogmas and hence to be free, no longer under any supervision. Anyone who knows something by having directly experienced it has no need to 'believe'; he 'knows', and is free. He will find himself *beyond* dogma, not *against* dogma. He will acknowledge the same things by a different route. And his 'orthodoxy' will be firmer than that of any other man because it

---

16 That is to say, to stray, to wander (Latin: *dis* = apart, *vagari* = to wander). René Guénon (1886–1951) — to whom Evola refers on more than one occasion as the 'master of modern times' — was a French writer, and one of the paramount defenders and explicators of the idea of Tradition. In Guénon's quest for a living tradition of initiation, he converted to Islam and moved to Cairo in 1930, where he remained until his death. He was the author of some thirty books on the occult sciences, spiritualism, symbology, and the plight of the modern West.

17 [Translator's footnote. —*Ed.*] Guénon, 'Initiation & Spiritual Realization', transl. by Henry D. Fohr, Sophia Perennis, Hillsdale NY, 2001, p. 90.

has inner roots; it would be impossible for him to 'divagate', even if he wanted to.

Such are the true relations normally existing between 'enlightenment' and dogma. One might even say that illumination justifies dogma (I am referring ever to the kind of dogma that truly relates to the metaphysical order), but also everything in a positive tradition that embodies a kind of authority or bond with respect to the masses. By contrast, a very serious perversion occurs when the need to go beyond dogma is affirmed on the basis of reason, a faculty that is merely human and hence incapable on its own of soaring towards anything transcendent. This is also the case when the possibility of going beyond dogma is extended to just anyone. It is at this stage that the dam breaks and that 'enlightenment' becomes a distinguishing feature of 'free thinkers', through a rationalist and critical thought which establishes itself as the ultimate judge in a domain governed inevitably by individualism — the very thing which tradition in specific circumstances has sought to prevent by taking on dogmatic forms. Such is the origin of the current yet distorted meaning acquired by the word 'enlightenment' in the history of ideas.

In view of all this, one can understand why the 'enlightened' — those who opposed the 'natural light' of unbridled human reason to 'dogmatic obscurantism' — sided with revolutionaries, liberals, intellectual and social subversives, modern Freemasons, anti-Catholic atheists and other anti-traditional forces. This peculiar state of affairs became particularly clear on the eve of the French Revolution, a period in which unbelievers and sceptics the likes of Voltaire, Diderot, d'Alembert and the other *Encyclopédistes* were joined by a group of self-proclaimed initiates and apostles of the supernatural, both groups operating under the aegis of the 'enlightenment'.[18]

---

18 Voltaire (1694–1778), Denis Diderot (1713–1784) and Jean le Rond d'Alembert (1717–1783) were three of the principle figures in the French Enlightenment. The last two co-edited the first encyclopedia, the *Encyclopédie*, whose original

After this clarifying digression, let us resume our previous reflections. The accentuation and predominance of the secularised intellect, of rationalism and of the other aforementioned abstract or technical and practical tendencies of Western thought, were ultimately destined to lead to an insurrection of all the forces of an existence that had been detached from any higher point of reference — forces which could no longer be contained by rational schemes and which had previously been disregarded and suppressed. But this is where the misunderstanding arose. Having lost all sense of that reality before which rationality represents only an unreal reflection and surrogate, people have turned not to the super-rational but to the sub-rational in search of what the intellect can no longer provide, insofar as this intellect has become synonymous with reasoning. The end result is the transition from one kind of error to another. The previous superstitious worship of *ratio* has been replaced with that of 'life', 'becoming' or 'the unconscious'. Worse still, the spirit has been mistaken for something which, ultimately, only corresponds to the naturalistic or even pre-personal part of the human being. René Guénon is perfectly right in noting that after the rationalism, materialism and positivism of the last century have led individuals to shut themselves off from what lies *above* man — and it is here that the contribution made by the distorted 'enlightenment' is to be found — these new currents are now opening man up to everything which lies *below* him. In particular, the unconscious has become a repository of all sorts of things. The fundamental methodological

---

contributors were known as the *Encyclopédistes*. Their work was to be a key step toward the universal enlightenment of man and the education of the citizens of new societies. Though the three men named here all died before the Revolution broke out in France, the *Encyclopédistes* were united in their hostility toward the *Ancien Régime*, and many of them contributed to the undermining of the aristocracy in one way or another. For more on the influence and nature of Freemasonry, see Chapter 10 of Evola's *Recognitions*. Evola adds the following note here: 'These ideas have further been developed in the last section of my book *The Mystery of the Grail*'.

distinction between the unconscious and the supra-conscious is utterly overlooked today. Hence too the distorted interpretation of the primordial world and the general confusion surrounding the various aspects and dimensions which, according to traditional teaching, pertain to symbolism and myth.

Finally, it is worth mentioning the latest outcome of the irrationalist regression, namely the myth of the 'leading idea'. Today we find a type of man who regards principles as meaningless abstractions and who assigns value to ideas only insofar as they have the power, as watchwords, to elicit certain emotional states. This is precisely the meaning that some people today assign to the word 'myth'. This 'myth' is understood as a complex which cannot be accounted for in rational terms and which must be evaluated not in terms of its objective content and truth but rather on the basis of its power to 'operate' as a centre crystallising irrational and emotional forces (i.e. those of individuals and the masses). In relation to this action, a leading role is often played — in an invisible and sinister way — by the 'corpses' of genuine, ancient myths (one might also refer here to the Jungian 'archetypes'). On this level, myths may also become conflated with the watchwords of politics, parties, democracy and demagogy. We thus witness a peculiar reversal: ancient humanity has been accused of being 'mythical', which is to say of having lived and acted according to fanciful and imaginary complexes. However, the truth of the matter is that, if there ever existed a 'mythical' humanity in this negative sense of the term, it is certainly contemporary humanity: those great words written with a capital letter — People, Progress, Humanity, Society, Freedom and the many others that have spawned incredible mass movements, causing the most disastrous consequences, paralysing all capacity for clear judgement and criticism in the individual — these words have the nature of myths. In fact, it would be more appropriate to describe them as 'fables', since etymologically 'fable', from the Latin *fari*, indicates that which amounts to mere talk, which is to say empty words. Such is the level of the so-called advanced and enlightened humanity of our day.

Let us recapitulate. From all the points made — according to a perspective which most contemporary men would necessarily find unusual — it emerges quite clearly just how important it is to have an idea of the correct and *central* direction to be followed, beyond the false antitheses produced by a process of dissociation. It would be necessary to rediscover the path leading to what is superior and anterior in man to both 'life' and *ratio*, and which has the nature of a bright, active presence. From the traditional point of view, this principle also has a form-giving and governing power, exercising as it does a moving and shaping action on all vital energies. On the basis of this, one witnesses in 'heroic ages' a single form-giving current at work in the domains of the sacred, of ethics, of law, and of the creative imagination. Of course, a reversal in this direction can hardly be envisaged today. Still, from the ideas just outlined it is possible to draw certain criteria of judgement and evaluation that may help one see more clearly, so as to prevent confusion and deviations, ensuring a space open to possible influences that may orient one in the right direction. The ultimate aim, then, is a new drive towards that inner region where man can find his true, bright and governing centre.

8. THE OLYMPIAN IDEAL AND NATURAL LAW

From the examples provided in the previous chapters, it is evident that in order to get a clear idea of many phenomena of the contemporary age, it is often necessary to take as one's point of reference ideals and principles belonging to a previous world — that which I usually refer to as the world of Tradition. This also holds true in the political and social domain. Today people hardly realise what a low level we have reached through the influence of those forces and myths which have gained the upper hand the modern West. People fail to grasp the inner dimension and deeper meaning of many structures and conceptions, precisely because they lack adequate points of reference and the kind of distance which is the *precondition* for any clear vision.

The decadence of the idea of State, the rise of democracy, the 'socialist' ideal, and even nationalism as a mass phenomenon fall within this complex. There is no perception of what all this means. I have already focused on this topic elsewhere,[1] recalling that the general view from which we need to set out in order to find our bearings is the dualism between 'form' and 'matter'. 'Form' classically had the meaning of spirit, and matter that of nature. The former is connected to the paternal, virile, luminous and Olympian element (according to the sense of 'Olympian' that the reader ought to be familiar with by now); the latter is connected to the feminine, material and purely vital ele-

---

1   [Evola's note. —*Ed.*] In my book *Men Among the Ruins*, Ch. 3.

ment. The State corresponds to 'form'; the people, the *demos*, and the masses correspond to 'matter'. In an ordinary situation, the principle of form, conceived as something self-existent and transcendent, orders, checks, limits and guides whatever is connected to the principle of matter towards a higher level. 'Democracy', in the broader sense, entails not only the breakdown of that synthesis between the two principles which is the hallmark of all higher forms of organisation, but also the establishment of the material principle — the people, the masses, society — as an autonomous and dominant principle which becomes the centre of gravity. Only a shadow of the State remains: a State which has been emptied and reduced to the merely 'representative' and administrative structure of the democratic regime; or the so-called 'State based on the rule of law', in which a series of abstract decrees, whose original meaning is lost, constitute the ultimate point of reference in normative terms; or, finally, the 'socialist labour State', 'workers' state', and so on. This mutilation is the origin of the underlying materialism and the purely 'physical' character of modern forms of social organisation. We are lacking the very foundations to ensure that every activity has a higher meaning, that 'life' may participate in what is more than life, following the paths and disciplines known to other ages. If the individual today is required to serve others and not to pursue his own selfish interests, this is only in the name of 'society' and 'the community' — which is to say of abstractions, or in any case of something which does not at all entail any elevation to a higher qualitative level. Materialism does not at all cease to exist in the passage from the individual to society or the community; rather, it may even be strengthened by this shift. I have further developed these ideas in the aforementioned book.

Here I will focus on a specific point, namely what is known as 'natural law', which has played a significant role in subversive modern ideologies.[2] The ultimate background of this idea is a utopian and optimistic conception of human nature. According to the theory of natural law, there exist, with regard to what is just and unjust, to what is lawful and unlawful, certain immutable principles which are innate to human nature, yet universal; and so-called 'right reason' can always grasp these directly. The sum of such principles makes up natural law, which by and large has the same characteristics as morality, and therefore possesses an authority, dignity and intrinsic force that 'positive law' — i.e. the law established by the State — does not. Thus, on the basis of 'natural law', it has been possible to challenge the State or at any rate cripple its authority: because its laws — according to this view — are justified by mere necessity and lack any superior investiture, their legitimacy ought to be assessed against 'natural law'. The Catholic Church itself has adopted this reasoning, and has done so, quite justifiably, for polemical purposes, to oppose the principle of pure political sovereignty in the name of the so-called 'natural rights of man', which in their modern version more or less coincide with the Jacobins' "immortal principles" of '89.[3] The Church has often acted as

---

2   The source of the idea of natural law can be traced back to the Ancients, and in particular to Plato and Aristotle, in whom, it might be said, the idea of 'nature', φύσις, first makes its appearance in philosophy — the same nature which Evola subsequently calls into question. The idea of 'natural law' (Ancient Greek: φυσικόν δίκαιον, lit. 'natural justice') stems primarily from Aristotle. Plato seems to have considered the concept somehow problematic; it appears rarely in his work, and its most dramatic appearance is in the longest speech given by that unapologetic praiser of the rights of the strong over the weak, Callicles (see *Gorgias*, 484). The concept appears to have undergone a substantial if not fundamental transformation in its transference to the Christian tradition. The concept did not play so evidently political a role before its absorption into Scholasticism, and it is interesting to speculate how this transformation might have contributed to the revolutionary politics of the most recent centuries.

3   The Jacobins were members of a political club which was most active during the French Revolution, which began in 1789. They were indeed one of the main

the guardian and advocate of natural law, precisely in order to claim a higher position for itself vis-à-vis the State.

That we are dealing here with mere abstractions is made clear by the fact that, despite centuries of controversies, no one has ever been able to exactly and unambiguously define 'human nature' (in the singular), the *naturalis ratio*,[4] nor any objective criterion to assess whether something truly agrees with that 'nature'. Essentially, mere reference has been made to a few basic principles that are tacitly regarded as being necessary in order to ensure life (thus Grotius speaks of 'consonance with the reasonable and *sociable* nature of man').[5] Yet herein lies the fallacy: ultimately, different kinds of social units are conceivable, and have existed, and the 'natural' assumptions of one group do not coincide — or only partly coincide — with those of other groups. Besides, when attempting to abandon the general formula and define natural

---

forces behind the bloody rise of that revolt, and the tyrant Robespierre himself issued from their ranks.

4   Latin: 'natural reason'. This idea plays an important role in Roman jurisprudence (it occurs, for instance, in the first paragraph of the first book the *Institutes*, by the influential jurist Gaius). This idea should not, however, be simply identified with the concept of human nature. The Ancients were perfectly familiar (one is tempted to say, more familiar than most of the moderns) with the complications, equivocations, and mysteries of this 'human nature', and none of the arguments made by Evola here was unknown to them. One should not forget that the existence of these problems might be inherent to that nature itself, so that the absence of an exact and unambiguous definition could prove indeed the contrary of what Evola believes: it might demonstrate, namely, that the classic concept is *not* an abstraction, but is rather a faithful representation of that nature itself.

5   Hugo Grotius (1583–1645) is, one might say, the least remembered of the most important figures of modern philosophy. He was a Dutch jurist who influenced John Locke and contributed enormously to the contemporary idea of international law; his own theories relied heavily, if not essentially, on the idea of natural law. The quotation which Evola here cites can be found in Grotius' *Rights of War and Peace*, Book I, Chapter I, §12.

law, which ought to be one and universal, this or that principle has been added or removed, depending on the author and the period. For instance, 17th- and 18th-century natural law theorists chose to ignore certain ideas that ancient authors had included in 'natural law': to take but one example, in the Classical world natural law often did not rule out the institution of slavery.[6]

However, it cannot be disputed that whenever we speak of natural law, we find a certain common denominator, a nucleus of distinguishing features which, moreover, does not at all correspond to human nature in general but only to a *certain* human nature, in relation to which 'society' itself acquires a very particular form and meaning. Natural law is not at all a single law, valid and evident everywhere and for everyone: it is only one kind of law, the particular conception of law developed by a certain type of civilisation and a certain type of man. As for the idea that, unlike political law, this kind of law corresponds to the divine will — whether this is seen as being normative in itself or rooted in the conscience of man as a rational being, as for instance Kant's so-called 'categorical imperative'[7] — this is nothing but a myth, a speculative smokescreen set up by those who defend and seek to affirm a view that reflects a particular outlook and ideal of society.[8]

---

6   On the contrary, a case could be made that it *depended on it*. See Aristotle's defense of natural slavery in his *Politics*, 1254a-1255a.

7   The idea of the categorical imperative was the central moral concept of the philosophy of Immanuel Kant (1724–1804). Kant famously expressed it thus: 'Act only according to that maxim whereby you can, at the same time, will that it should become an universal law' (*Grounding for the Metaphysics of Morals*, translation by James W. Ellington). That is to say, one should only act in such a way that, if all of humanity were to act in the same way, the result would be the propogation and flourishing of humanity.

8   [Evola's note. —*Ed.*] It is worth mentioning a significant example of the origin of a certain kind of natural law. The British Crown gradually came to assign citizens certain rights in the purely political sphere as a consequence of conflicts and various other vicissitudes. These rights were made absolute by Locke and

The ethical, if not purely sacred, character attributed to natural law is instead denied to positive law, which is said to spring from 'necessity' or even violence — indeed, the institutions of positive political law have often come to be regarded as being *magis violentiae quam leges.*[9] It is quite evident that this view reflects a civilisation which has already entered the secular and rationalistic stage. It is an established fact that primordially there was no purely political law, no purely 'positive' law; primordially, all law was a *ius sacrum*[10] that derived much of its normative authority from a supra-human sphere. This is true of a wide range of different political constitutions, in cities as much as in States and empires — as is readily acknowledged by contemporary historians of antiquity. The situation must have already become confused in people's minds via a process of involution the moment an opposition emerged between natural law and positive law, so that an ethical and spiritual value was assigned to the former yet denied to the latter. It is also worth mentioning, in passing, that we are faced here with a paradoxical reversal of values: given the distinction between men living *more barbarorum,*[11] naturalistically, outside the influence of any higher civilisation, and those living within a positive, well-structured and hierarchical order centred on the idea of the State, it is concluded that the former have an advantage over the latter, insofar as it is they who live according to the *naturalis ratio* and follow the so-called 'law of God written in the hearts of men', whereas the latter only obey revocable and man-imposed norms sprung from necessity. The logical

---

the American Declaration of Independence, and even given a theological foundation: thus these historical rights were transformed into inalienable 'natural rights' anterior and superior to any political society and conferred upon each creature by God.

9   Latin: 'acts of violence rather than laws'.

10   Latin: 'sacred law'.

11   Latin which means, literally, 'after the custom of the barbarians'.

consequences of all this were drawn by the champions of the 'noble savage', Rousseau and those of his ilk.[12]

Having established that the opposition between natural law and positive law does not apply to the particular laws of ancient States, and that so-called natural law possesses no particular dignity but is only a special kind of law intended for a given kind of society, we must now turn to consider that which, in a way, constitutes the recurrent feature of all theories of natural law: namely *egalitarianism*. According to natural law, all men are equal; indeed, according to one perspective, equality is not limited to human beings alone, but also extends to all living beings. Natural law proclaims the indiscriminate, intangible and innate freedom of every individual. Thus in antiquity Ulpian himself decried the juridical absurdity of *manumissio*, which is to say the freeing of slaves, since according to his view of natural law there is no such thing as slavehood.[13] In its more moderate forms, natural law is connected to a communal conception of property — *communis omnium possessio*[14] — which logically derives from the idea that equals have

---

12 The quotation regarding God's law written on the heart is a reference to Romans 2:15. Jean-Jacques Rousseau (1712–1778) was one of the most influential philosophers of modernity, and his philosophy contributed decisively to the French Revolution. His work might be regarded both as a radical protest against modernity, and a passionate continuation of the same. The protest involved a reworking of the idea of the state of nature (concept which had already been introduced by Hobbes and subsequently developed by Locke), and it is here that one should turn to understand his ideas on the human being in his primitive state — what Evola refers to as the 'noble savage', a term which however does not appear in Rousseau. See *Discourse on the Origin of Human Inequality*, Part I.

13 Ulpian (170–223) was one of the most important Roman jurists of his era. Ulpian's ancestors hailed from the ancient Phoenician city of Tyre, as Evola shortly reminds us. Evola probably references Justinian's *Digest*, in which several fragments of Ulpian have survived. See Digest 1.1.4, in which Ulpian states that manumissions 'had their origin in positive law (*a iure gentium*), since by the natural law all men are born free'. (Translation mine.)

14 Latin: 'the possession of all in common'.

equal rights. One detail here, as we shall soon see, proves revealing: according to the ancient idea of natural law, anyone born out of wedlock was to be considered the son, not of his father, but of his mother alone, just as in those cases where it was difficult to establish the paternity of a child.

J. J. Bachofen, a brilliant scholar of antiquity who has been almost completely forgotten by contemporary culture, was the first to identify the key idea from which this whole outlook has sprung:[15] the 'physical-maternal' conception of existence. The reference here is to a kind of civilisation incapable of conceiving anything higher than the physical principle of generation and natural fecundity, personified — on the religious and mythological level — by maternal deities and especially Mother Earth, *Magna Mater* (the Great Mother). Before the generating Mother, all beings are equal. Her law knows no exclusivism or differences; her love shuns all limits; and her sovereignty does not allow any individual to claim a special right over that which 'by nature' belongs to all beings collectively. The quality of being a 'child of the Mother' ensures intangible, sacred, equal rights to all. Equality goes hand in hand with physical intangibility and a specifically brotherly-social ideal of organised life is defined as being 'in compliance with nature'. All this is not necessarily associated with an explicit matriarchy. The origins may be forgotten, the chthonic background (i.e. the background related to the 'earth') may become utterly invisible, yet live on in a particular spirit and *pathos*, in an inner character: this is the case, for instance,

---

15   The Italian editor makes reference to the Italian translation of one of Bachofen's books: *Das Mutterrecht: eine Untersuchung über die Gynaikokratie der alten Welt nach ihrer religiösen und rechtlichen Natur* (Stuttgart: Verlag von Krais und Hoffmann, 1861). Johann Jakob Bachofen (1815–1887) was a Swiss jurist, philologist, and anthropologist, whom Evola held in high respect. A selection of his writings have been offered in English in the volume *Myth, Religion, and Mother Right*.

when the principles of natural law are applied in themselves, in the abstract, on a rationalistic level.

It is clear what aspects of the more ancient law of Rome are irreducible to this outlook: *patria potestas*, virile, aristocratic, senatorial and consular authority, the very conception of the State and, ultimately, the theology of *imperium*.[16] Thus Rome is marked by an antithesis: alongside laws and institutions of this sort we find individual elements that, as the counterpart to particular cults, attest to layers reflecting that ancient Mediterranean civilisation which can generally be described as *Pelasgian*.[17] At its centre stands, in various forms, the cult of the Great Mothers of nature, life, and fecundity. If we return to the legal background positively embodied by the Roman State, we find that up until a certain period the upper strata of Roman society were also shaped by a religious conception, only one opposite to the chtonic religious just outlined: for the State and its law expressed the same kind of sovereignty that the ancient Indo-European man assigned to the *paternal* forces of Light and of the luminous sky in contrast to the maternal deities of the Earth and even of the Heavens. Christoph Steding has rightly spoken of the 'luminous deities of the political world'.[18] I have already mentioned how the heavenly and Olympian deities were

16 *Patria potestas* is Latin for 'the power of the father'; that is, the legal and social authority which was vested in the *pater familias* (see note 10 to Chapter 5 above). *Imperium*, which of course subsequently came to mean Empire as we understand the word today, originally signified the power or the authority to rule.

17 The Pelasgians, according to Greek mythology, were the descendants of Pelasgus, who was by certain versions of the myth the first man. Evola is referring to the somewhat mysterious pre-Roman inhabitants of the Aegean Sea region, from whom the Greeks inherited several of their deities, including Zeus and Hephaestus, though the Pelasgians themselves worshiped a Mother Goddess over all other deities.

18 Steding (1903–1938) was a German historian. He was the author three works, all published during the reign of the Third Reich; none of these has been translated

also seen to govern the world as *cosmos* and *ordo*. The higher Hellenic conception of *cosmos*, i.e. of an orderly and articulated whole, equivalent to the Indo-European conception of *rta*, also informs the Roman ideal of the State and of law.[19] An etymological correspondence here (*rta*, *ritus*) reveals the most profound meaning of the strict, specific ritualism that constituted the counterpart of Roman patrician law.

This law was differentiated and, by contrast to natural law, encompassed the principle of hierarchy. Instead of the equality of individuals vis-à-vis the Great Mother, what applied here was the principle of different degrees of dignity based on one's origin, one's particular position within a given stock or people, one's relations with the *res publica*, and one's specific vocations.[20] The *plebs* instead obeyed a kind of law and idea of community where neither the individual himself nor his origins or clan[21] carried much weight — a community that originally stood for the most part under the aegis of avenging female and chtonic deities.

It was chiefly deities of this sort that the *plebs* of the ancient Roman State had worshipped even in rather remote times. According to an ancient description in the legal field, the plebeians were precisely the 'Children of the Earth'. The relation between certain peculiar features of these cults and the 'natural law' atmosphere associated with them

---

into English. The present quotation is taken from his 1938 *Das Reich und die Krankheit der europäischen Kultur.*

19 For *cosmos*, see note 7 to Chapter 7 above. *Ordo* is a Latin word meaning order, in the sense of rank and hierarchy. For *rta*, see note 30 to Chapter 5 above.

20 The *res publica*, from which we derive our word 'republic', meant literally the 'public thing', that to which every citizen should look in his communal interest. Our English word 'commonwealth' preserves something of the sense of this, though with a peculiarly Anglo-Saxon flavor. The *plebs* were the free commoners (as distinguished from the patriciate).

21 [Translator's note. —*Ed.*] Here and elsewhere, Evola uses the Italian word '*gente*', referring to the Roman concept of '*gens*'. In English, this essentially coincides with a 'clan', and it will be translated in that way throughout the present chapter.

is also significant. In Rome too the celebrations devoted to such goddesses often entailed a kind of return to the state of justice, as conceived by primordial natural law, with the temporary abrogation of the criteria of positive law: participants celebrated the return to the kind of universal equality that knows no privileges or distinctions in terms of clan, blood, gender or caste. Moreover, the temple of one of these Mothers, the goddess Feronia, housed the stone throne upon which slaves would sit during the manumission ceremony, when the goddess would acknowledge their natural equality vis-à-vis freemen.[22] Fides and Fidonia were another two similar goddesses who, as noted by Bachofen, maternally protected the plebs from the *invida iura* and *malignae leges* (coinciding with the forms of positive political and patrician law).[23] Hence we find a temple built in their honour by freedmen. Other female deities or legendary figures are associated with the early demands made by the *plebs* and with the cults of the Aventine, the hill so dear to the *plebs*.[24] And when Ulpian justifies the practice of assigning children born without the sanction of positive law to their

---

22 Feronia was a goddess associated with fertility and the natural world. She owed her popularity to her role as the goddess of liberated slaves and protectress of the lower elements of society. Fides (which is the Latin word for 'faith' or 'trust') was the goddess who oversaw the honouring of contracts and agreements. Fidonia was very similar to Feronia, and may well be simply a variant spelling of that goddess' name.

23 [Translator's note. —*Ed.*] 'Jealous laws' and 'spiteful laws': a quote from Ovid, *Metamorphoses* book 10 (l. 329–331).

24 The Aventine is one of the Seven Hills of Rome, and was indeed particularly favored by the *plebs*, perhaps because the land on it was public property. It became an entry point for new cults and for the introduction of new gods — many of whom, like the Pelasgian mother goddesses that Evola references in this chapter, were dear to the *plebs*, in part for their opposition to the patriciate. In one of those extremely suggestive echoes which sometimes come richocheting down the annals of history, the Aventine was also the place where a number of deputies retired to protest the Fascist regime after the murder of Giacomo Matteotti in 1924.

mothers, he is echoing the archaic matriarchal view (a view which had remained particularly strong among the Etruscans), according to which children belonged first and foremost to their mother rather than father, and would take her name. It would be possible to provide many other details of this sort, all leading us to the same point.

The 'natural law' elements that increasingly came into force in decadent, late Roman times are to be regarded as a counterpart to the predominance acquired in Rome by lower, bastard social strata and by their spirit. The crucial point, therefore, is that we are dealing not with the view of a given school of law, but rather with that of a given *ethnos* and civilisation, which regained strength in the period of universalistic crumbling of the Empire. The figure of Ulpian, a man of Phoenician blood, is highly significant. Alleged 'natural law' may be regarded as one episode in the counteroffensive which the Asian-Pelasgian Mediterranean world launched against Rome — a counteroffensive waged also through the increasing spread of exotic cults and mores in late Roman times. In several respects, Christianity continued this course: given its theological sanctioning of the principle of the equality of all men, the place assigned to natural law by Catholicism is little wonder.

I shall not take these references to primordial times any further. The point is that, generally speaking, the principles of natural law are not indispensable for the existence of a society; rather, these principles tend to establish and give sanction to a *given type* of society. In modern terms, they correspond to a 'social ethic' opposed to a 'political ethic'. Certain principles and values that not only differ from those of natural law but partly contradict them, while preserving a degree of uniformity and universality, have always been 'in accordance with nature' and constituted an inner imperative for a particular type of man. Instead of equality, freedom and brotherhood, what comes to the forefront here is the principle of difference, inequality and justice (in the sense of '*suum cuique*'),[25] along with the principle of hierarchy — the ideal of a kind of unity which is not fraternal, communitarian and naturalistic but heroic and virile, and an ethic not of 'love' but of honour. My work *Revolt Against the Modern World* illustrates precisely the endurance of typical orientations and forms based on these points of reference, which a certain kind of humanity held to be evident and acknowledged on essentially spiritual grounds, establishing them as the foundation of a *different* kind of civilisation and society.

It cannot be denied, however, that in later ages 'positive law' acquired features that have often coincided precisely with that which natural law theorists would argue it has always been. It has come to embody the codification of forms imposed by a formless power, devoid of any real charisma; even more often, it has been reduced to the kind of common law that regulates bourgeois society through the 'routine' of the administrative State. As for the so-called 'State based on the rule of law', this rests, as already noted, on a sort of fetishism of an emptied and soulless positive law, which is assigned an immutable character and absolute validity — as though it had descended from heaven, and were not the crystallisation of a particular socio-political situation, the creation of a given historical human group. All these are but sub-products and deviations. This necessary acknowledgement, however, in no way undermines my argument regarding those demands which are inspired by 'natural law' within the context of democracy, the ide-

---

25 Latin: 'to each his own', meaning classically that each member of the common-weal should receive that which is fit to him by his nature and his quality. As a philosophical precept it traces its origins to Plato and in particular to the *Republic* (Cf. Book 4, 443a). The Latin phrase comes from Cicero (see *De Rerum Natura*, Book III, 38). It is strictly related to the idea of 'distributive justice', which was one of Aristotle's political themes (see *Nichomachean Ethics*, Book III, 9.1280a7–22). Aristotle understood by distributive justice 'giving the equal to equals, and the unequal to unequals', concept connected strictly with the idea of merit, and tied to the aristocratic regime which Aristotle calls the best or second best regime.

ology of social life, and even a certain form of Christianity, by contrast to the political and ethical idea of the State. The necessarily succinct overview just provided exposes the deep meaning of these subversive developments, not merely in abstract and philosophical terms, but in terms of the revealing signs of regression, of the emergence and predominance of a specific inner race in man, the decline of a higher human type along with its symbols and law. The crisis of the traditional world brought about the resurfacing of the 'matriarchal' and naturalistic substrate, to the detriment of the prestige hitherto enjoyed by the symbol of paternity, which endured in the major dynastic civilisations of Europe — those that ruled by 'divine right'. 'Matter' has now broken free from 'form' and become sovereign. This reversal takes a variety of forms: democracy, the masses, 'the people', 'the nation' and the community based on blood and ethnicity in opposition to everything that the State embodies. The principles governing the ideal of politics and human bonds are no longer the paternal, spiritual ideals, but others that essentially may be traced back to a naturalistic substance, to the world of quantity, and even to the irrationality of collective sentiments fuelled by 'myths'. It is indisputably true that, to quote the aforementioned Steding, spiritually feminine or 'matriarchal' natures speak out in support of the 'people' and 'society', conceiving democracy as the pinnacle of world history.

We will see how other currents of our age converge in the same direction when, in a subsequent chapter, we examine the level of certain contemporary claims pertaining to the sexual domain (the so-called 'sexual revolution').

9. THE TASTE FOR VULGARITY

The regressive processes I have repeatedly clarified in the previous pages have also had an impact on the general domain of social mores and tastes. One of the most typical indicators of this is the taste for vulgarity and its more or less subconscious background, which is constituted by the enjoyment of degradation and self-contamination. A certain tendency towards deformation and a taste for the ugly and base is related to this. A few considerations on the matter might be of interest.

I shall only mention in passing that, as far as words are concerned, this tendency is certainly evident in certain new forms of literary realism. In terms of their subject matter, these deal not with social or individual 'reality' as a whole — as the name might suggest — but rather with its most vulgar, wretched, dirty or squalid aspects. A real 'effort' is shown in this direction, to the point that the expression 'engaged literature' is often used to describe the authors from this current, who combine their choice of such subjects with the specific aims of socio-political agitation. But what matters most here is the fact that, generally speaking, the representatives of this tendency do not come from the world on which they morbidly or tendentiously focus their attention. Rather, they are members of the bourgeoisie, or even of the *haute bourgeoisie* with intellectual pretensions.[1] So it is evident that

---

1 *Haute bourgeoisie* is French for 'high bourgeoisie', something like our 'upper middle class'. In particular, this is the class which owns the means of production

they find pleasure in exploring what is base or feel an unhealthy attraction for what is inferior.

The same feature emerges in a much wider field in different forms, such as the vulgar manner of speaking. This has become so common that people have few scruples to resort to it, not only in novels and short stories, but even on the radio and television. The observation just made also applies to this kind of phenomenon. Given that such speech does not belong to one's class or social milieu, and given that now young people, young women and even elderly men from the middle classes, the *haute bourgeoisie* or even certain segments of the aristocracy believe that they are showing open-mindedness, freedom and 'modernness' by ostentatiously using this language, the phenomenon in question reveals simply the pleasure of self-degradation, self-abasement, and self-contamination. And to anyone who might wish to speak of freedom from convention here, it should be replied that the conventional presents different aspects; whether conventional or not, certain customs are — or were — intrinsic to a particular class, and are — or were — its 'style' or hallmark. Taking pleasure in violating them simply means shattering all bounds or limits, exposing oneself to what lies below. Until recent times, the opposite tendency was common: many male and female individuals from the lower classes would, more or less artificially and clumsily, imitate the mannerisms, speech and behaviour of the upper classes. Today people are doing the very opposite, and they believe themselves unconventional in doing so, when in fact they are nothing but vulgar imbeciles.

In this connection, it is worth mentioning a related phenomenon, namely that of the taste for the ugly, vulgar and shabby in one's way of dressing, which has even become fashionable in certain milieus: workers' or cyclists' jerseys, peasants' overcoats and trousers, untucked

---

and gains its income from that ownership, without being reduced to dirtying its own hands in work, as is potentially the fate of the *petite bourgeoisie*.

knotted shirts, and so on. These find their counterpart in long, un-kempt hair, and in the uncouth, coarse manners and attitudes that these loutish youths have learned from American films, with their whiskey shots and double gin. Most remarkable of all is the still partly ongoing trend among young or even married women of wearing blue jeans — which is to say work trousers. The passiveness and tolerance exhibited by men in this respect is truly astonishing. These girls ought to have been sent to concentration or labour camps: these, and not luxurious existentialist apartments, would have been the appropriate setting for them and for the 'functionality' of their way of dressing, and might even have ensured a salutary re-education.

In a different field, the fad of 'howling' singers, which unfortunately is widespread in Italy, is another expression of this taste for the vulgar.[2] The tendency is much the same. One enjoys stepping down onto the level of the street, the alleyway, the corner market: the primitivism of a coarse voice, in the best of cases an almost animal-like instinctive-ness in the field of self-expression and emotion. The ecstasy that for some time now the hoarse and ungraceful singing of the Negro has been inducing in men and women of the White race reflects the same tendency. In the period of this writing, the band known as the *Beatles*, who have filled the youth with delirious enthusiasm, forms a particu-lar case. Leaving aside their hairdos — which match the description I have already given — the very name they have chosen for themselves is revealing: these shouters have chosen as their symbol one of the most disgusting insects, which once again perfectly illustrates the pleasure

---

2   The word '*urlatori*', or howlers, was used to describe a style of certain Italian singers principally in the 1960s. Though rather tame by contemporary stand-ards, these singers scandalised their epoch by singing in a way which broke from the rather civil style preceding them. They are given their name for their tendency to feature a single loud, often grating and classically untrained voice, as well as for the fact that in some of their songs the musicians themselves oc-casionally erupt into a crescendo of wild screams.

of abjection.[3] On the other hand, one might mention as a counterpart the fact that a member of the Roman aristocracy who had opened a nightclub had originally intended to give it the name 'La Cloaca' ('The Sewer'), but was prevented from doing so by the police. Besides, have the Beatles themselves not been knighted members of the Order of the British Empire by Queen Elizabeth?[4] These are signs of the times. The mire has reached even the royal palaces, which in any case are merely empty, faded remnants.

As I was saying, what lies at the basis of these and other phenomena is the pleasure of stooping to a lower level. This is the same sort of pleasure that, in the sexological field, distinguishes masochism and self-sadism. In terms of 'depth psychology', we are dealing with a destructive tendency directed against oneself. Hence, one should consider the role played in such phenomena by an unconscious, yet nonetheless active, 'guilt complex'. This is perhaps the most interesting and, in a way, positive aspect. It is as though one had perceived one's failure to live up to oneself, had perceived that foregoing of any higher meaning of life which characterises the modern age, and had felt — as a counterpart — an obscure sense of guilt or betrayal. It is as though one found pleasure in degrading, damaging and contaminating oneself.

However, there are some cases in which the destructive impulse is directed not inwards, which is to say towards oneself, but outwards, or toward that point at which the two directions meet and intersect. In

---

3   [Translator's note. —Ed.] The author is here referring of course to the intended assonance between the band's name (Beatles) and that of the insect (beetle).

4   In point of fact, only Paul McCartney (as if this were not enough) was truly knighted—honour which he shares with such luminaries of our contemporary 'culture' as Elton John, Bill Gates, Mick Jagger, and Bono. Evola is correct, however, that in 1965 all four of the Beatles were appointed Members of the Order of the British Empire, a separate honour which had hitherto been reserved primarily for military veterans and eminent public servicemen. The Beatles' appointment caused something of a scandal in those still rather innocent days, and several older members resigned from the Order in protest.

this regard, a different range of typically modern phenomena might come into play, which extend from trivial life to the level of culture. In general terms, the sadistic tendency also manifests itself in one aspect of the kind of art and literature which enjoys highlighting those human types and situations that reflect a shattered, broken-down or corrupted mankind. As is well known, one invokes the pretext here that 'this too is part of life', or that one only wishes to bring all this to light in order to elicit a reaction. What is really at work here is what the Germans call *Schadenfreude*, a malicious pleasure — which is to say, a kind of sadism, a sadistic enjoyment. One enjoys gazing not at the upright man, but at the falling, failed or degenerate man: the lower — not higher — limit of the human condition (to some extent, one might also refer here to what I will argue with regard to 'the laughter of the gods'). In the past, Jewish (and Russian) writers were particularly active in this sense; nowadays, it has become a general trend.

Analogous phenomena, with an analogous background, are also to be found outside the field of literature: in music, for example, and in the figurative arts. Here too interpreters and critics have invoked various pretexts: they speak of an 'existential revolt' as the meaning of these displays, and in some cases the socio-political motives of engagé Left-wing intellectuals also come into play. In a well-known work on the philosophy of modern music, Adorno has sought to interpret atonal music precisely in such terms:[5] the inrush of sounds shattering

---

5   The Italian editor gives the following reference: Theodore W. Adorno, *Philosophy of Modern Music* (Continuum, 2007). Adorno (1903–1969) was one of the various Jewish founders of the Frankfurt School, which surely stands among the forces most responsible for insinuating Marxist thought into the contemporary West, both Europe and the United States. Adorno was a pianist and a student of music theory (Thomas Mann, while writing his *Doctor Faustus*, frequently had recourse to Adorno's counsel), and his *Philosophy of Modern Music* treats in particular the dodecaphony developed by the Jewish composer Schoenberg, which was nothing if not a thoroughgoing rebellion against traditional harmony and classical tonality (I almost said *beauty*) in music.

traditional harmony and rebelling against the canon of the 'harmonic triad' is seen as the counterpart to the existential revolt against the false ideals and conventions of bourgeois and capitalist society. However, in this case we must be careful not to oversimplify things; in order to make an assessment, it is necessary to take the whole range of possible orientations into account. In addition to what I have argued about the most modern forms of music in my book *Ride the Tiger*,[6] I will also return to the matter in one of the following chapters. Still, in many cases the kind of 'value' I have tried to discover in this phenomenon is non-existent. Rather, we might refer in such cases to what an American author, John Hemming Fry, has written with regard to the sadistic and destructive background that emerges in relation to many other sectors of contemporary art. In a book published in the inter-war period, under the title of *The Revolt Against Beauty*,[7] Fry has pointed to the deformations, distortions and primitivism that play a significant role in many contemporary works of figurative art, both paintings and sculptures. In some cases, elective affinities with the art of savages and Negroes constitute an additional and most eloquent indicator.[8]

Naturally, we should not take academic beauty, which is empty and conventional, as a positive point of reference. Rather, we should refer to the opposition between form and formlessness, the idea that any genuine creative process consists in the predominance of form over

6   See *Ride the Tiger*, Part 6, Chapter 23.

7   Fry (1860–1946) was an author and a figurative and landscape artist whose work is characterised by subdued colors and a certain soft fluidity of form reminiscent of early Renaissance painters, though it is considerably more minimalist in its treatment of its subjects. His figurative paintings reference European mythology and symbolism. The book cited here was published in 1934.

8   [Evola's note. —*Ed.*] It is important to note that authentic Negro and primitive works have nothing to do with the adoption of a particular artistic style: more often, deformations and distortions form part of a 'magical art' which is based not on the subjective imagination but on the actual perception of dark, elementary forces.

the formless, in terms of the Greek idea of the transition from chaos to cosmos. In a higher sense, acknowledged not just by Classical authors but even by Nietzsche, 'beauty' corresponds to complete and dominant form, to 'style', to the law expressing the sovereignty of an idea and will.[9] As regards the rise of the formless, chaotic and 'ugly', what we find is a destructive process: not power but impotence. This phenomenon has a regressive character. Psychologically, the background is always the same: a sadistic tendency, a taste for contamination on the part of the artist and of those who appreciate and enjoy this kind of art (supposing it is a matter of real taste, and not a foolish reverse conformism, as in most cases). Significantly, in all fairytale or superstitious representations of demons the grotesque deformation of the human figure is a predominant element — just as in the works of some of the most popular modern authors.

Typically self-sadistic traits are also presented by some very recent dances in which we no longer find merely 'syncopated', intense elementary rhythms (one might even find something positive in this — as I have noted elsewhere),[10] but rather a grotesquely epileptic and monkey-like pattern: almost a pleasure in distorting to the utmost degree all that is noble in the human figure through violent, puppet-like contortions, leaps and convolutions. If we wish to sink as low as this level, we might mention as its counterpart the genuine sadism which distinguishes the so-called 'arrangements' practised by almost all fashionable orchestras today. These specialise in anarchic 'solos' and in the cutting up, altering, deforming and decomposing of Jazz or Pop pieces from the past — which in themselves may have been nearly acceptable — to the point of making them unrecognisable.

---

9   For relevant passages from the work of the philosopher Friedrich Nietzsche (1844–1900), see *The Birth of Tragedy* §3, *The Genealogy of Morals*, Second Essay, §12, and *The Will to Power* §803.

10   Here too see *Ride the Tiger*, Part 6, Chapter 23.

Finally, the sphere of pornography and the obscene is particularly worth taking into consideration, as they have become so widespread nowadays. There is no need to offer examples here. Heated debates, also related to the problem of censorship, have been raging with regard to texts regarded as obscene, although no clear ideas have been reached on the matter. It might be interesting to briefly mention the 'obscenity' trial against D. H. Lawrence's famous novel *Lady Chatterley's Lover*.[11] This was held in London about thirty-two years after the publication of a paperback edition of the book in England, where it was regarded as an exceedingly racy novel and had hitherto been banned.

As in other countries, the law of England describes as obscene whatever can corrupt and pervert. However, it does not regard as prosecutable 'obscene' works that are valuable for art, science 'or any other field of public interest'. Two things were at issue in the case of Lawrence's novel: the obscene language, and certain descriptions of erotic scenes that 'left nothing to the imagination'.

For our purposes, the two points are to be clearly distinguished. With regard to the latter, the general problem emerges of the degree to which sex is something 'obscene' and impure in itself, so that focusing on it and drawing attention to sexual experience has a corrupting effect. As is well known, Lawrence not only rejects this perception of sex, but even makes a sort of religion of sex itself: in sexual experience

---

11   Lawrence (1885–1930) was an English novelist and playwright who made a stir with the publication of his *Lady Chatterley's Lover*, long considered an obscene work for its explicit sexual scenes and offensive language. The book was originally published in censored form in the United States in 1928; Penguin Books risked an unexpurgated edition in Britain in 1960, and was swiftly brought to trial. The *R v Penguin Books Ltd* case marked a turning point in artistic censorship in British society, after the jury (three women and nine men) found unanimously for the defendant.

he sees a means to realise 'the living wholeness and living unison' of the person.[12]

As regards the nature of the various contemporary currents that extol sex and champion sexual freedom, I will examine all this rather extensively in another chapter. Here I will only note that the point of view of bourgeois puritanism, with all its taboos, is quite alien to me. It is also possible to go beyond the prejudices typical of sexophobic Christian moralism and to acknowledge that in several higher civilisations sex was not at all regarded as something impure, shameful or 'obscene'. The problem is quite another one. Today, it is necessary rather to take a stand against everything which serves only to trigger a sort of chronic obsession with sex and women, and which ultimately represents a systematic, wide-scale attack against virile values: for wherever love and sex predominate, it will always be womankind that, in some way or other, predominates. This obsession is nourished in a thousand ways by means that are not, strictly speaking, 'obscene', such as the images in magazines, ads and films, beauty pageants, 'sexual enlightenment' literature with its scientific pretensions, female immodesty, stripteases, the display of women's underwear in shop windows, and so on. Racy novels and stories are only one particular case. It is the overall phenomenon that one ought to keep in mind, in order to recognise its corrupting action, not from the standpoint of petty morals, but in the aforementioned terms — which is to say as an implicit action of corrosion and attack directed against those interests and values that ought to remain dominant in any higher civilisation.

In relation to the specific topic we are now exploring, however, it is genuine 'obscenity' that we ought to consider. In order to correctly define 'the obscene' and 'the pornographic', we need only turn to etymology. 'Pornographic' comes from the Greek πόρνη, meaning

---

12   The quotation is probably taken from Lawrence's last work, *Apocalypse and the Writings on Revelation* (Cambridge University Press, 2002), pg. 149.

prostitute (i.e. a low-rank prostitute, as opposed to a hetaira);[13] hence, it would be arbitrary to apply the term to texts that do not exclusively concern low-level prostitution. Instead, the term 'obscene' comes from the Latin *caenum*, meaning dirtiness, filth and mud (or even excrement). Hence, it may be used to describe one aspect of the most recent erotic literature, which leads us back to our main topic, the taste for all that is dirty, inferior and vulgar. What comes into play here is the choice made by many authors, starting from Lawrence, to employ the most trivial, slum-worthy words — that is, 'obscene' words — to describe sexual organs and acts, when dealing with sexual matters.

What has been written in defence of the obscene by Henry Miller, another author who is openly regarded a 'pornographic', is particularly revealing in this respect, not least for the typical misunderstandings it reflects.[14] According to Miller, 'the obscene' in literature — meaning the use of the most trivial erotic language — is a form of protest, of rebellion, of liberating destruction, intended to free man though a nonconformism verging on sacrilege. 'Ultimately, then, [the artist] stands among his own obscene objurgations like the conqueror midst the ruins of a

---

13   There were traditionally two kinds of prostitutes in Greek society: the *pornai*, who worked the streets or brothels and provided their services more or less indiscriminately, and the *hetairai*, which might be translated as 'courtesans', who often had dedicated clients in the upper classes of Greek society. The *hetairai* were hired for companionship as well as sexual intercourse, and in consequence were often well educated, trained in the social graces and intellectual discourse.

14   Miller (1891–1980) was an American novelist of some notoriety who passed a number of years in Europe. He is most often remembered for his *Tropic of Cancer* and *Tropic of Capricorn*, published in 1934 and 1939 respectively. His works faced censorship in several countries, and he, too, found himself on trial for the obscenity of his *Tropic of Cancer*. This case was brought to court in the United States in 1961, just a year after *Lady Chatterley's Lover* in Britain. The Supreme Court ruled in favor of Miller in 1964 (*Grove Press, Inc., v. Gerstein*), finding that his book is a 'work of literature'; just as in the Lawrence case, this led to a general loosening of censorship laws throughout the country.

devastated city ... he knocked to awaken.' This is ridiculous.[15] First of all, given that Miller is not a theoretician but essentially a novelist, he should provide some convincing examples of these miraculous powers of 'obscenity'. But his books are not even exciting in the manner of certain risqué literature; instead, it all boils down to the grotesque and the dirty when he treats subject matter of this kind or describes erotic scenes. All that remains is the satisfaction in pure and simple obscenity in the above-mentioned etymological sense, the reference to sex being secondary, and, for our purposes, irrelevant, since it is possible to speak of even the most risqué matters while avoiding vulgarity and obscenity. A short book generally assigned to the genre of pornographic literature, *Gamiani*, is said to have been written by Alfred de Musset to win a bet that he could describe the wildest and most perverse erotic scenes in a way 'that leaves nothing to the imagination' without using a single trivial word. Certain anonymous works of French literature that are sold under the counter (for instance, *Vingtquatre nuits charnelles*) offer further examples of the same kind.[16] Thus, all moralistic sexual

---

15 [The translator provides the following reference for the Miller quote: *On Writing* (New Directions Publishing, 1964), p. 187. The following note is Evola's. —Ed.] With regard to the misuse of words, it may be noted that Miller himself states that 'the whole edifice of civilisation as we know it' is 'obscene', which is nonsense, since that edifice is, if anything, absurd and meaningless. For Miller, who is an extreme pacifist, modern mechanised warfare is particularly 'obscene', and war in general: another absurdity that points to the same overwhelming tendency to emphasise only the inferior characteristics in any given experience. The negative, and sometimes degrading and demoralising aspects of modern warfare — the only ones described and highlighted by authors like Barbusse and Remarque — can be contrasted with what men like the young Ernst Jünger and Drieu La Rochelle personally experienced in the same 'total war'.

16 Musset (1810–1857) was a French dramatist, poet, and novelist. The full title of the work referenced here is *Gamiani, or Two Nights of Excess*. I have been unable to find any information on *Vingtquatre nuits charnelles*, but the title alone (*Twenty-four Carnal Nights*, as compared to Musset's mere pair) is probably sufficiently informative for the present context.

taboos aside, the salient point is precisely 'obscenity' — and the current use of obscene language, regardless of absurd pretexts like those used by Miller and Lawrence, essentially reflects the tendency towards self-degradation and contamination, of which we have enumerated a series of typical expressions. And it is certainly peculiar that the extolling and exalting of sex is associated with obscene language that can only make sex disgusting and repellent. Nonconformist rebelliousness, extending from Nietzsche's level down to that of solidarity with the Negro, has found a worthy counterpart in those who resort to the dirty and vulgar language of street folk. If the aforementioned justifications of obscenity are made in good faith, we must simply conclude that those who make them do not even realise the nature of the influences they are subject to, that they merely undergo them and are used by them, following an underlying current whose many manifestations all rigorously converge in a single direction.

Discerning observers will have no difficulty in extending the list of phenomena mentioned here, all of which betray the same origin and signify a widespread atmosphere. There is no need for me to repeat that any form of conformism is alien to me: generally speaking, there are some residues of bourgeois mores and culture that do not deserve to survive, and which are increasingly affected by irreversible processes of dissolution. Under certain conditions, these processes might even be a prerequisite for a new and better order. But this certainly does not apply to everything we have discussed here so far. With regard to the present matter, one must speak of nothing but debasement, vulgarity and pure degradation as essential components of the predominant taste and mores today.

10. THE LAUGHTER OF THE GODS

I t is obvious that modern civilisation in all its aspects has an essentially anti-aristocratic character on the political and social level. However, this is also true on the spiritual level, on the level of culture and people's outlook, even though the anti-aristocratic trait is harder to detect here because the necessary points of reference have been lost almost entirely.

Here I wish to highlight a particular aspect of the situation related to the rise of 'humanism'. I will use this term in a broad sense, distinguishing it from historical humanism in the period of the so-called Renaissance, even though this kind of humanism constituted a crucial turning point in the upheaval to which I am referring. What I mean by 'humanism', strictly speaking, is a general perspective centred merely on man, on the human condition, that makes everything human into a cult object — a genuine fetish. Here I will not consider the more degraded forms of this cult, such as 'Marxist humanism' and 'labour humanism'. Instead, I will focus on those forms which are related to the so-called 'tragic view of life', insofar as they tend to assign much 'human' worth to rebellious or subversive historical or mythical figures, and to side with them — this being the ideal and romantic counterpart to the plebeian and subversive revolutionary ideologies of recent times.

According to a certain mentality, being human — and nothing but human — is a glory in itself. The wretched, dark, painful and broken aspects of the human condition are termed 'tragic', and are praised consistently with the premises adopted. The prototype of the 'noble' human spirit is found in whomever rebels against higher forces, in the Titans, or in Prometheus.[1]

Therefore, one speaks of 'deeply humane works', of 'humane awareness', of a 'vivid and deep sense of humaneness'. One admires the 'tragic greatness' of a given life, or a face brightened by 'inner tragedy'. Finally, one praises the 'Promethean spirit', the 'noble spirit of rebellion', the 'Titanism of the will', and so on. The same tendency is also reflected by Carducci's *Hymn to Satan* and by certain forms of Faustianism.[2] This

---

1   The Titans were the children and grandchildren of the primordial Greek gods. According to Hesiod, they ruled during the Golden Age, and were subsequently overthrown by their own descendants, the Olympian deities, whose king was Zeus. Prometheus was unambiguously regarded as a Titan. This fact might complicate Evola's analysis, insofar as Prometheus, as a Titan descended of Titans, in a certain sense belongs more to the 'origins' than does the pretender Zeus. There is some reason to think that this was the position held by Aeschylus in his *Prometheus* trilogy, for instance, in which Zeus is portrayed as a tyrant and Prometheus the divine benefactor of humanity (see *Prometheus Bound*, lines 148–151 and 198–199); it is difficult to say with certainty what Aeschylus thought, as the last two plays of his trilogy have been almost entirely lost. Hesiod's portrayal of Prometheus is akin to Evola's (see *Theogony*, lines 507–616, and *Works and Days*, 42–105). According to all versions of the myth, Prometheus is responsible for stealing fire from the gods and bringing it to man; according to some versions, Zeus retaliated against mankind by sending them Pandora, who brought down her famous box, in which all ills were contained. Prometheus, in penalty for his transgression, was bound to a rock by Zeus; each day, an eagle came to eat his liver, which each night regrew, only to be eaten anew the following day.

2   The parallels between Lucifer (the light-bearer) and Prometheus have not been lost on modernity. Giosuè Carducci (1835–1907) was an Italian poet, and the first Italian to win the Nobel Prize in Literature. His *Inno a Satana* reveals an 'Enlightened' anti-clericalism in full swing: in this poem, Michael's sword rusts and the archangel is thrown into the void; the panoply of God's heaven is depopulated, including even 'the Jehovah of the priests', and only Satan remains, as a symbol of triumphant anti-Catholic and anti-authoritarian rationalistic humanism. Evola's reference to Faustianism is not so much to the legend of

sort of lingo was common among intellectuals, men of letters and the champions of a historicist and progressive philosophy which they had largely inherited from the Enlightenment. Its ridiculous and rhetorical nature went quite undetected, until an even further step down was taken with the aforementioned 'integral humanism' of collectivist and materialist Marxists, which dismisses even these superstructures in order to proclaim the mystique of the beast of burden and production. What we have here are clear indicators of the spiritually anti-aristocratic character of a typically modern view of life.

To get a vivid idea of the drop in level behind all this one might turn to the Classical world, to aspects, myths and symbols that are specific to it — provided these are not examined in the distorted or irrelevant form that is common to the latest expositions. It may be useful here to refer to what Karl Kerényi has written with regard to the meaning of Prometheus and the titanic spirit in his work *La religione antica nelle sue linee fondamentali*.[3]

As a preliminary step, Kerényi emphasises two points. The first is that the ancient Classical world, in its loftiest and most original aspects, was ignorant of 'faith' in the current sense of the term, since its religiosity was essentially based on a sense of reality and of the actual presence of divine powers. 'Faith presupposes doubt and ignorance, which are overcome by believing.' 'Faith' did not play any relevant role in the world-view of ancient men, because the perception of divine forces was as natural and direct a part of their experience and life as the data from the sensible world. For this reason — I should note

---

Faust as to certain of that legend's interpretations; in all the major renditions of that legend, Faust is portrayed as a deeply problematic figure. Faustianism rather tends against these representations to glorify Faust, seeing in him the symbol of the tirelessly striving and daring aspect of the human or the Western spirit.

3   For Kerényi, see note 34 to Chapter 5 above. The work mentioned here (*The Ancient Religion in its Fundamental Outline*) has not been translated into English.

in passing — a deplorable confusion is produced whenever the term 'religion', understood in its current, Christian sense, with faith as the centre, is indiscriminately applied to ancient spirituality and to primordial spirituality more generally. In this connection, one may refer to what I have already argued with regard to traditional 'myths' and to what I will argue later when defining the concept of initiation.

The second point concerns the idea of the primordial unity between gods and men. 'Gods and men have the same origin', Hesiod tells us, echoed by Pindar. Two races, the same 'blood'. Vis-à-vis divine powers, the Orphic initiate states: 'Mine is a heavenly race, and you know this too.'[4] Many other similar testimonies could be adduced. En echo of this is even to be found in the Gospel, albeit in strident contrast with the climate that distinguishes it, in the saying 'You are gods.'[5] That the gods *are looking at* men, that they are even present at their feasts and ritual banquets (the Romans had the distinctive ceremony of the *lectisternium*),[6] that they appear and take a seat alongside men, and so on — these images from the ancient world are not mere fantasies. They

---

4   Hesiod was a Greek poet thought to have lived somewhere between the eighth and the seventh centuries BC. I have been unable to find the source for the present reference. In *Works and Days*, Hesiod lays forth the generations of men in 109–173, attributing their origin to Zeus. In the *Theogony* he several times calls Zeus 'father of men and gods' (see for instance 457). Pindar (c. 522–c. 443) was a Greek lyric poet. His position on the origin of the men and the gods can be seen in his sixth Nemean Ode, in which he speaks of a common mother of men and gods, and of the possibility of man's rising to a godlike greatness. The Orphic mysteries were associated with the mythical poet Orpheus, who, upon the death of his newly wed bride, descended to Hades to recover her and returned, failing however to bring her back. These mysteries are associated with the mysteries of Dionysus, which according to the tradition were also the work of Orpheus.

5   See John 10:34, in which this startling phrase is uttered by Jesus, who is in fact alluding to Psalm 82:6.

6   *Lectisternium* is Latin, from *lectum sternere*: 'to spread on a couch'. The *lectisternium* were thus propitiatory meals offered to the gods and goddesses, originally

attest, in a figurative way, to man's sense of being with the gods. They are testimonies of a particular existential condition.

Nor are we to think of any 'mysticism' here. Kerényi states: 'Starting from Homer and Hesiod, this absolute form of a non-mythical being-together might be defined as follows: to sit together, to perceive and know oneself by reciprocally gazing into the primordial state of existence.' Kerényi speaks of a primordial state of existence on account of the antiquity of the testimonies that express this way of perceiving things.

Over time, the feeling in question waned and had to be reawakened through specific cultural actions, ultimately only manifesting itself sporadically. Already Homer mentions the fact that the feeling of actually being with the gods, as in the primordial state, is only experienced by special peoples 'whose existence fluctuates between divinity and humanity — indeed, they are closer to the gods than to men.'[7]

We must not necessarily think here of races belonging to a mythical antiquity. Even in ancient Rome specific and significant testimonies are to be found. One might mention the figure of the *flamen dialis*, who was regarded as a 'living statue' of the Olympian deity, and of Livy's description of some figures from the period of the Gaulish invasion, who were 'more similar to gods than men': *praeter ornatum*

---

accompanied by a seven day festival during which, according to Livy, quarrels were stopped and prisoners were released.

7   On numerous occasions throughout the *Iliad*, the Homeric heroes are seen to interact or fight with the gods in single combat. These heroes are described with a rich lexicon of epithets and adjectives deriving from the Greek word for 'god' or from the name of Zeus. Arguably the strongest of these 'divine' epithets is δῖος, deriving as it does directly from the genitive form of the name of Zeus himself; it might be translated as 'godly', meaning essentially 'like to the God'. Homer uses this term in reference to some twenty heroes in the *Iliad*, and above all to Achilleus, Hektor, and Odysseus. His use seems to follow the 'fluctuation' which is mentioned here; these 'divine' epithets indicate the movement of the mortal into the sphere of the gods.

habitumque humano augustiorem, maiestate etiam ... simillimos dis.[8]
Caesar himself — to whom many assign the profane attributes of a 'dictator' or Napoleon-like conqueror — is a man who in his youth could, according to Suetonius, claim that his lineage exhibited 'the majesty of kings and sacredness of the gods, in whose power also those who rule men lie'.[9] Even in the demonic practices of the late Roman Empire ideas and customs survived that, almost like murky glimmers, point to the natural perception of divine forces.

'Peoples whose existence fluctuated between the divine and the human' — this is the fundamental point. After this stage, different vocations emerged. Those who fluctuated between the divine and the human ultimately chose the latter, and made a boast of it. They were not aware of the degradation this implied, *nor of the laughter of the gods*. Here one may refer to Kerényi's reflections on the consideration that was originally given to the titanic spirit Classical world.

Hesiod defines this spirit very clearly through the epithets he gives Prometheus: these are all designations of the active, inventive and cunning mind that seeks to deceive Zeus' νοῦς, which is to say the Olympian mind.[10] But this mind can neither be deceived nor shaken. It is as firm and untroubled as a mirror; it discloses everything without

---

8   The Flamen Dialis was the high priest of Jupiter. The quotation is taken from Book V, section 41 of the *Histories* of the Roman historian Livy (BC 64 or 59-AD 12 or 17). The full translation is as follows: 'more than human in the dignity of their apparel and bearing, but also in majesty...like to the gods'.

9   Taken from §6 of the first of the *Twelve Lives of the Caesars* by the Roman historian Suetonius (c. 69–122). This first life is dedicated to Caesar (BC 100–44), the Roman general and subsequently dictator whose famous crossing of the Rubicon in 49 precipitated a civil war that led directly to the fall of the Roman Republic and the rise of the Empire. The passage which Evola quotes here is actually merely reported by Suetonius; in the historian's account, it is Caesar himself who speaks these words.

10   For a definition of this Greek term, see note 6 to Chapter 7 above, as well as Evola's considerations in the related passage.

searching for anything — everything is disclosed within it. By contrast, the titanic spirit is restless, inventive and always in search of something, by cunning and intuition. The object of the Olympian mind is what is real, being, that which is as it truly is. The object of the titanic spirit, instead, is *invention*, but this is only a well-construed lie.

It is worth quoting Kerényi's expressions. The Olympian mind corresponds to ἀλήθεια, which is to say non-concealment (the term means truth in Greek),[11] whereas the titanic spirit loves what is crooked, because a lie is intrinsically crooked (ἀγκύλος), as is too an intelligent invention like the lasso or noose (ἀγκύλη). The natural counterpart to the Olympian mind, or νοῦς, is the transparency of being; when the νοῦς fades, all that remains is being in its dark reality. The natural counterpart to the titanic spirit is instead spiritual misery: foolishness, imprudence, and clumsiness. What remains in the world after all of Prometheus' inventions is more misery for mankind; when the sacrifice is accomplished (the sacrifice through which Prometheus has sought to deceive the Olympian mind), Zeus takes fire back from mortals. And when, after stealing the fire, Prometheus himself is removed from mankind and made to suffer his penalty,[12] Epimetheus alone remains as the representative of the race of mortals: in place of the cunning one the fool remains, as his counterpart. The deep affinity between these two figures of Greek myth is expressed by the fact that

---

11   [Evola's note. —*Ed.*] The term can also be interpreted as 'oblivionless' or as the destruction of oblivion = 'recollection' or 'awakening', in the sense of knowledge of the truth. Later on (in Ch. 11) we will see how this is yet another element which distinguishes an opposite type of spirituality compared to the world of 'faith'.

12   [Evola's note; for the reference here, see *Revolt Against the Modern World*, Part 2, Chapter 7. —*Ed.*] Elsewhere I have mentioned an 'esoteric' interpretation of the myth, according to which the rock to which Prometheus is bound is the body, corporeality, and his punishment is not a penalty imposed by a mightier external power: the animal that gnaws at him while he is chained to the rock is only a symbol of the same transcendent power which Prometheus has sought to appropriate, but which is bound to act in him as something that tears and consumes him.

they are brothers. One might almost say that 'a single and primordial being, both cunning and foolish, here appears to split into two different brothers'. Prometheus is the cunning and far-sighted one, Epimetheus he who reflects too late.[13] The latter, in his imprudence, will accept as a gift from the gods woman, the last inexhaustible source of misery for mankind. According to Hesiod's account of this last and crucial episode in the struggle between the two spirits, Zeus laughs, knowing that men will enjoy the gift and love their misfortune.[14]

Thus Kerényi. This laughter marks the ultimate defeat of the titan and usurper. Kerényi clearly highlights this fundamental idea governing the ancient world. Olympian laughter is lethal. Yet no one, strictly speaking, dies from it; nothing is changed in the human being, a being who is filled with contradictions, a being exemplified by both Prometheus and Epimetheus. So what is destroyed by this laughter? The very importance of titanic misery, its allegedly tragical quality. In the face of Zeus, a laughing spectator, the eternal race of men plays out its eternal human comedy.

Even when a heroic element comes into play, the situation does not change at all, as far as the relation between these values is concerned. Kerényi makes this quite clear. According to the ancient conception of the world, the primordial titanic substratum of being and the laughter of the gods are interconnected. Insofar as human existence remains a prisoner to that primordial substratum, it is miserable and, from an Olympian

---

13   The name Prometheus according to the classic understanding means 'fore-thinker', while the name of his brother Epithemeus means 'afterthinker' — that is, he who acts blindly and understands his errors only in hindsight. According to Hesiod, it was the foolish Epithemeus who accepted the gift of Pandora.

14   [Evola's note. —*Ed.*] In this respect, however, one must take account of the ambivalence of the desire aroused by women and by sexual experiences. On this, I will refer to my book *Eros and the Mysteries of Love*. For instance, the opposite value is suggested by Plato's interpretation of love, based on the myth of the androgyne.

point of view, ridiculous and devoid of importance. This meaning is only confirmed when human gestures acquire an epic character. According to this ancient perspective, the gravity of discord and tension, struggle and slaughter, among the unhappy race of men — once the brothers of the gods — may even have cosmic consequences. Precisely in order to emphasise the magnitude of this tragedy, Homer even allows nature to take part by breaking its own laws through prodigies. Everything seems to contribute to augmenting the tragic importance of the hero.

Yet, according to the point of view of the ancient spirituality I am here referring to, which is to say according to what we might call the point of view of the 'primordial state of existence' — the state that existed before the consolidation of the human and Promethean illusion — does not move or deceive the νοῦς, the Olympian mind, any more than titanic cunning does. Kerényi notes that, according to the ancient conception in question, the only illusion which was acceptable in the relations between man and God was the tragic importance of a heroic existence as a spectacle for the gods (as Seneca too repeatedly states).[15] But the most tragic side of this importance lies in the fact that, as long as the spiritual eye of the tragic hero is not fully open, it too must break down and vanish before divine laughter. For this laughter is not, as the human perspective might suggest, the laughter of an empty 'absolute beatitude', but rather the hallmark of a full existence: the laughter of eternal forms.

Nietzsche, who in several respects was himself a victim of the titanic illusion, would say that it is precisely here that the *profoundness* of the ancient and Classical soul lies.[16]

---

15   The reference is to Seneca the Younger (c. BC 4-AD 65), the Roman philosopher, statesman, and dramatist. As an example of Seneca's statements to this effect, see *On Providence*, Chapter 2: 'But lo! here is a spectacle worthy of the regard of God as he contemplates his work; lo! here a contest worthy of God, — a brave man matched against ill-fortune' (translation by John W. Basore).

16   In this context it might be worth considering §1 of *The Birth of Tragedy*.

All this pertains to the mythical domain. But mythology is not a rambling fantasy. Myth in this context — leaving aside what I have argued in a previous chapter with regard to the strictly metaphysical and atemporal dimensions of myth — is 'the mirror of profound experiences that shape civilisations'. The ideas just evoked point in two directions by suggesting the *other* possibility, the opposite orientation from that embodied by the Promethean and titanic myth which humanism embraces.

The mythological framework — Zeus, gods, divine bonds of kinship, etc. — should not obscure the essential point by eliciting any fanciful feeling of unfamiliarity and anachronism. In principle, the spirit always has the possibility of orienting itself according to one or the other of these two opposite conceptions, and of drawing from this a yardstick as well as an underlying tone for its existence. The 'Olympian' orientation is just as possible as the Promethean one. Leaving ancient symbols and myths aside, it can translate into a way of being, a well-defined attitude to internal and external events, to the human and spiritual world, to history and thought.

This orientation plays a crucial role in all that is truly aristocratic. As we have seen, Prometheanism instead has a fundamentally plebeian character and at best amounts to a sort of usurpation. In the ancient world — not just the Classical world, but the Indo-European one in general — all the main deities of sovereignty, of *imperium*, order, law and rights had a chiefly Olympian character. By contrast, the historical manifestation of the Promethean line is closely related to everything that attacked all forms of higher authority, which it tends to abusively replace with principles and values associated with the lower strata of the social organism. As already emphasised in other chapters, these strata correspond to the 'physical' and merely human part of the individual.

Of these two freedoms, that of the sovereign and that of the rebel, it is generally speaking the latter which humanism and Prometheanism choose. This is true even when people purport to be celebrating the affirmation of human personality and its 'dignity', freedom of thought', and the 'boundlessness' of the spirit.

Besides, this significant choice is clearly visible even in the more trivial forms of the revolutionary ideology. Let us suppose that traditional hierarchies really did possess the character suggested by this ideology, i.e. that they were not also based on a natural authority and free acknowledgement but only on might, and that for instance in the 'dark Middle Ages' man and human thought suffered in political and spiritual shackles. *But in the person of whom?* Certainly not that of the alleged despots, those who administer dogma and who, generally speaking, to paraphrase Aristotle, are not themselves subject to the law they prescribe. These people were free. Thus even on this level it is clear what the foundation of the 'noble ideologies' of freedom and of the corresponding elective affinities is: an instinctual identification not with what is high but with what is low; an aspiration not towards the lord's freedom but towards that of the emancipated slave (assuming that, in the periods under consideration, most of the men in question were actually slaves in the pejorative and distorted sense). Even if we were to accept such a materialistic, one-sided and largely fanciful picture of hierarchical societies, the plebeian foundation of social Prometheanism, the quality of its elective affinities and the 'race of the spirit' it betrays are unmistakable.

Ultimately, things are no different in the cultural domain, where humanism and Prometheanism have celebrated the emancipation of thought and glorified the spirit that 'has broken all chains, becoming aware of its irrepressible freedom'. This has brought about a transition to rationalism, humanism and progressivism, often against the background of the aforementioned 'tragic view of life' and of the myth of Prometheus as a creator. It has fostered the illusion of the 'achievements of thought', particularly of the kind of thought that invents, builds, discovers — the applied thought of the ingenious and restless Titan of Antiquity.

What we have, then, is a movement from below that has led to the fading or destruction of what, in Western history and civilisation, was still associated with the opposite Apollonian pole of the aristocracy of the spirit, which is to say with the kind of sovereignty possessed by those who feel removed from the merely human, those who have the 'civilisation of being' (cf. Ch. 1) as their ideal, those whose lives and actions testify to a higher world and its calm — and not tragic — power.

Under the influence of increasingly rapid developments, 'humanism' was to follow the course leading from Prometheus to Epimetheus, to use the symbols just evoked. The modern world that is taking shape does not know Prometheus unbound in a positive sense, which is to say the Prometheus who has been unbound by Heracles (he who in Antiquity embodied man, the hero, who has made the *other* choice, that of allying himself with the Olympian powers).[17] The modern world only knows the Prometheus who has been unchained and allowed to go his own way, to bask in his misery and in the tragedy of a merely human existence — or, rather, an existence regarded from a merely human perspective. Ultimately, having lost the taste for this kind of self-sadism of 'tragic greatness', he plunges into the dull existence of Epimethean humanity. The latter, while surrounded by the splendid, titanic spectacle of the latest human achievements, only knows the kind of disciplines suited to animals of burden and the demonic rule of economics. The formula used by a well-known ideology is precisely 'integral humanism', meaning 'labour humanism', conceived as 'the meaning of history'. With this, we have come full circle.

---

17   [Evola's note. —*Ed.*] With regard to the hero of the Heraclean type, who is untouched by the 'laughter of the gods', see *Revolt against the Modern World*, Second Part, §7; and *The Mystery of the Grail*, §§ 6 and 18.

11. THE CONCEPT OF INITIATION

I t is not easy today to give an exact idea of what is meant by *initiation*, or to define the figure of the 'initiate'. The main difficulty lies in the need to refer here to a vision of the world and man and to structures which belong essentially to traditional civilisations which are distant from the present one—distant not only from the modern mentality and culture, but also, to a large extent, from the religion which has come to predominate in the West. In addition, there is the lamentable circumstance that if one still hears of initiation today, outside of the empty ritualistic residues of modern Freemasonry and such amateur-ish literary exercises as, for example, the well-known book *The Great Initiates* by E. Schuré,[1] one hears of it on the sidelines of the various theosophical, anthroposophical, or more generally occultist sects. The discredit which has rightly become attached to these frivolous 'neo-spiritualistic' forms, which are sometimes outright hoaxes, is bound to create a prejudice impeding the understanding of what initiation

---

1   Édouard Schuré (1841–1929) was a celebrated French author whose most widely read book is probably his first, the one that Evola here mentions. Evola provides the following reference: Schuré, *The Great Initiates: A Study of the Secret History of Religions* (Steinerbooks, New York, 1961). This book proposed to reveal the path taken by certain great 'mystics' in their quest for truth. Schuré himself was a follower of the theosophy and anthroposophy that Evola here derides (Schuré personally knew the founders of both these movements, Madame Blavatsky and Rudolf Steiner), both of which movements were linked to a decidedly humanis-tic vision of the world, and associated with a variety of questionable figures and events.

really is. This state of affairs has provided those who claim to represent 'modern critical thought' and contemporary 'culture' with a pretext to assimilate the world of initiation into that of the 'magicians' and 'clairvoyants' and like figures of the lower classes, and to disregard the fact that, historically, initiation was an integral and frequently essential part of the great traditions and civilisations of the past to which, in other regards, we pay respect and gratitude.

Nevertheless there is a set of modern disciplines — including the history of religions, ethnology, Asian studies, and Classics — in which certain momentous confusions are almost inevitable if the concept of initiation is not precisely defined. It may be noted that, in the face of the rich material which is now available, even highly esteemed scholars such as Frazer and Van der Leeuw find themselves at a loss.[2] Thus modern disciplines are often seen to conflate the figures of the initiate, the medicine man, the mystic, the yogi and even the wizard, whereas very precise distinctions must be drawn between these general types. Let us not even speak of what has happened with the psychoanalytical manipulations of this material: the comments I have already made with regard to the views of C. G. Jung — one of the main persons responsible for such manipulations — will suffice.

The only positive contribution to be found today is offered by the Traditionalist current spawned by René Guénon.[3] He is the most serious researcher in this field and he bases himself on much first-hand and authentic knowledge. Certainly, his horizons have their limits; however, he has proceeded with a certain rigour, while maintaining

---

2   Reference to James George Frazer (1854–1941) and Gerardus van der Leeuw (1890–1950), respectively. Frazer was an influential anthropologist and the author of the famous twelve-volume work on comparative study of mythology and religion, *The Golden Bough*. Van der Leeuw was a philosopher of religion who sought to apply phenomenology to theology.

3   For Jung, see note 9 to Chapter 4 above, and also Evola's analysis in Chapter 7. For Guénon, see note 16 to Chapter 7, as well as the related passage.

his distance from the aforementioned 'neo-spiritualists', as well as from so-called specialist 'scholarly' research, which is of external and profane nature.

Having described the situation in these terms, I will set out in what follows to briefly elucidate the meaning of 'initiation' and the spiritual framework to which it belongs. This will mean defining the concept of initiation in itself, in its pure state, so to speak, as a 'spiritual category'. Readers who are familiar with other works of mine will probably find this to be a summary of things they already know; readers who are not so familiar will experience a broadening of horizons, because the vision of the highest ideals conceived by mankind would be rendered incomplete if the initiatory ideal were excluded or ignored. To the first group of readers it will be self-evident just to what extent I follow the views of the aforementioned Traditionalist current, and to what extent I have deemed it necessary to distance myself from them.

1 — Etymologically, 'to initiate' means to establish a new beginning. In this respect, one might also speak of a 'rebirth'; but then it would be necessary to give this term a strictly ontological meaning. Indeed, the fundamental premise of initiation is that the human condition, along with the limits which define the common individuality, can be surpassed. It is a change of state, a passage from one way of being to another, in the most objective sense. This is why in some testimonies initiation is described almost as a physical event, so as to stress its real, ontological character. The opposition between 'superman' and 'initiate' can be helpful to explain the concept of initiation. The term 'superman' has been presented as the extreme and problematic strengthening of the species 'man'. However, in principle, the initiate no longer belongs to this species at all. With reference to high initiation, it may be said that the 'superman' belongs to a Promethean plane (man remains as he is but illegitimately seeks to gain a superior dignity and power), while

the Initiate in the proper sense belongs to an Olympian plane (he has acquired a different, innate and legitimate dignity).

The premise of the concept of initiation is therefore formed by the theory which holds that there are multiple states of being, of which the human is only one. However, one must take account not just of superior states of being, but also of states which are inferior to the one distinguishing the ordinary and normal human personality. Thus we can conceive of a double possibility in the opening of this personality — it can open either upwards or downwards. Consequently, an 'ascending' transcendence (in conformity with the strict etymological sense of the term 'to transcend', i.e. 'to go beyond by rising') must clearly be distinguished from a 'descending' transcendence.[4]

This is why I have spoken specifically of 'high initiation', and the distinction just drawn refers also to what I have said elsewhere about

---

4   [Evola's note. —Ed.] Precisely these two tendencies, almost as a reflection, can
     be identified on a more exterior plane, and even outside the initiatory domain, in
     the life itself of the man of our days. Thus, A. Huxley (along with also Jean Wal),
     referring to this man, has spoken of an 'upward self-transcendence' and a 'de-
     scending self-transcendence', adding a third direction, which he calls 'horizon-
     tal' or 'lateral self-transcendence'. For Huxley, the most widespread experiences
     in the descending direction are today linked to the use of alcohol, of drugs and
     of a pandemic sexuality; horizontal or lateral self-transcendence manifests itself
     in collectivistic phenomena, in the passive and irrational identification of the
     individual with various fanatical currents or movements or ideologies, with the
     manias of the day. For the man of today, both the descending self-transcendence
     and the lateral one are, according to Huxley, forms of escapism (and, I would
     add, of regression). However, the two become blurred because 'infernal' powers,
     which is to say powers of the sub-personal level, always operate in whatever is
     collective, and come to the surface. To give everyone his due, Jung is right to
     say that the ancient demons against whose possession people sought to defend
     themselves in the past have not disappeared in the 'enlightened and advanced'
     world, but rather continue to operate under the disguise of — and at the root
     of — the various 'isms' (nationalism, progressivism, communism, racism, and
     so on), as collectivising forces of 'horizontal' escapism.

primitive peoples constituting a special domain. The tribal initiations of the primitives and their so-called 'age cohort' initiations[5] in general operate in the descending direction. The individual opens himself up to the mystical-vital force of his stock, is integrated in it, and makes it his own. Or the integration may concern the deep powers which work formatively in the organism in the various periods of existence. However, whatever results from this for the individual, whatever new faculties he might thus acquire, contain almost always something collective and sub-personal. There is no need to dwell on this case any further. It presents itself in some typical forms, for example, in totemism and in some varieties of the primitive worship of the dead.

It is worth also mentioning a distinction in the area of the higher civilisations. This pertains to the division of initiation into the Lesser Mysteries, which can generically be called Demetrian-Chthonic, and the Greater Mysteries, which can be called Ouranic or Olympian.[6] Sometimes the Lesser Mysteries have been presented as a preliminary stage and the Greater Mysteries as a culmination. However, at other times, the Lesser and Greater Mysteries, along with many other forms of initiation with other names, which can be referred respectively to the former and the latter, have not shown this character of stages but have been distinct from and even opposed to each other. Indeed, these terms can refer to different orientations, vocations and meanings. To put it simply, it may be said that the Lesser Mysteries have a 'cosmic'

---

5   As for instance in rites of passage.

6   Demetrian-Chthonic: that is, connected on the one hand the goddess of the harvest Demeter, who was associated with the underworld, and on the other with the chthonic, meaning the realm lying beneath the earth. Olympian refers obviously to the gods of Olympus (for more on this, see the preceding chapter), while Ouranic refers to the god Ouranos (usually spelled Uranus), one of the first deities, the god of the sky, born either of Gaia (as Hesiod relates) or of the heavenly light and air, Aether. In his coupling with Gaia, he became the father of all — Titans, gods, and thus also men, alike.

and, in a certain sense, pantheistic character. Their limit is φύσις in the broadest and most original sense of the word, i.e. nature, Mater Natura, Mater Magna, the manifested world.[7] The Greater Mysteries instead stand under the sign of transcendence, of what is not 'life', even in the cosmic sense, but rather supra-life or being. One could thus speak of a rebirth into Life and a rebirth into Being as the respective aims of these initiations. Yet, the concept of initiation acquires the fullness of its higher significance essentially with respect to the second direction.

The initiations aimed at establishing or renewing a contact with particular forces of nature should be considered on their own, as a variety of the Lesser Mysteries. In the traditional world, this type is illustrated by various initiations that serve as a counterpart to specific crafts.

2 — Next, it is worth distinguishing, first of all, between the world of religion and that of initiation. Here a certain degree of schematisation cannot be avoided. There are religions in which an initiation is present, and from the point of view of the history of religion it is a fact that some religions developed from a domain which originally had an initiatory character, through a process of popularisation, of levelling, and of externalisation of the original teachings and practices. A typical example of this is Buddhism: there is a real gulf between what can be called the pure 'doctrine of awakening' and the related practices of

---

7　Φύσις and *natura* are the Greek and Latin words respectively for nature. This nature, however, was understood much differently than our own concept, which signifies either 'the whole of what exists', or else 'everything not produced by man'. The term φύσις originates in the Greek word meaning 'to grow, to spring forth, to become'; φύσις would thus mean that which springs forth in a specific way, in accord with its specific inner constitution. Its first recorded use in antiquity was in reference to the moly plant in Homer's *Odyssey* (see Book X, lines 302–306). In classical Antiquity, the term was used in distinction to νόμος, law or custom, and came to mean that which pertains to the character of a thing. *Natura*, similarly, also meant 'birth' or 'character'.

early Buddhism, and the religion which spread subsequently. It can be stated, however, that in a complete traditional system, religion and initiation are two hierarchically ordered degrees, whose relation in the doctrinal field is expressed by the terms exotericism and esotericism, mere faith and gnosis, devotion and spiritual realisation, the level of the dogmas and myths and the level of metaphysics. The present history of religions hardly brings out, or does not bring out at all, this essential articulation. The way of conceiving religion which has become predominant in the West — and which influences many unwitting independent scholars — shows that 'religion' can indeed represent a distinct category in itself, defined in opposition to everything which is initiatory and metaphysical. This conception derives to a large extent from the beliefs of the Semitic peoples, Judaism, Christianity and Islam, which are characterised, in their positive forms, by theism, creationism and the concept of man as generated *per iatum* (i.e., generated by the deity as a detached being).[8] Islam indeed possesses an esoteric and initiatory tradition in the contexts of Shiism and Sufism; and Judaism has a corresponding tradition in the Kabbala; but these currents are in a certain manner separated from orthodoxy.[9]

---

8 The phrase is Latin, and means literally 'by a throw'.

9 Shiism, or Shia Islam, is one of the two major branches of contemporary Islam, the other being Sunni Islam. The basic point of dispute between these two branches concerns the question of succession following Muhammad; the Shia believe that Muhammad appointed a successor, while the Sunnis believe that he did not. The consequences of this dispute have been, putting it mildly, impactful on the history of certain regions of the globe. Sufism, which is commonly refered to as 'Islamic mysticism', is connected with various forms of asceticism. René Guénon was initiated into this order. The Kabbala refers to a tradition of mysticism and esotericism originating in Judaism. It is complex and multifaceted, but it centers on the investigation of secret teachings originally of the Hebrew Bible, concentrating on the interpretation of those texts and on the numerical significance ascribed to the letters of the Hebrew alphabet.

Catholicism is instead completely lacking in anything equivalent, since instead of esotericism and the initiatory experience it has on the one hand mere mysticism, and on the other — as we shall note below — the curious phenomenon of structures which, in form, are of the initiatory type, but which are applied to a non-initiatic level.

It is possible to succinctly define the specific character of the religious perspective in itself as opposed to the initiatory one by saying that the former is centred on the conception of the deity as person (= theism) and is defined by an essential, ontological distance between this God-person and man, and therefore by a transcendence of the sort that only admits relations of dependence, of devotion, or, at best, of transport and mystical ecstasy, while the limit corresponding to the relation human I - divine You remains firm. By contrast, initiation takes as its premise the removal of this limit, and in its place posits the principle of 'supreme identity', whose counterpart is a supra-personal conception of the First Principle. Beyond God-as-person there stands the Unconditioned, a reality superior to both Being and non-Being, and to any specifically religious representation (some have spoken of a 'Supergod'). As is well-known, in both Hindu metaphysics and in the original forms of Buddhism, for instance, the personal God, the gods and the celestial kingdoms were acknowledged, but an inferior degree of reality was accorded to them and they were considered as belonging themselves to the realm of the conditioned. The absolute lies beyond all these. In Neoplatonism, whose links with the world of the Greek Mysteries are well attested, we find analogous conceptions.[10] This shows how arbitrary it is to speak indiscriminately of 'religion' when dealing with man's relation to a supra-human world.

3 — From the practical point of view, the metaphysical principle of identity leads to the transition from relations of a moral and devotional

---

10   For more on Neoplatonism, see note 13 to Chapter 7 above.

nature to relations based on knowledge. This finds its main expression in the idea that what defines the human state with all its conditions is not an ontological distance, but only 'ignorance' or 'oblivion'. This truth has sometimes been sensed also by high mysticism (Meister Eckhart: man is God, but 'does not know' he is such — which corresponds precisely to the Hindu theory of *avidya*, or 'ignorance').[11] The concept of salvation or redemption is thus replaced by that of *awakening*, by a metaphysical awareness of the dimension of transcendence as such. It is in these terms that the specific realisation of the initiate can be defined. 'Centrality' is its essential character. Thus, some have opposed to the concept of ecstasy that of *en-stasy*, indicative of the opposite direction, not of a 'going out', but of a reconvergence towards the centre. Besides, mysticism itself is cognisant of the saying: 'You have not found Me because you have sought Me outside of yourself, while I (the deity) was within you.' Another formula is that of the centre uniting with the centre, of the one uniting with the One.

The essential distinction that has just been drawn between the religious horizon and the initiatory one would seem nevertheless compromised by the fact that, even in salvation religions, the aim seems to be the overcoming of mortal and transient nature. But, again, it is necessary to acknowledge that these terms may have a different meaning

---

11   Eckhart von Hochheim (c. 1260-c. 1328) was a renowned German mystic who during the course of his Christian vocation was nominated a Prior at a Dominican convent and *twice* called to be *magister*, or teacher, in Paris (honour which he shared at that time with Thomas Aquinas alone), before finally being accused and tried as a heretic. He was found guilty on several counts, though not before he passed away. Several of his Latin writings have come down to us, and through these he has enjoyed an abiding influence; his importance is indicated by the fact that he is almost universally remembered as *Meister* Eckhart. *Avidya* was the ignorant error about reality which, according to Buddhism, lies at the root of suffering. Just as our word 'ignorance' means etymologically 'not knowing', so *a- vidya* means 'un- seeing, un- knowing'. Cf. note 15 to Chapter 7 above.

there, and also that various historical factors have interacted and given rise to a promiscuity which does not allow us to clearly distinguish the component parts. This point may be elucidated by considering the special problem of existence in the afterlife.

What is peculiar to the traditional 'inner (i.e. esoteric) doctrines' is the distinction between immortality and survival in a generic sense. The difference between the initiatory orientation and the religious conception has been adequately expressed by a scholar of the Far Eastern tradition (Granet),[12] who noted that in the religious conception the concept of an intrinsically immortal soul is never questioned, and the only alternative is the passing of this immortal soul after death into either positive or negative states ('heavens' or 'hells') — an alternative decided on the basis of a moral criterion. On the other hand, according to the aforementioned 'inner doctrines', immortality is something problematic and uncertain, and the alternative is rather between survival and non-survival — not so much at the moment of physical death as at the moment which is referred to as a 'second death'. Immortality in the proper sense is an exceptional possibility and coincides with the 'deconditioning' of being. The 'Great Liberation', the passage beyond any transient state, be it even supra-terrestrial, is the aim of high initiation. As is well-known, the concept of 'second death' recurs especially in the ancient Egyptian texts pertaining to the afterlife,[13] and it may be assumed that similar references found in the Old Testament are an echo of such initiatory teaching. Another example, albeit somewhat mythologised, is provided by the Greek tradition with the opposition between the privileged and Olympian immortality of initiates and 'heroes' identified with demi-gods) and the destiny of Hades reserved for the 'great number'. Arguably, however, it is in operative (as opposed

---

12   Reference to the French ethnologist Marcel Granet (1884–1940), who spent some years in China and wrote several books on that country's religion and civilisation.

13   In particular, see the so-called *Egyptian Book of the Dead*.

to speculative) Taoism that this doctrine — the problematic nature of immortality and the initiatory conditions for it — finds its most precise formulation. The teachings expounded in the so-called *Tibetan Book of the Dead* (*Bardo Thodol*) ultimately extend these fundamental ideas on an objective level;[14] they present the phenomenology of the possible experiences of the world beyond the grave, ever opposing the realisation of the unconditioned to the passage into one or another of the possible human or non-human forms of existence, none of which has the attribute of immortality, of non-transience, of stability, or of transcendent centrality. Here the alternative is once again determined by 'knowledge' in the aforementioned metaphysical sense, and by actions of the spirit that are only possible if one has such knowledge.

The common theme of these various examples stands in obvious opposition to exoteric religious views regarding a naturally immortal soul and its destiny in the afterlife, views which are often linked to the democratisation and degradation of a previous initiatory teaching. This is the case in Egypt and even in Greece. In relation to Greece, Rohde rightly noted how, following the decline of the original conception of the 'hero', people ended up regarding as 'heroes' those who had no other merit than that of being dead.[15]

---

14 Taoism is a philosophical tradition of Chinese origin. According to Tibetan tradition, the *Bardo Thodol* was composed in the 8th century. The title by which it is generally known was in fact given to it by its English translator, Walter Evans-Wentz; the original is literally translated as *Liberation Through Hearing During the Intermediate State*. Like the *Egyptian Book of the Dead*, it is a kind of guide for those entering the afterlife, and it lays forth a number of articulated and distinctive possibilities for the soul in that realm, along with indications on how to confront these.

15 Probably a reference to the German classical scholar Erwin Rohde (1845–1898), who made a distinguished contribution to his field with his 1894 work *Psyche: The Cult of Souls and the Belief in Immortality among the Greeks*. In all likelihood, Evola's reference here can be sourced to that work.

It is worth noting that the ancient tradition of the Mysteries (which contemporary historians of religions often confuse with salvation religions, the so-called *Erlösungsreligionen*)[16] brings out the essential ontological aspect by which the initiatory conception is opposed to the religious one. Diogenes Laertius informs us of the scandal provoked in certain 'enlightened' Greek circles by the Mystery doctrine according to which even a criminal could enjoy a privileged destiny after death, a destiny to which men of such high moral standing as Agesilaus and Epaminondas could not have access, insofar as they were not initiates.[17] In this regard, one can speak of a 'transcendental realism', which is confirmed also in the conception of the objective effectiveness of the initiatory rite: it is admitted that its power is, on the spiritual plane, objective and impersonal, and as detached from morality on that plane, as the action of a given craft is on the material plane. Like a craft, the rite only requires that certain objective conditions be met; then the effect will follow by necessity, no

---

16 The Mysteries refer to a variety of religious cults in Ancient Greece and Rome, so named for their initiatory aspect; those who had not been initiated into them could not know their secrets, nor participate in their rites. There were many different mystery cults in antiquity, some of them showing a remarkable longevity (the Eleusian Mysteries, for instance, survived for over a thousand years). They formed an important part of the culture of the ancient world. The last word Evola uses in the parenthetical here is German, meaning 'redemption-religions'.

17 Diogenes Laertius (not to be confused with the peculiarly entertaining cynic philosopher, Diogenes of Sinope) was a biographer of the ancient philosophers, to whom we owe the survival of much of our knowledge of antiquity. Agesilaus here probably refers to Agesilaus II (c. 444-c. 360), the Spartan King whose life has been immortalised in writings by Plutarch and Xenophon — the last of whom was indeed a close friend to the King. Epimanondas, whose birth is unknown but whose death befell in the year BC 362, was a Theban general, whose illustrious career is indicated by Cicero's nominating him 'the first man of Greece'. Plutarch wrote a life on him which has, sadly, been lost.

matter the subject.[18] Besides, even in the first centuries of Christianity this opposition was still felt to some extent, insofar as a distinction was drawn between *divinificatio* (deification) and *sanctificatio* (sanctification). *Divinificatio* is an ontological concept: it is defined in terms of a change of essence, like the initiatory transformation of being. *Sanctificatio* instead has a moral and subjective character, which pertains essentially to the attitudes of the individual and to a certain life conduct. In the development of Christian mysticism, after the beginnings (in which, especially in the Greek Church Fathers, remnants of esoteric and Mystery traditions survived), the concept of sanctification became almost exclusively predominant (Augustinism, Spanish mysticism).[19]

The conception just outlined nonetheless seems to be contradicted by the fact that, even in what is known to us of initiatory traditions, yoga and similar disciplines, strict precepts of a moral character can often be found.[20] But it is precisely in this respect that an essential difference between the world of religion and the world of initiation, between the religious attitude and the initiatory one, emerges, because precepts

---

18   [Evola's note. —*Ed.*] Naturally, different subjects will produce different effects — just as the action of fire is different according to whether it is exerted on water, wood or metal.

19   The term 'Church Fathers' refers to the ancient theological teachers of the Christian religion, and the *Greek* Church Fathers were those who wrote in Greek, rather than Latin. (There is also a third group, the Apostolic Fathers, who according to the tradition were direct pupils of the Apostles.) Augustinism refers to the tradition founded by one of the most important of the Church Fathers, St. Augustine (354–430), author of the *Confessions* and the *City of God*. The Spanish Mystics were the members of an influential movement during the Catholic Reformation.

20   Yoga refers to any number of spiritual practices (the word itself means simply 'to bind' or 'to join') originating in ancient India, and its genesis may date back to as long as four thousand years ago. It is generally tied to a regime of physical and spiritual self-mastery aiming at liberation.

which may be identical in both cases acquire a different meaning in each. In the first case, they are given an intrinsic imperative power, either because they are considered parts of a revealed divine law, or because an absolute validity is claimed for them, analogous to Kant's categorical moral law.[21] In the second case, they instead represent means towards an end; they only apply provisionally, insofar as to follow them creates in the individual certain favourable dispositions for initiatory transformation. The classical expression of this instrumental conception of moral precepts is given by the well-known Buddhist metaphor of the raft: it is said that the *sila*, i.e. the sum of moral precepts, may be compared to a raft built and used to cross a current. Once the raft has served its purpose, it is absurd to carry it any further (and one might add that it would be equally absurd to build it, if one did not intend to cross any waterway).

In this way too it is possible to define the relationship between initiation and morality. In general and in every tradition, it is necessary from the initiatory point of view to distinguish a part which has an exclusively social and mundane value, and which acts as a factor to hold in check the human animal, and a part which is really turned upwards, towards transcendence. The relativity of moral precepts is evident in both of these areas. In the first case, moral precepts in the various traditions undergo the influence of ethnic and historical conditions, making it impossible to find anything really constant and invariable, and hence intrinsically valid, in the wide range of norms which we find prescribed in different times and places. In the second case, when moral precepts are assigned a purely instrumental value, the only criterion is the extent to which the means adopted — whatever that may be — allows the goal to be reached. Not only are very different initiatory paths indicated in view of the predominant dispositions of this or that individual, but the chosen means may also be in complete

---

21   For the categorical imperative, see note 7 to Chapter 8 above.

contrast to the moral precepts which a tradition in its exoteric aspects prescribes for most people's lives in the world. The most typical cases are the so-called 'Left-Hand Path' of the Tantric *vâmâcâra* (which presents some points of contact with Dionysianism — for example, when it comes to the use of sex and the orgiastic and destructive element), and the 'heroic path' (*vîra-mârga*). Under the sign of pure transcendence, both of these rest on a genuine form of *anomia*,[22] which is to say scorn for the common moral and religious rules, although the ultimate end is not different from that of the 'Right-Hand Path', which instead uses such rules as a support ('the rules which do not chain but support those who do not know how to proceed on their own'). Generally speaking, 'antinomianism' (a word designating the rejection of the rules of the current religion), which almost always indicates connections with the world of initiation or of esotericism, is well attested in the history of religions.

4 — It is also clear from what has been argued so far that a line must be drawn between mysticism and initiation. This point is generally overlooked, and confusion between the two domains is common. Some brief considerations are therefore in order. To be accurate in terms of mere etymology, mysticism refers to the initiatory world, because the 'mystes' (which gives us the word 'mysticism') was the follower of the ancient Mysteries. But, once again, we are faced with a typical case of

---

22 The Left-Hand Path and the Right-Hand Path refer to two approaches to the esoteric. The terms originate in Tantra, word which means 'weave' or 'system'. Tantra today indicates a wide variety of vastly disparate practices. The Right-Hand Path has traditionally been associated with adherence to the law and to social convention, while the Left-Hand Path (following the eternal association of 'left' with something problematic or unusual or even sinister) has rather indicated a rupture from whatever is common and generally normative. This, however, does not exclude that the Left-Hand Path itself includes a certain set of rules, its own structured initiatic practices. *Anomia* is from the Greek ἀνομία, meaning literally 'without law'.

the corruption of words. In its now current sense, the word 'mysticism' can legitimately be used only to designate a phenomenon with specific features of its own, a phenomenon which may be regarded as the ultimate limit of the world of religion alone. First of all, this is a matter of fundamental orientation. To use the terms already employed, mysticism stands under the sign of ecstasy, initiation under the sign of en-stasy: an extroverted motion in the former case, an introverted motion in the latter. In accordance with the structure of the religious spirit, the position of the mystic with respect to transcendence is essentially 'eccentric' (= decentred). Hence, mysticism is predominantly passive, while initiation is active. A very common symbol in mysticism, especially in the West, is that of the spiritual wedding, in which the human soul plays the feminine role of the bride, which would be absurd on the initiatory plane. From a different perspective, the passivity of the mystic is inherent in the prevalence of the emotional and sub-intellectual element. It is reflected in the prevailing character of mystical experiences, which overwhelm the conscious principle of the I, rather than being controlled and dominated by it. Thus, almost invariably, the mystic has no precise idea of the road covered, and is unable to grasp or indicate the real and objective content of his experiences. Subjectiveness here prevails through elements that are still merely human, and the soul has ascendancy over the spirit (this is what makes the texts of the vast majority of Christian mystics, with their monotonous emotional effusions, almost unbearable — as can be seen by skimming, for instance, through E. Zolla's anthology *The Mystics*).[23] Therefore, one can legitimately speak, in a symbolic fashion, of the mystical path as an essentially *humid* one, as opposed to the dry initiatory one. It is undeniable that some mystics have occasionally reached metaphysical heights, yet without any true transparency, so to

23   Reference to the multiple volumes of the enormous anthology of mystical writings from the West, *I mistici dell'Occidente*, edited by the Italian historian of religions Elémire Zolla (1926–2002).

speak — through flashes and raptures, through the momentary lifting up of a curtain which then immediately fell down again.

Moreover, the mystic as such is a lonely wanderer. He ventures into the domain of the supra-sensible without having true principles to orient himself or any real protection. Once he has left the ground of his positive and dogmatic tradition, he is on his own. There are no chains of mystics — that is to say, of masters who transmit the mystical tradition in an unbroken manner, with an adequate doctrine and practice. Indeed, mysticism chiefly presents itself as a sporadic and irregular phenomenon.

Mysticism has flourished above all in traditions of an incomplete character, that is to say traditions in which mere religion and exotericism do not find their integration and crowning in initiation and esotericism. In opposition to the character of the merely mystical experience, it is necessary to highlight the conscious, noetic, and intellectual character attributed to the true initiatory experience, with the supra-rational clarity it bestows.

5 — At this point, one may mention the essential pattern of what, according to certain milieus, constitutes a 'regular' initiation. A discrepancy between the aforementioned theoretical premise (i.e. the fact that initiatory teaching, insofar as it denies the concept of 'creature', also denies the idea of a hiatus or ontological distance between being and the principle of the I) and the practical attitude seems to arise on account of the fact that the initiatory experience, which consists in an overcoming of the human condition and a passage to superior states, usually cannot be achieved through the means at the disposal of an isolated individual. However, this is not a matter of principle, but rather of historical and practical considerations, which take into account the existential situation in which the vast majority of individuals find themselves, owing to the process of involution that, according to all traditional doctrines, has occurred over the course of history.

Thus, according to the aforementioned pattern, initiation requires the transmission to the initiand of a special force by the representative of an organisation which is its holder and which is also the custodian of esoteric and initiatory teachings. In this context, 'tradition' takes the objective and technical form of an unbroken 'chain' which refers to an original centre. Wherever the present situation makes it possible, this is held to be the 'regular' form of initiation, a form which, on its own level, presents some similarities with baptism and even more with priestly ordination in Catholicism. But the general premise concerning the ontological connections between the human and the supra-human is here taken to imply that in the case of initiation, we find ultimately the passage from potency to act (brought about by the initiatory operation) of a deep dimension of the very being of the initiand. Thus the concept of 'virtual initiation' has been developed, an initiation which remains inefficient and ineffective (as in the case of the quality which is supposed to be infused by mere Catholic baptism), unless a personal action intervenes and is added to it. However, it cannot be ruled out that, in principle, this action alone may, if only in exceptional cases, bring about a breakthrough to a new level and the initiatory opening up of consciousness, even without the aforementioned 'regular' and, to a certain extent, external ritual connection with an organisation.

In relation to these exceptional cases, certain conditions, existential or otherwise, apply, although I cannot dwell on the matter here, given the complexity of the topic. Furthermore, it would be necessary to examine the connection between asceticism and initiation. In the cases just mentioned, this connection is real, provided asceticism is not considered in its mortifying, penitential forms, burdened by secondary moral and religious elements. Rather, ascesis may be conceived as an action undertaken by the individual through his own means, which can provoke the 'descent' and the grafting upon him of a force from above (in this case we will have a 'vertical' or direct connection, as opposed to the 'horizontal' connection through the medium of an initiatory chain). An integrative encounter takes place between the force which proceeds upwards from below and the supra-individual and supra-human one which proceeds downwards from above (on the religious level, one would speak of the grafting of 'grace'; but, setting other considerations aside, there is an essential difference here due to the crucial influence of the 'ascetic' action, insofar as this creates in man a quality like that of the lodestone which draws a metal, by attracting the transcendent influence: the saying that 'the Kingdom of Heaven can be taken by storm' may also be understood in these terms). This encounter makes initiatory development possible: the premise for an autonomous change of state is fulfilled.

However, there are also certain conditions for 'regular' initiation with its 'horizontal' connection, with respect to the qualification required of the initiand. This qualification has nothing to do with qualities of a profane sort: it may be that an eminent intellectual, scientist or modern philosopher is less qualified for initiation than an almost illiterate person. As far as moral qualities are concerned, I have already explained in what sense they can come into play and carry some value on the initiatory plane. In general, the qualification for initiation pertains to a special existential situation, and refers to a virtual tendency to self-transcendence, to an active opening to what lies beyond the human realm. When this is lacking, the individual is not open to initiation because the initiatory action would prove either ineffective or dangerous and destructive. It would not have any effect in the case of 'virtual initiation', i.e. when what is transmitted is merely a germ-like spiritual influence which the individual must develop on his own (thereby immediately acquiring an active autonomous role in his own self-realisation — which corresponds to a more or less articulated development in the initiatory process). It would act in a destructive manner in the case of a direct and solid initiation by a master. There is a power attributed to some personalities, especially in the East, to directly bring about an initiatory opening of consciousness by means of a certain technique; it this power met a rigidity in the structure of the I of the neophyte, the effect would be a trauma, a destruction of the unity of the person. Hence the importance of various preliminary initiatory tests, which are sometimes described in spectacular terms; these are always aimed at testing the capacity for self-transcendence and may even bring the individual to the verge of death and madness. The affinity between initiation and death has always been emphasised. A classic example of this is provided by the expressions which can be found in Plutarch and Porphyry.[24] Essentially, the initiatory qualification is that which is required to be able to actively and 'triumphantly' face an experience akin to death while still alive.

Often, a certain unification and harmonisation of being is required for initiation. The reason is that when there are imbalances and splits in the individual, these become exacerbated through contact with transcendent forces and, instead of the integration of being, the effect can be its disintegration and ruin. Incidentally, this reveals the fallacy of psychoanalytical interpretations, which have 'given value' to some initiatory processes by regarding them as equivalent to psychoanalytic

---

24   Plutarch (46–120), a Greek writer best known for his *Parallel Lives* and the *Moralia*, was also the author of a number of texts on the afterlife and esoteric questions. His dialogue *De facie quae in orbe lunae apparet* (Latin: 'On the Face which Appears in the Orb of the Moon') treats of cosmology, including spiritual and eschatological problems; he also wrote a tract entitled *De sera numinis vindicta*, 'On the Delays of Divine Justice', an investigation into the problem of Providence, given the fact that the unjust are not immediately punished, nor sometimes even during the course of their lifetimes. Evola here refers to a work which has come down to us only in fragments, Plutarch's *On the Soul*. Stobaeus (*Florigelium* 120) quotes from this work as follows: 'Death and initiation closely correspond'. Porphyry (c. 234-c. 305) was a Tyrian philosopher, one of the first Neoplatonists. He wrote a great many works, some of which have been lost; among them are learned tracts on the philosophers and the oracles, and an extensive polemical against the Christians (fifteen books in length). He speaks on initiation in particular in his work *De antro nympharum* ('The Cave of the Nymphs').

therapy: it is claimed that 'pre-scientific' initiations aim to restore a split individuality, an I grappling with the unconscious, with the libido and so on. In fact, every higher initiation requires as a point of departure and 'qualification' a healthy, unified and perfectly conscious man. The sole exception is constituted by cases in which certain diseases offer some virtual possibilities of self-transcendence, and have the character of diseases only because these possibilities do not work as such. Initiatory techniques then make use of them by giving them the right direction and integrating them into the process as a whole. This is attested in the specific case of shamanistic initiations. To some extent, one could also refer to what were described as 'sacred diseases' in Antiquity. Here the task would be to clarify things with respect to those 'positivist' psychiatric interpretations which, especially in the past, have engendered serious misunderstandings by claiming to be able to throw a scientific light on many aspects of ancient initiations, of mysticism, and even of demonology.

6 — The fact that I have spoken of a noetic (intellectual in the superior sense)[25] content of initiatory — as opposed to mystical — experience should not be taken to suggest something like the theoretical understanding of a teaching, even of a special or secret character. The attribute here is only meant to indicate the distinctive feature of this experience — always, essentially, as the experience of a state. What is at play here is the superior character of lucidity which in Antiquity was assigned to the νοῦς, the intellect in the eminent sense: here the reader may refer to what I have argued in the chapter about the fallacy of irrationalism. Nevertheless, the new state created by initiatory rebirth has always been considered the indispensable premise and the beginning of a superior kind of knowledge. It is a knowledge for which es-

---

25 'Noetic' is derived from the Greek νοῦς; see note 6 to Chapter 7 above, as well as the relevant passage, beyond Evola statements here.

pecially symbols, myths and signs (the 'language of silence') represent paths — and this reveals their true significance. For such knowledge, the word 'realisation' is often used, with reference to the direct grasping of essences via identification, by overcoming the dualistic state on account of which ordinary knowledge, when it does not amount to mere conceptual abstraction, is always governed by the object-subject law. But here it is necessary to emphasise once again the noetic character of the experience, so as to distinguish the kind of union that is being discussed here from that which is peculiar to a sub-intellectual, vital and emotional identification, of the sort promoted by modern irrationalism. When the cognitive aspects of initiatory development have been considered in a particular and systematic manner — one can refer, for example, to the classic *jnâna-yoga* and its divisions[26] — a process has occurred which leads gradually to the achievement of that *intuitio intellectualis*, or noumenal knowledge. This last represents a limiting notion in Kant, who introduced it only to oppose it to what in his view is the one possible form of knowledge for man.

Knowledge as realisation is described as knowledge which transforms and enlightens. In this respect, we might consider 'esotericism' under a special light. Esotericism does not deal with a knowledge monopolised and held secret in an artificial way, but rather with a truth which becomes obvious only at a level of consciousness which is different from that of the ordinary man, of the profane man, and also of the simple believer. The 'secrecy' in which esoteric truth can be shrouded pertains precisely to the fact that, in relation to the ordinary man, this truth ceases to be true and rather becomes dangerous and even ruinous. It is claimed that the conviction and execution of some

---

26   Reference to one of the three principle kinds of yoga as laid forth in the *Bhagavad Gita*, the so-called 'path of knowledge', whose practitioners seek liberation through meditation, contemplation, and the quest for gain self-knowledge. For *intuitio intellectualis* in the following part of this sentence, see note 15 to Chapter 7 above.

initiates, whose dignity was far from unknown (a typical case would be that of Al-Hâllaj in Islam),[27] was due to their not having recognised this requirement: this is not a question of 'heresy', but of practical and pragmatic considerations. A typical saying in this respect states: 'Let the wise man with his wisdom not trouble the minds of those who do not know.'

However, when initiatory knowledge is applied to the disclosure of traditional material, a particular effect occurs which is analogous to the acquisitions of the science of comparative religion on the cultural level. On the initiatory level, 'the transcendent unity of religions', as a modern representative of the Traditionalist current has called it, applies; although in this connection the word 'religion' has too restrictive a character. Different symbols, myths, rites, dogmas and teachings reveal a constant content, according to an identity which does not derive from any extrinsic process of borrowing and historical transmission, but essentially from a common metaphysical and a-temporal content. Since the point of departure, in the case of esotericism, is the direct, experiential perception of this content, the correspondences which can be established here acquire a special character as evidence, which distinguishes them clearly from exterior comparisons based on a quantitative approach, so to speak, of the sort be found in the expositions by scholars of comparative religion. Anyone of adequate sensitivity is bound to detect the difference between the two.

---

27 Mansur Al-Hâllaj (c. 858–922) was a well-followed Persian teacher of Sufism who toward the end of his life began to make public proclamations deemed blasphemous by certain authorities. His teachings became a political problem when they began to inspire rebelliousness in Baghdad. After a failed attempt on the caliphate undertaken by some who had been influenced by Al-Hallaj, this dangerous teacher was jailed for nine years before being publically beaten and executed. There is some debate as to whether his execution was finally brought strictly on account of his heretical religious teachings, or rather on account of the political unrest which emanated from them; but one way or another, Evola's point here stands.

As a counterpart to this intuitive penetration of the constant content lying beyond the wide array of historical and exoteric forms, what has been called the 'gift of tongues' is generally regarded as a hallmark of the true initiate (some people would say that there is an allegorical and exoteric reference to it in the well-known episode from the Old Testament). Just as the one who knows many languages knows how to express the same concept in the words of one language or another, so it is possible to express the same content in the words of one tradition or another, starting from a level which is anterior and superior to the multiplicity of these traditions. However, it should be borne in mind that not every language has the same expressive possibility, nor an equally complete vocabulary.

7 — The last point to which I will allude in these short notes no longer pertains to the definition of the pure concept of initiation in itself, but rather to the connection between the level of initiation and that of mundane reality and history. Particularly in recent times the conception of the secret character of the quality of the initiate has prevailed. The following saying of a Sufi (Islamic initiate) could be cited: 'That I am a Sufi is a secret between me and God.' The 'hermetic' character of the initiate is clear, moreover, from the initiatory current from which this adjective is specifically derived — alchemical Hermeticism, one of the main currents in the post-Christian West.[28] But if we go further back in time, a different possibility is also attested. If we focus our gaze on those civilisations which, in an eminent sense, we may call traditional — those civilisations which had an organic and sacred character and in which 'all activities were adequately ordered from top

---

28 Hermeticism is an esoteric tradition which takes its name from Hermes Trismegistus ('thrice-great Hermes'), the god who is said to have penned the *Hermetic Corpus*. This enigmatic text subsequently became the basis for the hermetic tradition, which had a deal of influence in the West, particularly beginning from the Renaissance.

down' — at the centre of such civilisations we often find, quite visibly, figures with features similar to those attributed to initiates. As this centre is constituted by an 'immanent transcendence', so to speak, meaning a real presence of the non-human in the human, which is expected of particular beings or elites, there is a corresponding form of spirituality which defines the initiate and distinguishes him from the priest, for example, because the priest, at best, is a mediator of the divine and the supernatural, but does not incorporate this element in himself through the character of 'centrality'. The 'divine royalty' at the origins of a great number of civilisations had precisely this metaphysical character.[29] A case in point is ancient Egypt, where the rites which established or confirmed the quality of the sovereign did not differ from the rites of Osirification and, in general, from the rites which ensured the change of nature, rebirth and privileged immortality.[30] Many other testimonies of the same sort could be adduced, even if

---

29 [Evola's note. —Ed.] With respect to the aforementioned character of 'centrality', of 'immanent transcendence', the sovereign of such civilisations is structurally more similar to the type of the initiate than to the type of the priest, even though his nature qualifies him for sacerdotal functions. This is something Guénon has failed to grasp, since he insists that, in normal traditional civilisations, the supreme representative of spiritual authority at the top and centre is the type of the priest, which entails the subordination of royalty to a sacerdotal caste. In reality, this does not at all apply to the primordial and higher state, but only to a situation which is to be considered abnormal from the traditional point of view.

30 Reference to the Mysteries of Osiris, the god of the afterlife and the dead — hence also, of resurrection, 'rebirth'. This cult, unsurprisingly, centered its interest on the survival of the spirit after death. According to the legend of Osiris, the god was murdered by his brother Set, who desired his throne. Osiris rose after his death to become the king of the underworld; his son, Horus, took his place as rightful king. The texts carved in pyramids at Saqqara consider the Egyptian Pharaohs to be the incarnations of both Horus and Osiris; Horus while they lived, and Osiris after they died — hence the Pharaonic connection to the Osirian mysteries. The Pharaohs, by reproducing the events preceding Osiris's resurrection, would arise in the same manner in the afterworld.

each individual case would require special consideration. Besides, residual traces of this primordial tradition are still attested in the Western Middle Ages, in the context of Christianity itself, because the rite of consecration of the king originally only differed in matters of detail from that of consecration of the bishops. This ritual was held to bring about a transformation of the nature of the one who was its object, the grafting onto him of a new *character indelebilis*[31] (in this comparison I am considering only the formal correspondence between the two rituals — which does not affect the aforementioned difference between the orientation of the priest and that of the initiate and primordial king).[32]

Thus, in other ages, besides the initiate of the secret or 'hermetic' type, a type is attested who, finding his natural and legitimate place at the top and centre of an organisation which was both sacred and political, also acted as a symbol, and who, insofar as he embodied a superior force, was in principle believed to be able to exercise a direct action — visible and invisible — on historical, political and social reality (this idea was particularly emphasised in the Far East). However, the type of civilisation which has come to predominate in historical times has increasingly ruled out the unity of the two powers — spiritual and political — and has therefore suppressed this function too, which, in general, was attributed to a visible leader known to have initiatory traits. Besides, in Europe, the character of the predominant religion, Christianity, has progressively driven underground any strands or centres of initiatory tradition which might have survived. Indeed, historical Christianity not only has no initiatory tradition, but its specifically religious orientation (in the main sense of the word 'religious'

---

31   The phrase *character indelebilis* is Latin, meaning 'indelible character', in reference to the irremovable spiritual seal conferred by three sacraments of the Church (Baptism, Confirmation, and Holy Orders). These sacraments thus can neither be erased nor repeated.

32   [Evola's note. —*Ed.*] On this, see the first chapters of my work *Revolt Against the Modern World*.

which I have defined above) has stood in opposition to the world of initiation. I have already mentioned the strange phenomenon that we find in Catholic Christianity, a sort of imitation of the initiatory pattern. Baptism conceived as a rite which will transmit a principle of supernatural life to the Christian by essentially distinguishing him from every non-Christian and providing the necessary condition for salvation; supernatural influences linked to the apostolic and pontifical traditions and claimed as basis for the efficacy of the sacraments; the objectivity of the *character indelebilis* created by priestly ordination; and so on — all this presents obvious formal analogies with initiatory structures. But the level is different, as is the orientation. It may be said that an image or reproduction has replaced reality and has been used to try to create an order on a different existential level.[33]

---

33 [Evola's note. —*Ed.*] The question of the existence or non-existence of a Christian initiation has recently been the object of discussion in some Traditionalist circles (see the review *Études Traditionnelles*, 1965. no. 389–390). Beyond what I have just argued — that is, that the sacramental Catholic *corpus* appears, in some respects, to be a kind of image of initiatory structures transposed onto the religious plane — some have added that such structures existed originally on the plane of true initiation, and even that they could also have maintained that character later on in Christianity. They have adduced, above all, certain excerpts of the Greek Church Fathers, in which the distinction between simple believers and those who are in possession of a superior knowledge ('perfect gnosis') is found, and in which an esoteric interpretation of the Christian Scripture is alluded to. In more recent times, they have turned to the Christianity of the Greek-Orthodox Church (because it is admitted that in the West, from the council of Nicaea onwards, the purely religious forms have completely prevailed), and in particular to the current of 'hesychasm', which some have chosen to describe as a 'Christian yoga'. Some expressions from one of the main representatives of this current, Saint Symeon the New Theologian (949–1022), have been cited, concerning a rite of transmission of a power (the 'holy spirit') through the laying on of hands, distinct from baptism — a rite which is thought to have the nature of an 'initiatory transmission'. However, originally, and especially in Greek Patristics, the mingling of Christianity with motifs essentially belonging to non-Christian mysteriosophy are obvious, and

It is not necessary to discuss this point here, nor the ordering function which Catholicism was able to provide in the Western world. This function, in any case, was not enough to prevent the birth of the modern world and of modern civilisation in the Christianised area, nor the progressive destruction of any traditional order and the affirmation of forms of subversion and materialism which, starting from the West, are becoming a worldwide phenomenon and are showing an increasing degree of irreversibility. A problem emerges when it is claimed that in the world of the most recent times true initiatory centres exist, and hence also people who virtually possess the powers derived from the

---

the example given by Origen shows what the alleged 'esoteric interpretation' really amounts to. While in the so-called apocryphal Gospels, and also in everything which has passed under the name of gnosticism in the history of religions, elements of a superior knowledge are found, all this falls outside the central and official current of positive Christianity — as does, for example, in later times, the current of the Brothers of the Free Spirit. Hesychasm itself must be regarded as an isolated vein of Greek-Orthodox Christianity, and the rite of the laying on of hands seems to us to have the generic character of a 'blessing', or at best of a 'virtual initiation', and not that of a real operation of initiatory opening of consciousness. These are all secondary phenomena. Naturally, within Christianity and sometimes even within certain regular religious orders, some individuals have occasionally managed to attain a level superior to that of theistic devotional religion (even in Protestantism). But this is another question, and by no means proves the existence and continuation of an initiatory tradition which, by its very nature, should have had its place *at the centre and top* of historical Christianity, especially of Catholic Christianity, acting as the keeper of an 'orthodoxy' in a superior sense. Against this, the aforementioned arguments have no force. On the other hand, the question can be resolved on the morphological and doctrinal plane: it is necessary to assess if what I have outlined thus far really corresponds to the essence of the initiatory reality. If it does correspond to this reality, one must ask whether it is compatible with what can be considered characteristic of the positive tradition and central conception of Christianity. The answer, I believe, is clear, and shows other considerations to be of no account. To put it drastically: in my opinion, what can be initiatory in Christianity is not Christian, and what is Christian in it is not initiatory.

very concept of initiation. We should then ask ourselves whether any connection exists between these people and historical developments generally. Given the course taken by such developments, no longer only in the West, the idea of a secret influence from behind the scenes becomes problematic. An action of this type would rather for various reasons be better attributed to opposite powers, to those of an anti-Traditional destructive force, which in certain milieus is referred to as 'counter-initiation'.

The idea of a 'withdrawal' of initiatory presences from the process of history is often adduced in this connection. But even without considering the domain of history, even limiting oneself to the spiritual plane alone, most of those who have some qualification to speak on this matter agree that the initiatory organisations in a position to claim an authentic filiation in Europe are now either non-existent or in a phase of degeneration (the possibility of such degeneration in turn poses a difficult problem); and that even the few existing outside Europe have become increasingly inaccessible, whereas falsifications and mystifications proliferate. This corresponds precisely to one of the features of what has been called the 'dark age'.

This situation has certain consequences for the very concept of initiation, in the sense that anyone with initiatory aspirations today, by force of necessity, should consider a different path from what is regarded as the 'regular' one, the one consisting, that is, in a 'horizontal' connection with an existing, living chain. In other words, it seems that we are left with the perspective of an essentially 'vertical' and autonomous connection by virtue on the one hand of an exceptional individual qualification and on the other of the kind of action — to a certain extent a violent action — which I have already mentioned when talking about the links between initiation and asceticism. Controversies have recently developed on this matter in circles interested in the problems of initiation, and those who insist on affirming exclusively the 'regular' patterns of initiation in abnormal times like ours have been accused — rightly so — of a formalist and unrealistic bureaucratism.

The whole issue is far from irrelevant. Aside from how important it is — for the reasons I indicated at the beginning — to get a clear idea of what initiation is and how it differs from other spiritual domains, it would be interesting to establish whether, to what extent and in what framework initiatory realisation is still possible at all today. The problem is essentially relevant for those who have made an absolutely negative assessment of all the cultural, social, ideological and religious values existing today, and who find themselves at a dead end; for them, perhaps, the superior freedom which has always been the aspiration of those who have ventured on the initiatory path constitutes the only alternative to the forms of revolt peculiar to a destructive, irrational and even criminal nihilism.

These last considerations naturally fall outside the topic of the theoretical definition of the concept of initiation (and it is this definition most of our readers will be interested in), but perhaps they can provide the necessary context for a comprehensive evaluation of it.

Since I have discussed the contribution made to the study of initiation by René Guénon and the Paris-based group inspired by him, it may be worth mentioning the special case constituted by a small group which has been established in Turin at the time of this writing, which aspires to be 'Traditional' and strictly Guénonian. While it cannot be reduced to the level of the many neo-spiritualistic conventicles, it turns Guénonianism into a veritable scholasticism (in the pejorative sense of the term). Like real 'teacher's pets', its members slavishly follow their master with tedious and stereotyped repetitions, to the point of stifling the more lively elements of his doctrine instead of developing them, delving deeper into them, or possibly revising and integrating them — particularly where, despite Guénon's efforts, these elements do not come from 'metaphysics' (in his sense), but rather from mere philosophy, and where certain consequences — often limiting consequences — of his personal equation can be felt.

In the meantime, the members of this group presume to start judging Traditionalist 'orthodoxy' ex cathedra in their journal, and labelling whoever does not follow their line 'profane' and deviationist, while never adducing any qualification which might justify their frivolous claims. Nobodies in every other respect, they are hardly authorised to regard themselves as 'non-profanes' on account of their passive, facile conformism, or their having joined — by their own claim — the Freemasons: for in Freemasonry there is no real, actual and experiential initiation whatsoever, but only empty, ineffective and degraded ritualistic remains, if not something even worse (consider what I have argued with regard to this matter in the last chapter of *The Mystery of the Grail*). All this shows a definite lack of sensibility and qualification.

This brief clarification may not be inappropriate as a means to orient the reader. However, one merit of the conventicle in question, whose existence is likely to be ephemeral, must be granted: its publication of Italian editions of some books and writings by Guénon — although it would have been useful to define the significance and limits of these writings with adequate introductions.[34]

---

34 [Translator's note. —*Ed.*] Evola is referring here to *Edizioni Studi Traditionali*, which, in the mid-1960s printed various hitherto unpublished works by Guénon in Italy (some of them later republished by Rusconi and Luna), and to their periodical, *Rivista di Studi Tradizionali*, which regularly featured articles critical of him, and with which he often exchanged polemics.

12. FREEDOM OF SEX AND FREEDOM FROM SEX

One defining feature of the present age is undoubtedly its emphasis on the realm of sex, combined with a regressive tendency that is evident to any keen observer. On the one hand, we see a struggle against the enduring moralistic and bourgeois limits to sexual life, and in psychology, sociology and philosophy an unprecedented degree of attention is being devoted to sex, verging on pansexualism and a sort of sex cult. On the other hand, this movement only approaches sex in its most trivial and ambiguous aspects — in this field too the predominant climate of 'democracy', promiscuity and decay is at work. Not only that, but starting from sex people have found a way to further the attack on the ideals, principles and structures of all higher forms of civilisation.

I have already discussed cases in which, in a certain kind of literature, the emphasis on sex is closely related to obscenity and the enjoyment of vulgarity. Leaving this aside, I will here examine how the tendency just outlined manifests itself in some contemporary authors, analysing its specific influences in terms of world-view, sociology and even political ideas. In particular, I will highlight the apparently paradoxical parallel between a sort of crusade in defence of sex and sexual freedom, and the drop in level occurring in the conception of sex.

1

We may start with an attempt to outline a morphology of civilisations and a historiography centred on sexuality. The range of perspectives according to which history has been interpreted more or less one-sid-edly are well known: materialist or spiritualist interpretations, which privilege the economy or great personalities and heroes, sociological, dialectical, purely political interpretations, and so on. The only thing we were missing was an interpretation with a sexual or, to be more pre-cise, sexual-psychoanalytical foundation. This gap has been bridged by an Englishman, G. Rattray Taylor, the author of a book entitled *Sex in History*.[1]

Taylor is a Freudian, and given that according to Freudianism sex constitutes a predominant and decisive driving force in human beings, he came up with the idea that an in-depth study of history is only possible by setting out from sex and people's attitude to sex. Therefore, Taylor set out to highlight the close connections allegedly existing between the main social, religious and cultural currents that have emerged in history on the one hand, and the predominance of one or the other attitude to sex on the other.

In this respect, the key to Tylor's historiographical interpretation is the opposition between 'patrists' and 'matrists'. The starting point is provided by a number of real fixations among psychoanalysts and Freudians. As is well known, these people believe that the sexual impulse is at work from early childhood and that it may even take one's father or mother as its object. However, this is not mere eroti-cism but a tendency to identify with the object. Thus on the one hand we have the type who tends to identify with his father (being jealous, mistrustful and antagonistic towards his mother, which is to say the other sex); on the other, we have the type who tends to identify with his mother, with corresponding negative feelings towards his father. The concepts of 'patrism' and 'matrism' are defined on this basis, and the idea is advanced that these primordial complexes are at work in

---

1   Taylor (1911–1981) was a British author and journalist. *The History of Sex* (1954) was his first book; he went on to write a number more having to do with biology, evolution, sexuality, and biotechnology.

history. According to Taylor, history is a stage on which two different civilisations, cultures, mores, moralities, and outlooks on life have alternated, clashed or merged — two conceptions of life deriving from the fundamental attitude of the 'patrists' and 'matrists'.

Each of these two attitudes has complex implications, which Taylor defines in the following terms. 'Patrism' is associated with the religion of the father, patriarchal rights, authoritarianism in the political domain, conservatism in the socio-political domain, mistrust towards research and enquiry, intolerance in sexual matters, emphasis on the distinction between the sexes, curtailing of women's freedom, the idea of the inferiority and sinfulness of women, asceticism and the condemnation of sexual pleasure, fear of spontaneity, and the idea that mankind is evil by nature. By contrast, 'matrism' is associated with the religion of the mother, a tendency towards social interaction, democracy in the political domain, progressivism and innovative ideas, tolerance in sexual matters, the downplaying of the distinction between the sexes (but also a privileged position and freedom for women), hedonism and a tendency towards pleasure, spontaneity, and the idea that mankind is good by nature. We find evident points of contact here with natural law theory and Rousseau's ideas, as outlined in a previous chapter.[2] On top of all this we have the typical phobias displayed by each of the two tendencies in relation to certain abnormal forms of sexuality — for example, matrists stigmatise incest in particular, and patrists homosexuality.

Here I will not dwell on the interpretation of the various historical ages that Taylor develops on the basis of these points of reference. The reader can easily imagine the one-sidedness of this kind of historiography. The Middle Ages fare worse of all, since they are presented as the stage for a repressive outburst of 'patrism' (embodied by the Catholic Church) and as the most striking combination of perversion, neurosis,

---

2   See Chapter 8 above.

hallucination, hysteria, arbitrariness and cruelty in history. However, medieval heresies are said to have often displayed a 'matrist' orientation: this is the case with the current of the Cathars, for instance, and even with that of the troubadours.[3] The creative and licentious Renaissance was also matrist, whereas the Reformation embodied a desperate reaction on the patrists' part, in the face of the increasing 'matrification' of the Church. However, the Counter-Reformation too was patrist, as was — obviously — Anglo-Saxon Puritanism. By contrast, Romanticism was matrist, and according to Taylor (who is no doubt correct in this respect) contemporary society, especially in America, essentially tends towards matrism.

The most obvious objection to this kind of historiography — which combines a few intelligent observations and analyses with a great deal of rambling — is that it ultimately explains very little, since the starting point remains obscure. For it would be necessary to determine why one or the other orientation, the paternal or the maternal, prevails in the individual, or rather the child, depending on the historical period. Besides, like all Freudian views, Taylor's represents a sort of caricature of some ideas that might even be valid when set in the right framework

---

3   The Cathars (from the Greek word meaning 'pure ones') were a group of European Christians in the period between the twelfth and fourteenth centuries who in many ways foreshadowed the coming of Protestantism in their protest against corruption in the Church and their attempt to reformulate Christian practices outside the sophisticated framework of Catholic theology. They believed in a kind of reincarnation, and held that the spirit is sexless; hence they did not set much store by gender. The troubadours were lyric poets in the Middle Ages, from the dawn of the second millennium to the middle of the fourteenth century. Their songs famously revolved around various aspects of romantic love, though they took on political and social themes as well. Over the centuries they developed an impressively differentiated classification of songs; there was a kind of song, for instance, devoted entirely to complaining over a lady's comportment, and another to detailing the declaration of love on the part of a knight to a shepherdess.

and given the right interpretation. Research, such as that carried out in the late 19th century by J. J. Bachofen (an author who is mentioned by Taylor yet assigned very little relevance), shows what an acceptable orientation might be.[4] I have already referred to this research elsewhere. It bears witness to the fruitfulness, for any morphological examination of ancient civilisations, of an interpretation setting out from that duality which on the human level manifests itself as the duality of the sexes. The difference lies in the fact that in the ancient world the starting point was metaphysics and the cosmos, not man understood in psychoanalytical terms with all his alleged complexes. Heaven and Earth, form and matter, spirit and nature, being and *bios*,[5] the eternal masculine and the eternal feminine, along with other dyads, were conceived as transcendental principles, anterior and superior to man. Setting out from these principles one might even embark on an analysis of civilisations, history and mores akin to Taylor's, while avoiding his absurd conclusions, one-sidedness and defiling explanations, that analyse what is higher in the light of what is lower. The opposition between civilisations of the father and civilisations of the mother, between androcratic and gynaecocratic societies (i.e. societies chiefly oriented towards the masculine pole or the feminine one), and between different cults, myths, ethics, political regimes, legal systems, forms of art, and so on, which may be traced back to these two opposite principles, is indeed at work in history, in its dynamic currents, in its underlying tensions, and in the forms it takes. In investigations of this sort deviation starts when one turns sex into something absolute after having reduced it to a purely human fact, instead of grasping the deeper meanings its reflects, meanings which establish essential links between the mystery of sex and that of the primordial forces at work both in the universe and in the spirit.

---

4   For Bachofen, see note 15 to Chapter 8 above.

5   From the Ancient Greek βίος, meaning life. It is most indicative that Evola should put this into contrast with 'being'.

2

We can now move on to briefly outline the theories of Wilhelm Reich, a Viennese pupil of Freud's who distanced himself from his master through a 'heterodox' re-evaluation of some of Freud's fundamental dogmas, making inroads into the general view of the world and the socio-political domain.[6]

In their final form, Reich's ideas revolve around the concept of *orgone* or *orgone energy* (a term coined with reference to the orgasm — the sexual orgasm). The idea is that in sexuality and in sexual experiences a super-individual energy manifests itself, a universal force. In principle, this is not wrong, and would lead us to a higher level than the one on which psychoanalysis operates. After all, a similar notion is expressed by a fundamental traditional teaching which has found its highest embodiment in the Hindu doctrine of *kundalini*: *kundalini* is a force — and not a merely biological force — that lies at the root of the human organism, and is related in particular to sex and the function of reproduction, as an immanent manifestation of the universal shakti in man. Shakti is one of the two terms in the aforementioned 'metaphysical dyad' or 'divine dyad'; it is the creative power of a god, figuratively represented as his 'bride'; it is a life-energy which

---

6   Reich (1897–1957) was a Jewish-Austrian psychoanalyst and, as Evola here reports, a pupil of Freud, who, perhaps even more than Freud himself, saw sexuality in everything. (One of his best known books, *The Mass Psychology of Fascism*, reduces the entirety of that historical period to an expression of supressed sexuality.) His theory of the 'orgone', which Evola here discusses, was roundly rejected by the scientific community (when it was not simply laughed out of court) but had an influence on authors such as William Burroughs, Saul Bellow, and Norman Mailer, the last of whom even became a rather enthusiastic advertiser for the so-called 'orgone accumulator' developed by Reich, which was supposed to concentrate the 'orgasmic power' which Reich believed was one of the fundamental forces in the universe.

represents the 'feminine' counterpart to the pure principle 'being', the 'divine male'.

This reference to traditional metaphysics is particularly important because, as we shall see, it clearly reveals how a confused intuition of something true in Reich is immediately associated with distortions and deviations. First of all, it must be noted that while Reich goes beyond the individual psychological level of current psychology and psychoanalysis and considers the super-individual level when he speaks of a cosmic 'orgone energy', he is not referring to the metaphysical level (as the traditional teaching just mentioned does). Rather, he searches for this power in the physical universe, in nature, as though it were a sot of electricity (indeed, he also speaks of a 'bio-electricity' and of the 'bion', conceived as an intermediate form between inorganic and organic matter), to the point that he believes it is suffused throughout the atmosphere. After conducting some expensive lab research on physical substances, he believed that he could even build 'orgone energy' condensers and 'orgone boxes' with therapeutic applications. Further developing the psychoanalytical theory of repression, Reich does not limit himself to arguing that neuroses, psychoses and other psychic disorders are caused by a stoppage or blocking ('stasis') of orgone energy due to obstructions ('armours') in an individual. These are essentially psychological and character obstructions, but they may also manifest themselves through muscular and physiological phenomena. But according to Reich even actual diseases of the organism, including cancer, are traced back to the same cause.[7]

---

7   [Evola's note. —*Ed.*] These therapeutic applications, for which Reich created an institute in the United States — the country where he settled, after various wanderings — lie at the root of his misadventures. Denounced by the American health authorities, who saw all this as a hoax, Reich refused to show up in court, claiming that he was ready to discuss and justify his practices only with experts, in a different setting. Charged with 'contempt of court', he was sentenced to two years of imprisonment and died of a cardiac arrest in prison. Meanwhile, in the

This generalising of the theory of repression is also based on the idea that repression may be due not just to forced sexual abstinence, caused by external circumstances, but also to 'orgastic impotence', which is to be considered alongside other, commonly acknowledged forms of impotence (from erectile impotence to ejaculatory impotence). Orgastic impotence would be due to an anxiety in relation to pleasure, which prevents one from reaching a full sexual orgasm and creates a protective character 'armour', or defence barrier of the I, thereby causing the aforementioned blocking of orgone energy — the source of all ills.

On the basis of these assumptions, Reich develops an *ad hoc* interpretation of the whole history of civilised humanity, which in his view has been characterised for millennia by large-scale barriers and armours of the aforementioned sort against the complete 'orgastic discharge' which true life pushes us towards. He speaks of the 'murder of life perpetrated by the armoured human animal', and he identifies the 'loss of paradise' with the 'loss of the full functioning of life in man' (which is instead ensured when sexuality runs its full course). 'Since, over the last millennia, all social life has been — for specific reasons — a kind of secondary armoured life which denies happiness [i.e. sexual happiness], it has made sure to eliminate and wipe out, through slander and degradation, all primary forms of life, which threaten its existence. It has realised in one way or the other … that it would collapse and would cease to exist if primordial life made its comeback on the bio-

---

United States, the promised land of democratic liberties and of psychoanalysis, a whole range of Reich's works were banned, including ones that had nothing to do with the controversial therapy, such as *The Sexual Revolution*, *Ether: God and Devil*, *The Mass Psychology of Fascism*, and *Character Analysis*. Nevertheless, the team of psychoanalysts and psychiatrists recruited by the Americans in Germany to carry out their democratic brainwashing after the War were considerably influenced by wacky ideas inspired by Reich on the 'sado-masochistic character', redubbed the 'authoritarian character'. See C. Schrenck-Notzing, *Charakterwäsche*, Stuttgart, 1965, pp. 113 ff. and 199.

sexual stage.' This hate towards, and well-planned struggle against, the force of life — that is to say, orgone energy, which coincides with the fundamental force of life and nature — stands at the root of the various disorderly expressions of a repressed and frustrated vitality, down to extreme manifestations such as psychosis, crime, and alcoholism. The blocking of orgastic discharge also engenders destructive frenzy, which is to say — as a reaction to an unbearable pressure — the impulse towards evasion and the yearning for nirvana (as Reich conceives it) as a surrogate for the liberation ensured by full sexual satisfaction.

Reich ends up with a sort of religion of life centred on sexuality and with an ethics that calls for complete surrender to the same, while stigmatising the structures of all higher civilisations and societies as hysterical and neuropathic defensive armours. The counterpart to all this is the call for a 'sexual revolution'. Here we clearly find the regressive quality which I have already highlighted in relation to all this modern sexology, with the flawed and one-sided conception that constitutes its foundation. Precisely for this reason, I previously recalled the traditional teaching that acknowledges a primordial force as the root of sexuality, but as one of the poles of the metaphysical dyad: the 'feminine' principle of pure life and nature — *shakti* or *prakrti* — that has its counterpart in the principle of 'being', Shiva or *purusha*.[8] Theories such as Reich's therefore represent a one-sided, anarchic adoption and absolutisation of what is only one of the two principles of the world. The result is the promoting of complete, un-

---

8   Evola discusses the *shakti* toward the beginning of the present chapter. The *prakrti* refers to the primal matter of the universe, and also to the feminine aspect in life, thus making an interesting connection between matter, nature, and the feminine. Shiva is one of the triad of supreme deities in Hinduism, which themselves are embodiments of the three fundamental aspects of the universe — creation, preservation, and destruction. Shiva corresponds to the last of these, and thus is sometimes referred to as the 'destroyer god'. *Purusha*, meanwhile, refers to the ubiquitous unchanging cosmic principle.

bridled sexual release, against everything which, in principle, is not at all the consequence of a 'neuropathic armour', but which rather usually corresponds to the action of the 'masculine' pole of that dyad on the human level — according to the mythical image of the male god who is the lord of *shakti*, which is to say the primordial life-force, and who finds his manifestation in everything that embodies 'form' in a higher sense, in all centrality and order above the level of nature.

One of the consequences of Reich's failure to realise all this (a failure evidently caused by his personal equation) is that he necessarily finds himself faced with an impenetrable mystery: for even if we were to grotesquely interpret all ethical, political, social and religious forms as barriers against 'life' and the cosmic organic impulse, given that these forms exist and somehow are part of life, we can only wonder what their true, profound origin might be. Reich admits his ignorance on the matter. He writes: 'The problem of how the human species, alone among all animal species, developed its armouring remains unsolved.' He gives up on the problem because 'it is too complicated: the concrete facts that might offer a solution lie in an all too remote past'. Actually, there is no need to provide an empirical historical explanation; rather, it would be necessary to elucidate, *a priori*, this possibility which manifests itself with such power and constancy in the human species in the face of that Life which Reich conceives as the one primordial foundation of the universe. The only real explanation lies in the existence of the other pole of the cosmic dyad, the principle personified in myth by the male deity, superordinate to the female one. This principle is at work in man, society and civilisation with an equally primordial power in all those areas where Reich only sees products of the armoured type suffering from orgiastic impotence and hysterically opposed to sex — the 'murderer of life'.

Even if we were to focus on the emotional factor — which hardly exerts a universal influence of the sort required by the totality of things it is supposed to account for — of the anxiety of the I vis-à-vis sexual pleasure, we would have to explain this anxiety. In one passage Reich speaks of the 'fear of dissolving into pleasure'. Man 'from the very beginning must have felt that his genital impulse made him lose control and reduced him to a flowing and convulsive fragment of nature. It may well be that this is the origin of orgasm anxiety', which must be identified as the origin of the religious condemnation of sexuality. Now, we are far here from any sort of pathology: what might be at play is simply the legitimate need to preserve one's personality against a complete, passive and naturalistic surrender to sex, which would represent an impairment and dissolution. Reich also writes: 'Orgiastic desire … now appears as an expression of this "drive beyond oneself" …. We tend to go beyond ourselves. Herein, perhaps, lies the solution to the problem of why the idea of death is so often used to refer to the orgasm. In death too biological energy (*sic*) escapes the boundaries of the material sheath that imprisons it. The religious idea of a "liberating death", of a "liberating passing away", thus acquires an objective basis. The function which in a normal organism is fulfilled by the orgasm reappears in the armoured organism as the principle of nirvana, or the mystical idea of salvation.' This is another example of a typical misunderstanding. The intuition is correct as regards the impulse towards transcendence which is intrinsic to eroticism and which manifests itself in the experience of intercourse (in its 'destructive' aspects, which however usually fall outside of these authors' primitivistic conception of sexuality). However, this is something quite different from a 'biological energy' — a biological energy which is brought into play in relation to death itself, through the 'flesh' and 'body' from which the armoured type seeks to break free, 'redeeming himself'. This is seen not as a reflection of his nature as a finite being in general, but as his very 'armour', 'the fabric which imprisons' that energy, preventing its 'natural' solution, orgastic discharge. Reich completely ignores the distinction between passive transcendence (which it is opportune to avoid) and genuine, active and ascending transcendence (in relation to which a particular use of sex is also called for in traditional teachings — see the material gathered in my work *Eros and the Mysteries of Love*). The surrender of the I and the discharging of the cosmic orgone energy in the individual through a complete orgasm: this is the limit of Reich's view of life and ethics.

After all this, let us examine in what way, in particular, Reich attacks the forms taken by Traditional society, based on his redefinition of Freud's theories. Freud had set out from the idea that the pleasure drive, the *Lustprinzip*, is the fundamental driving force of the human psyche. Later, however, he also came to acknowledge the existence of another equally basic drive, the drive towards destruction (*Todestrieb*).[9] Moreover, he developed a general theory of repression, to show that when the pathways to the satisfaction of the latter drive, the destructive drive, are barred, it changes level and finds two possible manifestations: if it turns outwards, towards others, it becomes sadism; if it turn inwards, towards oneself, it becomes masochism. Reich instead denies Freud's duality of drives. In his view what is primary is only the orgastic pleasure drive, the discharge of primordial orgone energy. The other drive, the drive towards destruction, in its twofold sadistic and masochistic aspects, merely derives from it: it only emerges following the repression of the former drive, when social structures, inhibitions

---

9   The two terms are taken from psychoanalysis, the psychological school invented by the Jewish Austrian Sigmund Freud (1856–1939). Both terms are German; the first is generally translated as the 'pleasure principle', though the word *Lust* is has decided connotations of desire and undertones even of sexuality, similar to the English 'lust'. Freud identified the 'pleasure principle' as being one of the two primary psychological principles in his 1911 work *Two Principles of Mental Functioning*; the other was the so-called 'reality principle', by which the 'pleasure principle' was limited — though it is safe to say that Freud generally viewed the 'pleasure principle' as being the greatest and most powerful principle in human life. In 1921 he published *Beyond the Pleasure Principle*, which introduced the *Todestrieb*, literally the 'death drive', the psychological urge toward self-destruction.

and orgastic impotence give rise to a complex accumulation of power which, through a deviation, manifests itself in a destructive sexopathic fashion, through sadism or masochism. The transposition of these sexopathic forms is what shapes the main features of a given type of society.

On the socio-political level, sadistic impulses, according to Reich, produce the authoritarian personality tendency, with a desire to dominate those under one's control and with the releasing of the destructive drive through the persecution of one's enemies (the 'capitalist', the 'Jew', the 'Communist', and so on, depending on the ideology). Instead, masochistic impulses give rise to the tendency towards a herd-like attitude, with the enjoyment of submission, a tendency towards 'personality worship', discipline, and even self-sacrifice. These two tendencies, the active and the passive one, are complementary in a way. According to Reich, they constitute the underlying foundation of all hierarchical systems and show that warrior tendencies, 'aggressive' attitudes, and so on, are phenomena with a clear sexopathic origin. Reich here lumps together the patriarchy, militaristic regimes, 'Fascist' ones, capitalism, Soviet communism (insofar as it is authoritative), and so on — more or less, the 'patrists'' world described by Rattray Taylor.

Some people have even sought to draw upon ethnology to find confirmation of these theories. Malinowski and an American-girl-turned-ethnologist, Margaret Mead, have compared two savage peoples living in similar environmental circumstances:[10] one, which was matriarchal and granted full sexual freedom from childhood, led a peaceful life, free of neuroses or other disorders, while the other,

---

10 The Pole Bronislaw Malinowski (1884–1942) and Margaret Mead (1901–1978) were both anthropologists who dedicated portions of their careers to exploring sexual customs among primitive peoples. Evola here probably references Malinowski's *Sexual Life of Savages in North-Western Melanesia* (1929) and Mead's *Coming of Age in Samoa* (1928), though both authors published other books on the same topic.

which had a patriarchal and authoritarian family organisation and limited sexual freedom, presented 'the same traits as European civilisation': aggressiveness, individualism, a warrior impulse, etc. Entirely sporadic observations of this sort, which rashly draw causal links, are certainly revealing for whomever takes it for granted that what is higher ought to be explained on the basis of what is lower — that civilised mankind ought to be explained on the basis of savages — and who ignore Dumézil's wise observation that, with a little effort, it is possible to find confirmation for just about anything in ethnology.[11]

However, as regards 'aggressiveness', conceived as a sort of rabid fury due to a suppressed pleasure drive, Reich and other people who hold similar views (like De Marchi, an author we shall soon be discussing) fail to explain the sexual social inhibitions or fear of losing oneself in pleasure that affects many dangerously aggressive wild animals. Furthermore, it would be ridiculous to seriously think that men like Alexander, Timur, Caesar, Napoleon or Frederick II would never have existed, had they received an adequate and uninhibited sexual education, outside a patriarchal family and 'armoured' society. It is indeed strange that practically no great conqueror, on a personal level, led a puritan life — unless Reich wishes to assume that, even though they made use of women, these great conquerors all suffered from 'orgastic impotence'. This is all foolish nonsense, and the regressive existential background of this kind of sexology applied to the interpretation of societies is evident. I do not wish to turn these authors' interpretative method against them by arguing that the impulse which has led them to pollute and degrade the forms of a higher civilisation — which always go hand in hand with the principles of authority, hierarchy,

11 Reference to the French philologist Georges Dumézil (1898–1986), who developed the 'trifunctional hypothesis' of Proto-Indo-European societies — the idea, namely, that these societies comprised three social hierarchies, the preistly, the warrior, and the commoners. See his 1940 work *Mitra-Varuna*, which has been translated into English.

virility, discipline and a warrior style (not to be confused with hysterical 'aggressiveness' and 'imperialism) — betrays, in the light of an analytical pseudo-science and a pansexual and unbridled view of life, precisely an unconscious aggressive instinct (either a sadistic or masochistic one), nor do I wish to conclude that Reich and other authors of his ilk are themselves in need of undergoing psychoanalysis and of being straightened out. It goes without saying that the inclination to command or to obey is inborn and usually has nothing to do with sexual matters: the *libido dominandi* and the *libido servendi* are merely degenerative forms of this.[12] Self-overcoming distinguishes both those in a position of authority who exercise their power as a duty and those who freely establish a relation of dependence, subordination and loyalty with a superior, as illustrated by the best aspects of the feudal world, both in Europe and beyond.

Secondly, this confirms what I mentioned at the beginning, namely that, contrary to what might seem to be the case, the background to these theories is a primitive and rather trivial conception of sex. Indeed, when Reich — against Freud — sets out to explain sadism and masochism as merely secondary sexophathic forms due to repression, he falls into a serious misunderstanding, insofar as he proves his ignorance of the actual dimensions of the sexual drive itself, taken in its deeper and most intense manifestations. While, in general, sadism and masochism do exist as perversions, they may also be simply the accentuation of aspects that are always to be found in any intense experience of sexual love, which entails a destructive element (with the impulse towards 'transcendence' that Reich only fleetingly and inadequately grasped). The themes of love-death and pleasure-destruction are not at all mere romantic and decadent psychopathic

---

12 For the *libido dominandi*, the 'lust or will to rule', see note 8 to Chapter 3 above. *Libido servendi* is Latin for the 'will to serve'. These terms might also be used in non-sexual contexts, but it is clear that Evola here intends them with sexual connotations.

projections. They occur throughout the history of eroticism. For instance, many ancient deities governing sex, pleasure and orgies were at the same time conceived as deities of death and destructive frenzy. One might mention here — among others — the goddess Ishtar for the Mediterranean area, the goddess Durga for the Hindu one, and the goddess Hathor-Sekhmet for Egypt: all of these, in one of their aspects, were goddesses both of death and of destructive frenzy (which also, incidentally, applies to Dionysianism).[13] On account of this other side, some of these deities were also goddesses of war. Rather ironically, then, these calls for complete sexual freedom have as their counterpart, or indeed premise, their conceiving the sexual impulse itself — which is established as the foundation of everything — in the most incomplete and uninteresting terms.

3

Luigi De Marchi, an Italian author with much the same ideas as Rattray Taylor and Reich (to the point that he has introduced and promoted the latter in Italy by publishing a translation of selected extracts entitled *La teoria dell'orgasmo*), has written a book entitled *Sesso e Civiltà*.[14]

---

13 Ishtar, the 'Queen of Heaven', was a goddess worshiped by the Akkadians, the Babylonians, and the Assyrians; she was later conflated with the Sumerian goddess of love and war Inanna. She makes appearance as the consort of the hero Gilgamesh in Book 3 of the *Epic of Gilgamesh*, in which she is called 'our lady of love and war' (see the Prologue). Durga is the warrior-mother goddess of India, often depicted as a multi-armed goddess riding a tiger or a lion. She was associated, as should be clear from this image, both with destruction and with creation. Hathor-Sekhmet was a warrior goddess and also the goddess of healing. She was the protectress of the Pharoahs themselves, and thus was their shield in battle.

14 De Marchi (1927–2010) was an Italian psychologist and an agitator for social change. The book which Evola here considers, *Sesso e Civiltà*, was the author's first, and has not been translated into English.

The background, determined by his personal equation, is always the same: while De Marchi lacks the general doctrinal points of references required to clearly examine many historical and spiritual aspects of sexuality, he displays the same animosity towards the ideals and structures of higher civilisations — an animosity which takes as its counterpart the call for promiscuous and naturalistic sexual freedom. In themselves, some of De Marchi's criticisms and suggestions for reform are acceptable. However, he slips into real absurdities on account of the egalitarian level to which he refers, in relation to which he displays an apostle's zeal. It may be useful to examine some of the ideas of this author, in order to define and develop some of the points already made in greater detail, and finally to wrap up the whole question.

Most of De Marchi's book is devoted to denouncing the 'sexophobic' complex, both in itself and in its historical manifestations. Without much difficulty, De Marchi shows that the idea of sexuality as something invariably shameful, sinful, impure and opposed to all spiritual values is, ultimately, an anomaly, since in the fields of history and ethnology peoples and civilisations are known that were ignorant of this notion, and even acknowledged the sacredness of sex. As previously acknowledged, it is certainly right to reject the puritanical and sexophobic equation between erotic repression and civilisation. Vilfredo Pareto had already made this point, adducing concrete examples to show that it is not at all true that a certain degree of freedom in sexual mores necessarily entails the decay and dissolution of all higher virtues in peoples or individuals, but that great historical figures also come into play here.[15]

While the idea in question is generally correct, certain reservations must be voiced with regard to De Marchi's attempt to look for supporting evidence among savage peoples, which is to say in ethnographic material. Rather, one ought to limit the enquiry to higher civilisations,

---

15   For Pareto, see note 3 to Chapter 5 above.

for two reasons: first of all because — it is worth repeating this once more — primitive peoples are not at all primordial peoples but, by and large, degenerate residues of primordial mankind and futureless side branches that have become detached from the central trunk of the human race and lost; secondly, because it would be easy to show that 'primitive peoples' often have inhibiting sexual taboos that are even worse than those of bourgeois society.

However, it is more important to note that in the context of actual civilisations certain distinctions are to be drawn. It is clear that the object of De Marchi's attention and sympathy is almost exclusively represented by the kind of civilisations and societies that Rattray Taylor calls 'matrist' and Bachofen calls gynaecocratic, Aphroditean or Demetrean. These civilisations and societies are characterised not by the mere acknowledgement of the value or even sacredness of sex, i.e. by anti-sexophobia, but rather by a naturalistic surrender to sex, by a 'physical' world-view that rules out transcendence, by the pre-eminence of women, and by a levelling promiscuity, with a pacifist orientation. In a previous chapter I pointed to the inner connection between the spirit of these degraded civilisations and 'natural law', which in Rome stood under the sign of female and plebeian deities. It is important to note that those who have established a relation between the decay of a civilisation and sexual promiscuity often refer to the spread of an Aphroditean, 'feminine' and devirilising sexuality of this sort. So one should not simply speak of sexophobia in this context.

One only needs to leaf through De Marchi's book to realise that his anti-sexophobic polemic rests on an ideal and world-view connected precisely to the naturalistic kind of civilisation just mentioned. For instance, he praises certain aspects of Etruscan civilisation (which closely recall the 'naturalistic communion' of some primitive peoples of the South Seas), by comparison to which the Romans may be seen as the 'Prussians of their age' (a rather fitting expression borrowed from R. Aldington,[16] but which could also be inverted by arguing that, in various respects, the Prussians were the Romans of their age, since they also reproduced some of the latter's fundamental virtues). Here the most serious fallacy comes to light, which invalidates everything which might be considered valid and acceptable in De Marchi's views: the idea — already affirmed by Rattray Taylor, as we have seen — that phenomena like sexophobic moralism, disdain for women and puritan repression are necessarily to be found in every virile, patriarchal, anti-democratic and warrior society. This is sheer nonsense. Rather, the point must be made that higher civilisations rejected all egalitarianism, cultivated strict ethical and warrior values, and kept women in their rightful place by denying them the role they play in Aphroditean and Demetrean societies, but without slipping thereby into puritan sexophobia. Since when is it true that 'in all militaristic civilisations there has never been any room for love' (to quote De Marchi)? Myth itself associates Mars and Venus, and it is a fact that all real women will always be more attracted to warriors than to the ambiguous, drunken virility of the Corybant.[17] Likewise, even in ordinary life it is a well-known fact that women are attracted to men in uniform. Moreover, it is one thing to put women in their rightful place, quite another to be moralistic misogynists. The subordination of women in all normal and androcratic civilisations does not imply any contempt or humiliation. Thousands of years of history also teach us that, generally speaking, women were quite happy in this position of alleged inferiority (*pace*

---

16   Reference to the English writer and poet Richard Aldington (1892–1962). I have been unable to source this reference.

17   The allusion to Venus and Mars is to their relationship; they were according to tradition lovers, despite the fact that Venus was (following Greek mythology) the wife or consort of Vulcan. The Corybants were ecstatic male attendants of the goddess Rhea or Cybele, whose initiation included dressing up in armor and participating in ritual dances.

Pierre Loti and his *Désenchantées*),[18] and were capable of fulfilling their potential as 'absolute women' and to develop an *ars amandi* that the emancipated women of today can hardly imagine; nor did they dream of any 'vindication' before the 'agitation' of recent years, akin to that which the so-called stirrers of 'class consciousness' have spread, like a virus, among the lower social strata.

Therefore, the fact that in certain civilisations sex received some acknowledgement and was even assigned some worth in the domain of the sacred does not mean that we should focus exclusively on those contexts in which all this led to the inferior, regressive, 'Aphroditean' and naturalistic forms just outlined. Rather, it is necessary to contend that in every complete traditional civilisation such forms were avoided, as ascetic and warrior values were cultivated alongside erotic ones, in relation to different paths and vocations. Thus in India, for example, we find the 'path of desire' (*kama-marga*), alongside the path of knowledge (*vidya-marga*), that of high ascesis (*tapas-marga*) and that of action (*karma-marga*).[19] Not just India but also China and Islam illustrate the coexistence of an 'androcratic' regime, i.e. one resting on male supremacy and on a highly developed erotic life. De Marchi too is forced to acknowledge this in the case of Islam, a civilisation marked by 'the extreme supremacy of men and almost complete nullification of woman' (I have already commented on this alleged 'nullification') and, at the same time, by a considerable emphasis on love and sexuality. To this one should add the warrior character of Islam (its 'aggressiveness',

---

18 Loti (1850–1923) was a French naval captain who wrote a number of exotic novels based on his voyages. The book mentioned here, *Les Désenchantées* (*The Disenchanted*, 1906) has not been translated into English, but appears to have been little more than a fictionalised plea for the emancipation of the women in the Turkish harems.

19 The paths in question are various routes toward self-mastery or self-knowledge in the Indian tradition, which are adopted for instance by certain variants of yoga.

to use De Marchi and Reich's terminology). Besides, one may refer to the case of ancient Rome, not just to note the dignity attributed to women, particularly as matriarchs, by these 'Prussians of their age', but also to make sure that puritanical sexophobia is not conflated with the need for measure, for a certain distance, for a certain masculine dignity. Cato himself, who is accused of 'militarist extremism' by De Marchi on account of his *Delenda Carthago*, exemplifies a tolerant yet dignified approach: as Pareto recalls, during the celebration of the *Floralia* he discretely withdrew instead of preaching fire and brimstone, lest the people be deprived of the sight of naked young women which these celebrations usually entailed; and when he noticed a young man trying to hide after leaving a brothel, not wishing to be seen, Cato told him that there was nothing to be ashamed of, provided he did not make such places his home.[20]

It goes without saying that De Marchi launches a massive attack against the sexophobia of Christianity and of the Christian civilisation, adducing evidence of all sorts, much along the same lines as Rattray Taylor: a theological hatred of sex, repression, mortification of the 'flesh' as the enemy of the spirit, and a conception of marriage almost as a regrettable necessity — a balm for the disease of lust (Augustine), tolerated only in view of reproduction. This sexophobic orientation only became even more accentuated in Protestantism and Calvinism. However, it is first necessary to clearly determine what is at stake in or-

---

20 More commonly known as Cato the Elder (234–149 BCE), this Cato is not to be confused with his great-grandson, Cato the Younger. Prior to the Third Punic War between Rome and Carthage, Cato the Elder took up the practice of ending all his speeches with some variant of the provocative expression *Carthago delenda est*, 'Carthage must be destroyed'. Such was his hatred for Carthage that he did this, evidently, even when the speech in question had nothing to do with the Carthaginians. As for the *Floralia*, either Evola or Pareto is in error here, for the anecdote refers, not to Cato the *Elder*, but to Cato the *Younger*. (See Valerius Maximus, *Factorum et Dictorum Memorabilium*, Book II, Part 10, Section 8.) The general point, of course, still stands.

der to ascertain whether one can speak of a deviation here. The deviation essentially derives from a misunderstanding. The pre-Christian and non-Christian world, as we have seen, often did not deny sex at all, or even assigned it a sacred and mystical character; however, it did not regard it as the only path allowing man to grasp the higher meaning of life, the only path leading him beyond the confines of his individuality, towards transcendence. For the most part, as a means to this goal, the path of ascesis and detachment was recommended, which is suitable only for some people and presupposes a particular qualification and vocation (besides, the same is true of the possibilities offered by sex, when a higher goal is what we have in mind). Those who follow this path must of course steer clear of sex and women, and regard these as a danger. Their precept will be abstinence, not as a repression and 'mortification of the flesh', but as an objective method to release a fundamental force of man and apply it to a different end.

Now, the misunderstanding on the part of Christianity lies in the fact that it establishes ascetic values as the foundation of a morality to be imposed on everyone: not only those who aspire towards otherwordly transcendence, but also those who live within the world and of whom one can expect, not an ascetic negation of existence, including sex, but only, at most, a certain 'sacralisation' of it. Besides, the same misunderstanding also lies at the basis of various other norms of original Christian morality, which can only apply in the field of ascetic disciplines — in fact, only in relation to ascetic disciplines of a particular sort. These norms include turning the other cheek, imitating the lilies of the valley, hating one's father, mother and siblings, leaving everything, and so on: precepts which outside the ascetic domain are sheer nonsense. Similar considerations apply to the indissolubility of ritual and sacramental marriage: as I have noted elsewhere,[21] this

---

21   The Italian editor here adds a reference to *Ride the Tiger* § 27 and *Eros and the Mysteries of Love* § 43.

can only concern an exceptional type of union, which is also known to other civilisations (at times even in more radical forms of 'heroic' indissolubility, as in the case of the woman following her husband in death). They do not apply to the kind of union established by the overwhelming majority of men and women — particularly in ages in which religion has ceased to be a living power, and, more than ever before, in bourgeois society. All the distortions, absurdities and pathological and puritanical forms of sexophobia that De Marchi denounces in his extensive overview of the history of sexual mores in the Christian area simply derive from this unwarranted conflating of very distinct domains. But at the same time one must, yet again, acknowledge the one-sidedness of a conception that extols sex alone and sees ascetic values as nothing but inhibitory and self-sadistic phenomena. Take the classic example of Shivaism: Shiva, the deity at the centre of certain orgiastic forms of worship, is also the god of ascetics, and his emblem, the *lingam* (*phallus*) is even worn by them because it symbolises not just reproductive, priapic animal virility, but also the spiritual virility at work in ascetics.

It is indisputable that, on account of the misunderstanding just discussed, Christianity is responsible for the Western distortion of the correct way of judging sex and its related problems. However, truly negative phenomena, in this respect, only emerged when the Western world started reducing religion to mere morality and came to approach the bourgeois age. It is then that 'virtuism' (the religion of 'virtue') emerged, to use a fitting expression by Pareto, who associates it with other 'secular religions' that are just as fanatical as the dogmatic ones: the religions of Progress, Democracy, Humanity, and so on. Before all this, the situation was not as grim as De Marchi and other authors suggest when they examine the Middle Ages, the Renaissance, and the 18th century. The Middle Ages were also marked by considerable sexual freedom and uninhibitedness. We know of the promiscuity associated with bathing, and we know that in castles — for the sake of hospitality — young women were expected to keep knights company in bed. Knightly epics also frequently mention women and girls taking the first step in sexual matters (something which should thrill De Marchi — see p. 252 of his book — but which, frankly, is a form of impudence which the differentiated type of man will not find very arousing). Finally, one — not wholly unpleasant — aspect of the golden age of knighthood and the wars of religion was the raping of reluctant women in conquered cities. One should also speak of so-called 'Platonic love' in the Middle Ages and of its 'mystery', because it is in fact something very different from what De Marchi and Rattray Taylor suppose and what we read in textbooks on literature and customs: as I have noted in my book *Eros and the Mysteries of Love*, these were often special forms of erotic initiation, with aspects unknown to 'simple and natural love', which is to say primitively carnal love, based on a 'complete orgastic discharge', to use Reich's terminology.[22]

De Marchi does not find much sexual freedom in the Renaissance and even in the 18th century, Casanova's century.[23] Here another absurd aspect of his ideas emerges. He states that we should not be misled by the proverbial frivolity of the 18th century, since 'corruption' and licentiousness were confined to an exclusivist class that 'took advantage of its hermetic isolation and age-old privileges', while formally honouring traditional social values and indeed attacking anyone who criticised them or 'sought to free the popular masses from their yoke'.

---

22 The Italian editor here refers to *Eros and the Mysteries of Love* § 48 and *The Mystery of the Grail* §§ 25 and 26.

23 Barbed reference to the Venetian Giacomo Casanova 1725–1798), the renowned adventurer of love, whose infamous *Histoire de ma vie* (*History of My Life*, a twelve-volume autobiography originally written in imperfect French) details in engaging and unabashadly frank language Casanova's endless adventures and conquests, most of them erotic. The point will not be lost on the reader: the idea that such a man could have lived, or such a book been written, in an age of prudish sexual contraint, rather defies credulity.

Here a few rectifications must be made; it should be noted, first of all, that this was often not so much a matter of hypocrisy as it later became in bourgeois society, as of a certain degree of irony, a certain detachment, with the veneer of good taste required by any free but not vulgar sexuality. However, generally speaking, it is most important to acknowledge that while a certain higher human type can afford a greater sexual freedom, it would be a terrible mistake to extend this freedom to everyone; and this not because of some artificial social privilege but because of the dangerous consequences that such freedom is bound to have for ordinary men and women. Even in Classical Antiquity we find the saying that 'not everyone can go to Kythera'.[24] It is always absurd to attack sexual taboos in the name of a democratically indiscriminate sexual freedom. Yet this is precisely De Marchi's approach. He even criticises Romantics like Byron and Nietzsche: for they rebelled and affirmed a nonconformist freedom 'beyond good and evil' for a privileged few, for exceptional beings, instead of promoting a renewal and general reform in sexual mores. Once again, this is utter nonsense: when freedom is extended to all, it is destined to result in licentiousness, dissoluteness and sheer, unbridled bestiality. Nietzsche himself had the final say on this, which is valid for all times, when he observed that the extent to which an individual can allow himself certain things, without falling into 'corruption' or 'decadence', is determined by his power to renounce them through the capacity to restrain himself at every moment.[25] Clearly, this only ever applies to a minority. But I will say more about this later on.

---

24 Kythera, by the tradition of Ancient Greece, was the island of Aphrodite, goddess of love.

25 Lord Byron (1788–1824) was the famous English Romantic poet, the author, among a great many other poems, of *Don Juan* and *Childe Harold's Pilgrimage*, and the play *Manfred*. His works often featured what has come to be known as the 'Byronic hero', who in many ways epitomises the Romantic era: this was a great man who, because of his exceptionality, could exclude himself from the

As elsewhere, in his analysis of Romanticism and the literature of Crepuscular and Decadent authors from the late 19th century De Marchi mixes right and wrong ideas. In his view, these currents did not achieve any 'progress' because they often exalted sex, yet only as a transgression, thereby implicitly acknowledging the negative and sinful character attributed to it by the puritanical conception — even exacerbating this character by associating sex with crime, cruelty, and perversion. De Marchi here speaks of an 'attempted sadistic escape from the grip of taboos' (we once again find Reich's quirks on the origins of sadism), of a phenomenon that ultimately has a psychopathic character: 'sexuality remains a sin — indeed, the sin par excellence' — except that it is enjoyed precisely for this reason. De Marchi is right in his criticism, insofar as doing something only because it is forbidden and 'bad' implies precisely an acknowledgement of the very criteria that lead most people to abstain from it. Yet one should not go any further than this: it is necessary to realise that a danger emerges the moment in which all tensions have been removed and everything seems lawful and natural. As for 'sadism', which may well not be sexopathic, I have already discussed it.[26]

We then come across not just absurdities but outrageous blunders, as when De Marchi describes the political transpositions of 'Romantic sadistic psychosis' in the form of the myth of the superman (notwithstanding all its problematic features) and when he applies the alleged equation between 'sexophobic moralism and militaristic imperialism' to currents such as Fascism, National Socialism, and so on. As regards Fascism, it would be difficult to deny that it presented many moral-

---

commonplace emotions and the customary ways of general humanity. Byron himself lived in a manner not much different from this; as but the most relevant example, he became a scandalous figure for the scope and liberty of his sexual liaisons, which including dalliances with both his cousin and his half-sister (it is probable he had a bastard child with the latter). For relevant passages from Nietzsche, see *Beyond Good and Evil* § 221 and *The Antichrist* §57.

26 See Chapter 9 above.

istic and bourgeois aspects and sexual prejudices not unlike those of the Christian democratic regime that is governing Italy at the time in which I am writing these lines. But what is most unbelievable is that De Marchi criticises the fact that 'when he wished to discredit persons and peoples Mussolini would accuse them of being feminine.' I wonder if De Marchi would have been flattered if I had opened my observations with the words: the same tendency is reflected by the book *Sesso e Civiltà* by the feminine, or effeminate, writer De Marchi. All this once again confirms the fact that this author conflates sexuality and promiscuity, given that the evident implication of his criticism of Mussolini is that being 'feminine' is an excellent thing, and not a degeneration, for a man (the logical counterpart to this being that it is an excellent thing for a woman to be masculine). Besides, what may partly be true as regards a certain degree of bourgeois puritanism exhibited by Fascism, does not really apply to National Socialism. Let us leave Hitler's personality aside here — although, once again, one wonders why De Marchi would want to quote Hitler's saying, 'the masses are like women', as evidence of his 'hysterical misogynism', given that women gladly obey real men and shun the weak (unfortunately, one should speak not of women but of whores today — as is shown, among many other things, by the transition from the 'oceanic gatherings' of the past to the current infatuation with democracy in Italy and Germany). Besides, Germany happily enjoyed a wide degree of sexual freedom under National Socialism, which even coined the motto *Das Kind adelt die Frau* to defend unmarried mothers, and which was the only regime in the modern world that had the courage to pursue certain ideas expressed, among others, by Plato in *The Republic* — something that De Marchi should be enthusiastic about, given that he calls for the establishment of 'free love circles and communities'.[27] Based on the idea

---

27   *Das Kind adelt die Frau* means, 'The child ennobles the woman'. This was also written *Das Kind adelt die Mutter* (the child ennobles *the mother*). This last was inscribed on the reverse side of the Mother's Cross of Honor, which was

that war operates a reverse selection, insofar as it chiefly cuts down a country's best, strongest and bravest men, Germany, to compensate for this in view of posterity, created three colonies during the War in which racially suitable girls could meet an elite of soldiers on leave. If sexual relationships were established, the couples could choose whether to marry or not. The State would take care of any children born through a special SS institution called *Lebensborn*.[28] It is clear, then, that De Marchi's antifascist assumptions led him to seriously one-sided views.

Other parts of De Marchi's book offer some acceptable criticism. For example, De Marchi psychoanalyses the creator of psychoanalysis, Freud, detecting in his 'science' a sort of smug revenge against the sexual taboos of which he himself was a passive victim, combined with the pleasure of polluting. On account of this, Freud, just like the Puritans, only saw the lowlier and dirtier aspects of sex. De Marchi states that Freud provides final 'scientific' confirmation 'of the satanic, filthy and evil nature of sex so emphatically preached by traditional religion and morality'; hence his conception of the human condition is even more gloomy than the Christian one 'since it lacks the ray of expiation and salvation'. De Marchi opportunely recalls Maurice Blondel's verdict on Freud: 'He saw the pig in man, and made him a sad pig'.[29] Along the same lines, De Marchi criticises a whole range of contemporary writers and novelists, down to Moravia and those of his ilk, who wallow in the same mire with their

officially awarded to German mothers for exceptional merit. For the reference to Plato, see in particular *Republic*, Book V, 457c — 461e.

28   The name literally means 'fount of life'. About 20,000 children were taken care of by this institution, mainly in Germany and occupied Norway, though not all of these children were born in the context that Evola here mentions. The general idea is not without interest in our own day of falling birth rates.

29   Blondel (1861–1949) was a French thinker, who attempted a kind of reconciliation between speculative philosophy and Christianity.

negative and distorted view of sex, which is highlighted in its basest aspects.[30]

Naturally, it would be all too easy to attack the mores of bourgeois society, and in particular those of the two 'world powers', Soviet Russia and America. De Marchi is right to note the sexual 'virtuism' that today brings together opposite political movements: it constitutes a sort of unspoken and unquestioned dogma which is not affected by all the calls for reform or revolution which certain exponents of these movements make in many other domains. As De Marchi states, the French Revolution, Socialism and Syndicalism were all sexophobic and puritanical; after the first stages of the Communist revolution, the Stalinist regime too towed the same line: the tendency here is to reduce the sphere of sex to a mere 'accident', to something devoid of any 'decadent complications', to a 'healthy' physical act which male and female comrades can resort to as a much needed release — the 'free' woman here is essentially reduced to her role as a worker and mother. All passion and profoundness are excluded from erotic love, for the sake of the 'Soviet motherland' and of various economic plans. De Marchi argues that Soviet Russia today has reached puritanical results that are more brilliant and on a wider scale than those ever reached by the clergy. Communist China has gone even further.

Equally correct is De Marchi's analysis of American mores and the profound unease that, all appearances aside, plagues life in the United States as far as sex is concerned. The origin of this trouble lies in the early Puritanical conception, which idealised woman on a sexophobic basis. As late as the Victorian period, woman was conceived as a superior, spiritual being. The 'supposition' that women could experience sexual emotions, or yield to them and derive pleasure

---

30 Alberto Moravia (born Alberto Pincherle, 1907–1990) was a Jewish Italian writer, and is considered one of the most important Italian writers of the twentieth century. His work, and perhaps most notably his 1960 novel *La Noia* (*Boredom*), was controversial in large part for its 'sexual realism'.

from them, was considered insulting. A cliché of 'dignity' and loftiness was thus imposed on women, who accepted it. In conjunction with female emancipation, this gave rise to a host of sexually inhibited, half-anaesthetised and frustrated beings, who find their counterpart in the materialist male that lets himself be dominated by women and 'respects' them in the most inane sense of the term, or — as a reaction — conforms to the stereotype of the 'tough guy', of the violent man, or of the gangster surrounded by 'babes'. Hence the lack of any meaningful encounter between the two parts, the two sexes. Hence, too, a whole series of counterbalances and outbursts, starting from the excesses of the beatniks, alcohol abuse, the frenzied enthusiasm for Jazz, and so on — which only worsen the situation.

The reader can easily imagine what De Marchi says when he focuses his enquiry on Italian mores. However, it is rather odd that he practically ignores central Europe and the Nordic countries, as well as a certain part of France, where the situation is quite different and approaches a somewhat satisfactory standard when it comes to well-informed sexual mores, marked by clarity and camaraderie.

Nevertheless, when De Marchi switches from his critique in the historical and more general field to the problem of sex in the present day, and attempts to lay down a new sexual morality, on the one hand he shows his ignorance of the actual situation, particularly as regards countries like Italy; on the other, absurdities emerge due to his failure to draw distinctions in relation to this ethics, which he applies to just anyone. Meanwhile, as regards certain related questions, De Marchi is in favour of divorce: here one can only agree with him, given what, in bourgeois society, the idea of an 'indissoluble union' championed by the Catholic Church — actually on the basis of the misunderstanding I previously highlighted — amounts to in practical terms.[31] Secondly, he

---

31   [Evola's note. —*Ed.*] In passing, one may mention that the most reasonable solution to the problem of divorce would be to admit two distinct forms of marriage: religious marriage, possessing a sacramental character (if only formally),

is in favour of birth control, which is something I can agree with, but not without noting a certain incongruity, since in practice most of the safest birth-control measures do not agree with the idea of naturalistic and instinctive sexual spontaneity upheld by De Marchi.[32] Again, one can agree with De Marchi when he opposes prostitution, seeing it as the logical counterpart to the present bourgeois virtuist regime, and concludes that the most effective way to overcome it would be: female emancipation + sexual freedom. Indeed, professional prostitution is very limited in central and northern European countries, insofar as this double condition has been fulfilled to some extent.

As far as sexual ethics is concerned, while a system of less conformism, greater sincerity and courage, greater realism, and clarity

---

and civil marriage. The former would be indissoluble and those who choose it should bear this in mind and ask themselves whether they are truly in a condition to live up to it. In relation to the latter kind of marriage, instead, divorce could be admitted, but only once — since it is conceivable and justifiable that a person may be mistaken once but not twice (this would rule out chain divorces of the sort common in America); the presence of offspring would constitute a serious prejudicial factor (this would lead people to think twice before having children). But although this would obviously be the wisest solution, it is one that the Church would find it difficult to accept, because one of the consequences of this solution would be a steep rise in the number of civil marriages. Thus the Church will in any case continue to oppose divorce, preferring 'indissoluble unions' that are such in name only — caricatures of what they ought to be.

32 [Evola's note. —Ed.] One can hardly consider a serious argument the fact that, in once again rummaging through ethnographic material, De Marchi has come across a certain savage people of the East that seems to combine full sexual freedom with very low birth rates; more weighty evidence is required. Rather, in relation to this matter one should note that intense and destructive sexual love is chiefly sterile — on this, see my book *Eros and the Mysteries of Love*. But, clearly, this does not apply to the kind of intercourse that the vast majority of women and men have — the irresponsibly instinctive and obtuse quality of that intercourse being the cause of the catastrophic and vermicular increase in the world population.

between the two sexes is desirable, one should not surpass a certain limit, especially by applying certain principles to everyone indiscriminately. As I have said, the prospect of a higher freedom in the field of sex can only be considered in relation to the ethics of a minority, whose inner structure shields them from the kind of dangers that this freedom would pose to other people.

It is almost comical on De Marchi's part to include sexual freedom among 'social demands' and the 'inalienable rights of the human person', alongside freedom of opinion, of worship, of assembly, of residence, and all the other fine 'achievements' of democracy, which would actually hardly be inclined to dispute this 'demand'. Here, as elsewhere, it is worth recalling the words of Nietzsche's Zarathustra, who was concerned not with freedom *from* something (i.e. restrictions) but with freedom *for* something, i.e. with the use of freedom, and who recalled that many people lose their last value the moment they cast off all yokes.[33] Free *for* what? To restore the climate of the ancient 'Aphroditean' societies, with their promiscuous, naturalistic, pacifist and humanitarian foundation and with the tacit and almost fatal pre-eminence they assign women? Besides, certain sectors of contemporary society are approaching an atmosphere of widespread and chronic sensuality, through a constant and insidious alluring of men on the part of sex and women, leading to the decay of all superior virile values and true spirituality, in line with what has always occurred at the final, twilight stages of many cycles of civilisation. Indiscriminate sexual freedom is all the more dangerous for a people such as the Italian one, which by race — rather than simply as a consequence of traditional prejudices — hardly has the best dispositions in the sexual field. For example, more sophisticated types aside, young Italian women find it almost impossible to move beyond the alternative between the bimbo

---

33 Taken from Chapter 17 ('On the Way of the Creator') of Part I in *Thus Spoke Zarathustra*. Consider also Chapter 1 ('On the Three Metamorphoses') of Part 1, and the difference between the lion and the child.

and the vulgar type. It is easy to speak of economic emancipation and sexual freedom as an antidote to prostitution: in actual fact, the only case in which this freedom does not prove detrimental is when women have acquired a special personality, something they have not even started to do today, despite all the achievements and demands of women on the material and practical level. In Italy the last War has merely led to a rise in petty, trivial or mercenary corruption. A recent survey on Italian call girls has found that the dominant outlook among them is no different from that of girls from the *petite bourgeoisie* who are in search of a husband and eager to 'settle down' — it is not at all the outlook of the young woman who aspires towards a greater, nonconformist freedom, and who makes use of it.

But even in the best case scenario, if we follow the views of De Marchi and other similar authors, the prospect is a transition from a gloomy, sadistic and puritanical sexophobia to a merry carelessness worthy of wild animals in 'nature'. What to think of De Marchi's suggestion that free sexuality is a recipe to increase sociability and mutual fellowship? Or his idea that one of the reasons why there is an urgent need for a sexual reform based on free love is the problem of how 'workers' will spend their spare time, when they will have so much of it thanks to the new technological advances? This is a fine perspective: a sensuous civilisation and 'Dionysianism' steeped in the atmosphere of today's after-work recreational centres or, even better, of their German equivalent in the past, *Kraft durch Freude* ('Strength through joy') — a formula that would seem to fittingly sum up the social aims of De Marchi's sexology. Ultimately, his utopianism only confirms the fact that he fails to grasp the more interesting, intense, transcendental and hence dangerous aspects that the sexual experience can present in the case of differentiated types of men and young women. De Marchi makes references such as: 'The problem was not to destroy the sensualising and dramatising of sexual facts by reducing these to essential physiological functions; rather, it was to exploit them for non-inhibitory and non-repulsive purposes'. He also acknowledges that the movement of reform seeking to promote the innocence of the naked female body by desexualising it, by detaching it from its sexual significance, 'strips sexuality even of that demonic power that it preserved in the Christian tradition.' Yet De Marchi opens these windows, only to close them immediately.

4

As one last point, let us consider, in particular, the demand for pre-marital and extra-marital sexual freedom, which is intended to do away with possessive sexual exclusiveness and the accompanying complex of jealousy. In relation to this, De Marchi's ideas can be associated with the views regarding a 'new sexual ethics' expounded by an Argentinian author of Yugoslav origin, Bosco Nedelcovic, in an open letter by this title, which he has also circulated in an Italian translation.[34]

Nedelcovic's purported starting point is a conception of sexual life which does not reduce it 'to a mere physiological necessity' and which places it on a higher level than the 'mere instinct of reproduction'. The author then affirms the possibility of a kind of 'polyamory' free from selfishness and exclusiveness, to replace conventional 'faithfulness' with 'responsible freedom'. In other words, he disputes the idea that the capacity to give 'one's best' in the erotic field requires having a relationship with a single person, to the exclusion of all others — a situation that in theory corresponds to the institution of monogamous marriage. The author, therefore, condemns the claim that a person can only belong to another alone (a reflection of the 'obscurantism of the patriarchy' — regrettably Nedelcovic, who offers some straightforward considerations, devoid of ideological encrustations, is evidently influ-

---

34 There is not much information available on this Nedelcovic, save that he was a linguist, a polyglot, and a utopistic visionary who died in the year 2000.

enced here by the absurd ideas of the authors considered thus far); hence, he also condemns the complex of possessive sexual jealousy. According to Nedelcovic, it is wrong to say that there can be nothing sincere and profound, if an individual focuses his love on several persons rather than just one. It is a grotesque bourgeois prejudice — he adds — 'to call a woman a slut if she has pre-marital or extra-marital relationships, and to call a man a poor "cuckold", if his woman is 'unfaithful' to him, whereby — in line with a more or less foolish interpretation of male pride — he will feel offended and jealous, beat, murder, and so on.'

These observations provide the starting point for the new sexual ethics endorsed by Nedelcovic (as well as De Marchi). But this is hardly a new suggestion in relation to man, as far as human history and institutions are concerned. Various civilisations practised polygamy, and even in Classical Antiquity concubinage was an unquestioned and legally recognised complement to marriage. In principle and existentially, all this implied the redirecting and multiplying of man's erotic interest in woman, as well as the non-existence or limited extension of exclusive possessive jealousy on woman's part. As a typical example one may consider the case of the wife of a Roman emperor who — it is said — would visit the slave market early in the day to choose one or two of the best slave girls for her husband, or the case of the Japanese women who would accompany their husbands and bid them farewell when they were leaving to spend the weekend with other women.

The defining feature of the sexual ethics championed by Nedelcovic, therefore, lies in the fact that it demands for women the kind of sexual freedom and non-exclusiveness that men had granted themselves in the institutions and societies just mentioned, and which they in any case practically grant themselves — de facto, if not formally — in present-day monogamous bourgeois society. Nedelcovic informs us that he has not confined himself to theory, but has led his wife to give herself over to other men, men in a state of 'conscious freedom'; and he reports that the outcome has not been the wrecking of their marriage, but an enrichment and intensification of their relationship.

In relation to all this, the following observations must be made. If this 'ethics' is widely applied, it becomes unclear what meaning or *raison d'être* marriage might still have. At most, it would be reduced to a 'preferential clause', a *ius eminens*, of one of the two spouses in favour of the other in their mutual relations, the two spouses being free to enjoy other sexual relationships. But even if this were the case, the problem remains that marriage, even when it does not have any sacramental and exclusive character, is generally connected with the idea of offspring. Hence, it would be necessary to establish a system of unions that rules out procreation (something which is only conceivable in relation to a small minority). Alternatively, one would have to envision a society in which the family no longer exists, in which free love rules and the State takes care of all offspring, as theorised by some early forms of utopian Socialism and Communism, which were soon abandoned. Be that as it may, it is clearly absurd to wish to apply the 'new ethics' to both sexes equally, unless we wish to end up with a degree of promiscuity which I believe even the most open-minded people would find it difficult to accept. Indeed, if in various countries the law is much harsher when it comes to female adultery, despite the democratic equality between the sexes, this is essentially due to the objective fact that, unlike in the case of male adultery, female adultery entails the possibility of the introduction of bastard offspring into the family via the wife's extra-marital relations.

The most important point, however, has to do with the title of the present chapter. One can acknowledge the ethical value of a system of sexual freedom without any exclusiveness only if this sexual freedom essentially presents itself as a freedom *from* sex, or is at least conducive towards such freedom. It is obvious that if we are truly capable of directing our erotic potential towards several persons to the same degree, without any jealousy and possessive exclusiveness, we have overcome the passivity that usually accompanies love, sex and passion, which is to say that we have freed ourselves from sex, without relinquishing it. Sexuality becomes something that is actively enjoyed, which is possessed and freely used, as opposed to something that we are possessed by and have to endure (along with bondage to women in general and to a particular woman). If this is the case, if this redirecting of sexual love in no way compromises the fullness and intensity of sexual experiences, it is evident that a higher level has been attained.

In this perspective, what I have already repeatedly noted, namely the absurdity of establishing the ethics of sexual freedom for everyone, becomes even clearer. It is clear that we cannot expect from ordinary men and women the kind of detachment that makes it possible to overcome all possessive exclusiveness, all bonds to a certain being, all jealousy. Most people cannot even conceive something of the sort. This only applies to exceptional cases, people with a particular constitution, or people who have taken upon themselves a special and rather difficult inner discipline.

Further particular restrictions apply to the female sex. Nedelcovic behaves like a gentleman when — in a spirit of fair play, so to speak — he demands for women the same kind of sexual freedom that men tacitly and egoistically grant themselves. Unfortunately, what stands in the way here are certain difficulties due not to the traditional privileges to which the male sex has laid claim, but rather to constitutive elements. The nature of women is such that typically they will find a serious erotic and sexual experience much more absorbing than men. Hence, we may conclude that it is far rarer for women to exhibit the superior inner level — or possibility to attain it — that allows freedom of sex to correspond to freedom from sex. Partly the situation may be less unfavourable among certain races, for example the central and northern European ones, where a stronger personality and greater inner freedom is more easily to be found among young women. In principle, however, the existential difference between the two sexes still applies, and it is necessary to draw the right conclusions from it: it must be acknowledged that the application of the 'new sexual ethics' to women is likely to entail, not an overcoming, not a higher freedom, but a decomposition, dissoluteness in the literal sense of the term — dissolution. The inevitable counterpart to all this is a drop in level and trivialising of sexuality itself — as I have already noted in relation to recent developments in sexual mores in Italy.

We may conclude, therefore, that the whole sexual reform movement, which calls for a 'sexual revolution', is compromised right from the start by the fallacies of egalitarianism and democracy. Its representatives have no sense of the level at which it is reasonable to affirm certain demands and values superior to those of petty, hypocritical and conformist bourgeois morality and all forms of 'sexophobia'. Many unmistakable clues show that the champions of the current in question have an utterly promiscuous, naturalistic and disintegrated type of sexuality as their starting point. All legitimate and partial demands asides, given that this call for sexual freedom goes hand in hand with an attack against the ideals of a hierarchical, virile and aristocratic civilisation, as well as against the general values not of a 'lesser morality' but of 'greater morality', we can certainly regard this movement as part of the general process of regression at work in the present age.

13. ROMANNESS, GERMANICNESS, AND THE 'LIGHT OF THE NORTH'

The ideas I will be presenting here may be mostly of retrospective, historical interest, insofar as the situation that could have given them a concrete and topical value no longer applies at present. I actually first formulated and defended these ideas in the period during which movements of renewal and reconstruction had affirmed themselves in Italy and Germany, movements that sided against the most advanced forms of modern socio-political subversion — Communism and democracy — and that were characterised by an impulse to return to the origins. In addition to purely political issues, they also addressed the need for a world-view that might serve as a foundation for an action designed to shape and rectify the human type of the two nations. The problematic and even negative aspects displayed by the two movements — the only aspects tendentiously emphasised in the present political climate — should not prevent objective spirits from acknowledging what can only be regarded as their valid potential, had they been adequately developed in the right circumstances. In the situation in question a specific problem also emerged — namely, the extent to which, in the reconstructive effort of these two movements, certain values and traditions of one people could integrate those of the other.

Today the preconditions for this problem are lacking. There is no need to state what the general socio-political and spiritual climate in Italy is like at the moment in which I am writing these lines; anyone can realise the wretched state in which this country finds itself through its infatuation with democracy and the growing gangrene of Socialism and Communism, notwithstanding the presence of certain dissident forces, which are however incapable of firmly uniting into a genuine front of the Right and defending a well-defined, profound and uncompromising doctrine of the State. Phenomena of the sort I have referred to when speaking of the breed of the elusive man, of the taste for vulgarity, of decayed and regressive sexology and the third sex, and so on, are particularly noticeable in the Italy of today. In Germany — in West Germany — the situation is even worse: while subversion, corruption and socio-political anarchy are not as advanced, and while there is more order and discipline, the whole past has been indiscriminately and almost hysterically thrown overboard, practical materialism is rampant, and the new generations utterly refuse to take interest in any superior idea. In many cases merely talking of a *Weltanschauung*[1] is considered suspect and one struggles to find something that resembles those groups which in Italy have not fully forgotten things, and which in a way continue to resist and react.

Nevertheless, I believe that it might be of some interest to recall the problems that I addressed when the aforementioned situation applied — the problem of the relations between Romanness and Germanicness, and of the possibility of a mutual interaction of the two — on account of certain intrinsically valid and normative elements, as well as from a retrospective and documentary standpoint.[2]

---

1   The German word means 'worldview', a term which was introduced into philosophy by Kant and cemented by Hegel. In distinction to the English term, a *Weltanschauung* refers in particular to the basic set of presuppositions or values through which a person interprets experiences and phenomena generally.

2   [Evola's note. —*Ed.*] The ideas I will be summing up here correspond to the most essential parts of a lecture I delivered in German under the auspices of the *Deutsch-Italienische Gesellschaft* and of the Minister of Foreign Affairs of the Reich in various cities across Germany — Berlin, Stuttgart, Hamburg, and Braunschweig. It may be interesting to recall one episode. My activity was opposed by a clique of the Italian Ministry of Foreign Affairs, which could not

As regards Italy, the main starting point was the need to gradually give shape, out of the essence of the people of this country, to a superior type that to some extent would embody the resurfacing, after centuries, of a fundamental component: the Roman or, more accurately, 'Aryan-Roman' one, as a means to overcome other less favourable components that are present and even predominant at times.[3] The term 'Aryan' here is a reference to the Indo-European origins. It should not be compromised by the arbitrary and superficial uses made of it by a certain form of political racism; it contains a fundamental and positive point of reference. Well-known comparative research has highlighted some common elements that, in terms of character and 'style', distinguished dominant stocks that shared the same origin, such as those of ancient Rome, Doric-Achaean Greece, and the Germanic populations in Europe. Now, there are some aspects of the German character in which the original dispositions have better been preserved. It is revealing that Prussia came to be referred to as 'the Rome of the North', while — as I have recalled in a previous chapter — some people have spoken of the

---

tolerate that mine was a 'free' undertaking and not one organised by those 'authorised' elements appointed by the people who had been put in charge of 'culture' at the time. I was even accused of perpetrating a kind of defamation of 'Italianness', because in a previous lecture held in Germany — again upon invitation of the German authorities — I had sought to make the public understand that Italy could not be reduced to the country of mandolin-players, *maccheroni*, 'Sole mio', fiery and jealous lovers, and gesticulating people — i.e. tourist Italy — and that an effort was being made to offer a higher ideal for the formation of a new kind of Italian. On account of this dangerous activity of mine, the aforementioned milieus had done their best to prevent me from speaking in Germany ever again, by trying to stop me from getting a visa. Things only got back on course when Mussolini personally stepped in. Instead, among the 'well-regarded' elements authorised to promote cultural relations between Italy and Germany, Guido Manacorda was chosen, an individual who — as I will later show — displayed a distorting animosity in his interpretation of Germanicness.

3   [Evola's note. —*Ed.*] On the aspects of this problem that are still relevant and on its solution, see J. Evola, *Men among the Ruins*, Ch. 16.

Romans as the 'Prussians of their age'.[4] Equally revealing is the nostalgia for the Dorian and Classical world harboured by Prussianism, as illustrated by the Dorianism of the famous Brandenburg Gate in Berlin.[5] The inclination towards discipline, disinterested service (the expression *travailler pour le roi de Prusse*[6] having become proverbial for every action not performed for personal gain), incorruptibility, sobriety, virility, active realism, reservedness, simple living, and clear and personal relationships based on command and obedience — all this has manifested itself in the best type of German and Prussian man to a far greater extent than in the Italian man, who is the physical heir to ancient Rome. Hence, when Italians, with their fixation for 'Latinness' and a certain 'Mediterraneanness', display an intolerance for all things German, it may well be argued that what are at work within them are dispositions and vocations that also oppose and distance Italians of this sort from the superior and original element in the history of the peninsula, namely the Aryan-Roman element. It was evident, therefore, that given a true aspiration to rectify and elevate the Italian type, to 'correct' it, any contact between the Italian people and the German one would lead not to any distortion or deformation of the former but, on the contrary, would help it to restore and bring

---

4   Probable reference to Spengler. See *Decline of the West*, Introduction, § 10.

5   This monument was erected between 1788 and 1791 on commission by the Prussian King Frederick William II. It was indeed built with intentional stylistic reference to the Dorians of Ancient Greece; in good Doric mode, it features a six-columned façade, and was even meant to evoke the gateway to the ancient Athenian Acropolis. The Brandenberg Gate has been the site of a great many important events in the history of Europe. It has seen the triumphal procession of Napoleon, and it became a symbol for the National Socialists; it was closed during the post-war partition of Berlin, only to be opened at the fall of the Berlin Wall. It has since then been regarded as a symbol of unity and peace, but given its history one might imagine any number of equally symbolic meanings which might be attached to it in some better tomorrow.

6   French: 'to work for the king of Prussia'.

into action its obscured heritage — in terms of character, inner and external formation, style, and ethics.

For my part, however, I paid just as much attention to the opposite problem, namely the problem of what aspects of our tradition, in a process of rapprochement, might, in turn, rectify and integrate the Germanic elements. But here it was necessary to take a different domain into account. While the field of character, ethics and life training essentially came into play in relation to the Germanic contribution, it was now necessary chiefly to refer to the higher level of the general view of life and even the idea of State. In this connection, it is also necessary to refer to the common origins of the two peoples. The Aryan-Roman element — which is to say the specifically Roman formulation of the common Indo-European heritage — presented itself as the essence of that which could promote a clarification, a rectification and a further development of the German spirit. As far as the essential task is concerned, with reference to the aforementioned situation, it may be expressed through the following formula: to rediscover the Olympian element of the North and promote the values and ideals deriving from them.

However, the preliminary condition, in this regard, was to clear various misunderstandings and distortions that, in Germany and Italy alike, informed the ideas of those who argued that while the two countries might have common contingent political interests, ultimately there is an unbridgeable gulf standing between Romanness and Nordic Germanicness. These ideas clearly derive from an arbitrary and one-sided conception, often a falsifying conception, of the Nordic-Germanic spirit, which finds its counterpart in a no less one-sided and contrived interpretation of Romanness. The animosity displayed by Catholic sectarianism also plays an important role here. Thus a well-established scholar of Germany, Guido Manacorda, drawing upon certain polemical motifs also shared by French Catholic nationalists, such as Henri Massis, believed that the opposition between Germanicness and Romanness can be summed up in the formula 'Forest and Temple'.[7] 'Forest', which is to say nature above the spirit; a search for truth in the sub-rational levels of being, freedom as elementary audacity, a tragic and romantic view of the world, the religion of eternal becoming, pantheism, immanentism, natural revelation, individualism, the affirmation of blood, folk and race against the State and any positive order, and so on — such would be the essence of Germanicness. 'Temple': the spirit above nature, the search for truth within the limits of human reason under the guidance of divine revelation, linearity, form, a Classical sense of measure, theistic transcendence, hierarchy, and so on — such would be the essence of Romanness.

Now, all this reflects a bias, a basic incapacity for objective discrimination. As regards facts in the field of concrete existential orientations and natural dispositions, the logical implications of an antithesis of this sort, assuming it is correct, are already contradicted by the elements that I have just highlighted in relation to Germanicness and Prussianism, elements I deem likely to exercise an integrative action upon the Italian spirit and character. Catholics stress the 'individualism' of Protestantism. But while this may be correct on a theological level, with reference to Luther's idea of 'free examination', on the practical level it is not correct at all, because despite the Reformation the central and northern European peoples have preserved their innate disposition towards discipline, order and the respecting of authority.[8]

---

7   Manacorda (1879–1965) was an Italian intellectual, philologist, editor of the journal *Biblioteca Sansoniana straniera*, and a decorated soldier during World War I. He converted to Catholicism in 1927, and became a prominent figure in the Catholic milieu, even acting as a mediator between Hitler and the Vatican in 1936 and 1937. He remained a strong adherent of the Church until his death. Massis (1886–1970) was a French writer, a convert to Catholicism and a conservative of the old guard (he refused, for instance, to collaborate with the Nazi regime).

8   The Reformation was the period of the Protestant-Catholic schism in the West, which was sparked by the 1517 publication of the famous *Ninety-five Theses*

Rather, as is well-known, it is precisely the Latin Catholic peoples that are distinguished by individualism, anarchy and a lack of discipline.

One wonders, moreover, to what extent Romanticism is an essential trait of the German spirit, along with what Spengler refers to as 'Faustianism', a concept he applies not just to the Germanic element, but to the whole cycle of 'Western' civilisation.[9] In my view, both orientations are to be regarded more as forms of decay than as primordial and original features of Germanicness. It is indisputable that Wagner and the infatuation with Wagnerianism played an important role in a certain kind of German culture, and even had political repercussions (for instance, through the prominence absurdly assigned to them within the framework of National Socialism).[10] However, it is significant and decisive that whenever Wagner dealt with motifs drawn from the ancient Nordic-Germanic and medieval German traditions (including the legends of the Grail and Lohegrin, the 'swan knight') — invoking the right of the artist (or at any rate of the modern artist) to treat a

---

of the Christian theologian Martin Luther (1483–1546). These *Theses* outlined abuses in the Catholic Church, and led to consequences both wide and enduring; among them was the emergence of the idea that each Christian should personally refer to the Bible in order to determine what Church doctrines are faithful to the original Christian teaching, and which are not — hence the idea of 'free expression' which Evola mentions here. This movement happened to coincide with the emergence of the printing press, thus making possible the wide distribution of translations of the Bible into various languages. Luther himself produced a German translation in 1534.

9   For Spengler, see note 4 to Chapter 4 above. For Faustianism, see note 2 to Chapter 10, as well as the relevant passage of that chapter itself.

10 The music of Richard Wagner (1813–1883) had an effect on German culture which it is difficult to overestimate, and this long before the National Socialists adopted his music. German music after him would never be the same, and philosophers, thinkers, and artists, Nietzsche and Thomas Mann among them, were basically changed by their encounter with Wagner's art. Hitler was a great admirer of Wagnerian music, and this accounts to some extent for its prominence in the National Socialist regime.

given subject matter as he pleases — he has been guilty of corrupting distortions and manipulations which are bound to strike and astonish anyone who, possessing adequate traditional points of reference, has any actual knowledge of such things.

This does not change the fact that, looking back at the origins, which is to say the ancient Nordic-Germanic traditions, two circumstances make any clarification difficult, while explaining in part, if not justifying, misunderstandings of the sort just illustrated. The first circumstance is the fragmentary and often spurious state in which some general Indo-European conceptions (often even ones of Hyperborean origin)[11] have been transmitted within the Nordic-Germanic traditions. The second circumstance refers to the repercussions that mythologised and transposed memories of primordial events have had upon these traditions.

For our purposes, it will be useful to briefly focus on the second point. 'Tragic heroism', that dark yet at the same time wild sense of life that some people regard as a congenital trait of the Nordic soul, constitutes an echo of something associated with the collapse of a very ancient civilisation. It is well known how much some followers of Wagner have gone on about the 'twilight of the gods'. The corresponding Nordic term, *ragna-rökkr*, is rather to be translated — less romantically but more adequately — as the 'obscuring of the divine' ('gods' and 'twilight' being merely mythologised images).[12] The reference here is not to the

---

11   Having origin, that is, with the Hyperboreans, the legendary race of men who lived in the far northern land of Hyperborea, where the sun never set. The Hyperboreans were physically powerful, exceptionally tall and long-lived, and were thought to be the most blessed of peoples. According to certain myths or legends, the Hyperboreans, in the wake perhaps of a great catastrophe, spread across the globe, and seeded the civilisations of Europe, Persia, and India.

12   It should probably be noted that the 'Wagnerian' translation is at least etymologically defensible, and indeed perhaps more than Evola's, insofar as Evola is making appeal, not so much to the literal meaning of the word, as rather to its esoteric meaning. *Ragna* quite literally means 'of the gods', though it might

specific view of the world of a given race or civilisation, but rather to episodes and events that fall within the historical and, partly, cosmic framework taken into account by ancient teachings pertaining to the four ages of the world, a concept also familiar to Classical Antiquity (Hesiod's Bronze Age and iron age, for example, correspond to the age of the 'Wolf' in the Nordic tradition of the *Eddas*).[13] But one point needs to be emphasised: beyond these memories and the tragic and wild aspect of those events, the Nordic soul too has known a higher truth. Anyone with an adequate education will easily acknowledge that in the mythology of the *Eddas* itself the essential element does not correspond to the *pathos* of the emergence and unleashing of elementary forces and of the struggle against them, nor to the particularities of sagas that even betray the influence of popular superstitions and external elements; the essential, in the tradition in question, is to be found in what are ultimately 'Olympian' meanings. These are implied,

---

also mean 'of the ruling powers'. Part of the trouble is that the word is written in two ways which Evola has here conflated into one: *ragnarök* and *ragnarøkkr* (as in the poem *Lokasenna*), the last of which would mean 'the growing dark of the gods', hence their twilight. The etymology of the first variant is indeed less clear; it appears to mean the destiny of the gods, the fate of the gods, which does not necessarily indicate their destruction nor even their disappearance. And according to the myth in question, not all the gods would perish in this period.

13　For Hesiod, see note 4 to Chapter 10. The present reference is to the ages of man which Hesiod presents in his *Works and Days*; the Iron and the Bronze ages, the last and the third to last respectively, were the worst ages of man, in which man would live in misery, families would fall into conflict and strife, and shame would disappear from the human heart. Hesiod believed he was living in the Iron Age, which makes one wonder what substance he might have chosen to describe our own. The *Eddas* refers to the works of Medieval Icelandic literature which has come down to us, commonly known as the *Prose Edda* and the *Poetic Edda*. The Wolf Age is likewise the last and worst of the ages in the *Edda*, as laid out in Stanza 45 of one of the poems of the *Poetic Edda*, the *Völuspá*; it, too, is characterised by fratricides and the turning of the child against his mother. The same section of the *Völuspá* speaks of *ragnarök*.

for instance, by the idea of Mitgard, which reflects the general idea of a supreme centre and fundamental order of the world, and which, in a way, may be considered the metaphysical basis of the idea of empire; by the symbolism of Valhalla as a mountain whose frozen and bright peak shines of an eternal light beyond all clouds; and, connected to this, the motif of the so-called Light of the North in its many variants. In relation to this, I should recall the symbolism of the golden realm of Gladsheim, 'brighter than the sun'; secondly, the royal castle of Oegier, which houses the Asen and in which gold — the traditional symbol for all that is incorruptible, royal and solar — manifests the power of a burning light; and, finally, the image of the celestial place of Gimle, 'more magnificent than any other and brighter than the sun', which 'will endure even when the heavens and earth pass away'.[14] In this and many other motifs, however fragmentarily recorded, a trained eye is bound to detect a testimony to a higher dimension in ancient Nordic mythology. We must conclude therefore that, like the men of Classical Antiquity, Nordic-Germanic men were familiar with the idea of an order existing beyond the world of becoming and of a tragic and elementary reality. According to the *Völuspá* and *Gylfagynning*, after *ragna-rökkr* a 'new sun' and 'new race' will arise; the 'divine heroes', or Asen, will return to Idafeld and find gold, which symbolises the primordial tradition of luminous Asgard and the original state. Beyond the mist of the 'Forest', then, a higher light shines. There is something greater than becoming and perishing, tragedy and fire, frost and death.

---

14   By the old northern mythologies, Mitgard was the name of the earth itself, the center of all things (the word later transformed into the basis for 'Middle Earth'). Valhalla ('hall of the slain') is the hall where deceased kings, and some of those who have fallen nobly in battle, go to pass their afterlife; it is ruled over by the god Odin. Glaðsheimr, which means, as Evola indicates, 'bright or shining home' was the location of Valhalla. The next two references here are presumably alternative transliterations of *Ásgarðr*, the abode of the *Æsir*, the gods. Gimlé was to be the home of those worthy men who survived *ragnarök*.

Let us recall Nietzsche's words: 'Beyond ice, the north, death — *our* life, *our* joy.'[15] This, truly, is the final profession of faith of the Nordic man, a profession of faith which, ultimately, may be regarded as Olympian and Classical.

Once we have clarified this point, we must acknowledge all the dross that the original tradition of the Light of the North has accumulated, partly as a consequences of the times, partly through poetic and romantic speculations. We will then be able to speak of a 'rediscovery of the Nordic Olympian world', which requires us to broaden our horizons and adopt higher points of reference. Indeed, even Günther has acknowledged that in order to learn about the true essence of the Nordic peoples we cannot refer to the beliefs of the Germanic peoples alone, for which — according to this scholar — 'we unfortunately have insufficient documents and from a period in which they had already more or less been influenced by religious conceptions from Asia Minor, the Mediterranean and Western Europe — the very Western Europe which through druidism had already become significantly removed from Indo-European religiosity of the purely Nordic sort.'[16] It is by looking at the purer and more primordial forms that the same spirit acquired among other peoples of the same stock that — according to Günther — we can find better elements to understand the true essence of the Germanic traditions. In this respect, the author refers not just to the ancient civilisations of India, Persia and Greece, but also to the ancient Italic traditions.[17]

---

15   *Völuspá* and *Gylfagynning* are both from the *Eddas*, the first from the *Poetic Edda* and the latter from the *Prose Edda*. The quotation from Nietzsche can be found in §1 of *The Antichrist*.

16   Hans Günther (1891–1968) was a German race researcher who came to prominence during the reign of the Third Reich. His theories had some influence on the racial practices of the Germans during that time.

17   [Evola's note. —*Ed.*] H. F. K. Günther, *Frömmigkeit nordischer Artung*, Jena, 1934, pp. 8–12.

On the basis of these conclusions, I argued that certain elements associated with Romanness might be helpful to a Germanic elite, insofar as it would allow it to regain awareness of the 'Olympian' component of the Nordic tradition, as a common basis for an action of restoration and rectification directed at the two civilisations and cultures. In certain German milieus this assessment of the Roman element often met with a strong resistance in the past — and may still meet some resistance today (should it even be possible to bring up such problems in the civilisation of the 'economic miracle' of present-day West Germany). It cannot be denied that German culture has displayed a certain anti-Roman animosity, and not just in the essentially political terms of the so-called *Kulturkampf* waged by Bismarck to reaffirm the authority of the State against any interferences from the Church of Rome and as a residual echo of Lutheran polemics — an animosity that has offered a pretext to those who, in Italy, are obsessed by the notion of a fundamental antithesis between Romanness and Germanicness.[18]

To clear all misunderstandings, however, it is necessary to draw a distinction by explaining what kind of Romanness I am referring to. All too often people in Italy have turned Rome into an abstract idea, a Humanist echo, a rhetorical object. All too often the primordial essence of Rome has been overlooked — the essence of that Rome whose origins lie in an august myth, that Rome which will always have an evocative power, that Rome which coincides not with a merely historical concept or ancient juridical structure, but rather with an order shaped by something more than simply human values — by divine powers, figures and dominions: a world of metaphysical tensions, a solar world marked by elitism, an Olympian and heroic reality, order, light, pure virility, and pure action. Closely related to all this is the idea of the State, of *Imperium*. Such is the Romanness which repre-

---

18 *Kulturkampf* literally means 'culture-struggle', and refers to the long and trying attempt on the part of Prussian Chancellor Otto von Bismarck (1815–1898) to make the Catholic Church submit to the rule of law in the German Empire.

sents a value for me, and it should not be regarded as the miracle of an isolated creation, sprung out of nothing, but rather as a peak in the overall cycle of the Indo-European peoples and civilisations: not a beginning but rather a rebirth, the mysterious re-emergence of a primordial heritage that, after growing dim through the contingencies and ethnic chaos of the archaic Mediterranean world, manifested itself once again, attaining a peak that Greece was never able to reach on account of the lack of a firm political idea — the deeds of Alexander the Great only possessing the fleeting brilliance of a meteor. Thus, the greatness of Rome is marked by what are also Nordic and Hyperborean symbols, such as the axe, wolf and eagle; the ancient *ius sacrum* and *ius civile*[19] of the Romans present some unmistakable affinities with the juridical forms of all ancient Indo-European civilisations; and the *flamen dialis*,[20] a particularly significant figure belonging to the more ancient forms of Roman priesthood, stood as a 'living statue of the deity' and was closely related to the Roman idea of the State, while presenting the same traits as the members of the highest sacred caste in the ancient Indo-Aryan civilisation. Despite various unfavourable circumstances and setbacks, this tradition endured for centuries and shines even in the late imperial period through many figures, myths and episodes. Thus — as I have already recalled[21] — alongside the Caesar who displays the traits of a dictator, we find the Caesar who, according to Suetonius, could claim as a young man that his lineage combined the majesty of kings and sacredness of the gods, in whose power also those who rule men lie. This Caesar was venerated not as an individual, but as 'perpetual victor', which is to say as a supra-personal power governing the destiny of the Romans. The ancient

---

19   Latin for 'sacred law' and 'civil law' respectively.

20   See note 8 to Chapter 10.

21   See Chapter 10 above, in which Evola speaks on many of the questions he presents here.

world saw Augustus as an equally momentous figure;[22] significantly, a relation was established between his person, the Delphic cult of light, the Apollonian idea of Hyperborean origins, and the symbolic figure of Orestes as the establisher of a new virile and celestial law, against the chtonic Pelasgian and pre-Indo-European world of the Mothers and of elemental forces.[23] Moreover, a confused yet powerful instinct led the Romans to detect a return in this stage of their history: the return of the primordial golden age, which is merely the mythologised memory of the original cycle of the stock from which the various ancient Indo-European races have sprung.

People have spoken of the *aeternitas Romae*,[24] which is more than mere rhetoric; one must think, here, of that which, being primordial, has eternal youth and is virtually superior in itself to the temporal condition, to 'history'. This has specific implications for historical and political reality. As already noted, the distinguishing feature of Rome compared to Greece lies in its close relation to the idea of empire and the principle of a universal order, something which allows us to draw a parallel with the impulse behind the ancient Aryan-Iranian civilisation, against the metaphysical background provided by Mazdaism.[25] The

---

22 Augustus, born Gaius Octavius (BC 63-AD 14) was Caesar's adopted son and heir, and the first Roman Emperor.

23 According to Ancient Greek mythology, Orestes was the son of Clytemnestra and Agamemnon. After the Trojan War, Agamemnon was slain upon his homecoming by his wife's lover Aegisthus, or by Clytemnestra herself. Orestes avenged the death by murdering both his mother and her lover, and was driven mad by his own deed; hounded by the Furies, he finally managed to purge himself of his guilt. The means of his redemption varies from version to version; in at least one version, Apollo himself presides over his purification. For the Pelasgians, see note 17 to Chapter 8.

24 Latin: 'The eternity of Rome'.

25 Another term for Persian Zoroastrianism, one of the world's oldest religions, which comes from the teachings of the prophet Zoroaster. Due to its conception of the world as being divided between two contrary forces of good and evil and

symbol of Rome is essentially that of an order which derives its highest legitimation precisely from Olympian aspects, and which therefore participates in the Aryan-Olympian light, yet also in something fateful and supra-temporal. At the same time, it represents an apex of human power and embodies an ideal of earthly justice and 'triumphal peace'.

When considering the political ideal of Rome, one must not lend too much weight to detached juridical forms, particularly the decayed and universalistic (in a negative sense) ones of the late Roman age, which later came to be fetishised. It is precisely these forms that fuelled a certain anti-Roman polemic in Germany, which criticised a legal system 'made up of clauses' (something unknown in early Roman law). On the political level, what is notable in Rome is rather the lofty character of the principle and ideal of State vis-à-vis the naturalistic order, which encompasses what pertains merely to the *ethnos*, folk, nation and race. Here there is no need to repeat what I have argued in a previous chapter with regard to 'form' and 'matter', the male and female principles which are at work in socio-political forms of organisation, and which differentiates these forms depending on which of the two is predominant.[26]

In the situation in the period under consideration, this was a particularly momentous point: the Roman ideal presented itself as a means to rectify one of the most problematic aspects of the German movement, insofar as it tended to emphasise the *Volk* and the *Völkische*—ambiguous terms, since *Volk* can mean both 'people' (the masses) and 'nation' or 'race'. A genuine mythology of the race/people took shape which, while keeping to an essentially naturalistic conception of the race/people, turned it into the primary element, the ultimate point of reference, which was expected to condition all political, ethical and cultural spheres. This myth was further extended in the

---

its monotheism, it is often taken as a forerunner of Christianity, though it would be a mistake to attempt too close a parallel between the two religions.

26   See Chapter 8.

sense that the ideal of the *Reich* itself was founded on it; the notion was developed of a guiding, ruling and ordering function exercised by a given nation/race which was not enhanced by a principle from above, not marked by any true grace. Thus populist and collectivist aspects came to be associated with what Vico refers to as the 'arrogance of the nations', a nationalist infatuation awkwardly modelled after Hegel's doctrine of the 'leading folk'.[27]

In this respect, however, the contrast between the new Reich — the Third Reich — and the previous German political tradition is evident, given first of all that Prussia originally emerged as the secular form of a State created by an Order, that of the Teutonic Knights, and second that the informing principle of Prussianism was later precisely the State, with the Hohenzollern ensuring the unity of Prussia.[28] When Bismarck founded the German empire, the Second Reich, the old conservative faction denounced the purely 'naturalistic' and subversive character of the ideology of the 'nation'. Bismarck himself, who did not believe in this ideology or in the *Volk* at all, saw dynastic loyalty as the true, solid, spiritual and ethical foundation of the empire. However, even in the National Socialist period some of those who had championed the so-called 'conservative revolution' and coined the concept of 'Third Reich', while endorsing National Socialism, consciously maintained these higher points of reference. One might mention, for example, Christoph Steding, who noted that 'only the State and the empire can lead a folk out of the condition of a dreamy being-in-itself and lend objective existence to the community of blood and race.' I have already quoted Steding's saying that 'men' uphold the State and empire,

---

27   For both Vico and Hegel, see note 28 to Chapter 5 above.

28   Much of the territory which was subsequently to become Prussia was conquered by the Catholic Order of the Teutonic Knights in 1226. During the wars that followed, the Order organised into a state, in part to deal with the threat of its enemies. The Hohenzollern dynasty was the ruling house of Prussia, which reigned there for many centuries.

whereas 'matriarchal' spirits uphold the 'people', the *Volk* — this being a deep difference, a matter of essence.[29] 'In order for a nation or race to reach that higher level which corresponds to the idea of State and empire, it must be struck and transformed by "Apollo's lightning bolt"' — and   there are no exceptions to this. 'Even Nordic-Aryan blood', Steding stated, 'needs this flash, this transformation, a catharsis leading it from regions of dark, naturalistic promiscuity to the level of the spirit, where the global political life of the State unfolds.'[30]

The 'race of Rome' may legitimately be counted among those which in the ancient world were permeated by 'Apollo's lightning', to the point of embodying a principle that the previous Mediterranean world had sought to affirm in vain. Here we may refer back to the brilliant reconstruction of the secret history of the ancient Mediterranean world provided by Bachofen.[31] If the paternal-Apollinean ideal, with its ethical, social, juridical and political values, was able to triumph for some time over the ambiguous world of paleo-Mediterranean tellurism, Dionysianism and the spiritual matriarchy, this is due precisely to the work of Rome.[32] What we have, then, is something very different from barren juridical positivism and 'State-worship'. The prominence accorded to the State and the law in Rome over the mere matter of the

---

29   See Chapter 8 above, and note 18 of the same.

30   [Evola's note. —*Ed.*] C. Steding, *Das Reich und die Krankheit der europäischen Kultur*, Hamburg, 1938, pp. 217–233, 292–293, 587.

31   For Bachofen, see note 15 to Chapter 8.

32   Apollo was the Greek god of music, and was classically considered the god also of order and form. Dionysus was the Greek god of inebriation and wine; his followers were renowned for their violence and drunken fury. The dichotomy between Apollo and Dionysus inevitably evokes Nietzsche, but Evola himself considered it in a somewhat different light than the German philosopher. For more, see Chapter 12 of Evola's *Recognitions*.

'people' was based on a sacred principle.[33] It marks the presence and victory of a race that had the virile and paternal element as its centre and which affirmed the luminous principle (connected to the figure of Iupiter Optimus Maximus)[34] — closely related to the Nordic idea of Mitgard and to the symbolic 'Light of the North'. This occurred not on the level of a spirituality such as the Hellenic one, in which myth was almost exclusively envisaged in relation to an overworldly realm and became subject to aetheticising forms of decay, but rather on the level of a global historical reality such as that of empire.

By adopting a point of view of this sort, one may view in a new light the encounters that occurred in history between the Roman tradition and the Nordic-Germanic one — in the Middle Ages, for instance. In relation to the Middle Ages as a whole, the situation may be described in the following terms: the strictly Germanic element helped reawaken in various parts of Italy the dispositions of a kindred heritage which had been present ever since the dawn of the Latin world; in turn, certain aspects of the Roman tradition helped revive a spiritual heritage that had often become obscured in the Nordic-Germanic peoples of the invasion period, a heritage that was equally kindred to the Roman one. This explains the appeal that Romanness, even in its twilight forms, exercised on the early Germanic peoples. In these early centuries, those races that burst onto the stage of history as new and still uncorrupted forces could certainly have swept away, not only whatever political power still endured, but Rome itself as a spiritual symbol, had they, as though following an obscure yet unfailing instinct, not perceived and found traces of a kindred spirit within

---

33 [Evola's note. —Ed.] It must be recalled that originally the word *popolus* in Rome referred not to the 'people' in the modern sense, the *demos*, but rather to the well-articulated community of citizens, more or less militarily organised into the *comitia curiata*.

34 Latin for 'Jupiter the Best and Greatest', referring to the father of the gods of the Roman pantheon.

it. This also holds true on the level of the ideal of the State, in relation to which the aforementioned author, Steding, writes: 'Since up until then in our Western world the Roman State had been the one which best embodied the idea of statehood and, as an almost ideal model, had realised the pure idea of the State according to the Nordic spirit, it is hardly surprising that it came to be acknowledged as a model also by many men who tended to keep to themselves, such as the Germans in the Middle Ages ... A glance at our predecessors' faces — through surviving images or statues — is enough to show that the so-called Roman "denaturalisation" was not at all harmful to them, since they appear far more virile, conscious, firm and healthy than those contemporaries of ours who wish to deny a fair share of our German past.' Here, Walter Franck noted, the heritage of Widukind, the leader of the Saxons, 'met that imperial tradition shaped after the image of Rome which with Charlemagne, in an iron-and-blood event, as is in any great upheaval in world history, united for the first time the disjointed and scattered world of the Germanic peoples.'[35] However, we should not overlook the spiritual counterpart to this process. While we may well speak of a denaturalisation, as far as the 'conversion' and Christianisation of the Germanic peoples are concerned, it is also true that a remote Nordic-Aryan heritage was awoken by the encounter with Rome, ultimately

---

35   The 'Walter Franck' here might be the German National Socialist historian Walter Frank (1905–1945) who committed suicide after the death of Hitler. Evola by way of reference notes: 'This quote comes from the introduction to Steding's work, p. XV'. Widukind (whose name literally means 'child of the wood') was the leader of the Saxons against Charlemagne. Nothing is known about his birth, and nothing remains to us regarding his death save legends, but his opposition to the Frankish invasion has won him a deal of symbolic fame, and thanks in part also to the mysterious nature of his life he has earned his place in legend. He is often regarded as a representative of Saxon independence.

leading to that grand Romano-Germanic civilisation expressed and animated by a metaphysical tension: the Ghibelline Middle Ages.[36]

According to this perspective, a Germanic as much as Roman tradition could provide some points of reference for mutual encounters, for the differentiation of vocations, and for the rectification of the ideological deviations marring yesterday's German movement. One such deviation is the attempt to call the idea of the First Reich, which is to say the Holy Roman Empire, into question on account of its transcendence and universality, which naturally conflict with the ideology of the *Volk*. What has just been argued helps clear this misunderstanding and distorted interpretation, while revealing the medieval imperial phenomenon as one of those cases in which the *Volk*, the nation/race, rather than being rejected is assigned a higher dimension, one constituting the precondition for any higher mission– a dimension that is symbolised by 'Apollo's lightning' and which is also attested by the sacred features displayed by the sovereigns of that age. Of course, in relation to modern times, this reappraisal was intended to prove influential at a deep level, by challenging the myth of the people/race as the primary and decisive element of a given political organisation and by leading a political structure headed by an almost populist figure who derived his charismatic power and authority from the *Volk* — in contrast to the legitimacy that distinguishes all traditional forms of sovereignty — to acknowledge its own involution.[37]

---

36 The Ghibellines were originally Italian supporters of Frederick Barbarossa, who subsequently sought to expand the Holy Roman Empire into the lands directly or indirectly controlled by the Pope, and thus to bring the Holy Roman Empire back into Rome, the point of its origin in the times of the Ancient Romans. The Ghibellines were opposed by the Guelfs, the supporters of the Pope, and the conflict between them became a centerpiece of Medieval politics, lasting some three hundred years, from the twelfth to the fifteenth century.

37 A reference, of course, to Hitler. This is a key part of Evola's unusual but most interesting critique of National Socialism, which he develops more at length elsewhere (see *Notes on the Third Reich*, available from Arktos).

In certain extremist milieus, moreover, one could observe the misunderstanding represented by certain neo-pagan aspirations. Certainly, the need expressed by the formula 'the struggle over world-view' (*Kampf um die Weltanschauung*) was legitimate. In order for a movement to have a truly creative character, leaving mere political ideologies aside, it must have a distinctive view of the world and of life. No less legitimate was the need to reassess the validity of certain generally acknowledged conceptions related to the beliefs which have become predominant in the West — which is to say, related to Christianity. In this sphere, the Italian counterpart to this movement had shown a lack of courage: while evoking the symbols of Romanness, it had consciously avoided addressing the question of the extent to which the adoption of these symbols as the foundation of a new world-view was compatible with Christian conceptions. Hence, it had limited itself to a conformist reverence for them and to compromises. By contrast, the German milieus in question had given proof of such courage. Regrettably, however, the 'paganism' they professed was something artificial and spurious, with almost no reference to the actual content of the traditions of the higher, pre-Christian or non-Christian Indo-European civilisations. In the 'struggle over world-view', no plans were made for a genuine return to the origins. The distortion of many themes and the heavy politicisation of others were evident, for example, in Alfred Rosenberg's famous work *The Myth of the Twentieth Century*, which was almost regarded as a touchstone.[38] The regressive tendency of this work was all to evident insofar as it sympathised with those proclaiming a so-called 'natural doctrine of

---

38 Rosenberg (1893–1946), one of the men sentenced to hanging at Nuremberg, was a German thinker whose influence was quite salient in the Third Reich. The book to which Evola makes reference here was a work on race which took its bearings in part from the racial theorists Gobineau and Chamberlain. *The Myth of the Twentieth Century* wished to establish race as a central element of a semi-pagan religion of the Third Reich (hence the work's title).

the spirit', associating this with the mystique of life and blood, with those professing the sort of irrationalism I have criticised in a previous chapter, and with those who deemed any doctrine of transcendence or higher asceticism 'non-Aryan', and so on. This neo-paganism was marked by a perfectly naturalistic view of existence, akin to that which had distinguished civilisation forms anterior to the appearance of the world of the Indo-European Olympian gods. Thus it is hardly surprising that in the ranks of those who professed themselves to be 'pagans' and who championed a new national German religion, people were to be found who also invoked a return to the matriarchy (Bergmann); nor is it surprising that Klages chose to refer to the view of life of the Pelasgians, i.e. the paleo-Mediterranean people to which Dorian and Apollonian Greece was opposed, and which in Italy came to be associated with the plebeian component of the Roman State.[39] Yet even the emphasis assigned to woman's role as mother in certain organisations of the German regime — the very organisations that simultaneously upheld the markedly virile ideal of the *Ordenstaat*, which is to say of a State governed by an Order, as opposed to a class of petty democratic politicians, party men or demagogues — was questionable, to say the least. Now, with regard to the German 'neo-pagan' tendency, insofar as it gave proof of these distortions, misunderstandings and primitivism, the important thing was to show that it was possible to react to it on the basis not of Christianity nor of fanciful notions such as that of 'Forest and Temple', but of the actual Indo-European, or Aryan,

---

39 Ernst Bergmann (1881–1945) was a German thinker, and yet another suicide after the death of Hitler. He wrote a work on the idea of a German National Church which was placed on the Catholic Index. Through research he carried out in the animal world, and particularly among social insects like ants and bees, he made the remarkable leap of concluding that the feminine element should have the upper hand in all normal and natural human societies. For Klages, see note 2 to Chapter 7 above. Evola has more to say about the stratification of the Roman state and the relation of its various elements (including the Pelasgian) in Chapter 9 of *Recognitions*.

origins. Within the perspective and limits just outlined, Romanness itself presented several valid points of reference that could provide a lift, rectification, and re-establishment of the required discipline of the spirit within the domain of the 'struggle over the world-view' and the — in principle legitimate — revisionism this entailed.

I will mention one more point. Throughout history, North and South have been the object of a mutual nostalgia that has rarely reached any balance. In this respect, one might note a curious circumstance. Whereas the nostalgia for the South has a prevalently 'physical' and sentimental character, the nostalgia for the North has a chiefly metaphysical and spiritual character. To this day the central or northern European man feels a nostalgia for the South, either as a humanist or as someone seeking sunlight, physical rest, and a certain picturesque environment that strikes him as exotic. The nature of the nostalgia for the North that at times manifested itself among the ancient Mediterranean peoples of the Classical age was of a different sort. In their view, the North was where the holy land of the Hyperboreans and Thule were located, conceived as the solar isle — *Tule a sole nomen habens*.[40] They believed that in the North Chronos still lived in a slumbering state: the god symbolising the golden age, which is to say the primordial times — which is why the Arctic Sea used to be known as the Sea of Chronos in antiquity. In the North the 'midnight sun' offered them a physical symbol of the highest mystery of Mediterranean antiquity, that of the inner light that rises where sensible light fades. Through

---

40 The last phrase is Latin: 'Thule takes its name from the sun'. According to ancient mythology Thule was an island located in the extreme north; Virgil used the expression *ultima Thule* to denote a distant place or goal. Strabo makes reference to the population of Thule as a people of fruit eaters, who get both nourishment and beverage (that is, beer and mead) from grain and honey. The land of Thule had a reputation for extreme fertility — most interesting fact from the point of view of 'prehistory', given that it was supposed to exist in what we now regard as the 'frozen north'. For Hyperborea, see note 11 above.

the phenomenon of an almost nightless day, this land struck them as the closest one to the land of perennial light. We are even told that a Roman Emperor led his legions to the northernmost areas of Britain not so much to earn the laurel wreath of military victory as to experience while still alive the union with the divine that awaited Roman sovereigns in the afterlife and to behold the king of the gods — who, according to another tradition and myth, however, resides in Latium, in Roman territory.

All this would appear to further confirm that the memory of the Nordic Olympian world, many aspects of which became obscured in later Germanic traditions, was kept alive by the Mediterranean races of the same stock. This primordial heritage — as we have seen — also encompasses the roots of those truly eternal aspects of Romanness. There was good reason to think, therefore, that to the extent that through *this* Romanness it was possible to help the Germanic man to acquire an anti-Romantic, clear, solemn, virile yet at the same time free and sovereign world-view, he would not become estranged from himself but would rather be brought back to the deepest and most original element in his own tradition. Aside from the fact that this would have served as a valid foundation for bringing out the positive elements of the German movement, paralysing the negative ones through an active retrieving of the symbol of a 'conservative revolution', the natural overcoming of one-sided and tendentious antitheses between the two cultures entailed by this would also set the ground for a true understanding between the elites of the two peoples. The nostalgia of the Nordic soul for the brightness of the Mediterranean can therefore overcome the level of aestheticism and naturalism, and acquire the deeper meaning of a spiritual impulse to grasp a metaphysical reality.

The Classicality of the action of ruling. Mistrust towards any yielding of one's spirit. The will towards a heroic catharsis. The affirmation of all the values of realism, discipline and sheer power, of order against chaos, of what transcends life vis-à-vis mere life, of a clear and bright vision by opposition to all that is darkly psychic, instinctual and naturalistic, form, hierarchy, limits as the expression of an infinite that possesses itself, State, Empire, the ideal of ascetic, warrior organisations as new Orders — all such things lie beyond North and South, all such things are 'Aryan' and 'Roman': they constitute the hallmarks of every great constructive cycle, of all great races in their period of high tension.

But unfortunately, in the present state of prostration that Europe now finds itself in, what significance can the presentation of such ideas and the evoking of such symbols still have?

14. SUBLIMINAL INFLUENCES AND 'INTELLIGENT STUPIDITY'

1

We have already had the chance to note the illusoriness of the claim that modern man, in general, has acquired an unprecedented degree of autonomy and self-consciousness. This illusion is partly due to the fact that attention today is primarily directed towards external conditions, on account of the disappearance of certain material limits to the freedom of the individual — limits that were often not without their *raison d'être*, and which almost invariably have come to be replaced by new ones — while ignoring the matter of inner (mental and spiritual) autonomy, and everything that is necessary in order to acquire it and defend it. In this respect, there is no reason at all to speak of progress; it would be far more legitimate to speak, once again, of a regression, since a range of processes have made man particularly vulnerable today to what could be described as 'subtle', hidden or subliminal influences, which in almost all cases have a collective nature. This is practically inevitable in a 'mass civilisation' of the sort that is increasingly becoming dominant in our world. The phenomenon is always the same and manifests itself on many different levels.

On the most trivial plane, the role now played by advertisement and propaganda would be inconceivable without the precondition of this passive opening up of the individual: an opening up which has either already de facto taken place, or which can easily be attained by means of this or that technique. It is well know that in the field of so-called MR (= motivational research) in the US, psychiatry and psychoanalysis have been recruited by the advertising industry to provide guidance as to which 'subtle' methods are the most effective in psychologically influencing the public. By operating on the unconscious and ancestral layers of the mind, it is possible to elicit decisions and choices in a desired direction, so as to arouse specific interests. In the US, all major companies have special MR departments; and if huge sums are spent on them, it mean that this system works, that the investment is a profitable one, and hence that defenceless passivity is indeed to be found in a vast number of men and women. It is telling that all this is taking place in the US, the country where, under the sign of democracy, it is claimed that man has achieved the highest degree of freedom, emancipation, and self-consciousness — when in fact the invisible coercion to shape society through the various forms of conformism and public opinion is often at least as great in this alleged 'land of the free' and 'free world', as the coercion exercised in visible and direct forms by the State in the so-called totalitarian systems of the 'unfree' world. Indeed, insofar as any difference between the two is to be found, it may not be to the advantage of the former, since people there are not aware that they are being influenced, whereas in the latter case the action is directly perceived, and is therefore more likely to elicit some kind of reaction.

I have spoken of advertising; but it is only a small leap from advertising to political propaganda. Thus, after an objective analysis some people in America have noted with indignation that the techniques used in the presidential elections do not differ significantly, from a structural point of view, from those used to foist a certain brand of soap or domestic appliance upon the public.

Besides, America is only an extreme case in this respect, as in so many others, insofar as it pushes processes that are also underway in other countries to the point of absurdity. Indeed, generally speaking, one could say that the success of the ideologies and slogans that almost completely dominate socio-political life today is simply due to the absence, in most individuals, of any real defence which might bar access to the sub-intellectual, irrational and 'physical' part of the psyche. If the threshold to this area were guarded, it would automatically thwart most of those methods which are applied on a vast scale nowadays by political and social agitators in order to rouse the masses and lead them in one direction or another, without depriving them of the illusion that they are simply acting in accordance to their own will and their own true interests.

Furthermore, collective currents arise in this climate, often quasi-autonomous currents that have a subtle, invisible substrate, and infective properties. This explains certain curious and unexpected consequences of conformism. There are some individuals who, in a given political and social system, agree to take part, while maintaining ideals and principles of a different or even opposite type. At a certain point these people may realise that their way of thinking has changed; but in most cases, they are not even aware of the change at all.

This can also occur to people who had initially adhered to a political system in a purely exterior, insincere and opportunistic way, based on ulterior motives or tactical considerations. This kind of adherence too places the individual in a kind of autonomous, collective psychic vortex; and if the individual lacks inner defences, reinforced by vigilance and an impersonal adherence to a higher idea, it is difficult in the long run to avoid the danger of infection. This usually goes unnoticed for the aforementioned reason: one remains within a superficial, external conception of the forces acting in a given society and historical climate, failing to grasp the deeper, 'psychic' dimension of the phenomenon.

Directly related to this is the 'charge' certain words or phrases have, and the contaminating effect they exercise on those who nonetheless agree to use them. But the intellectual cowardice of spineless men also plays its part here. The predominant climate in Italy at the time of this writing offers prime examples of this. I am essentially referring to the whole terminology promoted by the forces of the Left, by democracy, Marxism, and communism, which is accepted by others in the senses that these same forces established.

First of all, let us take the very word 'democracy'. Infatuation and passiveness have reached the point that this word has become a sort of taboo, accepted and repeated *ad nauseam*. Today there seems to be a kind of anxiety when one does not promote democracy and does not declare oneself to be democratic in one way or another. The surrender becomes obvious when, instead of absolutely refusing from the very beginning to take part in this game, one excuses oneself with this or that adjective by speaking of *true* democracy, *national* democracy, *healthy* democracy, and so on, thereby forgetting Goethe's saying — 'From those spirits which you have summoned, you will free yourself with difficulty'[1] — and without detecting the contamination.

Other fetishised words of the same kind, and with the same hidden infective properties, are 'socialism', 'work', 'the working class', 'sociality', 'social justice', 'the meaning of history', and, on the opposite side of the spectrum, 'reaction', 'obscurantism', 'immobility', etc. At a certain point, one may realise that one no longer has the courage to take a stand against these formulas; it may seem natural to use them, and regardless of any mental reservations on the part of those who do not completely belong to the front of global subversion, these expressions preserve its essential 'effective direction', a direction established by the ideologies to which these formulas properly belong, and from which they originate and derive their meaning. It is enough to observe what is being said and written today even in milieus that do not at all belong to the Left, and which claim to be a force of 'opposition', in order to

---

1   Most certainly a reference to Goethe's *Faust*, possibly to Wagner's warning to Faust in lines 1126–1129. Cf. 624–625 and 1428–1429.

realise how much they have lent themselves to this insidious game, and to the gradual and unnoticed surrender it entails.

Here I will limit myself to a couple of examples. With regard to 'reaction', I will not repeat what I have stated on many other occasions concerning some people's impudent attempt to turn the term 'reaction' into a synonym for abomination — as if, when certain parties 'act', others should refrain from reacting and instead turn the other cheek like good Christians and say 'Well done, keep it up!', thereby allowing legitimate self-defence to be labelled a 'provocation'. Biology and medicine teach us that when a tissue no longer 'reacts' to a stimulus, it is considered dead or nearly dead. This, unfortunately, might be the diagnosis of the current situation.

I have already discussed the myth of 'work' and the 'worker' in the previous pages. Another instance of stupid acquiescence is the acceptance of the leftists' appropriation of the term 'engagé'. The implication is that anyone who is not a leftist is not 'engagé' as a writer, intellectual or man of action, but is rather frivolous, superficial, irresolute, lacking in vigour, and with no real cause to defend. It seems as though this logical implication completely escapes those who nonetheless accept the equating of the terms 'engagé' and 'leftist'. Again, they allow themselves to be carried away by the current. It goes without saying that the opposite is true, i.e. that the only truly 'engagé' person is he who defends those higher ideals and transcendent aims that the the leftist rabble — intellectual or otherwise — covers with contempt and disrepute.

Other cases of intellectual surrender and cowardice ought to be noted with regard to the so-called 'meaning of history', understood in the subversive sense. Naturally, the current that has come to dominate recent history is, unfortunately, precisely the one highlighted by the progressive Left, but it must be interpreted differently. The direction and meaning of this current is one of collapse, of a gradual disintegration of every higher and legitimate order. Thus, as regards the concrete course of history, it is necessary to distinguish the description of events from their evaluation. Intellectual surrender occurs when one grants what exists the character of what should exist, of what is good, thereby stripping reaction of all moral justification. The origin of this deviation lies in Hegelian historicism, with its well-known identification of the real with the rational.[2] Now, regardless of the extent to which it is still possible to divert the process now underway, and even if this process were to prove irreversible, one should speak not of the meaning of history but of its meaninglessness, and one should categorically refuse to acknowledge this idol. Unfortunately, today an example of surrender comes even from above, from what according to some people is the highest positive spiritual authority in the West: the Catholic Church. By accepting the 'meaning of history', the Church is trying to bring itself up to date, to catch up with the times, to open itself up to the Left. Besides, there are some Catholics who have gone so far as to state that, ultimately, true Christianity today is alive and active precisely in democratic, Marxist, and even communist movements — hence the appearance of the so-called 'new priests' and, at a higher level, the formula of 'dialogue' with the kind of forces and ideologies that in his *Syllabus* Pope Pius IX had openly stigmatised and condemned.[3] The modernist Jesuit Teilhard de Chardin has already developed a doctrine serving as a framework for all this, a doctrine which is now

---

2   For Hegel, see note 28 to Chapter 5 above.

3   Reference to an annex to the encyclical *Quanta cura* (1864) of Pope Pius IX (1792–1878). The *Syllabus of Errors*, as it was called in its full title, lists eighty heresies or theological errors, and reads as a thoroughgoing condemnation of the humanism, liberalism, rationalism, communism, etc. which even in the Pope's day was gaining fast ground in all of Europe. The Pierre Teilhard de Chardin (1881–1955) mentioned in the next sentence was a French Jesuit priest and intellectual. He studied geology and paleontology (he was involved in the discovery of Peking man, an early human skeleton) and dedicated much of his academic work toward the synthesis of his scientific and religious beliefs. His works however have happily received no imprimatur.

in the course of being rehabilitated: he has more or less redefined the Christian idea of a providential direction of the course of history in terms of a progressive and linear evolutionism, encompassing science, technology, and social achievements. Naturally, one prefers to forget certain essential themes of the original Christian conception of history and of the times to come, a conception that is much less linear and which is far from offering a 'happy ending': the end times were spoken of in rather catastrophic and 'apocalyptic' terms, with the appearance of false prophets, the coming of Antichrist, the terrible Last Judgement, and the separation between the elect and the damned, rather than in terms of the universal redemption of an exclusively 'earthly' mankind through 'progress' and other such things. These themes found in early Christianity ultimately reflected some valid traditional teachings — all deformations and mythologisations aside.

Associated with the allegedly sacrosanct 'meaning of history', we find the term 'immobilism' in contemporary parlance, a term which is passively accepted in the negative sense it has acquired. To defend one's position is considered tantamount to 'immobilism', while changing one's position, naturally in the sense of following the lead of one's adversary, in such a way as to favour his action, is supposed to be the right thing to do. Leaving aside its crudest aspects, in its ultimate implication this position is also based on the myth of progress — as though any change, as such, necessarily meant something positive, a true advancement, an improvement. Bruce Marshall has aptly written: 'So-called backward [one might say immobilist'] societies are those that have the good sense to stop when they reach their destination, whereas progressive societies are those that are so blind that they pass it, rushing on madly.'[4] Generally speaking, one may refer here to what I already noted, with regard to a higher level, in Chapter 1: nowadays

---

4   Marshall (1899–1987) was a Scottish writer who wrote numerous books during the course of his life. I have been unable to source the present quotation.

no one seems to realise that there is such a thing as 'stability', which has nothing to do with immobility, and that one must absolutely oppose the conflation of the two. In political struggle, 'immobilism' is yet another bugbear associated with 'reaction'. Even men supposedly of the Right now accept this jargon and fear being accused of it. Moreover, should we be surprised at this, seeing that — as already stated — the Church itself is 'changing', no doubt fearing that otherwise it would be engulfed and displaced by the current of history, and deluding itself that flexibility and 'openness' can help it escape this possible fate?

Let us take another example: 'paternalism'. Here too we can note the acquiescence to the negative sense bestowed upon the term by the ideologies of subversion, while forgetting what this implies: the devaluation of the very concept of any family worthy of the name. Indeed, it is the very centre of the family that is devalued here: the authority and the natural and positive function of the father. The solicitude and care of the father, which is affectionate, of course, but also strict when necessary, his offering protection and granting things spontaneously, on the basis of personal relationships, with judiciousness and justice — all this, when transposed onto the social plane, is considered deplorable, intolerable, and injurious to the dignity of the 'working class'. The objective here is twofold: on the one hand, to undermine the traditional ideal of the family; on the other, to attack everything that in a normal society could have — and indeed once did have — a natural and organic, personal and 'human' character, as opposed to a state of latent civil war and a system of 'claims', which should ultimately be called by their true name: blackmail.

With regard to the acquiescence to new new 'trends' in language, one might refer, in passing, to a case that this time involves feminist 'claims', even though the particular domain here is rather banal. In Italy, it has become common to use masculine terms to refer to offices and professions performed by women. Some people no longer dare say *avvocatessa* [the feminine form of *avvocato*, 'lawyer'] instead of *avvocato* for a woman who exercises this profession, and the same is starting to happen with *dottore* [doctor], *ambasciatore* [ambassador], and so on. If the trend continues, even *maestra* [school mistress], *professoressa* [teacher/professor] and *poetessa* [poet] will be banned as injurious to the dignity of women.[5] The fact that this nonsense implies exactly the opposite of what people would like it to imply seems to escape women themselves. Indeed, women do not realise that in laying claim to the masculine form of these designations, what they attain is not equality (while remaining women), but the opposite, assimilation to man. It would be different if Italian had a neuter gender, in addition to the masculine and feminine ones, and all those terms could be used in the neuter rather than in the feminine form: only then would it be possible to emphasise activities and professions, the male prerogative to which one wishes to dispute. But what also plays a part in this silly new trend is the influence that people unwittingly undergo from the English language, which lacks a feminine form for many professions and occupations, making it necessary to add 'lady', or similar expressions, to 'doctor', 'secretary', 'barrister', etc.; by contrast, Italian almost always has a feminine form (*dottoressa*, *segretaria*, *avvocatessa*, *poetessa*, etc.), and there is no reason not to use such forms, other than complying with a silly democratic and egalitarian infatuation.

Here one should also blame the surrender and acquiescence of most men, who ought to have ridiculed this new jargon, along with many other recent 'achievements'. As for those women who, evidently

---

5   It might be of interest to the reader to learn that in the present climate this absurdity has taken precisely the opposite form as it did in Evola's day. Many professions in Italian are naturally masculine, as for instance *ministro* and *deputato*; recently an attempt has been made to arbitrarily invent a 'feminine form' for these by substituting the final 'o' with an 'a'. This has been much more powerfully resisted here in Italy than the analogous (and analogously absurd) alterations which are even now so offensively being foisted onto English pronouns.

ashamed of being women, encourage the application of this linguistic distortion, they should in a normal society be entrusted to specialists in diabolical hormonal manipulations, so that through adequate treatment they could be transformed into exponents of the 'third sex', thus fulfilling their aspirations on every level. However, to be fair, one wonders whether such treatment would not be appropriate also for men whenever the aforementioned acquiescence is due not so much to the subtle influences of the environment and to the unconscious processes that operate on the sub-intellectual part of the psyche of the ordinary man, but rather to an inability to react and to demonstrate true virility through moral courage and lucid, resolute judgement.

2

A qualified exponent of traditional thought, F. Schuon, has coined the expression 'intelligent stupidity' (though G. Bernanos had already used a similar expression, *l'intelligence des sots*, while another Frenchman had written: *Le drame de notre temps, c'est que la bêtise se soit mise à penser*).[6] Schuon used this expression to describe the nature of the kind of intellectuality that has come to predominate in broad sectors of modern culture and which is widely represented in Italy. This kind of intellectuality thrives in particular in journalism — that calamity of our times — and essay writing. One of its main channels by which it spreads is the 'cultural pages' of leading newspapers, since it is chiefly practised in the field of so-called 'criticism'.

The main feature of this kind of intellectuality is its lack of principles, higher interests, and any genuine commitment, and its concern with 'brilliance' and 'originality', along with an emphasis on professional 'fine writing', form rather than substance, and *esprit*

---

6   For Schuon, see note 5 to Chapter 4. For Bernanos, see note 1 to Chapter 1. The last quotation is from Jean Cocteau, and means: 'The tragedy of our times is that foolishness has started thinking'.

in the frivolous and mundane meaning the French give to this term. For the representatives of this 'intellectuality', brilliant phrases and impressive dialectical and polemical positions are far more important than the truth. If ideas are drawn upon at all, it is only as a pretext: what matters is to stand out, to appear very intelligent — just as for the petty politicians of today a party ideology is simply a means for advancement. Thus the 'vanity fair', the worst kind of subjectivism, or indeed narcissism, is an essential aspect of this phenomenon. This aspect becomes particularly noticeable when these intellectual cliques take on a mundane veneer (as in the case of 'salons' and cultural associations). It is not far off the mark to say that, of all possible kinds of stupidity, the most annoying one is that of intelligent people. When, upon an in-depth analysis of a person, what emerges is a nonentity, it would be better for there not to be any intelligence. But the question cannot be reduced to the annoying nature of this sort of people: one must also take into account their harmfulness, insofar as 'intelligent stupidity' — particularly in contemporary Italy — is highly organised: it is a sort of freemasonry, variously structured, which holds all key positions in advertising, wherever these are not already presided over and controlled by leftists. Its representatives immediately sense and ostracise anyone who has a different nature. Let us take a trivial yet telling example from today. There is a group gravitating around a rather widespread and well-made magazine which purports to be nonconformist and readily criticises the current political regime and social mores. Yet this group has made sure not to establish any contact with those few authors who could provide a positive foundation for it today — if it were earnest in its task — as far as principles and the traditional view of the world are concerned.[7] The group in question

---

7   [The Italian editor provides the following note. —*Ed.*] The magazine referred to
     is *Il Borghese*, which up until the mid-1970s was the most widespread right-wing
     periodical. On account of the cultural-political background of its editors and
     chief columnists, the magazine always ignored the 'traditional Right', including

ignores, or indeed ostracises, these authors every bit as much as the press from the opposite side of the political spectrum, precisely because the group can sense that they are of a different ilk. This clearly shows that this brilliant nonconformism is only a way to show off and 'stand out', since everything remains on an amateurish level. Besides, the founder of the magazine, who passed away a few years ago,[8] once unequivocally stated that if a different regime were en force today, he would probably switch sides, in order to be able to continue to be part of the 'opposition' — evidently, always with the aim of 'standing out' and showing his 'intelligence'. By contrast, the group I was mentioning has readily come to accept some individuals who initially displayed a certain awareness of higher values and ideas, only to then brush them aside. These people marketed their writing skills and, by foregoing any intransigence, easily fell in line with this 'intelligent stupidity', which can only make an impression on the spiritually inexperienced and provincial.

There is no need to point out that the counterpart to 'intelligent stupidity' is the almost invariable lack of character on the part of those who embody it. This is evident, in particular, whenever such people were politically active in the bygone years, in the previous period: opportunism and a chameleon-like adaptability are recurrent traits of theirs, since in the past they were Fascists out of self-interest, while today they claim to be anti-Fascists, when they should have the decency to keep silent and not touch upon such subjects.

Julius Evola. This attitude changed with the 'student protests' that broke out in Italy, as in other countries: Evola was asked to write about the subject and published a dozen articles in the years 1968–9, some of which were reprinted as an appendix to *Men among the Ruins*. Evola then continued his collaboration with the monthly magazine *Il Conciliatore*, after it became associated with *Il Borghese*.

8 [The Italian editor provides the following note. —*Ed.*] The reference here is to Leo Longanesi (1905–1957), who founded the magazine in 1950.

I have already mentioned the fact that 'criticism' is one of the main provinces of intelligent stupidity: it is in this sphere that its most pernicious varieties prosper. Here, as we shall see, it is possible to refer to what I have already argued at the beginning of this chapter with regard to the role played today by the vulnerability to certain environmental influences. There would be much to say on this topic. Generally speaking, 'criticism' should be seen as one of the scourges of modern culture, a scourge that has taken shape in bourgeois society in parallel to the 'news press' and the commercialisation of culture. Today the phenomenon has spread like a cancer: in any normal, traditional, society there was essentially no such thing as 'criticism'. Civilisations of this sort had creators and artists, and people who judged or appreciated their work directly, with no intermediaries: sovereigns, patrons, and common folk. By contrast, nowadays the 'critic' has sneaked in between the public and the creators like a petulant and presumptuous parasite.

By this I do not mean to say that all judgement about artistic works should be ruled out. However, I believe that, if judgement is to be passed, it should be formulated from a higher point of view, by those who are vested with the authority bestowed by true principles and a tradition: that is to say, by the kind of people who are practically non-existent nowadays and who in any case, even if they were to be found, would be given little voice. *Pace* those who defend the theory of *l'art pour l'art*, and despite Croce's horror for any judgement not focusing merely on the forms of expression to be found in a given work, judgements of such kind would in any case be formulated from a higher level than that of art:[9] they would be value judgements concerning the

---

9   *L'art pour l'art* means literally 'art for art', that is 'art for art's sake', and refers to an aesthetic theory which gained some currency in the nineteenth century, according to which art should exist only for itself, rather than for any kind of moral, didactic, social, or pragmatic function. This phrase or others like it appear in the work of numerous artists, from Poe to Stefan George; perhaps the most concise and elegant statement of the 'philosophy' behind it is to be found

meaning of this or that work within the overall context of a civilisation, and not in a separate domain, which is to say on the merely aesthetic level.

Far removed from all this, contemporary 'criticism' is condemned to pure subjectivism, which is to say arbitrariness. Often today it is critics themselves who manipulate values according to 'intelligent stupidity', inventing them where they do not exist, or concealing them where they do — calling the shots one way or another. As for the public, what we find here once again, if only in another form, is the passiveness and impressionability typical of our contemporaries (who, according to the democratic fad, have become 'adults') — as discussed in the previous pages. Indeed, a situation similar to the one we find in the field of advertising and propaganda is taking shape in the artistic and intellectual field. New moments of fame and new masterpieces are emerging, with *battages* giving rise to new vogues and trends. Hence, this particular public confirms what has been stated with regard to trend followers in general: they are ridiculous out of fear of appearing ridiculous. They undergo certain influences, and do not dare to openly express their thoughts and feelings out of fear that, should they pass judgement on one or the other work of contemporary art or literature, they will be labelled clueless amateurs by the high priests of 'criticism' — a field in which polemical divergences essentially make no difference, but only serve to make the offering more palatable, by increasing people's interest.

The same applies to many authors who, thanks to 'criticism', are now en vogue, including Nobel laureates and best-selling authors. Their insignificance would become quite evident if only people had a free spirit, possessed some serious, higher points of reference, and de-

---

in Oscar Wilde's Preface to *The Picture of Dorian Gray*. Given Evola's closing to this chapter, it is not irrelevant to remind that Wilde was a homosexual — one who belonged, surely, to the 'third sex' of which Evola speaks in Chapter 3. For Benedetto Croce, see note 11 to Chapter 7.

nied right from the start any authority to the high priests of 'criticism'. As far as clothing and personal appearances are concerned, passively and uncritically following the latest fashion — i.e. some new trend concocted by a nobody in some capital or other — must be regarded as an essentially feminine characteristic. As the phenomenon presents much the same traits in the artistic and literary domains, this confirms, from yet another perspective, the mindset that has come to dominate broad strata of the so-called cultured public of today, leaving aside the manifestations of the phenomenon in the spheres of everyday life and politics. Once gain, this is a sign of the times.

15. THE MYTH OF EAST AND WEST AND THE 'MEETING OF RELIGIONS'

1

I t goes without saying that with the following short remarks I do not claim to embark on any in-depth study of such a complex topic as the one indicated in the title. I will only provide some observations on certain aspects of the problem, which I will investigate more at length in the second part of the chapter, in order to further clarify the point I made on religion being one traditional form to be distinguished from other traditional forms.

In referring to East and West, I have spoken of 'myth': this term is to be understood in two senses, a negative one ('myth' as that which has no real content) and one that is at least partly positive ('myth' as a guiding idea). Naturally, it is necessary to examine the relations between East and West as civilisations and general spiritual orientations. However, the problem of such relations in our day seems increasingly destined to lose its relevance. Indeed, if we identify the West with that modern civilisation which essentially emerged in Europe (America only serving as a kind of appendix, insofar as it presents itself as the extreme, monstrous development of various aspects of the last European civilisation),[1] along with the general world-view, mores, interests and

---

1   The Italian editor supplies the following reference here: *Revolt against the Modern World*, Part 2, § 16.

socio-political forms associated with this civilisation, it is clear that the increasing modernisation of the East will progressively reduce these differences. They might become limited in the East to residual elements which can no longer be regarded as genuine traditional and formative forces.

It is ironic to think that until recently people were speaking of an Eastern threat to the West. They ought on the contrary to have spoken of the peril which the West represented for the East, a peril that fully manifested itself especially — and precisely — the moment the East emancipated itself materially and politically, and cast off the more or less colonialist tutelage of the West, only to passively be seduced and influenced by modern Western civilisation, foolishly adopting its values and its very concept of civilisation, thereby betraying or casting aside its own traditions.[2] The only example of a miraculous balance between one's own tradition and outer modernisation (i.e. Westernisation), namely Japan, already belongs to the past. After the catastrophe of the Second World War, this balance was broken and the all-out Westernisation of democraticised Japan is in full swing, in all domains. The counterpart to this is Communist China, which has erased thousands of years of history with a staggering speed. If we still wished to speak of an 'Asiatic peril', this could only refer to the possible danger represented by masses that have assimilated the forms of organisation, technological and industrial structures, and means to power developed by Westerners (since the latter, in the name of the 'universality of science', have irresponsibly made such things available to everyone, instead of reserving and preserving them for themselves, as a monopoly whose secrets are to be jealously guarded). These Asian masses might bring their full weight to bear on world politics and

---

2   [Evola's note. —Ed.] One should also note the attempt made by certain 'progressive' milieus in the East to promote traditions such as Buddhism (in Communist China) and Islam in a Marxist, which is to say subversive, sense, based on the claim that these two traditions advocate a classless and casteless society.

on the so-called 'course of history'. But on this level, qualitative and spiritual antitheses no longer apply; all that would remain are brute power relations.

Hence, in the present context and for the foreseeable future, we can only speak of a 'myth' of East and West in the negative sense of the term, whereby myth signifies a formula with no actual content. The considerations offered some time ago by René Guénon in his book *East and West* and, to a lesser degree, in *The Crisis of the Modern World* — texts already compromised by their evident one-sidedness — may be regarded as outdated.[3] The same applies to the one-sided thesis of the opposition between 'Eastern spirituality' and 'Western materialism', which has as its corollary the claim that the West should turn to the East to find the points of reference required for a rectification and reintegration of its own civilisation. By now this could only be meaningful retrospectively, in relation to an abstract East, with reference to the lore transmitted by those of its texts which pertain to traditional doctrines, wisdom, metaphysics and high ascesis. In the East some centres may well exist that continue to preserve this heritage in a living and genuine way. However, the course of events has forced them to become increasingly withdrawn and closed off, so that they no longer play any decisive role with respect to the historical forces that are now shaping the East. Besides, if we were to refer to those Easterners who in recent times have presented themselves as exponents and exporters of Eastern spirituality in the West, more or less on the margins of 'neo-spiritualism', their intellectual level — generally speaking — is such that it can only discredit their tradition and

---

3   References to two important works of René Guénon. The first offers a comparison of the East and the West, which concludes with a round castigation of what has become of the West, and urges a re-orientation of the West on the basis of Eastern principles. The second is a thorough critique of the modern West on the basis of the principles of the Tradition. See note 16 to Chapter 7 for more on Guénon, as well as the related passage.

seriously embarrass those Westerners who, having turned to original, authentic sources, have come to understand and appreciate Eastern spirituality and metaphysics.

On the other hand, the considerations put forward by Guénon in the aforementioned works could have been particularly significant on the level of a morphology of civilisations. Yet, on such a level the antithesis between East and West has from a historical perspective become relative. What Guénon had in mind was the East as an example of a 'traditional' civilisation, which is to say a civilisation in which all the main aspects of existence are oriented from above and upwards. India and part of the Islamic world in particular offered prime examples of this up until recently. But it is evident that the problem or antithesis comes to be redefined in this way: what one means by the West is actually only the modern West; hence, the opposition no longer concerns East and West, but modern civilisation and traditional civilisation. In historical terms, traditional civilisation cannot be described as either Eastern or Western. The medieval Europe of the Holy Roman Empire, medieval Christendom, was equally 'traditional', as was Rome, a centre of gravity and organising force in the West. The argument becomes, then, that in the context of a global civilisation the traditional orientation endured more, and with more complete expressions, in the East. However, it may be that in Asia everything will soon be reduced to distorted, folk residues, not unlike those that are still to be found today in certain 'underdeveloped' pockets of Europe, particularly in the South, where a traditional religiosity is combined with superstitions and a strong attachment to a non-'modernised' and rather primitive lifestyle.

Leaving aside the level of factuality and of current events, the term 'myth' — as already noted — can have another meaning in relation to East and West, pertaining to two universal ideas and symbols. At this higher level many investigations have been conducted on very treacherous terrain, and the one-sidedness of many of their assumptions is evident. The limits of an inferior and amateurish thought are illustrated by those intellectuals who have identified the West with Latin Catholicism. This, for instance, is the thesis put forward by Henri Massis in two of his books, *La défense de l'Occident* and *L'Occident et son destin*.[4] It is amazing that such books have received any consideration at all. Strictly speaking, the whole of non-Latin and non-Catholic Europe according to this thesis is not 'Western'. Indeed, Massis goes so far as to state that 'Germanicness and Slavicness are the two springs nourishing everything which constitutes a revolt against the West', adding that they bring back to life 'the old Asian heresies'. I have already referred to the analogous theses advanced by Manacorda (Ch. 13). Catholicism allows him to use Rome and Romanness as mystifying alibis: no attempt is made to establish the nature of the actual relations between Latinness and Romanness; and since (Latin) Catholicism is still Christian despite being 'Roman', it would be necessary to show that Christianity is conceivable without Judaism, without the legacy of a tradition which is Semitic rather than Western in its innermost spirit. The fact that Christianity has become the dominant religion in the West cannot change this. Looking back at the origins of Christianity, it is clear that it could never have taken root in the Roman world if the ground had not already been laid by Asiaticisation and inner dissolution. On the other hand, leaving aside the (often essential) rectification that Christianity underwent in order to establish itself in Europe, particularly after the appearance of the Germanic peoples on the stage of the great history of our continent, through various compromises and unstable combinations — and leaving aside too all mere superstructures — the predominance of Christianity in itself tells us nothing about the problem of values.

One of the less extremist theses used to build the myth of the West combines the Judaeo-Christian tradition with the Roman element and the Greek heritage. This combination is just as problematic and

---

4   For Massis, see note 7 to Chapter 13.

precarious. If one wishes to rigorously examine it, it is necessary to analyse its various components. Finally, one should not not forget that Christianity by now has ceased to be what for a rather long time it was — de facto if not explicitly: namely the religion brought by Europe, by the White European race; a religion frequently used to assert its hegemony, or even its colonialist purposes. In the face of the remarkable disintegration that is affecting Catholicism in particular in our days, with the extensive presence of people of colour in its highest echelons and its pseudo-ecumenism (to which we shall soon return), the 'universalist' character of the Christian faith has resurfaced. In keeping with this character, Christianity originally proposed to make no distinctions between peoples, between Roman and Hebrew, Hebrew and barbarian, but indiscriminately addressed all men. In view of this, it is not clear on what grounds one can affirm the 'Westernness' of Christianity and Catholicism, if not by assuming that its adoption amounts to a distortion of the nature of non-Westerners, who somehow become Westerners through their conversion. And the assumption here is always that it is possible to doctrinally prove the actual Westernness of Christianity as such. I will be discussing the arguments drawn from theism, pantheism and monism in support of the East-West opposition later on.

If we wish to consider the issue of origins, there is another consideration to be made, precisely in relation to those of Christianity. Whether we like it or not, the ideas of East and West have spatial and geographical implications (in this respect, it would be more appropriate to speak of Europe and Asia). If, however, we take not the geographical position of the two continents but their peoples and races as an essential basis, the opposition between East and West once again becomes an ambiguous one: for as a fundamental point of reference we ought to take the overall cycle of Indo-European civilisations, a cycle which has extended across Europe but also across part of Asia, which is to say the East. From this perspective, the opposition to be taken into account would be a different one — namely that standing between those general views of the world and of sacredness, ethical values, laws and customs, and so on, which have an Indo-European character, and other views and conceptions which have a non-Indo-European character, in Asia as much as in Europe. In the light of this criterion, it becomes evident just how precarious the definition of the myth of the West is when it is based on the mingling of the Judaeo-Christian tradition with the Roman and Greek components, since the former is foreign to that ideal Indo-European world which instead encompasses the other two components. It would be possible to point to further discrepancies, aside from the geographical opposition between East and West. For instance, Buddhism originally had a perfectly Indo-European character, a character that the Semitic roots of Christianity completely lack.[5] Thus the issue of race adds to the complexity of the problem and of the definition of the 'myth' of East and West.

I will refer in passing, chiefly for the sake of curiosity, to a thesis that the champions of the West and of Christianity might be tempted to adduce in support of their cause. This thesis has best been formulated by a well-known theologian, Romano Guardini.[6] The starting point is the idea that as a 'saviour' Christ was the first to break the cycle of nature and to release man from its bonds. By virtue of Christ's redemption, man freed himself from this cycle and acquired a detached superiority that constituted the precondition for acquiring knowledge of nature

---

5   The Italian editor here references *The Doctrine of Awakening*.

6   Guardini (1885–1968) was a priest and author whose work had a great influence on the intellectual strata of Catholicism in the last century. Though born in Italy, he lived nearly his entire life in Germany, and he wrote in German. His *Spirit of the Liturgy* had some effect on Vatican II, while others of his works included explorations of philosophy from a modern standpoint. Evola here offers the following reference: R. Guardini, *Der Heilbringer im Mythos, Offenbarung und Geschichte*, Zürich, 1946, which does not appear to have been translated into English.

and dominating it — something which in the 'natural' development of humanity would never have been possible without the new and unrepeatable event of redemption. The paradoxical outcome of this thesis is the bridging of Christianity and the world of positivist science, nature and modern technology: the two elements are viewed not in terms of an opposition, but in terms of a causal relation. This is but one example of the kind of absurdities one runs into when, instead of preserving the dogma of a particular faith within its valid limits, defined by its 'internal use', one experiences it as a fixed idea that inhibits any objectiveness and clarity of thought.

As a premise, Guardini has set the idea of the unique and unrepeatable burst of true transcendence into the world (with the incarnation of the 'Son of God') in contrast to the 'cyclical' conception. In the text to which I am referring, the author is forced to acknowledge that the non-Christian world too has its 'saviours', divine figures showing man the path to spiritual rebirth. However, in his view these are figures who fall within the cycle of nature, which experiences birth and death, ascent and descent, and which repeats itself in man and on the spiritual level. It is according to this perspective that one should consider 'solar' gods like Osiris, Mithras, Dionysus, and Baldur (it is evident how close this idea is to the notorious 'agricultural' interpretations of these deities as 'spirits of vegetation', and so on).[7] They would thus fall within the circle of nature and the liberation announced or provided

---

7   For Osiris, see footnote 30 to Chapter 11, and for Dionysus, note 32 to Chapter 13. Mithras was originally a Persian god, Mithra, but made an important entrance into Roman society somewhere around the first century AD. His cult included a complex initiation rite redolent with symbolism which Evola discusses at some length in Chapter 17 of *Recognitions*. The worship of Mithras became enormously popular in the first several centuries after Christ, and the god was long regarded as the Empire's defender. His role was so central to Roman society that some authors have speculated that Mithras, and not Christ, might have become the official deity of the Roman Empire — a most suggestive 'alternative history' which truly makes one contemplate what might have been. Baldur is one of the

by them would be a relative one, a mere foreshadowing of the absolute liberation of Christ, which is associated with true transcendence. For the sake of his strategy, Guardini has coined the term *innerweltlich*, meaning internal to the world, worldly, as opposed to *überweltlich*, supra-worldly: in the first category (that of *innerweltlich*) he includes all non-Christian forms of 'redemption', of *Erlösung*. He thus speaks of an *innerweltlich Lösungen des Lebens aus der Fessel des Todes*, which is to say of an 'inner-wordly' release of life from the bonds of death (opposed to the 'supra-worldly' release): an obviously contrived and inconsistent concept. Here I will only note that both the non-Christian West and the East were familiar with the idea of this 'circle' and that in the East, especially with Hinduism, it was seen to include various subordinate, theistic and 'non-supreme' deities; yet beyond this circle, and indeed precisely in opposition to it, they conceived the notion of transcendence. There is nothing more absolute, for instance, than the ideal of transcendence and of the deconditioning of being conceived and realised by early Buddhism, just as ancient Greece conceived both of a turning away from the 'cycle of generation' or 'necessity', which is to say nature, and also of an impulse to transcend it.[8] Guardini's

---

Norse Æsir; he is the god of light and the sun, whose death would be one of the harbingers of the coming of ragnarök.

8   [Evola's note. —*Ed.*] It is extremely important to bear in mind that the symbolism of the circle may be interpreted in two distinct, or indeed opposite, ways. On the one hand, the circle may symbolise the irrelevance of life, the eternal return of the same situations in different guises whenever one is subject to the bonds of nature — thus in Hinduism *samsara*, the current of conditioned forms, of endless becoming and perishing, has often been presented as a circle. Another image used is that of an animal tied to a central pole and eternally going round it, without ever realising it. But a different interpretation is equally possible: the circle may symbolise victory over becoming, over this indefinite and boundless flow, which is checked and brought back to its origin — I have already mentioned this interpretation when discussing the 'civilisation of space' (Ch. 1). The circle then becomes — to borrow a Platonic expression — the 'mov-

theory, then, is only one example of the kind of apologetic, sophistic manipulations that distort the truth. It certainly does not do justice to the scholarly earnestness of a theologian who, in other respects, is far from being an amateur.

Getting back to our main topic, which pertains to the West, if one wishes to characterise Christianity as a doctrine of transcendence absolutely opposed to 'nature' (a claim that is not wholly legitimate from a historical perspective, since one should then exclude Thomism, for instance, with its use of Aristotelianism and its attempt to view nature in relation to a divine and rational order which is not opposed to the supra-natural one of revelation),[9] strictly speaking, one would have to associate Christianity only with the inferior aspects of modern Western civilisation. The revulsion towards and violent detachment from nature leads to its desecration, to the destruction of the organic conception of the world as a cosmos, as an order of forms reflecting a higher meaning, as the 'visible manifestation of the invisible' — a conception (of Indo-European origin) which is an integral part of the Classical view of the world and which also lies at the basis of various

---

ing image of eternity': by contrast to the insignificance of the mere flowing and becoming in a linear and irreversible direction, it 'eternalises itself' at each individual moment. This is what Nietzsche poetically grasped when speaking of the 'great midday' and of the circle, at each moment of which we find 'being', that which transcends time. On the doctrine of absolute transcendence in early Buddhism, see J. Evola, *The Doctrine of Awakening*.

9   Thomism is the doctrine of St. Thomas Aquinas. Evola's point here is both interesting and valid, though it might be considered in a different light: Aquinas attempted a reconciliation between classical philosophy and Christian faith which could not help but result in tension on both sides; on the philosophical, insofar as philosophy must eternally chafe at being the 'handmaiden to faith', and on the Christian-theological, insofar as Christian theology might in all its 'otherworldiness' find itself acknowledging aspects of the existent natural world which have the power to chain or bind it — the problem that Evola here indicates.

forms of knowledge of a different sort compared to profane, modern science. Nature has thus become detached and soulless, a sum of mere 'phenomena' — the very phenomena which are the exclusive focus of modern science and technology. The counterpart to this is an abstract 'inwardness' or spirituality, the 'subjectivity' which according to a certain neo-Hegelian philosophy of history was 'discovered' by Christianity and which stands in dialectical opposition to the previous ancient spirituality or civilisation, which was marked by 'objectiveness' (another fanciful digression). Actually, what stands under the sign of this 'providential' dualism is only the split structure of the last man, who with his 'subjectivity' moves through the diabolical world of devices he has created as a 'sovereign', ultimately becoming trapped in a process that has become almost independent and which drags him further and further away. If anything, this is what may be inferred from Guardini's thesis of the Christian foundations of science and technology in the modern world, which is to say in the modern West.[10]

Besides, already in Hegel's philosophy of history we find an idea that agrees with Guardini's theory and which occurs, with some variations, in many of the authors who have spoken of an opposition between East and West.[11] According to Hegel, the experience of nature as such is still foreign to the East: nature is not yet perceived as a reality; it is simply *māyā*, something which lacks autonomous existence.[12]

---

10 [Evola's note. —*Ed.*] The emergence of exterior science and technology from the distinctive character of the Christian doctrine of transcendence and its original dualism is something that I had sought to illustrate — many years before the publication of the aforementioned work by Guardini and within the framework of a contingent, extremist position— in *Imperialismo pagano* [*Pagan Imperialism*] (Atanòr, Todi-Rome, 1928).

11 For Hegel, see note 28 to Chapter 5 above.

12 The word *maya* literally means 'illusion', also 'magic', and is used to describe what Western philosophy might term the 'world of becoming' — the grand pageant of phenomena which confronts us in our common experience, and which seems characterised fundamentally by change and transience; hence the

Between spirit and nature there is a sort of promiscuity; hence, in man we find a sort of dreamy consciousness which cannot yet be described as genuine self-consciousness (this being the 'in-itself' stage or stage of mere 'being' of the Absolute Spirit in universal history). In order to attain self-consciousness, what is required is the contrast between the I and nature. In addition to this, some have spoken of a nostalgia for a lost spiritual world, the world of the One-All, the obscuring of which afflicts us (hence the meaning of *māyā* as deceptive illusion), associated with the theme of withdrawal from the world, of pure, formless ascetic liberation. We shall soon see what can be gathered from this thesis. In passing, I should mention that alongside this theory of the Eastern 'dreamy consciousness' and of a self-conscious and free personality that is foreign to the East, some people have added the fanciful notion of Christian supremacy, which they even seek to affirm in the initiatory field. Merely to give an example — for fancies of this sort hardly deserve much mention — I will note that Rudolf Steiner, the creator of 'anthroposophy', a variant of contemporary theosophism, went so far as to claim that the East never experienced a truly conscious form of initiation, which only became possible — as a 'modern' and 'individual initiation' — after the advent of Christ; the latter, becoming man through incarnation, revealed 'the I', something unknown to the dreamy Eastern consciousness.[13]

---

illusory character ascribed to it by certain Eastern doctrines. The idea of nature (see note 7 to Chapter 11 above) is indeed characteristic of Western philosophy, and though certain rough parallels might be found in other traditions, it is arguably unique to the Occident.

13 The Austrian Steiner (1861–1925) was much involved in a number of those 'spiritual movements' which Evola, in various places throughout his oeuvre, takes to task. As Evola notes here, he was the founder of the awkwardly named 'anthroposophy' (which is supposed to mean 'human wisdom' or else 'knowledge of the nature of man') — the same anthroposophy which Evola mentions in dismissive passing in Chapter 11 (see the passage connected to note 1 of that chapter).

All this nonsense aside, the underlying motif also resurfaces in the thesis of those who assign pure spirituality to the East and a concrete knowledge of nature to the West, and who look forward to the 'happy ending' of a future synthesis between the two, not realising that a synthesis of this sort has already been achieved in the only conceivable form within the framework of the world-view of every 'traditional' civilisation. I say 'in the only conceivable form' because otherwise such a synthesis becomes a mere fancy, insofar as the concrete knowledge of nature, i.e. the kind of knowledge which distinguishes positive and profane Western science, presupposes a well-defined philosophy and world-view, a specific intellectual and methodological orientation within a self-enclosed system where true spirituality would only represent a nuisance, a profoundly disturbing element — if it were given any attention at all. The world of modern science strictly maintains the character of a non-I, of an external reality that can only be perceived through the 'phenomena' grasped by the physical senses and their extensions (i.e. scientific instruments), simply in order to be translated into handy algebraic formulas and laws of a merely statistical sort. 'Spirituality' cannot be added to such world to create a 'synthesis', but can only be superimposed as something detached and more or less unrealistic: precisely as in the case of certain scientists and, more generally, of those modern Westerners who are not entirely atheist, but who combine an absolutely secular and profane kind of knowledge which serves essentially practical purposes with the world of faith and devotion which distinguishes mere religion, or with some vague form of spiritualism.

As regards the 'dreamy consciousness' of the East and the idea of the world as *māyā*, it must be noted that references of this sort can only concern, at most, a part of India, and not the East in general. In relation to India, they exclusively apply to extreme and 'illusionistic' forms of Vedanta (and Nagarjuna's doctrine, which was influenced by it), which in any case are only imperfectly understood by the aforementioned authors.[14] In the *Veda*, a tradition of Indo-Aryan origin, nothing of the sort is to be found and one cannot speak of a consciousness that 'is ignorant of nature' at all; instead, what we have is a hymnic and evocative glorification of the divine powers at work in the universe. Samkhya, another Hindu spiritual current, affirms a clear-cut dualism between the spirit, *purusha*, conceived in terms of a detached sovereignty opposed to 'nature', as the male principle opposed to the female one, in a way that is often reminiscent of Aristotelianism.[15] Moreover, it is worth mentioning Tantric theory, another Hindu current, which is distinguished by a metaphysics based on the 'active Brahman', on 'power', *shakti*.[16] This as far as India is concerned. But there is more to the East than India (with its variety of spiritual forms just outlined). The East also includes Iran, whose ancient religion had an essentially active and warrior character; China, whose metaphysical tradition revolves around the notion of the Tao as an 'immanent transcendence' with no dreamy or escapist overtones;[17] Japan, whose religiosity is associated with an equally active and concrete Spirit — and so on, down to the remnants of traditions of Hyperborean origin to be found, if only in incomplete and obscured forms, in central and central-northern Asia. This variety of forms explodes the tendentious myth of the East I have

---

14   Vedanta is one of the six schools of Hinduism, which takes its bearings by the ancient Sanskrit writings known as the *Upanishads* or *Vedānta*, the most generally known part of the wider body of *Vedas* that Evola mentions in the following sentence. Nāgārjuna (c. 150-c. 250) was a teacher of Mahāyāna Buddhism, whose thought insisted on the radical emptiness or non-existence of phenomena.

15   Samkhya is another of the six schools of Hinduism which, put into Western terms (recognising, naturally, the limitations implied by this), tended to rely on logic and rational demonstrations as the basis for its doctrines. The opposition to which Evola refers is between *purusha* (spirit, awareness, consciousness) and *prakrti* (matter, the stuff of which phenomena are made). For more on this distinction, see note 8 to Chapter 12 above, as well as the connected passage.

16   For Tantra, see note 22 to Chapter 11 above. For the Shakti, see Chapter 12.

17   For Taoism, see note 14 to Chapter 11.

just mentioned ('dreamy consciousness', pantheistic escapism, etc.). Those who have formulated this myth have displayed a one-sidedness that reflects an unbelievable degree of ignorance — unless we are to assume that a sort of spiritual blindness is at work, which prevented them from seeing what they do not wish to see; for otherwise the irrational impulse that governed them would be blocked.

Are we, then, to draw a negative balance at the end of our analysis of the consistency of the myth of East and West, even leaving aside the orientations that have de facto increasingly come to dominate the swiftly modernising West?

One of the themes that some people have sought to bring into play in this context is the dualism between action and contemplation. Guénon himself referred to it. The East would chiefly stand under the sign of contemplation, the West under that of action. This too is a somewhat one-sided thesis, because — as I have just recalled — the East also encompasses the Iranian and Japanese civilisations, both of which are essentially oriented towards action. By contrast, if one were to insist on defining the West with reference to Christianity, it is indisputable that in the best aspects of this religion the contemplative life is predominant over the active life. There is also one curious saying, whose origin I have not been able to ascertain: *Ex Oriente lux, ex Occidente dux*.[18] This would partly be associated with the same sort of ideas; perhaps the reference is to Rome or to the medieval Holy Roman Empire (in relation to which Dante evoked precisely the

---

18   Latin: 'From the East the light, from the West a leader'. The first part of this expression appears to have been a common saying both during the Middle Ages and perhaps also during the time of the Romans; it might have originated simply in recognition of the direction in which the sun rises, though it indubitably came later to have a deeper significance. The phrase has had several variants, including, in the Middle Ages, *Ex Oriente lux, ex Occidente lex* — 'From the East the light, from the West the law'.

figure of the DVX),[19] according to its universal ordering function, with a clear emphasis on action and on a warrior tradition.[20] Here too, however, some conditions apply, because it is necessary to bear in mind that the imperial idea is attested in the East itself, for instance in Iran and China, as well as in India — although the latter did not historically achieve it, it was familiar with the ideal of the *Chakravarti*, or Universal Sovereign.[21] Nevertheless, this context is perhaps the only one that can suggest a basis — however relative — to distinguish the two fundamental orientations.

As our starting point we can take the world-view of those who have attributed to the East a dreamy consciousness and an impulse towards evasiveness, a tendency to flee the world. I have already noted that in this respect one should not speak of the East as a whole, but at most of one of the spiritual currents of India, namely Vedantic monism, chiefly embodied by Shankara. The essence of this doctrine is that Brahman, the Principle, which is everything and 'without a second', is immutable and immobile, does not act, and has no determinations (*Nirguna-Brahman*). It remains such even in its manifestation, in the

---

19   Reference to the *Divina Commedia* of the divine poet Dante Alighieri (c. 1265–1321). The passage in question is found in Canto XXXIII of the *Purgatorio*, lines 40–45, in which Dante makes characteristically eliptical reference to the renewal of the Holy Roman Empire and the coming of a 'five hundred ten and five', which in Roman numerals would be DXV; rearranged, this makes DVX, *dux*.

20   [Evola's note. —*Ed.*] An acquaintance of mine has ironically changed the saying *Ex Oriente lux, ex Occidente dux* into *Occidente crux* ['in the Occident the cross'], on account of the calamity that the West (understood as the modern world) has brought upon the East. As for *Ex Oriente lux*, this formula is valid up to a point if we go back in time, insofar as the Indo-European civilisations of the East were created by waves of people of western and north-western origin, i.e. *ex Occidente*.

21   The word comes from Sanskrit, and indicates a ruler who, beyond being universal, is also benevolent and just.

unfolding of the universe, which, compared to Brahman, is 'strictly nothing': it is a 'modification' that in no way alters Brahman. The latter encompasses all possibilities: manifestation is but an accidental fact that actualises some of them. Yet, strictly speaking, as particular determinations these possibilities represent a negation of the perfect totality of the Principle (the same view is expressed by the famous axiom of Spinoza's monism: *omnis determinatio negatio est*).[22] Furthermore, the same transition from potency to act in these possibilities, which gives rise to the universe, can only be regarded as a development or movement when it is considered from the outside, from the perspective of manifestation: for, otherwise, one cannot speak of movement or development. Hence, only from the point of view of man, who is confined within manifestation, can the latter appear real in all its processes, determinations and transformations. Metaphysically, this is an illusion: it is *māyā*, the effect of a primordial ignorance, *avidya*[23] — just as, to take Shankara's classic comparison, one might see a rope on the ground and mistake it for a snake. Hence, this wisdom aims to free man from the illusion of the world by leading him to acknowledge that everything is Brahman, the immutable Brahman which knows no duality and is devoid of attributes.

This whole system presents itself as a 'philosophy of God', a view *sub specie aeternitatis*[24] which is only plausible and flawless from the point of view of the Principle itself, of Brahman, and not that of man, unless man is united with Brahman as one. Otherwise, serious incongruities immediately emerge. First of all, the universe is described as that

---

22 The phrase is Latin meaning 'Every determination is a negation', and it originally appears in a letter written by Baruch Spinoza (1632–1677). Spinoza was a Jewish Dutch philosopher who, while dutifully carrying out his work as a lens-grinder, simultaneously wrote a number of books which were to become indispensible for the European Enlightenment.

23 For *avidya*, see note 11 to Chapter 11 above.

24 Latin: 'from the perspective of eternity'.

which derives from the development — from the actualisation — of certain possibilities contained within the Principle. But, at the same time, it is claimed that within the Principle all possibilities are already actualised *ab aeterno*,[25] that within it the possible (i.e. possibilities) and the real are one and the same, a seamless whole. Therefore, the same thing (i.e. the universe) would exist, at the same time and according to the same relation, both in potency and in act: one could not speak of development or even of manifestation at all, insofar as this concept implies a possibility as its starting point, i.e. something which is not yet actualised; yet, according to this view, everything is already actualised in the Principle.

From an external point of view — such as that of a finite being who finds himself confined within manifestation, and for whom the process of development or manifestation appears real — the argument does not hold, given its monistic premise. It would only be consistent if one were to admit, as creationist religions do, that man is a being removed from the Principle and mysteriously projected *per iatum*[26] outside it, a being that therefore can consider the world process from the outside, according to a relative and illusory perspective — i.e. that can see the world as a real process. But this stands in complete contrast to the doctrine of non-duality, the doctrine of the 'Supreme Identity', which distinguishes Hindu metaphysics as a whole and especially Vedanta, according to which there is no difference between the I as *ātman* (the I in its transcendent dimension) and Brahman, and there is nothing at all outside Brahman. We would be forced to conclude, then, that in man the Principle itself, as man's *ātman*, is subject to illusion, to *māyā*, which would mean reintroducing — in some mysterious and absurd fashion — a duality within the Principle.

---

25   Latin: 'from eternity, since the beginning of time'.

26   Latin: 'by a throw'. Evola indicates what he means by this phrase in a passage of Chapter 11 above; see the sentence attached to note 8.

If instead we were to abandon the point of view of absolute non-duality, this would only worsen the situation. If we argue that only *Nirguna-Brahman*, which is to say the Principle with no attribute or determination whatsoever, which cannot even be regarded as a 'cause', is real, and that everything else is merely a semblance, illusion, unreality and fallacy — i.e. *māyā* — and that therefore the finite (i.e. determined beings, all living beings) and the absolute stand in mutual contradiction, with no possible connection between the two, the question emerges of what, in practical terms, the person who makes this claim *is*: whether Brahman itself or a finite being that finds himself in the realm of *māyā*. In the latter case, i.e. as long as a person is referring to an I that cannot be identified with the stark, shapeless One, or indeed with that which lies beyond being and non-being (for this is the highest point of reference of the metaphysics in question), not just himself but everything he affirms will be *māyā* — an illusion, chimera and fallacy — including the claim that only *Nirguna-Brahman* is real and that the rest is pure illusion, i.e. the very doctrine of Vedanta in this extremist and 'illusionist' form. It is interesting to note that a critique of this sort has been advanced not by some subtle, modern and profane philosophy, but in India itself: it may be found in a Tantric treatise, Shiva Chandra's *Tantratattva*, which was published in an English edition by A. Avalon in 1914.[27]

All these difficulties are essentially due to the fact that an attempt has been made to give conceptual expression to supra-rational experiences within a philosophical system that is unreservedly presented as the only valid one. This system is compromised by its static conception of the Principle. There is no reason why 'manifestation' should be

---

27   The work in question goes under the English title *Principles of Tantra*. I have been unable to find any information about the author, other than his impressive full name (Shriyukta Shiva Chandra Vidyarnava Bhattacharyya Mahodaya), and the fact that he was an English-educated Hindu. Evola offers the following note: 'This critique is further explored in J. Evola, *The Yoga of Power*'.

considered something illusory and negative, as a negation, simply by virtue of the fact that it clearly does not exhaust the endless possibilities of the Principle. The idea that every determination (i.e. everything which has a form, everything which is defined, including man taken not as pure *ātman* but in his concreteness) is a negation can only apply to an immobile substance and to a poorly understood notion of infinity—and this, only in the case of a determination that is passively experienced, not of self-determination. As I have already noted on several occasions, this is an absurd idea if it is also applied to the Principle understood as *potestas*, i.e. as the capacity to unconditionally be that which it wants to be. The principle is that which it wants to be, and what it wants to be no doubt reflects the absolute, the infinite. Manifestation—hence, everything that amounts to form, determination, individuation and cosmos—does not stand in contradiction to the infinite as an illusion and semblance, as *māyā*, but rather is precisely what the term 'manifestation' ultimately means, namely the act whereby a supreme, free *potestas* affirms itself. And this action does not have a purely illusory character (according to extremist Vedanta, if the Principle were to affirm 'I create, I act, I am the cause', it would be under an illusion, since all this falls within *māyā*), but is actually real: indeed, it is the element linking the unconditioned (as cause) to the conditioned (as effect).

With this, it might seem as though we have embarked on a philosophical digression, drifting away from our main topic, the myth of East and West. But the reference just made to action shows that this way of understanding the Principle entails a different assessment of the meaning of action and contemplation. According to our outline, it is possible to define two essential spiritual orientations. To make things clearer, let us take the image of rays projected from a centre—this is one possible way of representing manifestation. The ray which issues forth and proceeds is the process and becoming of the world. If the I, the human person, is placed on this ray or identified with it, two orientations become possible: to look back or to look forward, to proceed or to withdraw, to adhere to the process of irradiation or, by turning back, to tend towards a return, a re-absorption into the Principle. The second orientation is the 'escapist' one, based on one-sided contemplation. It is generally associated with a pessimistic view of the world, existential angst, the idea that life is all pain and gloom — that we find ourselves down here on account of some guilt or dark destiny — and a yearning for redemption and liberation. This is precisely the prevailing climate in religious mysticism. The psychoanalytical interpretation, according to which the mystical orientation is ultimately based on the memory of and nostalgia for prenatal existence within the maternal womb, with its safe and protective warmth, and hence on the impulse to return to this womb and abandon oneself to it, is obviously a joke; but if this idea is transposed onto the right plane, there is some truth to it: the highest aspiration is reabsorption within the indeterminate pre-cosmic infinite, in the formless that precedes manifestation.

As regards the other orientation, that which affirms and preserves the forward direction of the ray, it clearly has positive value only provided that a connection with the origin and centre of irradiation is maintained, i.e. only provided that, while not withdrawing from the world, while preserving one's *presence* in the world and on the path of action, one remains aware of the dimension of transcendence in itself and of its role as the centre. Otherwise, we would have a movement that loses itself in indeterminateness — to use a Buddhist simile: like an arrow cast into the night. Bearing this specific reservation in mind, the orientation in question is a metaphysically valid one. It may be said that just as the other orientation is defined by the exclusive ideal of *liberation*, this one is characterised by the ideal of *freedom*. Action finds justification here, as it were, in the right balance with a form of contemplation which does not amount to an escapist *pathos*, but which must rather be understood as a way to bear in mind and revitalise one's contact with the origin.

If, then, despite the complex range of elements to be taken into account, we still wish to develop a myth of the East and a myth of the West, we can do so by referring precisely to the two orientations just outlined: proceeding or withdrawing in the process of manifestation; freedom and liberation; the affirmation of form in view of the power that it freely manifests and which determines it, and impatience towards it or its rejection; the predominance of action in the terms just illustrated and the predominance of a form of contemplation detached from the world. Naturally, this is a very general outline: various factual and historical data may not agree with it (I have already mentioned some of them). For example, the aspects associated with a pessimistic view of the world presented by Orphism and, partly, even by Platonism — both of which fall within the West — would, according to our outline, be under the sign of the 'East'.[28] This would certainly apply to early Christianity, with its conception of life in the world as a valley of tears, its theory of original sin, its yearning for redemption, and its expectation of a Kingdom not of this world.[29] However, those aspects of the pre-Christian Classical and Western Indo-European world that may be traced back to the 'myth of the West' are undeniable and predominant. And it is equally evident that the myth in question is associated with all those influences which shaped original Christianity,

---

28 For Orphism, see note 4 to Chapter 10 above. I am uncertain what Evola has in mind when he speaks of pessimism here. One indication of what he might intend is offered by the fact that, according to certain Orphic hymns, the satyr Silenus was identified as the tutor of Dionysus, a god who had particular importance in Orphism. This Silenus was a drunkard who grew prophetic in his inebriation; when the Phrygian King Midas captured him to force him to share his wisdom, the satyr responded: 'Best of all is it to not have been born; and if born, to die as soon as possible'. This is recounted in Plutarch's *Moralia*, 'Consolation to Apollonius'.

29 The references here can be found in the Bible. See, for instance, Psalm 84:6; Romans 5:12–13 and 1 Corinthians 15:22 (the Pauline interpretation of the Fall); 1 John 2:2 and 1 Corinthians 15:17; and John 18:36.

particularly in the Romano-Germanic medieval cycle, rectifying it and giving it forms that are often very removed from the initial spirit of this faith.

It is quite obvious that, generally speaking, the West stands under the sign of action. Yet, if we focus our gaze on more recent times, what we find is a degenerative form of the orientation and myth just described. The basis of the 'modern world', which until recently was synonymous with the West, has certainly been action. However, this is a dissociated and autonomous kind of action; to use the simile previously adopted, it is as though the ray, streaming on, had gradually lost all contact with its origin; or, to use a different simile, it is as though an object in motion had strayed from its orbit and set off on a tangent, to the point of losing every centre and hurtling into endless space. Hence the linear and historicist conception of time which distinguishes the most recent West, with its myths of evolution and indefinite progress: a rectilinear motion that continues further and further, endlessly, with an acceleration that recalls that of a falling body. Metaphysically, this motion signifies a flight, because it no longer sets out from an immobile transcendence, but is rather driven by a kind of fever or vertigo. Hence the angst which from time to time seizes the modern West, despite all its 'achievements'.

So as not to end our analysis on a negative note, we might say that the myth of the East, that of the West and the degenerative forms of the latter, which correspond to the central myth of the modern world, can be defined according to the morphological outline we have summarily traced.

2

In connection with the Second Vatican Council we have witnessed the spread of what some people have referred to as 'ecumenical euphoria'. It is believed that in parallel to the doctrinal weakening of Catholicism which occurred under John XXIII and Paul VI — possibly the most baleful popes in the recent apostolic tradition[30] — the exclusivism of Rome is also losing ground, that relations of mutual understanding and 'dialogue' are being established, and that on the spiritual level too we are approaching the kind of unification that is materially being achieved among the peoples of the Earth: 'a unitary embrace of the men of all continents and all faiths, both Christian and non-Christian.'

Now, the conditions are such that, if we were ever to get as far as this, the result would be only a regressive phenomenon. On the spiritual level this alleged ecumenism is bound to reflect the character of the unification that is being pursued on the temporal and material level in the present age. This is a mockery of true unification, because the latter can only be achieved at the summit and not at the base, and only within an organic framework. Today all we find in the political and social field are traces of a formless democratic unity deriving from a flattening and breakdown, not from the integration of any higher principle. Considering that the two aforementioned popes have gone so far as to welcome and almost bless the UN — a bastard and promiscuous organisation of democraticised peoples standing alongside communistised ones — as a prefiguration of the hoped for future unity of mankind, there should be no doubt as to what kind of orientation we can expect to find, as a counterpart to all this, on the spiritual level.

Politically speaking, there can only be true unity within a structure that, in one way or another, reproduces that of the medieval Holy

---

30   Pope John XXIII (1881–1963) held the papacy from 1958–1963, becoming in that period one of the most popular Popes of history. He was responsible for the infamous Vatican II, which has been widely criticised as a worrying if not unacceptable capitulation on the part of the Church to liberal modernity, under the guise of attempting to improve the Church's relevance. It led to a great many changes to Church practice, as for instance the substitution of vernacular for Latin during masses. Paul VI was Pope John's close friend and successor, who continued the previous Pope's tendencies — what Evola in various places refers to as the Church's 'opening to the Left'.

Roman Empire: a sum of particular political units that are firmly organised and differentiated, above which stands a supra-national, spiritual and transcendent principle of authority, providing unification from on high. Much the same scenario is envisaged by the doctrine that Dante expounds in his *De monarchia*, which preserves a timeless normative value, aside from those elements in it which belong to a past that cannot be brought back to life.[31] Consequently, only a transcendent unity, achieved from above, can have any value on the religious level: this is the kind of unity which stems from the acknowledgement of the One Tradition that exists beyond its various particular and historical forms, of the constant metaphysical elements that present themselves in various guises — as though translated into different 'languages' — across the various religions and sacred traditions of the world. The essential precondition, here, is the 'esoteric' admission of what presents itself according to the opaque and often even contrasting variety of exoteric, external and historical forms taken by religions and traditions. The encounter, therefore, can only take place at the summit, on the level of elites capable of grasping the inner and transcendent dimension of different traditions, in the light of which unity would automatically follow and 'dialogue' could take place without disturbing the limits that distinguish each religion at the level of its 'base' and external doctrine.

Nothing of the sort is to be found in the recent reformist events that have awoken this 'ecumenical enthusiasm'. Rather, what we find here is essentially defeatist tolerance. It is vaguely acknowledged that non-Catholics too do not wholly find themselves in error and are

---

31   *De Monarchia* was Dante's 1312–1313 political treatise on secular versus religious (that is, Catholic) authority in government, defending the former over the latter. (Some centuries on, the work was banned by the Church.) The Pope, from Dante's point of view, should concern himself with the eternal life, that is, the afterlife of men; while it is the role of the Emperor to concern himself with *this* life. One might say that Dante provides the theoretical grounding for the Christian utterance, 'Give unto Caesar what is Caesar's, and God what is God's'.

not unavoidably destined to damnation (according to the old axiom: *extra Ecclesiam nulla salus*).[32] Christians are invited to take into account and respect the dogmas of other traditions as 'facts', with the recommendation of emphasising not so much the dogmas themselves as any common moral and social principles that might help bring men together as brothers. This means stressing the lower and almost 'profane' part of every religion and tradition — not that which directs man upwards, towards transcendence, but those elements of religious superstructures that can be used to order or restrain social life, as a merely social and rational moral system could also do. In other words, what is emphasised is the secondary rather than the essential, since in every religion worthy of this name morality is only justified in view of a higher, transcendent aim. On the other hand, the invitation to consider the chief doctrinal content of every religion empirically, as a mere 'fact', i.e. as something that simply is as it is, amounts to an *a priori* refusal to understand, amounts to genuine agnosticism — the very opposite of the kind of approach that can lead to the only existential level on which a true higher unity can be discovered and affirmed. Thus these fanciful 'encounters' and this tendency to display inter-faith tolerance are of no spiritual interest at all. If this direction were truly to be followed, all we would witness is a new contribution to the kind of flattening, decay and 'democracy' that are taking root in vast areas of the planet on all levels (the only small inconvenience being the prospect of a good old atomic war), as genuine values are forgotten, along with all that has form, all that is organic and qualitative.

It is peculiar that alongside these new tendencies, the opposite tendency endures at a higher level, namely as sectarian intransigence, which also uses the formula 'meeting of religions', but actually draws upon all the polemical and exclusivist themes mentioned before. In

---

32 Latin, taken from the writings of Saint Cyprian (c. 200–258): 'outside the Church, no salvation', meaning that only those who have been baptised into the Catholic tradition will be saved.

this respect, it might be useful to focus on a specific case: the theses put forward by the Swiss writer Jacques-Albert Cuttat in his book *La Rencontre des Religions*, published in Paris in 1957, as well as in various articles and lectures, such as *Asiens Incognito im europäischen Geistesleben* and *Vergeistigungstechnik und Umgestaltung in Christus*.[33] These theses are relevant also from a particular point of view. Cuttat had formerly adhered to the French traditionalist current headed by René Guénon (under the pseudonym Jean Thamar he had even published various articles in this group's magazine, *Études Traditionnelles*) and had acquired a certain special culture by studying hesychasm, which is to say the mysticism of Greek-Orthodox orientation, and Islamic Sufism. His later return to the theses of sectarian Christianity has a peculiar polemical character, as it is marked by an opposition not just to Eastern traditions but also, and especially, to traditional metaphysics and the initiatory path in general. His ideas have proven attractive to some who, having stopped halfway along the traditionalist path or having even turned back, have felt the need to find some excuse to justify their failure or lack of qualification.

Thanks to his past experiences, Cuttat has been capable of bringing together more extensive and serious information related to the history of religion than Massis, Guardini or any other militant apologist. Yet he has deployed this solid arsenal to defend much the same theory, to denounce the alleged Eastern peril, to put forward an exclusivist defence of theistic and devotional religion, and to affirm its superiority compared to any other form of spirituality. What we find, then, is the

---

33 Cuttat (1909–1989) was a diplomat and orientalist who served for a time as the Swiss ambassador to India. He dedicated much of his life to improving the relations between the Christians and the Hindus, before falling out of a window in Colombo and suffering severe head trauma which evidently impaired his functioning thereafter and brought a quick end to his career. The first book that Evola mentions here, *La Rencontre des Religions* (*The Meeting of Religions*) was probably his best known.

very opposite of what might be suggested by the formula he himself uses, 'meeting of religions'. Cuttat's positive contribution rather lies — as we shall see — in his detailed examination and justification of the irreconcilability of divergent spiritual orientations, i.e. the impossibility of any dialogue between them. I am consciously using the expression 'spiritual orientations' here rather than religions. As will soon become clear, Cuttat's most serious misunderstandings derive from his arbitrary inclusion within the category 'religion' of spiritual forms which do not belong to the same level. One wonders here whether Cuttat is not acting in bad faith: whether, to suit his purposes, he might not have chosen to ignore what, by virtue of his past experiences, he well knows regarding the essential morphological differences between religious thought and metaphysical thought, between esotericism and exotericism, between 'metaphysics' and mere faith — differences I have already outlined in Chapter 1. Cuttat confuses and distorts these categories in order to exalt the originality and superiority of what has become the predominant religion in the West, considered in its most limiting and exterior aspects. This calls for one additional clarification.

In examining the relations between East and West, Cuttat lays out a series of oppositions that are partly true, but which ought to simply be subjected to a morphological and existential analysis, exterior to any value judgement, since — as we have seen — these are terms that cannot be placed on the same level, terms which do not admit a common criterion. The problem is presented in the following way.

On the one hand, we would have a 'spiritual hemisphere' that includes Jews, Christians and Muslims, in which the Absolute is conceived as a person. This is set in contrast to another spiritual hemisphere that includes Buddhism, Hinduism, Taoism, Confucianism and Shintoism, and in which the Principle is impersonal in its ultimate and transcendent expression, and only personal in its relative aspects or manifestation. The more sophisticated nature of Cuttat's polemical arsenal is revealed by the fact that, unlike many of his colleagues, he does not employ the derogatory and arbitrary label of 'pantheism' (= everything is God) for the East; he admits that 'even the East does not ignore divine transcendence and does not at all deify nature as such. In reality, this is a kind of *pantheism* (= everything is God) which instead of leading to the personal God, as in monotheism, culminates with what Rudolf Otto has called *theopantism* (= God is everything, He is the only reality).'[34]

Therefore, the question is no longer the presence or non-presence of the conception of God as a person, but rather the place that this conception is assigned within a given system. The alternative appears to be between systems that allow a non-personal or supra-personal Absolute (a super-God, so to speak) and systems that ignore, rule out or deny this truly transcendent dimension of the Principle. However, when posed in such terms, the question carries its own answer — an answer that goes in the direction contrary to what Cuttat suggests.

Before explaining why this is the case, it must be noted that Cuttat cannot refer the opposition between these two systems to East and West, as he regards as non-essential, foreign and accidental certain doctrines that are equally present in the traditions he includes within the 'non-Eastern spiritual hemisphere' — Judaism, Christianity, and Islam. (We shall not dwell here on the unwarrantedness of considering Judaism and Islam non-Eastern.) Indeed, Judaism is familiar with the Kabbala, Islam with Sufism, and — as regards ancient traditions — Neoplatonism and various mystery traditions have equally been characterised by the acknowledgement of the Principle which transcends the theistic personal God.[35] As regards Christianity, bearing in mind what I have repeatedly observed with regard to the essential

---

34   Otto, Rudolf (1869–1937) was a German Lutheran theologian and a student of comparative theology. He wrote numberous works, some of which have been translated into English.

35   For both the Kabbala and Sufism, see note 9 to Chapter 11 above. For Neoplatonism, see note 13 to Chapter 7.

character of this belief, it may be noted that both in its early stages (especially with Greek patristics, Dionysius the Areopagite, Irenaeus, Synesius, and a few others)[36] and with some mystics and theologians who partly approached what we may refer to as the 'dry path' (Scotus Eriugena, Meister Eckhart, Ruysbroek, and Tauler),[37] a few higher points of references have emerged here and there. Given that he is not ignorant of all this, Cuttat resorts to a peculiar strategy: with a sort of unconditional sentence, he states that what we have here is the intrusion or interference of a foreign current within the spirituality of the 'Western hemisphere'. He speaks of an 'Asia present incognito', and, with a zeal worthy of the Holy Inquisition, he goes about unmasking and denouncing this in relation not just to the aforementioned theological doctrines and mystics, but also to a whole range of Western thinkers down to Kant, Schopenhauer, Hegel and the existentialists, so as to mark out what in his view is purely 'Western' — but which, as

---

36 The three names presented here are all of Church Fathers. According to tradition, Dionysius the Areopagite lived in the first century AD and was converted to Christianity by Paul himself. He was reputedly the first Bishop of Athens. His writings are of a mystical and Neoplatonic tone. Iranaeus may have been martyred around the opening of the third century. He too was a bishop, and he was dedicated to attacking the gnostics and other early heresies. As a curiosity, he was the first to introduce the infamous number 666 into Christian theology. Synesius (c. 373-c. 414) was yet another bishop, though one who interested himself in science (he was a correspondent with the Neoplatonic astronomer Hypatia).

37 Scotus Eriugena (c. 815-c. 877) was an Irish theologian. A Christian Neoplatonist, he was steeped in the ancient philosophies and wrote several philosophical works, foremost among which is his classic synthesis of previous philosophy, *The Division of Nature*. For Meister Eckhart, see note 11 to Chapter 11. The Blessed John van Ruysbroeck (1293 or 1294–1381) was a Flemish mystic whose works dwell on questions of asceticism, virtue, and divine matters. Johannes Tauler (c. 1300–1361) was a German mystic, a disciple of Meister Eckhart and a man of certain Neoplatonist tendencies. He wrote no tracts nor treatises; some eighty of his sermons have come down to us.

we shall see, is thereby reduced to something very meagre and empty indeed.

The truth is that here too in this respect it is absurd to use the geographical-cultural categories of 'East' and 'West'. We are not dealing with interferences external to a given system, but rather with an esotericism that in the West too has established itself, if only sporadically, beyond exotericism (i.e. the more exterior forms of the corresponding tradition); it is a matter of a gnosis and 'metaphysics' soaring above the level of mere faith and theism. Hence, as I was saying, what we have is not one 'religion' meeting (or not meeting) another kind of religiosity at the same level, but rather spiritual categories or realms that are actually different. To be more precise, we are dealing with the formal difference between systems that are familiar with a metaphysical teaching beyond 'religion' on the one hand, and systems that instead are limited to the level of devotional religion on the other. Cuttat has done his best to confine the *whole* tradition of the 'Western hemisphere' to a system of the latter sort — an operation as arbitrary as it is one-sided. In any case, given that he was forced to acknowledge the existence of an Eastern metaphysics far removed from any sort of 'pantheism', he finds himself in an impossible position when he attempts to present things in terms favourable to theism.

It would be consistent to argue that an impersonal Principle beyond the personal is inconceivable and to describe any doctrine based on it as an illusion and aberration. But if no such argument is advanced — if one admits that, beyond the theistic God, one can conceive of a reality superior and anterior to any divinity conceived in the likeness of man, with human feelings — then it is truly absurd to wish to assign theism any primacy. Thus Cuttat is forced to resort to mere word play to lend a veneer of consistency to his attempt to invert the two parts. Ultimately, when he avoids following those who casually dismiss non-Christian spirituality as 'naturalistic' or 'pantheistic mysticism'; when in relation to the East he speaks instead of an 'impersonal deity who is ontological and metaphysical, yet not supernatural' (as only the theistic deity is supernatural according to his argument), Cuttat twists the meaning of words: for in the literal sense of the term, 'metaphysical' (from *physis* = nature) means precisely 'supernatural', 'metacosmic'. And since Cuttat was forced to acknowledge that the 'East' is familiar with a metacosmic principle, he coins a new and bizarre term, 'transmetacosmic' for the theistic God, believing that this absurd verbal device is enough to lend a foundation to his thesis of the superiority of theistic theology.

According to Cuttat, the 'transmetacosmic' principle lies at the origin of relations of a superior kind between man and the Principle, relations that are not ontological but personal and 'truly spiritual', and which are unknown in the 'East'. Here too he shows an uncommon ability to turn the tables, since he gives the impression of having taken into account everything refering to 'Eastern' spirituality, but only in order to assign it an inferior, subordinate position. We here enter the domain of inner experiences. Some have characterised the 'Eastern' path as a centripetal movement, a movement of detachment of the mind from the exterior and phenomenal world, and of convergence into a deeper I, or divine Self (the *ātman* of the Upanishads). Cuttat eagerly adopts this idea. In his view, this is the 'primordial gesture of the East'. Yet, this would only amount to travelling half of the way. Having come to the centre of himself, man ought to acknowledge 'vertical transcendence' and follow the movement towards God as a person who is 'unattainable transcendence', above all inwardness, including the most profound and detached from the world. Only 'moral' categories of Christian origin or of a Christian sort would come into play here, no longer 'Eastern' ones: the category of the relation between an 'I' and a divine 'Thou', between a human person and the divine person, supernatural love or *communio*, trust in the redemption brought about by Christ (which, however, would place Judaism and Islam outside of the non-Eastern 'Western hemisphere', insofar as they do not acknowledge this redemption at all), faith, humbleness, and 'tremendous astonishment' as man's answer to God, who wishes to 'give himself to him', an amazement which is infused into creatures by God as a means for him to reveal himself to them — and so on. Cuttat concludes, in a remarkable casual way, that 'The Orientals have not explicitly discovered that the ultimate inwardness of the spirit culminates with the extreme transcendence of the Creator.' In other words: what is distinctive of the 'East' ultimately amounts to nothing more than a preparatory stage, and only beyond this stage does the truly supernatural manifest itself.

All this amounts to an intentional muddying of the waters to suit Cuttat's own cause. He acts as though he did not know what he does in fact know: he is aware of how the path is truly structured in 'metaphysical' doctrines; he learned this, if not directly from the traditions in question, then from the clear exposition of their true meaning provided by the traditionalist group he used to be a member of. These doctrines take both directions into account, associating one with the symbolism of the centre and the other with that of the axis. The first movement is an inward one, by which the deepest and most original core of one's being is reached, detached from all 'nature'. However, the Self as a centre is not at all the point of arrival; it is in turn a point of departure for the 'vertical' realisation of transcendent and super-individual states of being, unfolding along the 'axis of the universe'. These are represented by different symbols in different traditions, and all culminate with the Unconditioned (the Principle superordinate to the theistic deity). This has clearly been grasped by every complete metaphysical teaching. Hence, the distinctive character of the view defended by Cuttat, which he attributes to the 'superior' spirituality of the 'West', merely consists in conceiving a *rift* between the two stages, a kind of break: the true path to realisation stops at the centre; being does not rise above this centre, in a vertical direction; as though he is kept back by some kind of fundamental impotence or angst, he objectifies all other states in the form of a transcendent person, the theistic God, God as an unreachable person. He thus passes from the level of metaphysical and intellectual realisation to that of sentimentality, love, devotion and all the rest, giving new life to all those merely human, and ultimately socially and emotionally conditioned, impulses (Cuttat speaks precisely of relationships akin to those between friends, husband and wife, father and son) — impulses that the preliminary process of purification and detachment ought to have burned off, leaving no residues. To be sure, the metaphysical path too acknowledges the possibility of there being some kind of discontinuity or hiatus between concentric realisation and vertical, ascending realisation; but the ability to actively overcome it without swerving and by transforming oneself is the mark of the true initiate. This is the fundamental point.

Here too the concessions that Cuttat is forced to make in relation to the 'Eastern' metaphysical path irreparably vitiate, from the very start, the thesis he wishes to uphold, namely the cause of the 'West'. He admits that the path in question is marked by depersonalisation, by the overcoming of the individual person, by the attainment of a pre-conceptual, pre-affective and pre-volitional pure I. How is it possible, then, to associate with a higher stage relations in which the crucial role is played by everything which is not just 'personal' but even sentimental, emotional and 'moral'? Do love relations — even mystical love relations — not imply the limit of personhood? Besides, how is it possible to find anything 'subjective' and 'individualistic' in a spirit that, through intellectual catharsis or some other form of purification, has attained the condition of depersonalised purity just mentioned?

I have argued that the 'Eastern' path (or, rather, the path of high initiation in general) does not ignore 'vertical transcendence', but rather conceives it as a form of realisation to be attained . Let us take an example to clarify just how absurd it is to present as something 'more' that which derives not from any transcendent realisation but from the halting of being *at the beginning* of the vertical direction, leading to the re-emergence and influence of sub-intellectual complexes. Try to picture a yogi or *siddha* bursting into tears (whereas in theistic mysticism the 'grace of tears' is often presented as one of the highest markers of a saint's perfection); a Buddha — an 'awoken one' — engaging in prayer or invocations; a *shenjen*, a 'transcendent man' of Taoism, or a Zen initiate repeating formulas akin to those of Greek Orthodox hesychasm: 'Jesus Christ, Son of God, have mercy on me!' — and so on. More than any dialectic, the very impossibility of imagining such things reveals the absurdity of Cuttat's views and the level to which they actually belong.

Ultimately, this author's only merit — as already noted — lies in the fact that he has fully thought out the implications of a purely religious position foreign to all metaphysics. He thus ends up denying the very value of that movement of realisation 'towards the centre of oneself' which he had granted as the first stage in a complete process. He finds the idea that 'God only unites with gods' dangerous (this is a saying by St Symeon, but it is also a Classical and Pythagorean conception);[38] *theosis*, preliminary deification, would ultimately be superfluous, or indeed dangerous, because 'we have already been redeemed in Christ' (once again, we should then rule out Islam and Judaism), and all that is required is humble and faithful adherence to our Redeemer. Cuttat writes: 'If we do not wish to elevate ourselves to God starting from our

---

38 St. Symeon the New Theologian (949–1022) was given the epithet 'Theologian', not for his teachings, but for his having had a personal vision of God. Symeon's direct experience of God gave him, he believed, authority to speak of God; and he denied that anyone who had not had such an experience could claim such authority. This view of his quite predictably got him into some trouble with the religious authories (who, one can well assume, had *not* had enjoyed such an experience), and he died in exile, though he was later recognised as a saint by the Orthodox Church. The Pythagoreans were followers of the Greek philosopher Pythagoras, whose views were founded on mathematics and spiritualism, which makes a most curious blend to our modern scientistic eyes. The word following this note, *theosis*, means (as Evola indicates) 'deification', and refers in particular to the Orthodox Christian belief that salvation consists in a reunification of the soul with God, that is, with *theosis*.

fallen soul, are we not trying to impose on God more than what he asks of us? Is it not to that nature, to the sick and the underprivileged, to sinners and even to the dead that Christ directly addresses his redeeming gesture? Does he set some other *sine qua non* condition for his highest promise, apart from the requirement of unreservedly surrendering ourselves, as he has found us, *with* our flaws, to the omnipotence of his essentially gratuitous and undeserved mercy?' 'If we believe that we can only reach and unite with him *after* we have cleansed all our wounds, are we not conditioning our surrender, refusing to put absolute faith in him, and doubting that *he alone* is responsible for our deifying redemption?' Thus the author even refuses to include, if only as a preparatory and subordinate stage, what the 'Eastern' path of realisation and asceticism had acknowledged as valid (which Cuttat here reduces to something very insignificant indeed). He more or less ends up with the Calvinist doctrine of the rejection of works and of faith as the only means for salvation — the ultimate limit of the merely religious direction.[39]

In this respect too, Cuttat turns the tables, in order to avoid having to gloss over facts he knows well but which would undermine his theses. The East too is familiar with the type of man who embraces the aforementioned views: the *bhakta*, the devotional man;[40] and the East

---

39 Calvanism is based on the teachings of John Calvin (1509–1564). It is one of the earliest non-Lutheran Protestant faiths, and held total sway for a time in the politics of Geneva. Evola is here referring to one of the most peculiar and characteristic elements of Calvin's teaching, that concerning predestination: by this view, God has predestined some souls to be saved, and some souls to be damned, which choice on God's part does not depend on any characteristic or action of the persons in question. Thus, a man might to all worldly appearances be a wretched sinner, and still find himself in heaven after he dies; likewise, a man who appears to all human eyes blameless and pious might yet be consigned to the flames.

40 *Bhakti*, the practice of the *bhakta* here mentioned, literally means 'attachment, love, worship'.

too is familiar with the corresponding path, *bhakti-marga*, which is marked more or less by the categories just described and which takes a personal deity as its point of reference. However, there are two points worth noting. The first is that in India the *bhakta* is essentially a type of man who, being characterised by the quality of *rajas*, is hierarchically inferior to the type of man who follows the path of pure metaphysical knowledge, characterised by the higher quality of *sattva* (what comes into play here is the doctrine of the three *guna*, the forces that give things and beings their defining features).[41] Secondly, the appearance of the *bhakti* current, both in India and elsewhere, is historically a relatively recent phenomenon; to be more exact, its predominance and emergence as something other than the orientation defining more popular and promiscuous forms of worship is recent. In the face of all this, Cuttat once again turns things round, invoking the 'Western' conception of time.

He speaks of the opposition that exists, in relation to time, between the Judaeo-Christian creationist view, from which the idea of linear historical development would derive, more or less in terms of progress (including progress from 'sin' to 'redemption', and from the latter to the 'consummation of time') and the 'Eastern' conception of the world as a changeless emanation and as the pure symbol and perpetual image of a metacosmic and timeless reality — a conception that rules out the idea of history and gives rise to the doctrine of cycles. I have already spoken of this view, which is also shared by Romano Guardini. More generally, many historians of religion, including Mircea Eliade, acknowledge the specific contribution made by Christianity to the

---

41 *Rajas* and *Sattva* are two of the three *Gunas* (as Evola notes, the word means something like 'qualities' or 'attributes'). *Rajas* is the quality of activeness, dynamism, motion, energy; *sattva* that of harmony, serenity, balance. The third quality, which Evola does not mention, is *tamas*, imbalance, chaos, disorder, violence. The Italian editor provides the following reference: *The Yoga of Power*, Chapter 4.

concept of history as 'history'.[42] For my part, I will refrain from noting that the other conception, the 'cyclical' and non-'linear' one, while not characteristic of Christianity (although it does surface in the Old Testament, in the *Ecclesiastes*), was also known to various ancient Western and Mediterranean doctrines.[43] For if I were to note this, Cuttat would hasten to say that it is an 'interference from Asia' or an 'incognito Asia' that has crept into the 'Western spiritual hemisphere'. Nor will I refer to what Celsus, with detached irony, noted in this regard: namely that it is because they are only familiar with a fragment of a particular cycle that Christians and Jews speak of 'history' and the 'end of the world', dramatising the latter and mistaking a recurrent element in every cycle for a unique one.[44] But even without aiming so high, even without referring to the great recurrences, but considering only the time span which encompasses present humanity and the ages generally known to us, the linear and 'evolutionary' conception (even that with a providential or eschatological background) may be set in contrast to the involutional conception of history — a contrast that corresponds to pure reality, regardless of what timeless and metaphysical openings may occur over the course of 'history'. No doubt, this represents a contrast between a mere fancy and the truth, since the West by now is providing a clear overall picture of the reality of the regressive process.

---

42 For Eliade, see note 2 to Chapter 1 above.

43 For the reference to Ecclesiastes, see for instance 1:1–11. For some indication of the 'various ancient Western and Mediterranean doctrines' to which Evola here alludes, see note 13 to Chapter 13, and the relevant passage.

44 Celsus was a Greek philosopher of the second century, and a powerful adversary of Christianity. For that reason, no doubt, the only part of his work which has reached us is that preserved in the Christian theologian Origen's refutation of him. For Celsus' views on the matter at hand, see for instance Origen's *Contra Celsum*, Book 1, Chapter 19.

Now, by resorting to the historico-evolutionist conception, Cuttat believes that he is elegantly overcoming the difficulty intrinsic to the aforementioned late appearance of the doctrine of *bhakti* (i.e. the theistic-devotional attitude) in the East, arguing that this reflects a progress towards a higher evolutionary stage: a 'divine economy' which has bestowed even on the East, at a later time, a truth and path analogous to those revealed by Christianity, insofar as the god of the *bhakti-marga*, of the path of devotion, is only a concealed and not yet fully conscious form of the god of 'monotheistic revelation'. One might say that it is 'Christ incognito'.

The actual truth of the matter is that the late appearance of the devotional doctrine in the East is one of the aspects of a regressive process (since it occurred at the height of the period known as the 'dark age', or *kali-yuga*).[45] Hence, historically speaking, it ought to be associated with the obscuring of original metaphysical doctrines, and with their polarisation. This is most evident in Buddhism and Taoism; only when they became polarised, when they opened up increasingly to the masses, did they take the form that is typical of all mere religions: reliance on the gods for salvation, the transformation of abstract metaphysical principles or great spiritual masters into 'divine person-

---

45 The *kali-yuga*, the age of the demon Kālī (not to be confused with the Goddess Kali; cf. note 6 to Chapter 18 below), is the last of the four ages of the world, as described in the Hindu scriptures. It is characterised by strife and war, the rise of unrighteous men and immodest women, the unworthy being raised up and the worthy being brought low, the domination of men by women, the reign of unmerited arrogance and blind mendacity, great vices leading to the decadence of rulers and teachers, and the constant restless displacement of peoples, both geographically and in terms of 'caste' — or, to describe the entire era in a word, 'modernity'. It is most interesting to compare this with the other conceptions of the cyclical nature of history which Evola mentions in the present book: see note 11 to Chapter 13, and the relevant passage. Evola treats of the *kali-yuga* more particularly in the Appendix to *Revolt Against the Modern World*, 'On the Dark Age'.

alities', the need for external spiritual help above all, faith, devotion, worship and group ceremonies. Only if we wish to describe the striking of a compromise with the merely human — and its accompanying illusions — as something 'providential', can we regard as providential those processes that in the various Eastern traditions have regressively led to this development (the most typical case being Amidism),[46] formally bringing them into line with Christianity. This is an instance of the general movement of involution of mankind (first in the West and later in the East), which today only those who close their eyes and refuse to see can fail to acknowledge, since it is becoming increasingly evident. The relative contemporaneousness of 'Western' devotionalism and the spread of bhaktism, Amidism, religious Taoism and so on is a coincidence that, as Cuttat notes, may have escaped Western orientalists and missionaries as much as those Easterners interested in the Christian West. However, it is something quite evident, and its meaning is strictly the one I have just indicated.[47]

One could go on and on denouncing all of Cuttat's manipulations. So I will not pause to describe how he deals with Islam, how he inverts things here too: with Sufism (which even goes so far as to acknowledge in man a condition whereby the Principle becomes aware of itself, and which professes the doctrine of Supreme Identity), Islam offers a clear

---

46   This most particular sect of Buddhism establishes as its center the worship of the 'celestial Buddha' named Amida. Through proper worship, the believer is thought to acquire the attributes of this celestial Buddha, so that after his death he will be reborn in the 'Pure Land'.

47   [Evola's note. —Ed.] Elsewhere I have noted that the defining feature of Christianity, a religion typical of the 'dark age', lies in the fact that it is a *desperate* theory of salvation, which is only conceivable in the light of the existential situation of the 'dark age', i.e. that of a kind of humanity which has fallen so low that most people can only hope to overcome death and damnation through a complete surrender, a longing for grace and redemption, coupled with faith in divine mercy. It is only in these terms that the *raison d'être* of a belief such as the Christian one can be explained on a 'providential' level.

and eloquent example of a system that, while encompassing a strictly theistic religious sphere, also acknowledges a higher truth and path to realisation. Here the emotional and devotional element, love and all the rest lose — as they do in authentic, original Buddhism — any 'moral' meaning and any intrinsic value, becoming merely one among many other techniques (as is also the case in bhaktism, or Eastern 'devotion', when correctly understood in its proper context).

To conclude, Cuttat's positive contribution lies in the aforementioned fact, namely: that he rigorously and coherently marks out what pertains to a purely religious and exclusivist doctrine vis-à-vis a metaphysical doctrine — which transforms the whole question of 'East' and 'West' into a secondary matter. From the point of view of purely religious doctrine, the oppositions he describes are indeed real: on the one hand we have moral (i.e. subjective) categories, on the other ontological categories; on the one hand the idea of deification or sacralisation, on the other that of mere sanctification; on the one hand, the theme of sin, on the other that of error and the theory of metaphysical 'ignorance' (Ch. 11); on the one hand, redemption and salvation, on the other the Great Liberation and spiritual awakening; on the one hand, objective techniques of high ascesis to foster realisation, on the other the 'answer' of the soul that surrenders itself to God as a person; on the one hand the theory of the incarnation of the 'Son of God' as a unique and unrepeatable event that marks a watershed in the spiritual history of the world, on the other the theory of avatara[48] and of multiple divine manifestations; on the one hand the experience of the world as a sacred and transparent symbol of the timeless metacosmos, on the other the acknowledgement of nature and of the brotherly and loving communio of all beings and creatures in God (as in St Francis' mystique of nature);[49] on the one hand the deconditioning of

---

48   The avatars, in the Hindu tradition, are deities embodied on earth.

49   Reference to Francis of Assisi (1181 or 1182–1226), the Catholic friar and preacher, remembered for his sentimentalistic love of the poor and the sick,

the person, on the other the acceptance of the inevitable finiteness of man as a creature; on the one hand the overcoming of 'history', on the other its eschatological magnification (which, once secularised, leads to the Western fantasy of 'progress'). All these oppositions are correct. To be more precise, they generally present themselves as oppositions if one adopts the religious point of view, which is characterised by the absolutising of what distinguishes an inferior type of man and his 'truths'. From a metaphysical and traditional perspective, these are instead two hierarchically ordered levels.

The state of affairs, then, is the very opposite of how Cuttat has sought to depict it by arguing that 'Western-Christian values include and complement Eastern ones, and not the other way round.' It is difficult to understand how, starting from his odd ideas and many misunderstandings, we may conclude that through the alleged new 'Euro-Asiatic renaissance' (pray, *what* renaissance?), and the corresponding 'irresistible interpenetration of East and West' (?), it is possible to attain something positive and speak of 'encounters', whereby 'the East does not help the West to deny, possibly involuntarily, its own values, but rather encourages it to concretely master them' — unless what we mean by 'master' is reinforcement of the more exclusivist, limited and even anomalous aspects of everything we presume to be 'Western' (an identification whose arbitrariness I have already highlighted).

Besides, this negative conclusion is explicit in the pages in which Cuttat takes a stance against 'traditionalism', i.e. against the very current to which he had hitherto subscribed. The foundation of 'traditionalism' is the aforementioned idea of the transcendent unity of all religions (or, to be more precise, of all the great spiritual traditions, since — as I have repeatedly stressed — it is more appropriate to limit the use of

---

and his compassion for the beasts. He is indeed recalled as the Patron Saint of Animals (whatever this is supposed to mean) and was known to preach to the birds, who were said to have a particular fondness for him.

the label 'religion' to particular forms of such traditions). From the traditional point of view, these present themselves as being mutually 'assimilable', as being different and more or less complete forms of a single wisdom, or *sapientia perennis*, as emanations of a timeless and primordial tradition: all differences concern the contingent, conditioned and ephemeral side of each great historical tradition, not the essential one, and no one tradition, as such, can claim to possess the monopoly on absolute truth.

Cuttat states: 'Of all religions, Christianity is the only one [once again, he forgets about Greek thought, Islam and everything else he had included within the 'non-Oriental spiritual hemisphere' of our planet, for the sake of broadening that hemisphere] that can only be either the total Truth or a nonsensical claim. *Tertium non datur*.'[50] A Christianity 'assimilable' to other traditions would only be one religion among many others, it would vanish as a pure chimaera. Either it is 'incomparable', or it is nothing at all. For Cuttat, the universal concordance, compatibility and transcendent equivalence of religions 'are not a recurrent religious feature but *only one aspect of non-monotheistic traditions*'. For the 'Western' believer to admit that his religion can be considered from this perspective, thereby becoming 'equivalent to the others vis-à-vis God', would be to deny his faith. From a Judaeo-Christian point of view — Cuttat adds — the only possible position with regard to other spiritual currents lies not in 'assimilation' but in the 'conversion' of their followers. This is tantamount to doing away for good with the formula of the 'encounter' between different religions (if one wishes to express oneself in such inappropriate terms) and to display a complete lack of any sense of boundaries: Cuttat seeks to make an absolute criterion, applicable from a universal objective perspective, of ideas that are simply part and parcel of a particular religion, and which outside this religion — i.e. beyond their 'internal

---

50   Latin: 'No third possibility is given'.

use' — become a 'nonsensical claim', as Cuttat himself states:[51] he never asks himself whether to adopt an attitude of this sort is not to be guilty of the sin of pride to which Christianity gives so much emphasis in other respects.

Positions of this sort appear to compensate for 'ecumenical euphoria' more than enough, as one fallacy, one deviation, serves as a counterpart to the other — a highly significant sign of our times. Incidentally, it becomes clear what certain 'defences of the West' ul-

---

51   [Evola's note. —Ed.] Theses similar to Cuttat's are put forward by R. C. Zaehner in the book *Mysticism, Sacred and Profane* (Oxford, 1937), especially in the chapters on theism and monism. Zaehner shares Cuttat's background as an orientalist; like him, he subsequently switched to militant theistic apologetics. To support his cause, he stresses the opposition between what he regards as truly 'sacred' mysticism (the one founded on theism, i.e. on God as a person) and a 'naturalistic' kind of mysticism (that of monism — just as Guardini had come up with the concept of a 'liberation which does not go beyond the world', *innerweltlich*). I would rather invert this thesis, arguing that, if anything, what is 'naturalistic' — insofar as it reflects purely human categories — is that kind of spirituality which rests on a 'social' and affective foundation, and is based on the relationship between a human 'I' and a divine 'Thou': a relationship which in mysticism acquires markedly erotic overtones, since — as Zaehner notes — the detached I can only overcome his isolation and communicate with God if the soul plays the role of a woman, that of a 'virgin who falls violently in love and desires nothing so much as to be 'ravished', 'annihilated' and assimilated into the beloved.' It seems to me that the very fact of *tutoyer* the divinity (i.e. of using the divine 'Thou') is almost an impertinence, a lack of the sense of distance and infinity. However, from the opposite point of view, namely that of metaphysical Unity, Zaehner is correct to observe that one cannot say that 'God is love' and speak of 'union', insofar as love and union imply a duality; and the One with no second can neither love nor be loved, given the lack of a second term. Indeed, as already noted (Ch. 11), on the metaphysical rather than devotional level one speaks neither of 'union' nor 'love', but rather of 'awakening', of a realisation of the dimension of transcendence itself. For authors such as Zaehner, the fact that a deity is not defined by 'moral' attributes, the fact that it lies beyond good and evil, makes it a 'naturalistic' deity, below the spiritual level of man. In actual fact, to assign such attributes to a God is merely to humanise and degrade him.

timately lead to — namely to forms that suggest that a sort of anxiety complex is at work with respect not so much to the 'East' as to broader spiritual horizons. My analysis of Cuttat's case, which I have conducted not on account of any intrinsic seriousness of his ideas but only because they serve as an example, is thus justified as a way to complement the exposition provided in the first part of the present chapter.

16. THE YOUTH, THE BEATS, AND RIGHT-WING ANARCHISTS

1

M uch — indeed, too much — has been written on the issue of the new generation and of 'young people'. In most cases, the topic does not deserve the interest it has received. The importance which is sometimes assigned to youth in general today, and which finds its counterpart in a sort of devaluation of all those who are not 'young', is absurd. No doubt, we are living in an age of dissolution; the increasingly prevailing condition, therefore, is that of the 'rootless' person, for whom 'society' has lost all meaning, as have the norms that used to govern life. Besides, for the age just before our own — which still endures in certain places — such norms merely coincided with those of the bourgeois world and morals. Naturally, the youth in particular have grown weary of this situation, so from this perspective it may be legitimate to address certain issues. Still, it is necessary to draw certain distinctions and to consider, first of all, the case in which the situation in question is experienced merely passively, and not by virtue of any active initiative of one's own, as may have been the case with the occasional intellectually-oriented and individualist rebel in the past.

A new generation, therefore, is simply accepting this state of affairs: it shows no real concern and makes foolish use of its unfettered condition, so to speak. When these young people claim that they are misunderstood, the only answer one can give them is that there is simply nothing to understand about them — that, if a normal order were en force, it would only be a matter of curtly putting them in their place, as one does with children when their foolishness becomes annoying, invasive, and impertinent. The alleged non-conformism of some of their attitudes, which are actually quite banal, reflects a sort of trend, a new convention: it is the very opposite of an expression of freedom. Many of the phenomena we have examined in the previous pages, such as the taste for vulgarity and certain new social mores, may largely be attributed to this youth. Examples would include the fanatic (male and female) fans of howlers — those epileptic 'folk singers' — and, at present, of the collective puppet-show known as 'yé-yé sessions' and of this or that 'album', with all that such interests entail in terms of behaviour. Their lack of any sense of the ridiculous makes it impossible to exert any influence upon them, so one can only leave them to their own devices and foolishness. One should consider that if any polemic with regard to things such as the sexual emancipation of minors or the sense of family were to appear among this type of youth, it would have no impact at all. As the years go by, the need for most of them to face the material and economic problems of life will no doubt ensure that this youth, having become adult, will adapt to the professional, productive and social routines of the contemporary world, thereby essentially passing from one form of nothingness to another. So there is no real problem.

This type of 'youth', defined by age alone (for one can hardly speak here of certain possibilities characteristic of youth in an inner, spiritual sense),[1] is particularly common in Italy. Federal Germany presents a very different phenomenon: the foolish and degenerated forms just mentioned are far less widespread there; the new generation would

---

1　[Evola's note. —Ed.] Cf. J. Evola, *Biological Youth and Political Youth*, Chapter 5 of *Recognitions*.

appear to have calmly accepted the idea of an existence in which no concerns should be raised, of a life about whose meaning or purpose one should not wonder. This generation is simply concerned with enjoying the comforts and eases offered by the new development of Germany. We may refer to this type of youth as being one 'without concerns', a type which may have shed many conventions and acquired new freedoms, without creating any conflicts, on a two-dimensional level of 'factuality', foreign to any higher interest in myths, disciplines or ideals.

This is probably only a transitional phase for Germany, because if we turn to consider countries that have gone further in the same direction, countries almost completely steeped in the atmosphere of a 'welfare society', where life is safe and everything is rationally regimented — we may refer in particular to Denmark, Sweden, and to some extent Norway too — we will notice that, from time to time, reactions take place in the form of violent and unexpected outbursts. These mainly concern the youth. In these cases, the phenomenon becomes more interesting and may be worth examining.

2

In order to grasp the most typical forms of this phenomenon, it is necessary to turn to America and, to some extent, England. In America, phenomena of spiritual trauma and revolt have already emerged on a wide scale among the new generation. I am referring to that generation which has been given the name of Beat Generation and which I have already discussed in the previous pages: Beats or Beatniks, also known as hipsters.[2] They have been the representatives of a sort of anarchistic

---

2   The name 'Beat' was given to this 'generation' by Jack Kerouac, whom Evola briefly discusses below. It is somewhat ambiguous, meaning as it does simultaneously 'beaten down', 'weary', and also of course the element of musical rhythm. Kerouac wanted to associate the name with 'beatitude' — the artificialness and

and anti-social existentialism, a sort more practical than intellectual (certain insignificant literary expressions aside). At the time of this writing, the movement is no longer en vogue or flourishing: it has practically disappeared from the scene or dissolved. Nonetheless, it retains a certain significance, because this phenomenon is intrinsically connected to the very nature of the last civilisation; so long as this civilisation endures, similar manifestations are bound to appear, albeit in different forms and under different names. In particular, as American society, more than any other, embodies the limits and the *reductio ad absurdum*[3] of the entire contemporary system, the Beat forms of the phenomenon of revolt have acquired a special paradigmatic character; and, of course, they should not be regarded in the same terms as that foolish youth that has just been discussed, chiefly with reference to Italy.[4]

From my perspective, a brief study of certain issues within this context is justified, because I agree with the claim made by some Beats that — contrary to what psychiatrists, psychoanalysts and 'social workers' believe — in a society and civilisation such as ours, and especially the American one, it is generally in the rebel, the misfit and the anti-social person that the healthy man is to be found. In an abnormal world, all values are inverted: it is precisely the one who appears abnormal in relation to the existing milieu who is most likely to be 'normal' and to preserve some vital energy. I cannot agree at all with those who would

---

obscurity of which connection is itself quite suggestive about the nature of the movement as a whole.

3   Latin: 'reduction to absurdity', meaning that the phenomenon in question takes the system so far as to reveal its inherent ridiculousness.

4   [Evola's note. —*Ed.*] At the moment I am writing these lines [1968], this silly and carnevalesque Italian youth has taken to describing itself as Beat, making widespread use of the term. On the level of engagement, there can be no comparison between the American Beat movement, problematic as it may have been, and the ridiculous 'protest' attitude of these Italian epigones of the Beats.

like to 'rehabilitate' such individuals, whom they regard as sick, and to 'readapt' them to 'society.' One psychoanalyst, Robert Lindner, had the courage to state this explicitly.[5] From our point of view, the only problem concerns the definition of what we might call the 'Right-wing anarchist'. We will examine the distance that separates this type from the problematic orientation that almost invariably distinguishes the non-conformism of Beats and hipsters.[6]

The starting point, which is to say the condition triggering the revolt of the Beats, is evident. Their target is a system that, without taking 'totalitarian' political forms, stifles life and damages personality. They sometimes bring up the issue of physical insecurity in the future, as they see the very existence of mankind as threatened by the prospects of a nuclear war (which are blown up to apocalyptic proportions). But what they chiefly feel is the danger of spiritual death inherent in any adaptation to the current system and to its variously conditioning power ('hetero-conditioning'). America is described as 'a

---

5   Lindner (1914–1956) was a psychologist who made some kind of important contribution to 'gambling psychology'. The film *Rebel Without a Cause* was named after one of his books, though in terms of material the two evidently had little if anything in common. It may well be in that book, however, that Lindner made the statements Evola here references, since his own *Rebel Without a Cause* was a case study of a troubled young criminal named Harold, whom Lindner was permitted to analyse over forty-six psychoanalytic sessions.

6   [Evola's note. —*Ed.*] In what follows I will partly be drawing upon testimonies and essays from the collected volume S. Krim (ed.), *The Beats*. The most important essays are those by H. Gold, Marc Reynold, and N. Podhoretz; to these one may add Norman Mailer's book *Advertisements for Myself*. Mailer has also been a spokesman of the Beats and hipsters, and it seems that he did not stop at mere theory, going so far as to 'gratuitously' stab his wife. As for the general climate, we may refer to Jack Kerouac's novels *On the Road* and *The Dharma Bums*, to which we may further add Colin Wilson's novel *Ritual in the Dark*, which tackles the same issues to some extent. In a book that had roused much interest, *The Outsider*, Wilson had already studied — from a general perspective — the figure of 'the outsider' (outsider to the 'normal' world and society).

rotten country, developing cancer in every one of its cells' — 'passivity (conformity), anxiety, and boredom: its three characteristics.' In such a climate, the condition of being rootless, a unit lost in the 'lonely crowd', is very vividly experienced: 'society: an empty, meaningless word'. Traditional values have been lost, the new myths have been debunked, and this 'demythologisation' undermines all new hopes: 'freedom, social revolution, peace — nothing but hypocritical lies'. The prospect of 'self-alienation as the ordinary condition' is a real threat.

Here, however, one can already point to the most important difference from the 'Right-wing anarchist' type: the Beat does not react or rebel from a positive standpoint — which is to say, by having a precise idea of what a normal and sensible order would be, and firmly keeping to certain fundamental values. He reacts against the prevailing situation as though by instinct, in a confused existential way reminiscent of certain biological reactions. By contrast, the 'Right-wing anarchist' knows what he wants, and has grounds for saying 'no'. The Beat, in his chaotic revolt, not only lacks any such grounds, but would probably reject them were they shown to him. Hence, the definition 'rebel without a flag' or 'rebel without a cause' fits him well. This implies a fundamental weakness, in that the Beats and hipsters who are so wary of being 'hetero-conditioned' — that is to say, controlled by external forces — ultimately run precisely this risk, insofar as their attitudes, as mere reactions, are provoked by the situation at hand. If anything, cold detachment would be a more coherent attitude.

Therefore, leaving aside the outwardly directed protest and revolt of the Beat, when this type considers the actual problem of his inner personal life and seeks to resolve it, he inevitably finds himself on slippery ground. Lacking a concrete inner centre, he throws himself into the fray, often driven by impulses which, instead of pressing him forward, make him regress, as he strives to fill the emptiness of a meaningless life in all possible ways. An illusionary solution had been found by one of the forerunners of the Beats, Thoreau, who had resurrected the Rousseau-esque myth of the natural man and of the flight into nature: an all too simplistic and, ultimately, insipid formula.[7] Then there are those who have taken the route of a new and cruder form of bohemian living, of nomadism and vagrancy (as in the case of Kerouac's characters),[8] of the disorder and unpredictability of an existence that shuns all pre-ordained lines of action and all discipline (as in the case of Henry Miller's early, party autobiographical novels),[9] in an attempt to grasp the fullness of life at every moment ('burning consciousness of the present, with neither 'good' nor 'evil').[10]

The situation becomes even more serious when extreme solutions are adopted: when an attempt is made to fill one's inner emptiness, to feel 'real' and to display a higher freedom ('the self under no law or obligation') through violent or even criminal actions which are conceived not just as acts of extreme resistance and protest against the established order, against what is normal and rational, but as a means

7   Henry David Thoreau (1817–1862) was an American philosopher and naturalist, who is perhaps one of the most consistently misinterpreted authors of American history. He is remembered as a tax evader, a proponent of pacifistic nonresistance, and the man who built a cabin by a pond on land that wasn't his, while living off the dole provided by certain wealthy friends — and in all three cases, his ideas and actions are generally understood badly and without any reference whatever to what he actually wrote on these matters. In any case, there is no question that he has been taken as a figurehead for the kind of inadequate and feeble revolt that Evola here denounces.

8   Jack Kerouac (1922–1969) was an American novelist most often remembered for his rambling 1957 book *On the Road*. He was one of the figureheads of the movements Evola here analyses, and his influence extended past his death to any number of popular folk singers and 'musical groups' who followed. He was a kind of posterchild of revolt who, after a short fierce life of rebellion, had his exhausted liver give out on him.

9   For Miller, see note 14 to Chapter 9 above.

10   The source of the present quotations is unknown; they have therefore been retranslated directly from Evola's Italian translation. All following quotations are taken from the original sources, unless otherwise noted.

to find self-confirmation. The 'moral' basis of gratuitous crimes has been affirmed along these lines, which is to say crimes carried out without any material or passionate motives, but simply out of 'a desperate need for value', to 'prove to oneself that one is a man', that 'one is not afraid of oneself', as a 'gamble with death and the afterlife'[11]. The use of everything frenetic, irrational and violent — the 'frenetic desire to create or destroy' — may be understood in much the same terms.

Here the illusory and equivocal nature of this kind of solution emerges quite clearly. It is evident that in such cases the search for a heightened vital feeling almost invariably serves as an illusory substitute for a real sense of the self. Besides, it is worth noting that extreme and irrational acts are not limited to things such as going out into the streets and shooting the first person one meets (as André Breton once proposed to the 'surrealists'),[12] or raping one's younger sister, but also includes acts such as, for instance, giving away or destroying everything one owns, and risking one's life to save a foolish stranger. It is a matter of being able to discern whether what one regards as a 'gratuitous' extreme act actually attests to and realises a superior freedom, or whether it is instead driven by hidden impulses to which one is enslaved. A serious misunderstanding on the part of anarchist individualists, generally speaking, is constituted by the idea that one is 'being oneself, free from bonds', when one is in fact enslaved to oneself. Herbert Gold's observation with regard to those cases in which this

11 One might mention here an episode to which Evola alludes in note 6 above. During a certain party that had been organised at their home, a drunken and probably high Norman Mailer stabbed his wife near the heart with a penknife. No motive for this incredible action was ever forthcoming (though that same evening his wife had, evidently, mentioned that Mailer's writing was inferior to Dostoevsky's).

12 Breton (1896–1966) was a French writer, and came to be considered the founder of Surrealism after publishing the *Surrealist Manifesto* in 1924. This, however, evidently did not suffice, so he later wrote a *Second Surrealist Manifesto*, in which the present 'proposal' is to be found.

self-examination is missing is certainly correct: 'The hipster is victim of the most hopeless condition of slavery — the slave who does not know that he is a slave and is proud of his slavery, calling it "freedom".'[13]

There is more to this. Many intense experiences that can give the Beat a fleeting sense of 'reality' ultimately make him even less 'real' as they condition him. Wilson very clearly brings this situation into light through one of the characters of his aforementioned book:[14] someone who, in a rather Beat setting, carries out a series of sadistic murders of women in order to 'become reintegrated' and escape frustration, 'because one has been defrauded of one's right to be a god', but in the end turns out to be a shattered, 'unreal' being. 'He's like a man with paralysis who needs stronger and stronger stimulants. He doesn't care any more.' 'I thought that [murder] was only an expression of revolt against the modern world and its mechanisms, because the more one speaks of order and society, the higher the crime rate rises. I thought his crimes were but an act of defiance . . . Instead that was not at all the case: he kills for the same reason that drives an alcoholic to drink: because he cannot do without it.'[15] The same also applies, of course, to any other 'extreme' experience.

In passing, in order to draw further precise distinctions, it is worth mentioning the fact that the world of Tradition too was familiar with the so-called 'Left-Hand Path' — a path I have already discussed

---

13 Gold was born in 1924, and is still living. He is a Jewish American novelist, who has written some two dozen books. The present quotation comes from his 1962 book of essays *The Age of Happy Problems*, where it occurs in Part 1 of an essay entitled 'Hip, Cool, Beat and Frantic'.

14 That is, the book mentioned in note 6 above: Wilson's 1960 work *Ritual in the Dark*. Colin Wilson (1931–2013) was an English novelist and thinker who called himself a philosopher.

15 The first of these two quotations, but not the second, has been reproduced from its original.

elsewhere:[16] it includes breaking the law, destruction and the orgiastic experience in various forms, yet starting from a positive, sacred and 'sacrificial' orientation that is directed 'upwards', towards the transcendence of all limits. This is the opposite of the pursuit of violent sensations merely because one is internally shattered and unstable, in an attempt to somehow remain on one's feet. The title of Wilson's book, *Ritual in the Dark*, is most appropriate: it almost conveys the idea of celebrating in the darkness and gloom what, in a different context, might have constituted a rite of transfiguration.

Likewise, the Beats often make use of certain drugs, seeking thereby to induce a rupture, an opening beyond ordinary consciousness. This, at any rate, according to the intentions of the best among them. But even one of the movement's leading representatives, Norman Mailer, has acknowledged the 'gamble' which drug use entails.[17] Alongside the 'higher clarity', the 'new, fresh and original perception of reality, by now unknown to common man', to which some aspire by the use of drugs, there is the danger of 'artificial paradises', of surrendering to forms of ecstatic delight, intense sensations and even visions, devoid of any spiritual or revealing content, which are followed by a state of depression once one returns to normality — thus only aggravating the existential crisis. What makes the difference here is, once again, the fundamental attitude of one's being: this almost invariably determines the action of certain drugs, in one sense or another. Confirmation of this comes from the effects of mescaline, as described by Aldous Huxley (an author already acquainted with traditional metaphysics), who draws an analogy with certain experiences of high mysticism, as opposed to the utterly banal effects described by Zaehner (an author I have already mentioned when criticising Cuttat), who sought to repeat

---

16   [Evola's note. —Ed.] *Eros and the Mysteries of Love*, § 28; *The Yoga of Power*, Ch. 5.

17   For Mailer, see note 6 and 11 above; also note 17 to Chapter 4 and its relevant passage.

Huxley's experiences, with the aim of 'controlling' them, but starting from a completely different personal equation and attitude.[18] Now, since the Beat presents himself as a profoundly traumatised being who has thrown himself into the confused pursuit of something, he cannot expect anything really positive from the use of drugs. The contrary alternative will almost inevitably prevail, thus reversing any initial effects.[19] Besides, the problem is not resolved by fleeting openings into 'Reality', following which one finds oneself plunged back into a meaningless life. That the prerequisites for venturing on this ground are

18 Huxley (1894–1963) was an English novelist and thinker who is best remembered as the author of *Brave New World*, though he wrote a great many worthy books during his life, as for instance *Point Counter Point*, an excellent critique of scientistic modernity. Huxley was grandson of the famous T. H. Huxley, 'Darwin's Bulldog', and indeed toward the beginning of his life seemed destined for a career of science as well. To his bad fortune, and perhaps to our good, he contracted an eye disease which left him almost blind, a fateful event in his life which was destined to set him later on the road to authorship. He wrote about his experimentation with mescaline most notably in *The Doors of Perception* (1954) and *Heaven and Hell* (1956), and about mysticism in *The Perennial Philosophy* (1946). The British academic Robert Charles Zaehner (1913–1974) is mentioned by Evola in note 48 of the previous chapter.

19 [Evola's note. —*Ed.*] One Beat, Jack Green, has provided (in the above-mentioned anthology) some interesting descriptions of his experiences with a particular drug, peyote. He ultimately acknowledges that this substance 'felt very nice but was no major liberation', and that if his eye had been trained, he would not have needed peyote. Moreover, regardless of what positive insights he may have reached, he shows an awareness of the *satori* doctrine of Zen. Finally, he states: 'I haven't had the true experience & I don't try for it often.' He also acknowledges the wide range of possible effects. He writes, among other things: 'it must be that the exhaustive preparation, especially the unconscious preparation involved in meditation, leads to a sudden split, which is perceived as a sudden unity.' Even after the decline of the Beat movement, American youths, and especially university students, have hardly abandoned the path of drugs. At the time of this writing, this is confirmed by the alarm caused by the growing spread among the youth of LSD 25 (lysergic acid diethylamide).

lacking is also made apparent by the fact that the vast majority of Beats and hipsters were young people who lacked the required maturity and who rejected all forms of self-discipline as a matter of principle.

Some people have claimed that what the Beats (or at any rate some of them) were seeking, deep down, was a new religion. Mailer, who stated 'I want God to show me his face', even claimed that they were the harbingers of a new religion, that their excesses and revolts were transitional forms, which 'tomorrow could give rise to a new religion, like Christianity.'[20] All this sounds like nonsense today, now that it is possible to draw an assessment and no developments of the sort are in sight. Certainly, these forces lack precisely superior and transcendent points of reference like those of religions, which might provide support and a right orientation. 'They are searching for a faith that will save them', someone has said; but according to Mailer 'God is in danger of dying' — the reference here being to the God of Western theistic religion. Thus so-called mystic Beats have looked elsewhere: they have been drawn to Eastern metaphysics, and especially Zen — as already mentioned in another chapter. However, with regard to this last point there are grounds for suspicion as to the motivations involved. Zen has exerted an influence on the individuals in question, particularly as a doctrine promising sudden and spontaneous, enlightening openings onto Reality (with so-called *satori*),[21] which may be produced through the undermining and rejection of all rational superstructures, through pure irrationality, the ruthless tearing down of every idol, and possibly the use of violent means. It is easy to see how all this might appeal to the young, rootless Westerner who cannot put up with any discipline

---

20 None of the quotations from Mailer here, except 'God is in danger of dying', are taken from the original English.

21 *Satori* is a Japanese term meaning 'awakening', the spontaneous and enigmatic enlightenment sought by the practitioners of Zen Buddhism. Evola addresses this question in Chapter 19 of *Recognitions*; the interested reader might also reference the work of D. T. Suzuki.

and leads a reckless, rebellious life. But the truth is that Zen tacitly presupposes a previous orientation, connected to an age-old tradition, and that harsh trials are not ruled out (we only need to read the biographies of certain Zen masters: Suzuki, who was the first to introduce these doctrines in the West, has literally spoken of a 'baptism of fire' as preparation to *satori*).[22] Arthur Rimbaud spoke of a method of becoming a seer through the systematic derangement of the senses, and the possibility cannot be excluded that, in a completely, mortally reckless life, in which one advances on his own, without any guidance, 'openings' of the sort alluded to by Zen may take place.[23] But these would always be exceptions, almost miraculous occurrences — as if certain individuals were predestined, or were under the protection of a good genius. One may suspect that the reason behind the attraction that Zen and similar doctrines exert on the Beats lies rather in the fact that these doctrines provide a sort of spiritual justification for their inclination towards a purely negative anarchy, towards the lack of restraint, while allowing them to avoid the primary task, which in their case would be to give themselves an inner form.

This confused need to achieve a higher, supra-rational point of reference, and — as someone has noted — to grasp 'the secret call of Being', is completely misdirected when this 'Being' is confused with 'Life', according to theories such as those of Jung and Reich.[24] This is

---

22 Daisetsu Teitaro Suzuki (1870–1966) was a Japanese author who wrote many books on Zen Buddhism.

23 Rimbaud (1854–1891) was a French poet best known for his 1873 prose poem *Une Saison en Enfer* (*A Season in Hell*). He was involved in a stormy affair with the poet Paul Verlaine (1844–1896), which culminated in Verlaine's attempting to shoot Rimbaud, thus landing the older man in prison. Rimbaud was precocious both in his beginnings (he was published already at the age of 16) and in his endings (he abruptly stopped writing at the age of thirty-one, and dedicated the remainder of his life to travelling and working).

24 For Jung, see note 9 to Chapter 4. For Reich, see note 6 to Chapter 12, as well as the relevant passage.

also the case when one sees in the sexual orgasm and in giving oneself over to the sort of degenerate and frenzied Dionysianism sometimes offered by Negro jazz other suitable paths for 'feeling real' and getting in touch with Reality.[25]

With regard to sex, I should repeat here what I have already stated in Chapter 12, when examining the perspectives of the apostles of the 'sexual revolution'. One of the characters in Wilson's aforementioned novel wonders whether 'the need for a woman is only the need to re-gain that intensity for a moment' — whether a higher impulse, towards a higher freedom, is not unconsciously channelled into the sexual drive. This question is a legitimate one. As has already been noted, the non-biological and non-sensualist but, in a sense, transcendent conception of sexuality actually finds specific and significant anteced-ents in traditional teachings. However, it is necessary to turn here to the issue I have examined in *Eros and the Mysteries of Love*, where I have highlighted the ambivalence of the sexual experience, which is to say both the positive possibilities it encloses and the regressive, 'derealising' and conditioning ones. Now, the starting point is a sort of existential anguish, so much so that the Beat seems to be obsessed with the idea of failing to attain 'the perfect orgasm' — according to the aforementioned views of Wilhelm Reich, and, partly, those of D. H. Lawrence, who claimed to see in sex a means to merge the primor-dial energy of life, taken for Being and the spirit.[26] There are therefore grounds for thinking that the negative and dissipating aspects of the sexual experience will predominate — once again, because the exis-tential prerequisites for the opposite course are missing: sex and the uncontrollable force of the orgasm will control the self and not vice-

---

25   [Evola's note. Quotation has been taken from the original. —*Ed.*] Casual re-marks such as the following one by Mailer are typical: 'The hipster, though he respects Zen, prefers to get his mystical illumination directly from the body of a woman'.

26   For Lawrence, see note 11 to Chapter 9 and the relevant passage.

versa, as ought to be the case for all of this to serve as a path. As in the case of drugs, experiences of this sort — which, incidentally, may also play a role in the Left-Hand Path — are not suitable for a decentred young generation. As for complete sexual freedom, it is trivial as a mere expression of revolt and non-conformity, and has nothing to do with the issue of spirituality.

The negative aspects are brought better into focus by the fact that the *Beats* turn jazz into a sort of religion and see it as a positive means to overcome their 'alienation', to grasp moments of liberating intensity. The Negro origins of jazz (which continue to serve as the basis even of the more elaborate forms of these rhythms, as in the case of swing and be-bop), are not seen as a matter of concern, but as something valuable. In another chapter I have already mentioned, as an aspect of the spiritual 'negrification' of America, the fact that in a famous essay Mailer assimilates the position of the Beat to that of the Negro: he speaks of the former as a 'white Negro', expressing appreciation for certain aspects of the irrational, 'natural', instinctual and violent Negro nature.[27] Moreover, the Beats have openly displayed a tendency towards promiscuity even on the sexual level, with white girls challenging 'prejudices' and conventions by giving themselves to Negroes. As for jazz, one can identify in its milieus an assimilation of certain elements that is more serious than the infatuation displayed by the foolish non-American youth mentioned at the beginning of this chapter. But this is precisely what makes the phenomenon more dangerous: there are reasons to believe that the identification with frenzied and elementary rhythms produces forms of 'downward self-transcendence' (to use an expression previously explained),[28] forms of sub-personal regression to what is merely vital and primitive, partial possessions that, following moments of violent intensity and quasi-ecstatic outbursts, leave one

---

27   See Chapter 4 above.

28   See Chapter 11 above.

feeling even more empty and estranged from reality than before. If we consider the atmosphere of Negro rites and group ceremonies of which jazz is reminiscent in its original and earliest forms, that direction seems quite evident: as in the case of the *macumba* and in the *candomblé* practised by Black Americans,[29] it is obvious that we are dealing with forms of demonism and trance, with obscure possessions which have nothing to do with any access to a higher realm.

Unfortunately, there is little more to be gleaned from an analysis of what Beats and hipsters have sought, on an individual and existential level, as a counterpart to a legitimate revolt against the present system, to fill a void and resolve the spiritual problem. The crisis endures. Only in exceptional cases does one find anything that, in the case of a 'Right-wing anarchist', may carry positive value. Ultimately, the issue here is the human material. Insofar as a new generation may choose to seriously follow the course of practical non-conformism, demythologisation and cold detachment from all bourgeois institutions, there is nothing to object. Following the suggestions of certain representatives of the Beat Generation, I have not dismissed their movement as a passing trend, but have rather focused on it in some detail, on account of its distinguishing aspects. The issues it addresses are a natural expression of the current age. The movement thus preserves its significance even

---

29 Reference to two practices among the Blacks of the Americas. The first, *macumba*, is a form of witchcraft which is obscurely connected with certain edifying local beliefs that river porpoises have the ability to transform into human males and have intercourse with young women. *Macumba* also has various malicious applications reminiscent of voodoo. The second, *candomblé*, is a form of ritual practice which immigrated to the Americas together with enslaved African shamans. It involves, among other things, dance ceremonies designed to open the practitioners to spiritual possession. These practices are also known by the name 'batuque', and in connection with the 'dance ceremonies' in question, the word has unsurprisingly come to be used in Brazil to indicate 'rhythm percussion music'.

though its specific forms have ceased to exist in America or to exert any real appeal.

3

After all this, I would like to briefly consider a specific case related to the younger generation. There are young people who are rebelling against the socio-political situation in Italy while, at the same time, showing an interest in what I usually refer to as the world of Tradition. While they oppose Left-wing forces and ideologies, which are making dangerous inroads, on a practical level, these youths also take an interest — at least in theory — in the teachings and disciplines of ancient lore in more positive terms than was the case with the Beats' confused approaches.

What we have, then, are potentially 'available' forces. The problem is finding suitable guidelines to lend their activity the right direction.

My book *Ride the Tiger*, which has been described as a 'manual for the Right-wing anarchist', only partially solves this problem, since it is essentially addressed to a specific differentiated type, with a high level of maturity — something which all too often people have failed to observe. So the guidelines provided in this book are not always suitable for the category of young people I have just mentioned.

The first advice to give these youths is to be wary of forms of interest and enthusiasm that might only be biologically conditioned, which is to say connected to age. One must see whether these young people will preserve the same outlook once they approach adulthood and come to face the concrete problems of life. Unfortunately, experience has shown me that this is only rarely the case. At the threshold of thirty, say, few keep their position.

I have spoken of a kind of youth which is not merely biological, but also has an inner, spiritual aspect, and hence is not conditioned by age. This higher youth may also manifest itself through biological youth. It is characterised not by 'idealism' — an inflated, equivocal term — since the capacity to undermine ideals to the point of approaching point zero of established values is a trait which these young people ought to share in common with other currents of a very different nature. I would rather speak of a certain capacity for enthusiasm and vigour, unconditional devotion, and detachment from bourgeois life and purely material and self-serving interests. The task, then, would be to assimilate these inclinations and make them one's own, so that they may become permanent qualities and counter the opposite influences to which one becomes fatally exposed with the passing of the years, and the need to face the concrete problems of contemporary life.[30] As for non-conformism, the first prerequisite is a strictly anti-bourgeois conduct of life. In his early days Ernst Jünger did not hesitate to write: 'Better a criminal than a bourgeois.'[31] I am not saying that this formula should be taken literally, but it does suggest a general orientation. In everyday life, moreover, one must look out for the snares of sentimental matters — marriage, the family and any other surviving structures belonging to a society whose absurdity one acknowledges. This is a crucial benchmark. By contrast, in the case of the type in question certain experiences which we have seen to be problematic in the case of Beats and hipsters may not pose the same dangers.

---

30 [Evola's note. —Ed.] In this respect, it may be interesting to provide a reference drawn from the ancient Arab-Persian civilisation. The term *futâva*, from *fatà* = 'young man', was used to describe the quality of 'being young' precisely in the spiritual sense just noted, one defined on the basis not of age but primarily of a special disposition of the spirit. Thus the *fityân* or *fityûh* (= 'the young') came to be conceived as an Order, whose members would undergo a rite connected to a kind of solemn vow always to maintain this quality of 'being young'.

31 Ernst Jünger (1895–1998) was a German soldier and writer. Few of his many books have been translated into English, nor indeed has the book that Evola wrote on Jünger and Jünger's idea of the 'Worker', a kind of heroic humanity of the future, hardened in the fires of our modern warfare and inured to an austere kind of existence.

As a counterpart to all this, the type in question ought to display an inclination towards self-discipline in free forms, removed from any social or 'pedagogical' requirement. In the case of young people, what is at stake is their development, in the most objective sense of the term. A difficulty emerges because every development entails certain values as a point of reference, but the young man in revolt rejects all values, all the 'morals' of existing society — and especially bourgeois society.

A distinction must be drawn in this respect. There are certain values which have a conformist character and a purely exterior, social justification — not to mention those values which have come to be regarded as such because their original foundations have been completely lost. Other values instead simply present themselves as a means to ensure a genuine form and steadfastness. Courage, loyalty, lack of deviousness, an aversion to falsehood, an incapacity to betray and superiority vis-à-vis any selfish pettiness or lowly interest may be counted among those values which, in a way, transcend 'good' and 'evil', as they are situated on an ontological rather than 'moral' level: precisely because they bestow or strengthen 'being', by contrast to the condition represented by a feeble, elusive and shapeless nature. No 'imperative' applies here. The individual's natural disposition is what counts. To use a simile, nature presents both substances which are fully crystallised and ones which are imperfect and incomplete crystals, mixed with crumbly gangue. Certainly, we will not call the former 'good' and the latter 'bad' in a moral sense. They present different degrees of 'reality'. The same holds true for human beings. The problem of young people's development and of their love for self-discipline must be approached on this level, above all criteria and values related to social morality. F. Thiess has justly written: 'There are vulgarity, meanness, baseness, bestiality and perfidy, just as there are the stupid practices of virtue, bigotry and conformist respect for the law. The former are worth as little as the latter.'[32]

Generally speaking, young people are characterised by an overflow of energy. Thus the problem emerges of what use this can be put to in a world such as ours. In this respect, one may first of all consider the fostering of the process of 'development' on the physical level. Here I can hardly recommend any modern sport at all. Indeed, sport is one of the leading causes of the degradation of the modern masses and almost inevitably has a vulgar character. However, some particular physical activities may be admitted. One example is high-altitude mountaineering, when it is brought back to its original form, without the technical aids and the tendency towards sheer acrobatics that have deformed it and stripped it of its spirit in recent times. Parachuting too can offer positive possibilities — in this case, as much as in the previous one, the risk factor is a useful support for inner strengthening. Another example might be Japanese martial arts, provided that there is the opportunity to learn them according to their original tradition and not in the forms which have become widespread in the West and which lack the spiritual counterpart that enabled these activities to be closely associated with subtle forms of inner and spiritual discipline. In relatively recent times, various possibilities were offered by certain student corporations in central Europe, the so-called *Korpsstudenten* practising *Mensur*[33] — cruel but non-fatal duels that followed specific rules (leaving facial scars as traces) — with the goal of developing courage, steadfastness, intrepidity and endurance to physical pain, while at

---

32 Taken from a work (I am uncertain which) by the German author Frank Thiess (1890–1977)

33 This is a kind of épée or rapier fencing which uses limited armor and undulled blades, and encourages, as Evola notes, character, courage, and camaraderie. It is practiced to this day in Germany and to a lesser extent in Poland, though it is likely in most if not all such cases that this practice has transformed in predictable ways to fit the tone of the times.

the same time upholding the values of a higher ethics, of honour and camaraderie, not without certain excesses. But as the corresponding socio-cultural contexts have disappeared, something of this sort is quite unthinkable today, especially in Italy.

This overflow of energy may also lead to various forms of 'activism' in the socio-political sphere. In these cases, what is required first of all is serious self-examination, to ascertain that a possible engagement with ideas opposed to the general climate may not simply be a means to release such energy (in which case, under different circumstances, even very different ideas might serve the same purpose). The starting point and driving force must rather be a true identification with these ideas, based on a thoughtful acknowledgement of their intrinsic value. Apart from this, in the case of activism a further difficulty emerges: for although the type of youth I have been referring to may have clearly discerned what ideas are worth fighting for, he could hardly find any fronts, parties or political groups which truly and staunchly defend ideas of that sort in the current climate. Another circumstance, namely the fact that the stage we have reached makes it unlikely for the struggle against currently dominant political and social movements to achieve any appreciable general results, ultimately has little weight: the norm here should be to do what must be done, while remaining ready to fight — even to fight, if necessary, a losing battle. At any rate, it will always be useful to affirm a certain 'presence' today, even by means of action.

As for the sort of anarchist activism that constitutes a mere act of protest, this could range from the kind of violent demonstrations that are commonly described as 'hooliganism' — such as those held by young people in certain countries (I have already mentioned the case of Northern European countries, where 'welfare society' is the rule) — to terrorist acts, such as those once used by nihilist, political anarchists. Leaving aside the motives of certain Beats, which is to say their desire to carry out violent actions simply for the thrill of it, such activism seems quite pointless even simply as a means to release energy. Certainly, if it were possible to set up a sort of 'Holy Vehme' today, so as to keep the main culprits of contemporary subversion in a constant state of physical insecurity, it would be an excellent thing.[34] But this is not something which the youth can organise; and, besides, the defence system of contemporary society is too well-built for such initiatives not to be quashed from the start and paid for at too high a price.

It is worth considering one last point. In the category of young people that we are presently discussing and who may be described as Right-wing anarchists in relation to the contemporary milieu, we find some individuals who at the same time are seriously drawn towards the prospects of spiritual realisation brought to their attention by earnest representatives of the traditionalist movement, with reference to ancient lore and initiatory doctrines. This is something more serious than the aforementioned ambiguous interest exerted by the irrationalism of a misunderstood Zen among certain American Beats, not least because of the different quality of the sources of information. Such an attraction is understandable, considering the spiritual vacuum that has been created by the decadence of the religious forms once dominant in the West, and the questioning of their value. It is not inconceivable that, once removed from these, young people may aspire towards something truly superior, rather than any worthless substitutes. Nonetheless, our aspirations with regard to the youth must not be too ambitious and removed from reality. Not only is a certain degree of maturity required, but one must also bear in mind that the path which I have also outlined in previous chapters (11 and 15) requires,

---

34 The Vehmic courts were an unofficial (some would say vigilante) and largely secret system of jurisprudence in the late Middle Ages. These courts were formed by the members of a kind of closed society who even had a form of initiation (obviously, in a mundane sense of the word) for entry. Their proceedings were equally secret, and often resulted in executions.

and has always required, special qualifications and something akin to what is known as a 'vocation' among religious Orders. As is well known, in such Orders the novice is allowed a certain amount of time to ascertain just how genuine his vocation is. Here I must repeat what I have stated before concerning the more general vocation that one may experience as a youth: it is necessary to see whether it will grow weaker or stronger with the passing years.

The doctrines to which I have referred must not give rise to the kind of illusions upheld by many spurious forms of contemporary neo-spiritualism — theosophy, anthroposophy, etc. — which is to say, to the idea that the highest goal is within everyone's reach and realisable by this or that expedient. Rather, it should appear as a distant mountain range, to be reached only through a long, difficult and dangerous trek. Certain preliminary tasks of considerable import nonetheless provide a real prospect for those nurturing a genuine interest. First of all, they should devote themselves to a series of studies concerning the general view of life and of the world which constitutes the natural counterpart to such doctrines, so as to acquire a new outlook, positively reinforcing the 'no' they utter in the face of everything that exists today, and elimi-nating the many and severe forms of intoxication arising from modern culture. The second phase, the second task, would be to surpass the merely intellectual level by lending 'organic' form to a certain set of ideas, in such a way that it may determine a fundamental existential orientation and thereby engender a permanent and unwavering sense of security. Any youths that had gradually attained as much would have already gone a very long way. They could leave the question of the 'if' and 'when' of the *third* phase undecided, in which, with the endur-ing of the original tension, one may attempt certain actions that are 'deconditioning' with respect to human limits. Imponderable factors come into play here, and the only sensible aim to pursue is an adequate preparation. It would be absurd to expect any immediate results in a youth.

Various personal experiences of mine confirm the the relevance of these final brief considerations and clarifications, which obviously concern a highly differentiated group within non-conformist youth: the group of those who have come to perceive the strictly spiritual problem within its appropriate framework.

These considerations have brought us well beyond what is commonly called the problem of young people. The 'Right-wing anarchist' may be conceived as a fairly distinct and comprehensible type, in opposition to both the stupefied youth and the 'rebels without a flag', and to all those who embrace reckless living and undertake experiences that can provide no real solution, no positive contribution, unless one already possesses an inner form. Strictly speaking, one could object that this form is a limitation, a bond which contradicts the initial aspiration, the absolute freedom of anarchism. However, it is highly unlikely that anyone formulating such an objection may do so by taking as his point of reference transcendence in the genuine and absolute sense of the term — the kind of sense, for example, it acquires in relation to high ascesis. Hence, one may reply that the other alternative concerns a youth that is so 'burned-out' that, as no significant core has survived the test represented by the general dissolution, it may well be regarded as a pure existential product of this very same dissolution: it is pure delusion for this youth to believe that it is really free. Such a youth, whether rebellious or not, is of very little interest to us — nor do we have anything to do with it. It can only serve as a case study within the overall framework of the pathology of an epoch.

17. INITIATIC CENTRES AND HISTORY

G iven the confusion in this area, it is opportune in the first place to clarify what we mean, in general, by 'initiatic centres' and 'initiatic organisations'.

I have already discussed initiation in some detail in a previous chapter.[1] Here I will only recall that, in its genuine and overall meaning, initiation consists in an opening of consciousness beyond human and individual forms of conditioning, entailing an alteration of the subject (of his 'ontological status'), who then participates in a higher freedom and a higher consciousness. This is related to the grafting upon the individual of an influence which is somehow transcendent, or not merely human. Generally speaking, this influence is transmitted, and the transmission is an essential function of an initiatic centre. What results from this is the idea of an uninterrupted 'chain' (the term used in Islam is *silsila*) of remote and mysterious origin, and parallel to a 'tradition'. According to the Guénonian school, initiatic centres — provided they are genuine and regular — are connected to a single centre and even originate from it. Though such an assumption is certainly valid, it raises, however some difficult problems.

What comes into play for the topic that I intend to discuss here is that aspect of spiritual influences that does not concern only 'knowledge', spiritual enlightenment, and the attainment of gnosis, but also

---

1   See Chapter 11 above.

a certain *power*. This power could even be considered by some — and justifiably so — a positive sign, given that certain illusions could emerge as long as we are dealing with a knowledge pertaining to higher spheres, which remains within a purely interior domain. The presence of some kind of power, which is verifiable as such, is an indirect yet rather positive proof of the concreteness and reality of the knowledge which one believes oneself to have attained by means of an initiation.

With regard to initiatic centres, Titus Burckhardt has therefore spoken of spiritual influences 'whose action, if not always apparent, incommensurably surpasses everything that is in the power of man'.[2] Let us move now into the domain of reality and history. I have had a friendly debate with Burckhardt about the existence and the state of initiatic organisations in today's world. I do not wish to claim that they no longer exist, but rather that they have become ever rarer and more difficult to access (the assumption is always that we are talking about *genuine* initiatic organisations, and not spurious groups that claim to possess such a character). It seems as though a progressive withdrawal of such organisations has occurred, and hence also of the forces that they manifested and conveyed. Moreover, keeping in mind certain noteworthy traditions, this phenomenon would not be a recent one. I will only mention those texts in which it is said that the quest for the Grail was accomplished, but that in accordance with a divine order the Templars of the Grail abandoned the West and moved — together with the mystical and magical object, which was no longer to remain 'among sinful peoples' — to a mysterious region, sometimes identified as the kingdom of 'Prester John'.[3] And the castle of the Grail,

---

2   Burckhardt (1908–1984) was a German Swiss student of the Wisdom Tradition and, like Guénon, a convert to Sufi Islam.

3   The Knights Templar were a religious military order of Christianity. They originated in the early twelfth century during the time of the Crusades, and originally dedicated themseves to the protection of Christian pilgrims to the Holy Land. The Order grew in prestige and influence in the centuries following,

Montsalvat would also have been magically relocated there. Naturally, one must take account of the symbolic dimension of all of this.

A second, more recent tradition concerns the Rosicrucians.[4] After causing quite a stir, especially with their manifestos, in which they made known their 'visible and invisible presence' and with their plans to restore a general higher order, the Rosicrucians also withdrew — this, at the beginning of the 18th century, which suggests that those groups which subsequently described themselves as 'Rosicrucian' were doing so illegitimately, as they lacked a regular traditional affiliation or continuity.

One could add an Islamic testimony provided by the Ismailist initiatic current, in particular that of the so-called Twelvers.[5] The cor-

---

becoming especially prominent in the wars to recover the Holy Land. Beyond the purely military aspect of their work, they followed a strict code of conduct. They were also said to be seekers of the Holy Grail, the lost vessel of mysterious power which appears in various legends. (It is popularly associated with the cup used by Christ at the Last Supper, but this is only one of its various interpretations.) Their name in full is *The Poor Knights of Christ and the Temple of Solomon*, hence *Templars*, due to the fact that their early headquarters was none other than the Temple Mount in Jerusalem, wherein certain rare and potent artefacts were said to be housed, including, according to some rumors, the Grail itself. Prester John was a legendary Christian King-Priest, perhaps a descendent of the Three Magi, perhaps residing in the East, in Central Asia or in India.

4   The Rosicrucians were members of an esoteric order connected to alchemy, the Kabbala, and Hermeticism. They made a rather ostentatious entry into Europe at the beginnig of the 17th century through a number of manifestos, in which they proclaimed their grandiose intent, as for instance to effect a 'universal reform of mankind'. As early as the Thirty Years War, which began in 1618, some said they had already departed in order to preserve themselves from the conflict; some century hence it was largely understood that they had gone away, perhaps to the East.

5   Ismailism is a branch of Shia Islam which derives its name from Isma'il ibn Jafar, the man it recognises as being the legitimate seventh Imam, or seventh successor to Muhammad. The Twelvers, however, who form the largest branch

responding view is that the Imam, the supreme head of the Order, the manifestation of a power from above and also the principle behind the initiations, has likewise withdrawn. They await for him to manifest himself again, but regard the current age as one marked by an 'absence'.

Nevertheless, in my view this does not imply that initiatic centres in the strict sense no longer exist. Without doubt, they still exist, even if in this respect the West hardly comes into play and one must turn to other areas, both in the Islamic world and in the East. Given this, the problem becomes the following: if, as Burckhardt claims, such centres were the repositories of spiritual influences par excellence and if, in addition to their initiatory function, they must also be regarded as the principle behind a possible external action that 'if not always apparent, incommensurably surpasses everything that is in the power of men', how must we conceive the relation between still existent centres of this sort (provided they exist as something more than mere remnants) and the course of recent history?

From the traditional point of view, this course has in general an absolutely involutional and disintegrating character. Now, in the face of the forces that are at work in these developments, what is the position of initiatic centres? If they still have the power to exert the aforementioned influences, must we assume that they have received a sort of order not to use them, not to prevent the process of involution? Or are we to conclude that the general process of 'solidification' and impermeability of the environment to the supra-sensible, having caused a sort of rift, limits all actions that go beyond the initiatic field in a purely spiritual and interior sense?

---

of Shia Islam, differ with them on this, and believe rather that Isma'il's younger brother was the true seventh Imam. The Twelvers get their name from the number of Imams they believe existed in the legitimate line of succession from Muhammad. According to their beliefs, the last Imam, Muhammad al-Mahdi, is not dead, and will return.

It is important to clarify, and to set aside, those cases that, from a historical perspective, are only the fruit of what was sown earlier. Men were granted a fundamental freedom. If they have used it for their ruin, the responsibility falls on them and there is no reason to intervene. Now, one can speak in such terms for the West, which has been following the path of anti-Tradition for some time and — through a chain of causes and effects sometimes quite visible, sometimes hidden to a superficial glance — has fatally reached its current state, which resembles the *kali-yuga*, the 'dark age' prophesied by ancient traditions.[6]

But in other cases, the situation is quite different. There are some civilisations that did not follow the same path or embrace the wrong vocations, but only found themselves subjected to external influences; as such, they ought to have been defended. Yet apparently they were not. For example, in the case of Islam there are certainly existing initiatic (Sufi) centres, but their presence has not actually prevented the evolution of Arabic countries in an anti-traditional, progressive, and modernist direction, with all the consequences this entails.

One crucial case is that of Tibet. Tibet never considered taking the same path as Western countries. It had maintained its traditional structures intact and was also considered a country in which, more than in any other, individuals and groups existed who were in contact with supra-extensible and divine powers. Still, this did not prevent it from being invaded, profaned and devastated by the Chinese Communist hordes, which also put an end to the 'myth' of Tibet which had exerted such great fascination on the Western spiritual milieu.[7]

---

6   For the *kali-yuga*, see note 45 to Chapter 15 above.

7   The Chinese have been interfering in Tibet since 1720, but Evola is here referring to the 1950 invasion on the part of the 'People's Republic of China' (as one is still compelled to call it). The incorporation of Tibet into China swiftly followed. The better part of the actions the Chinese committed against the native Tibetans have fallen under the deep shroud of Chinese propaganda, but in the remaining part of this chapter Evola relates some of the news which has reached us.

Yet, in principle, there ought to have been the preconditions for the use of the concrete powers of what was attributed to influences of more than merely human and material order.

It is worth clarifying that what I have in mind here are not invisible and magical barriers of protection that might have blocked the invaders of Tibet. It is sufficient to refer to something far less spectacular. For example, in the field of so-called modern parapsychological research, performed under strict control, the reality of 'paranormal phenomena' has been verified — that is, the possibility for objects to be displaced, moved or levitated from a distance for no explainable reason. However, given the matter with which paranormal research almost exclusively deals, these are sporadic spontaneous processes which cannot be willingly produced, and they are often mediumistic. Nevertheless, it has been ascertained that a psychic agent can cause phenomena, such as the levitation of a heavy object, which imply an undoubtedly superior force to the one required to cause, for example, deadly brain damage. Even the phenomenon of bilocation, which is to say the projection of one's own image in a distant place, has been verified (incidentally, this would also appear to have occurred with Padre Pio).[8]

So, from everything that has been reported by travellers and observers worthy of credence, starting from A. David-Néel,[9] similar phenomena have been verified in Tibet, yet not as phenomena of a me-

---

8   Padre Pio (1887–1968) was a friar who became a celebrity in Italy around the age of thirty, when he began to report stigmata — a phenomenon which he continued to report for some fifty years, until his death. He was also ascribed remarkable spiritual powers by those surrounding him, including (as Evola here indicates) the ability to appear in two places simultaneously.

9   Alexandra David-Néel (1868–1969) was a Belgian-French explorer of the East who wrote numerous books chronicling her voyages, including several about her travels in Tibet, best known of which is *Magic and Mystery in Tibet* (1929). In this last book, she speaks of her first-hand experiences of some of the phenomena that Evola mentions here.

diumistic and unconscious sort, but rather as ones governed by consciousness and will, and made possible by disciplines and initiations.

Now, it would have sufficed to use powers of this sort to cause, for example, a cerebral lesion and thereby strike down Mao Zedong the very moment in which the first Communist division made its way across the Tibetan border.[10] Or the power of projection of one's own image could have been used to manifest a warning apparition before the Chinese Communist leader.

All this should not seem like a mere digressive fantasy to those who have a conception of initiatic centres of the sort outlined in the aforementioned words by Burckhardt and who believe that similar initiation centres still exist. Do Tibetan traditions not speak of the famous Milarepa,[11] who in the first period of his life — before setting out on the path to the Great Liberation — was an outlaw who devoted himself to black magic, and, in fact, caused a massacre of his adversaries by magical means? Instead, we have witnessed the end of Tibet, and it is not possible to explain this through the idea of a sort of Nemesis (as for the West).[12] A book that has recently been published in an Italian translation by Borla[13] speaks of the odyssey

---

10   Mao Zedong (1893–1976) was one of the founders of Communist China, and was Chairman of the Communist Party of China (more aptly described as the dictator of China) during the time of the Chinese invation of Tibet.

11   Jetsun Milarepa (1052–1135) was one of the most famous Tibetan yogis. According to one account of the incident Evola reports here, Milarepa summoned a hailstorm and killed thirty-five individuals to avenge the theft of his dead father's wealth.

12   Nemesis was the Greek goddess who brought retribution against men for their hubris, or their overweening pride and their exceptional good fortune. She has been connected with the ideas of equilibrium and law. She was the daughter of Night, and was thought to bring a just leveling to the overly-blessed. She was thus seen as a balance against the excesses of Fate and Fortune.

13   [Evola's note. —Ed.] Chögyam Trungpa, *Nato in Tibet*, Borla, Turin, 1969 (Eng. ed. *Born in Tibet*, Shambala, Boston, 2000).

of those Lamas who were only able to escape in order to save their lives, as people were being massacred in the country, in an attempt to eradicate everything that had a holy character and to commence the Communist atheist indoctrination of the local inhabitants. The only resistance were those Tibetan guerrilla partisans who withdrew to inaccessible area. It goes without saying what an occult defence of the sort just mentioned would have meant. Its significance would have made all the marvels of the voyages and amazing explorations boasted about in the modern Western world appear quite banal and insipid.

So the problem just posed remains, as apparently no adequate clarification of it is possible. The only idea that one could put forward, perhaps, is that of a sort of fracturing of what exists, a kind of autonomising of a part of reality, and hence of history, entailing a sort of impermeability with regard to extrasensory influences. We could also refer to the doctrine of cycles — to that which is characteristic of the closing of a cycle. Yet, in the case in question, there would be little room for moral values. We should think of a general process in which everyone is implicated, even those who have not contributed to it. And we could also refer to a kind of watchword transmitted to initiatic centres, in order that they might allow destiny to take its course.

Ideas of this kind would lead us quite far, to the very conception of an inscrutable direction of the world and, in another respect, to the relation existing between freedom and necessity. According to this perspective, necessity could be associated only with the factual domain of existence, freedom with the various attitudes that can be adopted vis-à-vis facts (or with one's reaction to those facts) — attitudes which, in principle, are not predetermined. Within this context, moreover, we could assign particular weight to what we can gain from certain experiences, even negative and dramatic ones, if we adopt a given attitude, to the point of envisaging them as a test. As we can see, this is a rather vast and complex range of problems, with which the theology of history too has grappled.[14] Here I have only referred to it as the general background for a more in-depth investigation of the specific subject of this essay.

---

14 [Evola's note. For more on the idea of modern experiences as a test, see *Ride the Tiger*, and in particular Chapters 6, 15, and 16 thereof. —*Ed.*] The traditional Catholic theology of history struggles to interpret events such as that of the so-called 'Invincible Spanish Armada': set up against the heretics, it set sail after the most solemn consecrations, only to be destroyed by the 'forces of nature' — a storm — even before getting the chance to engage in combat.

18. THE METAPHYSICS OF SEX AND THE 'ONE'

Generally speaking, I believe that discussions are only meaningful and significant if they essentially aim to provide a clarification, on the basis of a shared assumption. If a writer is capable of recognising the ultimate assumptions of his own thought (whether they are related to his 'personal equation' or not), and grasps the fundamental difference between them and those of another writer, the only sensible thing for him to do is to follow his own path without seeking to interfere with an intellectual world that is foreign to him. However, this rarely happens, owing to the lack of the aforementioned preliminary self-analysis; writers do not even limit themselves to providing an immanent critique of other people's views (which would certainly be something acceptable and worthwhile), but engage in confused polemics — precisely because of the divergence in underlying conceptions. This ultimately demonstrates the influence of sub-rational motivations.

Given all this, I would never have taken into account a book such as Giulio Cogni's *Io sono te — sesso e oblazione* (*I Am You — Sex and Offering*).[1] But the author thought it would be a good idea to include an essay in his book on my work, *Metafisica del sesso* (*Eros and the*

---

1   Giulio Cogni (1908–1983) was an Italian writer and composer, most of whose written works seem to revolve around the questions of race and love. None of his works has been translated into English. The translator gives the original publishing information on *Io sono te — sesso e oblazione*, as follows, for anyone

Mysteries of Love). That is not as important as the fact that in these circumstances grave confusions and distortions have weighed on a domain that goes beyond the ideas that I have espoused on various occasions. Hence, it is opportune to provide a clarification that, all polemics aside, may shed light on a few clusters of potentially interesting ideas.

The views of *Io sono te* essentially reproduce those which Cogni had already expressed in another book, *Saggio sull'amore* (*An Essay on Love*), published in 1933. At that time, someone wisely said that Cogni, who was then a follower of Gentile through and through, had translated Gentile's theory of the 'spirit as pure act' into a more sapid 'theory of the spirit as impure act', since he saw sexual union as a prominent and concrete form of the identification of the subject with the object postulated by Gentile's actualism.[2] Moreover, Cogni formulated a 'phagic' or 'anthropophagic' theory: loving would mean eating oneself, devouring oneself. His new book expounds a similar thesis through the 'equations hunger-sex and hunger-love'. Previously, Cogni had presented things in rather masochistic terms: man is 'eaten' by the woman in whom he is absorbed and loses his individuality. In his more recent exposition, this 'erotic anthropophagy' seems to be conceived as something reciprocal — a rather unlikely prospect since,

---

interested in pursuing the references made here by Evola: Ceschina, Milan, 1970.

2 'Actualism' is the idealistic philosophy of Giovanni Gentile (1875–1944), the neo-Hegelian intellectual of the Fascist Period. Gentile was a principle intellectual and political figure during Mussolini's rule, and remained a rigorous proponent of the fascist regime throughout all its vicissitudes, for which loyalty Evola elsewhere praises him. Gentile eventually lost his life for his beliefs, for he refused to turn against the regime in its failing, and in consequence was shot to death in his car by partisans. He came to be known as the 'philosopher of fascism', though Evola strongly contested this epithet (see Chapters 1 and 34 of *Recognitions*). 'Actualism' emphasised the primacy of the 'pure act' of thinking, so much so that this act is seen to produce the world of phenomena itself.

ironically, it leads us to think that in the end all that remains of the lovers is two mouths, each lover having been entirely ingested and consumed by the other.

If his entire theory ended here, with 'phagia', we might say that Cogni was inspired only by the crudest aspects of sexuality: the 'hunger' of bodies, simple lustful desire. But he immediately moves on to things that are in complete contrast with what, by way of analogy, 'eating' and hunger might suggest. Cogni always gets back to 'dedication', to 'sacrificial offering', the self-abandonment that in his view occurs in eroticism and sexual union. Carnal pleasure would be a 'complete renunciation of oneself in order to make oneself the other' (p. 16).

Cogni even switches to a sort of mysticism: 'the sexual act is a form of humility based on self-annihilation and the sacrificing of oneself to the universal life that is seen in the body of the beloved' (p. 111). 'Love is "phagic" because only through the gift of the body, through devouring and letting oneself be devoured, does one realise the most powerful symbol of Unity: any alleged individual separation is removed.' The ultimate goal is 'immersion into the cosmic One without a second' (*ibid.*). All this seems like a pure digression to me, even one with a slight paranoid tinge.

First of all, with regard to the incongruence of his points of view, it must be noted that in 'hunger' and in 'phagia', which are presented as the key to sex, there is no trace of this 'sacrificial' orientation, this self-abandonment and 'sweet' identification ('sweet' being a word that often recurs in Cogni, even in connection to sadomasochistic situations. One might say, not without malice, that he displays a marked preference — of the sort usually found among women — for confectionery products rather than the prevalently manly taste for spicy and peppered food). Indeed, what is at work in hunger is the neediness of an individual suffering from deprivation, an individual that by eating only pursues his self-preservation and satiety: exactly the opposite of self-abandonment and of the sacrificial gift of oneself.

Besides, there is nothing 'sweet' about an absolute, devouring hunger. And since Cogni even makes of anthropophagy in its proper sense a sort of mysticism, he does not realise that, in general, it reflects the same sort of situation: as has been widely demonstrated, if the savage feeds himself with the flesh of others, he does not do so for any 'sweet' identification, but only — and more gloomily — because he believes he is absorbing the other person's powers to his own advantage. As for eating the flesh of sacrificial victims, it is fanciful to say that what is at work within it is the tendency to immerse oneself in the cosmic One. In general, here everything boils down to 'totemic' participation (the victim incarnating the totem), and hence to a rather restricted order, adumbrated by the sorcery and demonism typical of totemism in general. This is therefore a very flimsy and inconsistent basis for the theses advocated with reference to sex. And the Eucharistic symbol — unless one wishes to totally contaminate it by discovering in it rather suspect roots — boils down to a mere allegory.

As far as I am concerned, the fundamental intention of my book *Metafisica del sesso* was to highlight the existence of a possible transcendent dimension of sex. I endeavoured to lead the 'transcendental' meaning of eros (in the almost Kantian sense) back to a dark, unconscious impulse to restore an original wholeness. Hence, I referred to the Platonic theory of the androgyne, as the most noted mythical formulation of this idea in the West.[3] Moreover, I noted that what may come into play in the erotic-sexual experience are phenomena of

---

3   For eros, see note 6 to Chapter 3 above. The 'Kantian' reference here is surely not to what the German philosopher Immanuel Kant (1724–1804) might have thought about love (one is permitted to suspect that whatever Kant wrote of love, the old clock of Königsberg knew not whereof he spoke), but rather to his idea of the transcendent versus the transcendental; the first refers to that which moves from the world understandable through rationality alone to the world which transcends reason; the second refers to that world itself. Evola's most interesting point here thus seems to be that there is an element of eros which does not even draw us to the super-rational, but which rather essentially

'transcendence', of a momentary traumatic removal of the common conditionings of individual consciousness. I showed that this was the precondition for the practices of certain milieus, especially Eastern ones, which make initiatic, magical or evocatory use of sex. But all that is quite far from Cogni's mystical-phagic digressions, and every confusion in this regard is deplorable.

First of all, we should not generalise by attributing the marked quality of 'transcendence' to what is typical of almost all sexual unions among human beings. What holds true in the metaphysical or transcendental realm cannot be applied to the phenomenological. A phenomenological examination disproves all the idealising, mystical and fanciful notions of a 'very sweet' sacrifice, or the sacrificial surpassing of oneself in the flesh of the other to which Cogni always returns. Factually, in most sexual intercourse, one partner seeks only *his or her own* pleasure, making the other a means to this, so that the situation is not very dissimilar — *sit venia verbis*[4] — from 'mutual masturbation'. Therefore, there is no overcoming of individual bonds. In the second place, existentially, often — and today more than ever — sex serves as a means of self-confirmation for the individual, to fulfil his need to 'be worth something' (*Geltungstrieb*, as Adler would say),[5] or to look for an illusory, turbid substitute for a true sense of existence, which he lacks. Hence, once again, there is no exit from the closed circle of the individual. Finally, as I have already noted — and also emphasised in my book — although sporadic phenomena of 'transcendence' can sometimes occur in the profane experience of sex, usually they are not

---

pertains to that realm. As for Plato, the reference is to his *Symposium*, and in particular the delightful speech of Aristophanes therein (see 189d-194e).

4 Latin: 'may I be pardoned the expression' (literally, 'may there be pardon for the word').

5 Alfred Adler (1870–1937) was a Jewish Austrian doctor and psychotherapist; one of his theorised psychological drives was the *Geltungstrieb, the instinct or drive to be validated or recognised.*

experienced as such. They are realised in traumatic, extreme forms of orgasm that for the most part represent a 'break' in the individual's consciousness, to which he or she returns feeling empty, instead of having had 'the dazzling experience of the One'. This experience rarely occurs in profane, carnal, or romantic love. It chiefly pertains to the magical and initiatic use of sex, the kind of use that — among other things — involves a special approach to sexual intercourse, and about which one thing is certain: intensive states of particular, destructive intoxication come into play (destructive, that is, in an almost onto-logical, not moral, sense). This excludes 'phagia', the abandonment of oneself to the other, self-sacrifice, and all the 'sweet' and pantheistic affectations so dear to Cogni. Besides, the *dangerous* — and far from idyllic, romantic and idealising — character of such practices has always been emphasised.

Cogni has also noticed the relation I have indicated — and which takes multiple forms — between eros and death, between sex deities and deities of destruction and death, but without understanding this relation in its true sense. Besides, it is significant that the secret Hindu orgiastic rites designed to lead to the aforementioned experience of transcendence were celebrated under the sign of goddesses like Durga and Kali, not in their maternal aspect but in the destructive one. Sekhmet, the Egyptian goddess of love, is also the goddess of destruc-tion and war (her leonine head refers to a beast whose manners are not exactly the sweetest). Something analogous applies to the ancient goddesses of the Mediterranean area, starting with Ishtar, also the god-dess of orgies.[6]

---

6 For all these goddesses but Kali, see note 13 to Chapter 12 above. Kali (not to be confused with the demon *Kāli*, who gives his name to the *kali-yuga*) is a Hindu goddess of destruction, but a destruction understood to lead potentially to liberation. She thus appears, for instance, as the destroyer of evil forces, and is sometimes portrayed dancing on the prostrate body of her consort Shiva.

Related to all this is the following point. I have indicated the magnetic foundation of every form of eros and every intense sexual experience.[7] It is the strengthening of such a foundation that serves as the basis for the aforementioned experiences. But this foundation is due precisely to the polarity of male and female as ontological principles, something that has always been acknowledged. Cogni denies that this polarity is an essential requirement of eros, which in his view only concerns the naturalistic plane, as in electricity and other similar phenomena. That means that for him all the documentation that I have brought together, in an entire chapter, from the most varied cultural areas, regarding the 'metaphysical dyad' might as well not exist because it contradicts his promiscuous pantheism.

Without dwelling on this domain, which is perhaps a little too specialistic, I will now provide a more general outline of the erotology proposed by Cogni. The theory of eros as pantheistic identification is nourished, in Cogni's work, by references to India and to Hindu philosophy through the Vedanta.[8] Clearly, Cogni has only seen of India what, given his temperament, he could appreciate: an India immersed in the 'dream of the One', the 'warm, all-embracing, all-justifying, supremely tolerant, loving and accepting sweetness of the people and land of India'. The *Mother India* discovered by certain humanitarian American authoresses who have worn out their femininity — the India associated with Gandhism, non-violence, and the alleged climate of 'loving equality' stemming from the feeling of a One above every illusory difference — would be the true India. But this image is partly one-sided, partly absurd.

First of all, Cogni seems to overlook the small flaw in this 'sweet tolerance', as represented by the massacres between the Hindu and Islamic inhabitants of India, including some that are recent, as well as

---

7   See Chapter 3 above.

8   For the Vedanta, see note 14 to Chapter 15.

the elimination of Gandhi — yet another delectable incident.[9] He then ignores the fact that, if there has ever been a social regime in the world that for millennia has rigidly enforced the principle of difference, it is the Hindu caste system. Standing in contrast to the alleged India that is all love, self-abandonment and pardon is the India of the great epics and of the *Bhagavad Gita*, a traditional text which in India enjoys the same popularity as the Bible does among Westerners.[10] It attributes to the supreme manifestation of the divine an overwhelming character of destructive transcendence, drawing from this a spiritual and metaphysical justification for the warrior's duty to fight and kill, sparing neither friends nor relatives should they be found in the enemy's ranks. And everyone knows that the Hindu Trimurti, which is much more familiar to the Hindu population than the abstractions of Vedantic speculation, attributes to Shiva the divine function of destruction.[11]

But it is little use stressing such things, since Cogni is visibly affected by a spiritual blindness that prevents him from seeing whatever does not support his inclinations. Thus Buddhism only interests him in its late and popular exoteric forms as a religion, with its 'love for all creatures', Amida the god of love, etc.,[12] by contrast to the rigorous individual ascetic techniques of the Buddhist doctrine of 'awakening'

---

9   Mahatma Gandhi (1869–1948), the famous non-violent opponent to British rule in India, was shot to death by a Hindu extremist.

10   The *Bhagavad Gita*, name which means 'Song of the Lord', is a part of the Hindu epic *Mahabharata*. It recounts a part of the events in the life of the hero and demi-god Arjuna.

11   The Trimurti is the Hindu trinity — though this word should not mislead: it bears no resemblance whatsoever to the Christian trinity. It can be understood fundamentally as a recognition of three fundamental forces in the universe — creation, conservation, and destruction — and thus proposes three divinities in mirror of these forces: Brahma the creator, Vishnu the preserver, and Shiva the destroyer.

12   See note 46 to Chapter 15, and more generally the entire second part of that chapter.

illustrated in the genuine texts of the original Buddhist canon — which I have presented by strict reference to these texts in a book that Cogni claims to be familiar with.[13] From that canon it becomes obvious that, among other things, if love and compassion figure (still only with an instrumental function) as preliminary stages in the sequence of the four phases of the highest Buddhist contemplation, of *dhyana*, they are ultimately left behind, since the summit is constituted by a state of sovereign, disembodied impassibility and imperturbability that, whether Cogni likes it or not, has something of the 'Olympian' quality to it and nothing of a soft humanitarianism.

De facto, our author does not dwell on the peaks, but on the trash heaps of India. Current devotion has certainly played a role in India, but only among the lower, popular strata of society, which are not unrelated to the pre-Indo-European substrate of the country. Only relatively recently has it corresponded to a philosophical system, that of Ramanuja.[14] Earlier, it was considered a 'path of devotion' and love, *bhakti-marga*, but it certainly was not assigned any prominence: the dignity of a spiritual 'royal path', *raja-marga*, was rather attributed to the path of knowledge', *jnana-marga* and *jnana-yoga*.

This character has chiefly been attributed to the Vedanta, which Cogni is enthusiastic about, seeing it however only as the theory of absolute Identity, of non-duality, of the One-All, of 'thou art that', a theory providing the basis for his ideas about an eros that embraces and reunites everything.

---

13   See Evola's *Doctrine of Awakening.*

14   Ramanuja (1017–1137) was an enormously influential Hindu theologian whose commentaries continue to be the basis for certain forms of Hindu devotional life. Evola's present reference is related perhaps to the fact that Ramanuja embraced a monist philosophy which reduced the entire universe to a single principle — though this is in his case a 'qualified monism', as he also recognised that the Vedas speak of plurality, as Evola subsequently mentions.

Now, it should be said that the primitivistically pantheistic version of Vedanta does not at all exhaust the Hindu spiritual world. First of all, we may note that a radical monism is not attested in the original tradition, in the Vedas, which present us with an articulated *pantheon*. In the second place, India has known some great speculative systems, like Samkhya, which emphasises the primordial duality of *purusha* and *prakrti*, and like metaphysical Tantrism, which criticises the 'illusionistic' Vedanta (the world is *maya*) and which along with the Kashmir School has formulated a highly differentiated cosmological doctrine.[15]

I will not dwell on these factual data about India. The essential point is that Cogni exchanges the metaphysical One with the pantheistic One, with that One which — according to the expression Hegel uses with regard to the 'philosophy of identity' of the later Schelling — is 'the night in which all cows are black'.[16] This is not the One that dominates a well-articulated order of differences (a *kosmos*, in the Hellenic sense) but rather a promiscuous 'naturalistic' unity which is to be associated with 'Life'. Such is Cogni's spiritual horizon.

From this confusion, much more serious confusions arise in the practical realm. Cogni has no sense of the fact that just as there exists an integrative 'ascending self-transcendence', so a 'descending self-transcendence' exists that is dissolving and regressive for one's true personality. In other words, the I can experience openings either upwards or downwards — which is to say, towards 'nature', the un-

---

15   For Samkhya, see note 15 to Chapter 15. For Tantra, see note 22 to Chapter 11 above. The Kashmir School refers to specific branches of Tantrism which originated in Kashmir in the centuries immediately preceding the end of the first millennium.

16   Hegel is briefly discussed in note 28 to Chapter 5 above. The present reference is to Hegel's *Phenomenology of the Spirit*, Preface, Part 4 §16, where Hegel critiques the idea that 'in the Absolute all is one'. Friedrich Schelling (1775–1854) was a German philosopher of the German idealist tradition; his 'identity philosophy' was his attempt to wrestle with the subject-object distinction with reference to the single Absolute.

conscious, and the formless ground of life. Only the former openings correspond to high ascesis, initiation, and authentic yoga. Ancient wisdom drew a distinction and contrast between 'higher waters' and 'lower waters', where the former are illuminating, the latter intoxicating and dissolving; and this basic doctrine, which was also taken up by thinkers from the Renaissance period, has opportunely been recalled by one of the few people today who are truly qualified in this field, namely René Guénon, in order to warn us of the danger and deviations of a certain contemporary 'spiritualism'.

To return to the field of eros, Cogni mentions the ambivalence that is present, from the spiritual point of view, in sexual experiences. If woman was seen as a danger in the past, if the saying *foemina mors animae* ('woman is the death of the soul') was used in Latin as a way to recommend continence, this is not attributable to any moralistic attitude, to the 'theological hatred for sex' that Vilfredo Pareto speaks of, or to the 'sexophobia' stressed by L. De Marchi.[17] The reference here was, rather, to the possibility that the experience of sex — in relation not to the need to restrain mere mortals and to moralise, but rather in relation to individuals with supernatural aspirations — could lead precisely in the negative direction of a 'descending self-transcendence'. And if we examine the predominant use of sex among the most recent generations, we find a reflection of this even on a very profane level: no 'sweet' sacrifice of oneself, no 'carnal offering' that redeems and leads to the One, but only intercourse used in the same way as drugs (or, to be more precise, in the same way as the current profane and pandemic use of drugs) to draw from the extreme feeling of the orgasm the illusory confirmation of the sense of self (the exact opposite of the upward direction).

---

17   For Pareto, see note 3 to Chapter 5 above. For De Marchi, see note 14 to Chapter 12, and also the relevant section of that chapter.

When the One is 'the night in which all cows are black', every difference is disputed and dismissed, and promiscuity in the name of that One becomes a norm even in the forms that are most repugnant for every well-born person. Cogni is explicit in this regard, and demonstrates, if nothing else, the courage of coherence. He claims, for example, that 'every doctrine that starts from the absolute and not relative point of view, from hierarchical inferiority or superiority, is erroneous in its very foundations, if it is true that the One is all and identical to Brahman'. Note that these words (p. 156) are stated with regard to the difference between species — for example, between men and animal species. We can only imagine how they apply to the human domain. Cogni will certainly not object if — to the greater glory of the Vedantic One — a young Nordic girl beds a Zulu Negro or an Australian aborigine whose morphological and mental level corresponds to the stone age. He is certainly a hardcore egalitarian, a fanatic 'integrationist' (he rushed to make an act of contrition, updating his views in relation to a 'past error', since he had been a racist in the Fascist period, albeit one subscribing to what in my view is a dubious racial theory),[18] an admirer of 'unisex' and the 'third sex', and so on. But the last straw is in the area of carnality. As a more audacious form of identification — whether 'phagic' or not — in the name of the One, he actually admits not only homosexuality and pederasty, but even intercourse with animals, sodomy with women, and so on. His theory explains why 'relationships of this sort, which are commonly considered to be against nature, have so much appeal for many people.' 'Only by accepting in principle what are ordinarily the most repugnant areas of the other [for his/her sexual use], is one certain of having reached absolute identity' (p. 134). At this rate, we believe that Cogni might end up endorsing even coprophagia (the eating of faeces as a form of eroticism) and sanctifying disgust-

---

18 The Italian editor provides the following references: C. Cogni, *Il razzismo*, Bocca, Milan, 1937; and *I valori della stirpe italiana*, Bocca, Milan, 1937.

ing actions, insofar as coprophagia is widely featured from an erotic perspective, along with other horrors, in the *120 Days of Sodom* by the Marquis de Sade.[19]

Naturally, in denouncing such aberrations on Cogni's part, I am not appealing to any conformist moralism but to what is called normal in a higher, not social, sense. For example, pederasty at the most can be tolerated when it arises from special constitutional situations of imperfect sexualisation, but it must be stigmatised as a vice, deviation, and perversion in all other cases. In this, as in all other instances of sexual psychopathy, one must deny the presence of the objective conditions required by a metaphysics of sex for actual experiences of a 'deconditioning intensity'. But there is no hope that Cogni has any understanding of such matters.

Finally, one must note another deviation in Cogni, which goes hand in hand with promiscuous sexuality and pantheism. Since — as we have seen — his reference point is not metaphysical reality but rather the promiscuous ground of 'Life', skirting the unconscious and the subconscious, Cogni in his more recent writings openly sympathises with psychoanalysis and 'metapsychics'. He goes so far as to say that 'parapsychology' 'still remains the great hope of the future' (p. 124). He engages in a duet of mutual adulation with Emilio Servadio, who has 'paved the way', 'knowing India in depth and every type of initiatic thought and psychic depth'.[20] This makes me smile. If Servadio ever

---

19 Marquis de Sade (1740–1814) was a French aristocrat and erotic novelist, who has made his permanent imprint on our language with the terms *sadism* and *sadist*. He was, and remains, famous for his immorality and blasphemy. *120 Days of Sodom was, by Sade's own judgement, 'the most impure tale ever told'. It was written while Sade was imprisoned in the Bastille, where he was being kept on account of his alleged insanity.*

20 Servadio (1904–1995) was a Jewish Italian psychoanalyst and esotericist, and evidently also a Mason. For two years, he participated in the Ur Group (the mysterious group headed by Evola beginning in the year 1927, which pursued

had any idea of initiatic matters and authentic wisdom, it was when, before the war, he was vividly interested in the publications of the 'Ur Group', which I directed. After the war, taking one step ahead and two back, he more or less set all this aside and immersed himself in psychoanalysis — what's more, on a lucrative professional level, seeking to gain as much publicity for himself as he could. He associated psychoanalysis with 'parapsychology', in place of initiatic knowledge and wisdom traditions, setting out to probe not the 'psychical depths' but rather the 'slums of the psyche'. Cogni had no trouble establishing a connection with psychoanalysis and metapsychics, insofar as his One can easily be associated with the 'deep unconscious that is one throughout the universe', thus explaining telepathic phenomena and metapsychics in general (p. 109), while being the field proper to psychoanalysis. In these new disciplines the unconscious becomes de facto a repository for all sorts of things. Such an elementary and basic distinction as that between the subconscious (or unconscious) and the superconscious is completely ignored, partly for the simple reason that psychoanalysts and metapsychists have no idea of the latter, and partly because it is unlikely to come into play in their experimental field, for obvious reasons. Hence too aberrant assimilations such as those of C. G. Jung,[21] who equates the figures perceived by psychopaths or dream visions with the symbols and mythical structures of the initiatic and religious field, reducing everything to the emergence of 'archetypes' out of the collective unconscious. Now, it still holds that, apart from psychoanalysis and its murky world, all modern 'parapsychology' only embraces the offal of the extra-normal and is foreign to anything that might possess an authentically spiritual value. It deals with 'slums'

---

questions of magic and esoteric studies), and afterward wrote for *La Torre*, also edited by Julius Evola.

21   For Jung, see note 9 to Chapter 4.

which will only impress the naïve.[22] But given what has been said, the reason for Cogni's interest in such things is evident: we are dealing here with true elective affinities. It is at this level that he situates what he calls the 'great hope' — signs of the times.

In conclusion, the present considerations have shown that Cogni's mentality, personal equation, elective affinities and theoretical points of reference have no contact with a spiritual world that we presume is not at all personal. In cases of this sort, as was stated at the beginning, discussions have little meaning. However, with these notes I have sought not so much to 'argue' as to clarify certain issues of unquestionable relevance for those readers who might have an interest in the topics under consideration.

---

22   [Evola's note. —*Ed.*] For a critique of metapsychical research and even psychoanalysis, see my book *Mask and Face of Modern Spiritualism* (1932).

19. WHAT 'TRADITION' IS

There are two reasons why it is still opportune today to clarify the concept of Tradition in that particular meaning, whereby it is quite common to employ the term with a capital letter.

The first reason is the burgeoning interest that this idea of Tradition has attracted — and continues to attract — as a point of reference in the milieus of Right-wing culture and opposition, particularly, among members of the new generation.

The second reason has to do with the fact that, at the same time, and — we might say — precisely because of this interest, attempts have been made to put forward a corrupt and watered-down interpretation of the concept of Tradition, as though to replace the original and integral one with less demanding and more accommodating content, so as to preserve the 'routines' of a more or less conformist mentality. In this respect, borrowing a French term, we might speak of an *escamotage*.[1]

For instance, people who were initially drawn to the concept of Tradition have fallen back into 'Catholic traditionalism'. With regard to the inner meaning of this retreat, rather significant words were spoken by a representative of this current in an interview with Gianfranco de Turris.[2] The author in question acknowledged that, like other men

---

1   The word literally means 'conjuring', and thus comes to have the sense of juggling or sleight of hand in English.

2   De Turris was born in 1944 and is still living. He is an Italian journalist and writer, and is the present secretary for the Julius Evola Foundation, as well as the editor for many of Evola's publications.

both of his generation and after, he had previously taken a positive interest in the idea of Tradition, especially in its political application, but subsequently distanced himself from it, feeling that it had served as a 'healthy heliotherapy': he needed 'to get away from the sun before getting burnt'.[3] Evidently, this is merely a clever, elegant way of saying that he could not cope with the potential of certain ideas in his present unfulfilled state — hence his retreat into 'Catholic traditionalism'.

Another notable case is a book published by Bombiani under the explicit title of *Che cosa è la tradizione* (*What Tradition Is*).[4] Leaving aside the fact that this is no systematic exposition but a collection of essays that often have little to do with the subject, the author again offers a pale version of Tradition, with visible religious and moralising concerns. His display of a range of citations from various cultural fields only makes things even murkier, given the lack of a systematic framework. It is quite evident that this book was written because of the aforementioned growing interest in the idea of Tradition. Practically speaking, it tends to replace that idea. There is one other feature worth noting: the author of the book in question, who claims to be telling us what Tradition is, would never have dreamt of approaching ideas of this sort only a short time ago, when he was still hanging out with Moravia and other representatives of a more or less lefty intelligentsia.[5] He feigns not to know that the integral concept of Tradition was clearly formulated by René Guénon and his group back in the 1920s, and then in my work *Revolt against the Modern World*, published in Italy in 1934 and in Germany in 1935, the first part of which is entitled precisely 'The World of Tradition'. Almost begrudgingly — and only a couple of times — the author mentions the contribution made by the Guénonian

3   [Translator's note. —*Ed.*] See G. de Turris, *Il 'tradizionalista' cattolico (11 domande a Primo Siena)*, in *Il Conciliatore*, no. 4, Milan, April 1971, p. 174.

4   [Translator's note. For Zolla, see note 23 to Chapter 11 above. —*Ed.*] E. Zolla, *Che cosa è la tradizione*, Bompiani, Milan, 1971.

5   For Moravia, see note 30 to Chapter 12 above.

current, while systematically ignoring my own. Regrettably, he has a rather broad readership, which on a practical level makes his flimsy presentation of what Tradition is rather pernicious.

The author in question loses himself in an almost theological-Scholastic field when he states that 'Tradition par excellence, to which a capital letter applies for the sake of exactness, and not as a rhetorical flourish, is the transmission of the knowledge of the best and greatest object, the knowledge of the most perfect being.' At most, this might hold true in the contemplative-religious domain; and only with reference to it can it be argued that Tradition 'finds concrete expression in a range of devices: sacraments, symbols, rites and discursive definitions whose aim is to develop in man that aspect or faculty or potency or vocation — however we wish to call it — that puts him in contact with the highest degree of being available to him, placing above his corporeal or psychic constitution the spirit or intellectual intuition.' In this respect, the author acknowledges the development of a hierarchy 'between relative and historical beings, based on their degree of distance from the idea of pure being.' However, it is evident that he does not go beyond the abstract sphere, as is confirmed by the fact that he displays a sort of idiosyncratic attitude towards the various forms of political reality, and hence too towards all expressions of the State, of political hierarchy and *imperium*, in keeping with certain distorted Christian-spiritualistic views (as is also clear in the case of the 'traditionalist' Leopold Ziegler).[6] But in fact, Tradition displays its full formative and animating power precisely in the domain of socio-political organisation, to which it lends a higher meaning and legitimacy. A prominent

---

6   Ziegler (1881–1958) was a German idealistic thinker and upholder of traditionalism who might be distinguished from such proponents of the tradition as Evola and René Guénon by his unequivocal embrace of Christianity. This seems to have led him to a certain interpretation of tradition in an egalitarian and universalist key; there is certainly nothing 'aristocratic' about his traditionalism.

example of this, which survived into the modern era, may be found in Japan.

It would be presumptuous on my part to seek to expound the integral meaning of Tradition in the present context. I can only provide a summary overview.

Two aspects of Tradition may be distinguished, one associated with a metaphysics of history and a morphology of civilisation, the other with its 'esoteric' interpretation, which is to say the deeper dimension of the various traditional elements.

As is well-known, the term 'tradition' comes from the Latin *tradere*, which is to say 'to transmit'. In this respect, it has an indeterminate character, allowing it to be used in the most diverse and profane contexts. 'Traditionalism' can mean conformism, and in this regard Chesterton stated that tradition is 'the democracy of the dead': just as in democracy one conforms to the opinion of a living majority, in conformist traditionalism one follows the majority of those who came before.[7] Few people are aware that the literal meaning of the term *Kabbala* is precisely 'tradition', understood in this case as the transmission of a metaphysical teaching and as the 'esoteric' interpretation of the corresponding tradition — a meaning which approaches the matter we are dealing with here.

As regards the historical domain, Tradition must be traced back to what may be termed *immanent transcendence*. This is the recurrent idea that a force from above is at work in this or that area or historical cycle, and hence that spiritual and supra-individual values constitute the axis and supreme point of reference for the overall organisation, formation and justification of every subordinate and simply human reality or activity. This *force* is a presence that is transmitted, and this transmission — supported precisely by the character of this force,

---

7   The quote is from the famous Catholic apologist G. K. Chesterton (1874–1936). It is to be found in Chapter 4 of his 1908 work *Orthodoxy*, one of his most popular books.

which transcends historical contingencies — is precisely Tradition. Normally, Tradition, conceived in this sense, is borne by those at the summit of their hierarchy of reference, i.e. by an elite. In their most original and complete forms, there is no separation between temporal power and spiritual authority, since the latter, in principle, constitutes the foundation of the former, its source of legitimation and consecration. As a typical example, one might mention the Far-Eastern conception of the sovereign as the 'third power between Heaven and Earth', a conception which also occurs in the Japanese tradition of regality, which survived almost unchanged throughout the centuries, until the recent past. I have referred to many similar examples, also drawn from the Western world, in my aforementioned work, highlighting the endurance of the underlying idea.

In the aspect of 'immanent transcendence' I have just indicated, this *tradere* or transmission (hence, Tradition) concerns not something abstract and contemplative but rather an energy that, while invisible, is nonetheless quite real. The leaders and elite have the duty to take care of this transmission within certain institutional frameworks, which vary yet share the same aim. It is quite evident that it is best guaranteed when it goes hand in hand with a continuity of stock and blood safeguarded by rigorous norms. Indeed, when the chain of transmission is broken, it is very difficult to re-establish it. There is hardly any need to emphasise the fact that, from this perspective, Tradition stands as the antithesis of all that amounts to democracy, egalitarianism, the primacy of society over the State, power from below, and so on.

As regards the second aspect of Tradition, one must refer to the doctrinal level. Here the point of reference is that which we may call the *hidden transcendent unity of the various traditions*. This includes both religious traditions and traditions of a different sort — wisdom or mystery traditions. What has been termed the 'traditional method' consists in discovering an essential unity or correspondence of symbols, forms, myths, dogmas and disciplines beyond the various expressions they may take in individual historical traditions. This unity can emerge through an in-depth examination of traditional material: an investigation — it is worth stressing — that constitutes something quite distinct from the research conducted in the so-called comparative study of universal religions, which is limited to the surface and hence has an empirical, as opposed to metaphysical, character. The faculty required is rather what may be called 'intellectual' or 'spiritual intuition', *intuitio intellectualis*.[8] Those with an adequate sensitivity will immediately notice whether it is at work or not on account of a sort of illuminating virtue it bestows, and which is nowhere to be found in the extrinsic and faltering approaches of certain profane enquiries or of those who pose as traditionalists without having any actual roots in Tradition. Here one may refer not just to the authors mentioned at the beginning of this chapter and other authors with a similar background, who simply flirt with the idea of Tradition as mere intellectuals, but also to certain psychoanalysts who have drifted into the fields of symbolism, mythology and religion. Besides, only the rare intellectual capacity I have just mentioned, which cannot be acquired, can give a *sense of measure* and prevent what may be called the 'superstition of Tradition'. Indeed, some people have given free rein to their imagination and have set out to discover traditional elements, including imaginary ones, just about everywhere, even in spurious and primitive contexts. This is the equivalent of the so-called 'interpretative delirium' (in a psychiatric sense) of the Freudians, who see sexual complexes at work everywhere.

The origin of traditional forms presents some rather complex problems. As regards the first of the two aspects just outlined, namely the historical one, the idea is often advanced of a *primordial tradition* from which all subsequent, particular traditions derive. But if we keep to the historical level, this concept must be better articulated. Thus the hypothesis of a primordial Hyperborean or Western-Nordic

---

8   See note 15 to Chapter 7 above, as well as the relevant passage.

tradition, which applies to the group of traditional civilisations of the Indo-European area, can hardly be brought into play in relation, for instance, to Far-Eastern traditions. The latter, in all likelihood, are to be traced back to a different original stock or nucleus. But what often prevails here is the point of view which ought to be followed for the second aspect of the problem, namely the explanation of essential concordances and correspondences between traditional elements. The idea that certain figures — 'initiates' and the like — consciously brought into being the various traditions is a simplistic and partly superstitious one. Although some people might find this difficult to accept, we ought rather to envisage a scenario whereby 'concealed' in-fluences — so to speak — have shaped the history and development of the various traditions, without their representatives really realising it.

There are also some cases in which the same influence may be seen to 'proliferate' in geographically or chronologically distant areas, with no apparent material transmission — like an eddy vanishing from a certain stretch of a river, only to resurface at a different point in its course. This explains many cases of traditional correspondences, both in terms of particular elements but also in terms of the overall structures of certain civilisations: no connections are to be found at the surface level, yet something imponderable comes into play that makes the greatest possible use of 'supporting' elements. For example, the genesis of ancient Romanness, with its reproduction of the various forms of the primordial Indo-European tradition, may be viewed in this light. Finally, we must consider those cases in which the influence in question operates at a later stage, which is to say in the further devel-opment as a tradition of some original material, which it transforms, enriches and even rectifies. To some extent, this would appear to have occurred in the formation of the Catholic tradition out of the material of primitive Christianity.

The introduction of the idea of Tradition helps free every particu-lar tradition from its isolation, precisely by tracing its general principle and essential content back to a broader context, in such a way as to effectively integrate it. This only goes to the detriment of the claims of sectarian exclusivism and privilege. Certainly, the notion may trouble and confuse those who felt confident within a restricted, fenced-off area. However, for others the traditional view will disclose broader, freer horizons, and bestow a higher confidence, provided one does not cheat — like those 'traditionalists' who have laid their hands on Tradition simply as a way to spice up their own particular tradition and reassert it with all its limits and exclusivism.

INDEX

0–9

120 Days of Sodom (Sade) 320

A

Adler, Alfred 312
Adorno, Theodore W. 101
Æsir. See Asen
Agesilaus 132
Aldington, Richard 170
ἀλήθεια (aletheia) 115
Alexander the Great 202
Al-Hâllaj, Mansur 143
Altheim, Franz 57–59
America. *See* United States
Amidism 269
anomia 135
anthroposophy 121, 241, 297
Apollo xv, 203–209
Aristotle 24, 70–95, 119
ἀρχαί (archai) 71–75
ascesis 138, 171–173, 232, 270, 298, 318
Asen 199
Ásgarðr. See Oergier
Asiens Incognito im europäischen Geistesleben (Cuttat) 256
ātman 247–249, 261
avatara 270
avidya 129, 246
Augustine 21, 133, 172
Aurelius, Marcus 45

B

Bachofen, Johann Jakob 90–93, 156, 169, 206
Baldur 237
Bardo Thodol. See *Tibetan Book of the Dead*
Beat generation 37
Beatles 99–100
Bergmann, Ernst 211
Bernanos, Georges 5, 224
Bhagavad Gita 142, 315
bhakti 266–268, 316
bhakti-marga 266–268, 316
Bismarck, Otto von 201–205
Blondel, Maurice 180
bodhi 77
Brahman 243–248, 319
Brandenburg Gate 193
Breton, André 282
Buddhism 13, 77, 126–129, 231–243, 257–270, 286–287, 315
Burckhardt, Titus 300–305
Burnham, James 38
Byron 176–177

C

Caesar 52, 114, 165, 202–203, 254
Calvanism 265
candomblé 290
Carducci, Giosuè 110
Casanova, Giacomo 175

categorical imperative 87, 134

Cathars 155

Catholicism xii, 49, 77, 94, 128–148, 195, 234–236, 252

Cato 172

Celsus 267

Chakravarti 245

Charlemagne 208

Che cosa è la tradizione (Zolla) 324

Chesterton, G. K. 326

China 1, 28, 130, 171–180, 231, 243–245, 303–305

Christ 49, 236–241, 261–268, 300

Christianity 94–96, 127–133, 146–147, 172–180, 203–221, 234–273, 286, 300, 325–329

Chronos 212

Cicero 48–56, 95, 132

Classical world 19, 87, 111–118, 193

Cogni, Giulio 308–322

Communism 187–191

Copernican Revolution 7

Corybants 170

cosmos 53–55, 71, 92–103, 156, 239–249

Counter-Reformation 155

Crisis of the Modern World, The (Guénon) 232

Croce, Benedetto 53, 72–73, 227

Cuttat, Jacques-Albert 256–284

D

d'Alembert, Jean le Rond 79

Dante 244–254

Darwinism 72

David-Néel, Alexandra 304

Deep Are the Roots 27

Défense de l'Occident, La (Massis) 234

De Marchi, Luigi 165–186, 318

democracy 10, 27, 81–83, 95–96, 152–154, 178–191, 216–218, 255, 326–327

De monarchia (Dante) 254

Descartes 75

Désenchantées (Loti) 171

de Turris, Gianfranco 323–324

dhyana 316

Diderot, Denis 79

Diogenes Laertius 132

Dionysianism 135, 167, 184, 206, 288

Dionysius the Areopagite 259

Dionysus 112, 206, 237, 251

Dumézil, Georges 165

Durga 167, 313

E

East, tradition in xi–xiv, 1–2, 35, 139–146, 182, 230–274, 300–304

East and West (Guénon) 230–258, 271

Ecclesiastes 267

Eckhart. *See* Meister Eckhart

Eddas 198–200

egalitarianism 89, 170, 189, 327

Egypt 1, 131, 145, 167

Einstein, Albert 7

Eisenhower, Dwight D. 33

Eliade, Mircea 5, 266–267

Elizabeth II (queen) 100

Encyclopédistes 79

England 33, 104, 277

Enlightenment 76–79, 111, 246

en-stasy 129–136

Epaminondas 132

Epimetheus 115–120

eros 20, 311–318

Eros and the Mysteries of Love (Evola) 16, 116, 163–182, 284–288, 308

esotericism 127–143, 257–260

Etruscans 94

Études Traditionnelles 147, 256
Europe x–xiii, 12, 31–36, 75, 96–106, 146–149, 166, 181–200, 214–236, 294–301
existentialism 14, 37–38, 278

F

Fascism 157–158, 178
fatum 54–60
Faustianism 3, 110, 196
Feronia 93
Fides 93
Fidonia 93
Fitzgerald, Ella 31–37
Fitzgerald, F. Scott 31–37
flamen dialis 113, 202
Floralia 172
fortuna 54–56
France 5, 36, 79, 181
Francis, Saint 270
Franck, Walter 208
Frank, Walter. *See* Franck, Walter 208, 294
Frazer, James George 122
freedom 14, 27–28, 56–67, 89–105, 119, 150–195, 215–216, 250–251, 276–306
Freemasons 79, 151
French Revolution 79–89, 180
Freud, Sigmund 32, 157–166, 179–180
Freudianism 153
Frobenius, Leo 29–32
Fry, John Hemming 102

G

Gamiani (Musset) 107
Gandhi, Mahatma 315
Gentile, Giovanni 53, 309
Germany 36, 53, 158, 178–204, 236, 276–277, 294, 324
spirit of 194–201, 212–214

Gershwin, George 30–31
Ghibellines 209
Gianfranceschi, Fausto 37
gift of tongues 144
Gimle 199
Gladsheim 199
gods 43–56, 74, 93–130, 197–213, 237, 264–268
man's relation to 55–60
Goethe 51, 218
Gold, Herbert 279–283
Gospel 71, 112
Grail 77–79, 120, 151, 175, 196, 300
Granet, Marcel 130
Greater Mysteries 125–126
Great Initiates, The (Schuré) 121
Greeks (Ancient) 16
Grotius, Hugo 86
Guardini, Romano 236–240, 256–273
Guénon, René xiv, 30, 78–80, 122–127, 145–151, 232–244, 256, 300, 318–325
guṇa 266
Günther, Hans 200
Gylfagynning 199–200

H

Hathor-Sekhmet 167
Hegel, Georg Wilhelm Friedrich 53, 191, 205, 220, 240, 259, 317
hegemonikon 10–11
Heracles xv–xvi, 120
Hermeticism 144, 301
Hesiod 110–125, 198
hesychasm 147, 256–264
Hinduism 77, 160, 238–243, 257
historicism 4, 53, 73, 220
Hitler, Adolf 178, 195–196, 208–211
Hohenzollern 205
Holy Roman Empire 209, 233–253
Holy Vehme. *See* Vehmic Courts
Homer 21, 113–126

homosexuality 16–24, 154, 319
howlers 99, 276
Hubert, Henri 5
humanism 47, 60, 109–120, 220
human nature. *See* nature
Humboldt, Wilhelm von 53
Huxley, Aldous 124, 284–285
Hymn to Satan (Carducci) 110
Hyperborean tradition 197, 202–203, 212, 243, 328

I

I Am You – Sex and Offering. See *Io sono te – sesso e oblazione*
Ibsen, Henrik 14
imperium 91, 118, 325
India 1, 28, 133, 167–171, 197–200, 233–266, 300, 314–320
Indians (American) 29–30
initiation x, 20, 78, 112–151, 170–175, 237–241, 263, 296–305, 318
intuitio intellectualis 77, 142, 328
Io sono te – sesso e oblazione (Cogni) 308–309
Iran 243–245
Irenaeus 259
Ishtar 167, 313
Islam 78, 127, 143, 171–172, 231, 258–272, 299–303
Ismailism 301
Italy viii, 14–16, 36, 48–57, 99, 151, 167–236, 276–278, 291–304, 324
ius civile 202
ius sacrum 88, 202

J

Jacobins 85
Jahn, Janheinz 36–37
Japan 1, 22, 231, 243, 326
jazz 31–38, 288–290
jnâna-yoga 142
John XXIII 253

Judaism 127, 234, 258–264
Jung, C. G. 32–33, 67–69, 122–124, 287, 321
Jünger, Ernst 107, 292
Jupiter 59, 114, 207
justice 43, 85–95, 204, 218–222, 239

K

Kabbala 127, 258, 301, 326
Kali 268, 313
kali-yuga 268, 303–313
kama-marga 171
Kant, Immanuel 87, 134–142, 191, 259, 311
karma-marga 171
Kashmir School 317
Kerényi, Károly 59, 111–117
Kerouac, Jack 277–281
Klages, Ludwig 66, 211
Knights Templar. *See* Templars
κόσμος. *See* cosmos
Kulturkampf 201
kundalini 157

L

Lady Chatterley's Lover (Lawrence) 104–106
Lawrence, D. H. xiv, 21, 104–108, 288
Lawrence, T. E. xiv, 21, 104–108, 288
Lebensborn 179
Left-Hand Path 135, 283–289
Lesser Mysteries 125–126
libido dominandi 21, 166
libido servendi 166
life x–xiii, 1–68, 80–263, 275–318
Lindner, Robert 279
Livy 44, 112–114
λόγος (logos) 70–71
Loti, Pierre 171
Lustprinzip 163
Luther, Martin 195

M

macumba 290
Mailer, Norman 37–38, 157, 279–289
Malinowski, Bronislaw 164
Manacorda, Guido 191–195, 234
Mao Zedong 305
Marquis de Sade. *See* Sade, Marquis de
marriage 172–187, 292
Mars 170
Marshall, Bruce 221
Marxism 218
Massis, Henri 194–195, 234, 256
matrism 154–155
Mauss, Marcel 5
māyā 240–249
Mazdaism 203
Mead, Margaret 164
Meister Eckhart 129, 259
Mensur 294
metanoia 9
Middle Ages 1, 34, 119, 146–155, 175, 207–209, 244, 296
Milarepa, Jetsun 305
Miller, Henry xiv, 106–108, 281
Mitgard 199–207
Mithras 237
Montsalvat 301
Moravia, Alberto 180, 324
mountaineering 62–65, 294
Muntu (Jahn) 36–37
Musset, Alfred de 107
Mussolini, Benito 178, 191, 309
Mysteries 16, 116–145, 163–182, 284–288, 309
Mystery of the Grail, The (Evola) 77–79, 120, 151, 175
mysticism 113, 127–141, 250–285, 310–311
Mystics, The (Zolla) 133–136
Myth of the Twentieth Century, The (Rosenberg) 210

N

Nagarjuna 242
National Socialism 178, 195–209
naturalis ratio 86–88
natural law 84–95, 154, 169
natural rights 85–87
nature xii, 1–19, 44–46, 69–131, 145–162, 179–195, 208–243, 257–293, 307–319
Nedelcovic, Bosco 185–188
négritude 36
Negro 27–38, 99–108, 288–290, 319
Nemesis 305
Neo-Hegelianism 53, 240, 309
Neoplatonism 75, 128, 258
Nietzsche, Friedrich xiii, 6–14, 38, 66–70, 103–117, 176–183, 196–206, 238
νοῦς (nous) x, 3, 29, 51, 70–91, 114–117, 136–142, 199–207

O

obscenity 104–108, 152
Occident et son destin, Le (Massis) 234
Oegier 199
Old Testament 30, 130, 144, 267
Olympian ideal 74
Orestes 203
orgone 157–163
Origen 147, 267
Orphism 251
Osirification 145
Osiris 145, 237
Ottoman Empire 21

P

Padre Pio 304
pantheism 195, 235, 258–260, 314–320
Pareto, Vilfredo 40, 168–174, 318
patrism 154–155
Paul VI 253

Pelasgians 91, 203–211
pietas 43, 56–57
Pindar 14–24, 112
Pius IX (pope) 220
Plato 11–21, 70–95, 116, 179, 311
Plutarch 132–140, 251
Porgy and Bess (Gershwin) 30–31
pornography 104
Porphyry 140
positive law 85–95
prakrti 160, 243, 317
prajñā 77
Prester John 300
primitive peoples 73, 125, 164–170
Prometheus xv–xvi, 110–120
Protestantism 147–155, 173, 195
Prussians 170–172, 193
psychoanalysis 22, 67, 157–166, 179,
    216, 320–322
Puritanism 155
purusha 160, 243, 317

R
ragna-rökkr 197–199
raja-marga 316
rajas 266
Ramanuja 316
ratio 66–67, 80–88
Reformation 133, 155, 195
Reich, Walter 91, 157–177, 191–210,
    287–288
Renaissance 7, 102–109, 144–155, 175,
    318
Rencontre des Religions, La
    (Cuttat) 256
Republic, The (Plato) 95, 114, 179, 303
Revolt Against Beauty, The (Fry) 102
Revolt Against the Modern World
    (Evola) viii–x, 61, 95, 115, 146, 268
Ride the Tiger (Evola) 9, 102–103, 174,
    291, 307

Right-Hand Path 135
Rimbaud, Arthur 287
Ritual in the Dark (Wilson) 279–284
Rohde, Erwin 131
Romanticism 155, 177, 196
Rome (Ancient) 41–59, 113, 172,
    192–193
    spirit of 201–214, 233–234, 329
Rosenberg, Alfred 210
Rosicrucians 301
Rousseau, Jean-Jacques 89, 154, 281
rta 55, 92
Ruysbroek, John van 259

S
Sade, Marquis de 320
Saggio sull'amore (Cogni) 309
Sallust 49
Samkhya 243, 317
satori 285–287
sattva 266
Schelling, Friedrich 317
Scholasticism 75–85
Schopenhauer, Arthur 17, 259
Schuon, Frithjof 29–30, 224
Schuré, Édouard 121
science 8, 104, 143, 166, 179, 221–242,
    259, 285
Scipio the Elder 48
Scotus Eriugena 75, 259
Second Vatican Council. *See* Vatican II
Sekhmet. *See* Hathor-Sekhmet
self-sadism 100, 120
Seneca 48–49, 117
Servadio, Emilio 320
Sesso e Civiltà (De Marchi) 168–178
Sex in History (Taylor) 153
sexophobia 169–189, 318
sexuation 22–24
Shankara 245–246
shakti 157–161, 243

shenjen 264
Shiism 127
Shiva 160, 174, 248, 313–315
Shiva Chandra 248
siddha 263
sila 134
silsila 299
Sombart, Werner 34–35
Soviet Russia 180
Spengler, Oswald 29–32, 66–69, 193–196
Spinoza, Baruch 246
sport 61–65, 294
State 10–15, 43–51, 83–96, 131, 179–216, 325–327
  modern conception of 15, 83–84, 95
  traditional conception of 10–11, 43, 49, 51, 88–92, 96, 191, 194–195, 325
Steding, Christoph 91–96, 205–208
Steiner, Rudolf 121, 241
Stirner, Max 14
Struggle for the World, The (Burnham) 38
Suetonius 114, 202
Sufism 127, 143, 256–269
Suzuki, Daisetsu Teitaro 286–287
Syllabus of Errors (Pius IX) 220
Symeon, Saint 147, 264
Synesius 259

T

Tantratattva 248
Tantrism 317
Taoism ix, 131, 243, 257–269
tapas-marga 171
Tauler, Johannes 259
Taylor, G. Rattray 153–175
technology 3, 35, 57, 221, 237–240
Teilhard de Chardin, Pierre 220
Templars 300
Teoria dell'orgasmo, La (Reich) 168

theosophism 241
Teutonic Knights 205
theosis 264
theosophy 121, 297
Thiess, Frank 293–294
Third Reich. *See* National Socialism
Thomism 239
Thoreau, Henry David 280–281
Thule 212
Thus Spoke Zarathustra (Nietzsche) 6, 183
Tibet 303–305
Tibetan Book of the Dead 131
Titans 110, 125
Todestrieb 163
Tradition xi–xv, 43, 78–83, 232, 254, 283–303, 323–330
Traditionalism 326
Trimurti 315
troubadours 155
Twelvers 301

U

Ulpian 89–94
UN (United Nations) 253
United States xi, 5, 26–38, 101–106, 155–158, 180–182, 216, 230, 277–291
Upanishads 243, 261
Ur Group 320–321

V

Valhalla 199
van der Leeuw, Gerardus 122
Vatican II 236, 253
Veda 243
Vedanta 242–249, 314–317
Vehmic Courts 296
Venus 170
Vergeistigungstechnik und Umgestaltung in Christus 256
Vico, Giambattista 53, 72–73, 205

vidya 77, 129, 171
vidya-marga 171
Vingtquatre nuits charnelles 107
vîra-mârga 135
virtuism 40, 174–180
Voltaire 79
Völuspá 198–200

W

Wagner, Richard 196–197, 218
Weininger, Otto 13–17
West xi–xiv, 29–44, 69–83, 101,
    121–149, 191–273, 287–311
Widukind 208
Wilson, Colin 279–288
World War II 27–33

Y

yoga 133–147, 171, 316–318

Z

Zaehner, R. C. 273–285
Zen 38, 264, 285–296
Zeus xv, 74, 91, 110–118
Ziegler, Leopold 325
Zolla, Elémire 136, 324

OTHER BOOKS PUBLISHED BY ARKTOS

SRI DHARMA PRAVARTAKA ACHARYA   *The Dharma Manifesto*

ALAIN DE BENOIST   *Beyond Human Rights*
Carl Schmitt Today
The Indo-Europeans
Manifesto for a European Renaissance
On the Brink of the Abyss
The Problem of Democracy
View from the Right (vol. 1–3)

ARTHUR MOELLER VAN DEN BRUCK   *Germany's Third Empire*

MATT BATTAGLIOLI   *The Consequences of Equality*

KERRY BOLTON   *Revolution from Above*
Yockey: A Fascist Odyssey

ISAC BOMAN   *Money Power*

RICARDO DUCHESNE   *Faustian Man in a Multicultural Age*

ALEXANDER DUGIN   *Ethnos and Society*
Eurasian Mission
The Fourth Political Theory
Last War of the World-Island
Putin vs Putin
The Rise of the Fourth Political Theory

KOENRAAD ELST   *Return of the Swastika*

JULIUS EVOLA   *Fascism Viewed from the Right*
A Handbook for Right-Wing Youth
Metaphysics of War
Notes on the Third Reich
The Path of Cinnabar
Recognitions
A Traditionalist Confronts Fascism

OTHER BOOKS PUBLISHED BY ARKTOS

GUILLAUME FAYE

Archeofuturism
Archeofuturism 2.0
The Colonisation of Europe
Convergence of Catastrophes
A Global Coup
Sex and Deviance
Understanding Islam
Why We Fight

DANIEL S. FORREST

Suprahumanism

ANDREW FRASER

Dissident Dispatches
The WASP Question

GÉNÉRATION IDENTITAIRE

We are Generation Identity

PAUL GOTTFRIED

War and Democracy

PORUS HOMI HAVEWALA

The Saga of the Aryan Race

RACHEL HAYWIRE

The New Reaction

LARS HOLGER HOLM

Hiding in Broad Daylight
Homo Maximus
Incidents of Travel in Latin America
The Owls of Afrasiab

ALEXANDER JACOB

De Naturae Natura

JASON REZA JORJANI

Prometheus and Atlas
World State of Emergency

RODERICK KAINE

Smart and SeXy

LANCE KENNEDY

Supranational Union and New Medievalism

PETER KING

Here and Now
Keeping Things Close

OTHER BOOKS PUBLISHED BY ARKTOS

OTHER BOOKS PUBLISHED BY ARKTOS

ERNST VON SALOMON — *It Cannot Be Stormed*
The Outlaws

SRI SRI RAVI SHANKAR — *Celebrating Silence*
Know Your Child
Management Mantras
Patanjali Yoga Sutras
Secrets of Relationships

TROY SOUTHGATE — *Tradition & Revolution*

OSWALD SPENGLER — *Man and Technics*

TOMISLAV SUNIC — *Against Democracy and Equality*
Postmortem Report
Titans are in Town

HANS-JÜRGEN SYBERBERG — *On the Fortunes and Misfortunes
of Art in Post-War Germany*

ABIR TAHA — *Defining Terrorism: The End
of Double Standards*
The Epic of Arya (2nd ed.)
*Nietzsche's Coming God, or the
Redemption of the Divine*
Verses of Light

BAL GANGADHAR TILAK — *The Arctic Home in the Vedas*

DOMINIQUE VENNER — *For a Positive Critique*
The Shock of History

MARKUS WILLINGER — *A Europe of Nations*
Generation Identity

Made in the USA
Las Vegas, NV
24 August 2023

76549651R00208